SPOTLIGHT ON SENTENCE AND PARAGRAPH SKILLS

CAROLE ANNE MAY

Camosun College

PEARSON
Prentice
Hall

Toronto

National Library of Canada Cataloguing in Publication

May, Carole Anne, 1948–
    Spotlight on sentence and paragraph skills / Carole Anne May.

Includes index.
ISBN 0-13-123485-4

    1. English language—Paragraphs. 2. English language—Sentences. I. Title.

PE1441.M394 2006   808'.042   C2005-901440-7

ISBN 0-13-123485-4

Vice President, Editorial Director: Michael J. Young
Acquisitions Editor: Patty Riediger
Marketing Manager: Toivo Pajo
Signing Representative: Carmen Batsford
Developmental Editor: Matthew Christian
Production Editor: Richard di Santo
Copy Editor: Karen Alliston
Proofreader: Nancy Carroll
Production Coordinator: Janis Raisen
Permissions Manager: Susan Wallace-Cox
Permissions Research: Lisa Brant
Page Layout: Janet Zanette
Art Director: Julia Hall
Cover and Interior Design: Gillian Tsintziras
Cover Images: Nonstock

1 2 3 4 5   10 09 08 07 06

Printed and bound in Canada.

This book is dedicated to Daniel and Christopher.

brief contents

contents

preface

Welcome to *Spotlight on Sentence and Paragraph Skills*. I have written this text in order to help encourage student writers, through its philosophy and structure, to become capable, confident, and eager to handle higher-level challenges in their writing. *Spotlight on Sentence and Paragraph Skills* teaches the fundamentals of sentence construction and paragraph basics, including structure and organization, through the reading and analyzing of various readings, along with grammar and mechanics. Many college composition textbooks develop the idea of writing in terms of a top-down or a bottom-up approach. This book takes a different tack by emphasizing the conception of writing as a complex process, as a recursive undertaking, and as an individual project having different stages.

The materials on which this text is based have been very popular with both teachers and students over the course of my three decades of teaching at four community colleges. Students consistently report their enjoyment with the approach and the nature of the exercises and assignments; they have expressed satisfaction over the improvement they have witnessed in their abilities to analyze, organize, and construct written material.

Spotlight on Sentence and Paragraph Skills has been designed with a clear sequence that builds application through varied exercises—both individual and collaborative—in sentence construction, detailing improvement of style and form, and in paragraph writing, featuring summary, narrative, descriptive, and explanatory modes. I have woven the thread of grammar and mechanics through the first fourteen chapters of the book. I have also included challenging exercises that develop critical thinking as students practise and apply foundational concepts. Since most college and university composition classes include many students whose native language is not English, *Spotlight on Sentence and Paragraph Skills* offers special ESL sections in the first fifteen chapters. These sections, called *ESL Pointers*, present ideas and practice in areas of common difficulty for ESL writers.

In addition, *Spotlight on Sentence and Paragraph Skills* provides an important element—readings—both at the paragraph and multi-paragraph levels. Chapters 15–19 all contain readings and samples for students. Chapter 19 is an entire chapter dedicated to readings and designed to develop students' analysis of structure and content by using specific questions as tools to enlarge critical thinking.

Key Features

Spotlight on Sentence and Paragraph Skills has several useful and important features:

It contains one chapter dedicated to particular parts of speech. This chapter lays the conceptual framework for sentence construction, form, and design.

It provides an entire chapter on subject-verb agreement. Most composition textbooks offer only short sections on subject-verb agreement, and yet this error is one of the most common amongst beginning college writers for both native and non-native speakers of English. *Spotlight on Sentence and Paragraph Skills* addresses the problem and provides extra explanation and practices.

It includes three full chapters dedicated to sentence style. Concentrating on sentence style by breaking it down into various elements and providing practice with those elements improves students' awareness of their own writing needs.

It offers one full chapter on developing writing vocabulary. Student writers gain confidence and competence in their writing as they begin to develop a stronger writing vocabulary, which is often the most difficult for students to develop without targeted practice.

It contains one chapter dedicated to summary writing. Summary writing is one of the most important skills college students require in their academic work. Chapter 15 assists students to develop deeper comprehension in regard to what they read, helps them to evaluate the importance of main ideas, and supports them as they learn to write more concisely. These stages lay the foundation of critical reading and thinking.

It offers focussed and engaging paragraph writing. To write effectively, students must be engaged. Chapters dedicated to narrative, descriptive, and explanatory paragraph writing provide interesting activities and topics that both encourage and engage students.

It presents readings throughout most of the book and in a dedicated readings chapter. The readings focus on interesting, current issues. At the same time, the readings will provide students with writing models.

It contains self-tests and review tests for 14 chapters. Self-tests provide students with instant feedback about their skill and knowledge regarding grammatical and mechanical elements in English. Review tests provide feedback to students and instructors. Review test keys are not contained in *Spotlight on Sentence and Paragraph Skills*; therefore, instructors can decide to use the reviews as evaluation tools in their courses. Review test keys are found in the Instructor's Manual.

It provides a *checkout* for each chapter. The *checkout* is a valuable study and learning tool for students. Students can read through a chapter's explanation and *checkout* feature to prepare for tests. They can also check out their own understanding, using this feature.

Faculty Supplements

Spotlight on Sentence and Paragraph Skills is accompanied by an Instructor's Manual, which is an invaluable resource for anyone using this textbook. Included in the Instructor's Manual are review test answers, suggested activities, and additional answers for exercises from the text. This supplement can be downloaded by instructors from a password-protected location on Pearson Education Canada's online catalogue (vig.pearsoned.ca). Simply search for the text, then click on "Instructor" under "Resources" in the left-hand menu. Contact your local sales representative for further information.

Acknowledgements

I am especially grateful to Pearson Education Canada for the opportunity to bring this series of books forward. Patty Riediger, Matthew Christian, Richard di Santo, Toivo Pajo, and Carmen Batsford have been outstanding in their encouragement and expert support. I also wish to acknowledge my students who have been the source of inspiration and instruction over my years as a college instructor. They have given me many meaningful learning experiences and joyful interactions. I am deeply indebted to them. Finally, I must thank my wonderful family for their love and support. I earnestly hope that *Spotlight on Sentence and Paragraph Skills* helps college writing students to become confident and competent in their composition skills as they engage in the sheer delight of learning.

Sentence Structure

One of the most important elements in writing is the sentence. It provides units of meaning to your reader. To develop clear sentences in your writing, you need to know what makes up basic sentence structure and to understand how to use various grammatical structures in conventional, yet interesting ways. This section will provide you with the fundamentals of English grammar through exercises in sentence writing.

chapter 1

Parts of Speech

Chapter Objectives

What will you have learned when you have completed this chapter? You will be able to

1. name eight basic parts of speech.

2. spot the function of basic parts of speech in sentences.

3. use word position to help determine part of speech.

4. see that word order in English sentences can change meaning.

5. recognize that sentence type can often set the tone.

English, like every other language, has a form and a structure. This form and structure is what we're talking about when we talk about grammar.

Grammar describes how words function in sentences and how they relate to one another. Words are classified according to how they function in sentences; these classifications are called the *parts of speech*. In English grammar the parts of speech are nouns, pronouns, verbs, adjectives, adverbs, prepositions, interjections, and conjunctions.

Chapter 1: Self-Test

Try this self-test to find out what you know about parts of speech in the English language. Check your answers with the Answer Key at the back of the book.

1. What does the term *part of speech* mean? Write a definition without looking up the term.

2. Complete the exercise below by adding a brief definition for each of the terms.

   Term Definition

   1. What is a noun? _____

   2. What is a pronoun? _____

   3. What is a verb? _____

   4. What is an adjective? _____

   5. What is an adverb? _____

   6. What is a prepositional phrase? _____

   7. What is a conjunction? _____

   8. What is an interjection? _____

Word Position

Often the position of a word in a sentence is a determining factor in deciding to what part of speech the word belongs. Notice how the word *flying* is used in the following three sentences.

> Trevor is <u>flying</u> to Toronto. His <u>flying</u> instructor is from Spain. <u>Flying</u> is scary.

In sentence 1, *flying* is expressing action: it is telling what Trevor is doing. Therefore, *flying* is a verb in sentence 1.

In sentence 2, however, no person named in the sentence is performing the action of flying. Instead, *flying* is describing the instructor. When you read the sentence, you notice that *flying* helps to describe the noun *instructor*—a *flying instructor*. Words that describe nouns are called *adjectives*; thus, *flying* is an adjective in sentence 2.

In sentence 3, *flying* is the subject of the sentence; it is what the sentence is all about. Nouns or pronouns can act as subjects of sentences, so you must assume that *flying* is a noun in sentence 3.

You can change the position of a word in a sentence, or you can change its form; when you do either, you might also be changing its part of speech. Later, you will practise with more parts of speech, but first read on to learn more about the basics.

Functions of Parts of Speech

It is important to know how these eight parts of speech can function in sentences.

1. Noun (concrete or abstract)

   Quick definition: person, place, thing
   Functions: as subject—who or what does the action
   as object—who or what receives the action

   subject   object
   The toad sat in the wicker basket.

2. Pronoun

   Quick definition: takes the place of a noun
   Functions: as subject—who or what does the action
   as object—who or what receives the action

   subject   object
   She called him for advice.

3. Verb

   Quick definition: shows action by describing what the subject does, or links the subject to the rest of the sentence
   Functions: as action
   as link

   action
   Her brother washed the car.

   links subject to the rest of the sentence
   Amil is tired after work.

4. Adjective

   Quick definition: describer or modifier of a noun
   Function: adds detail

   The red wool cap belongs to Ramon.

5. Adverb

   Quick definition: describes or modifies verbs, adjectives, or other adverbs
   Function: adds colour or detail to verbs, adjectives, or other adverbs

   The street worker tries hard to help the homeless.
   Several of the dogs were happily chasing the frightened skunk.

6. Prepositional phrase

   Quick definition: describes or modifies nouns, adjectives, or adverbs in the sentence
   Functions: works like an adjective or adverb
   adds colour or detail in the sentence

   Madeleine will take the volleyball team to the beach after school.

7. Conjunction

Quick definition: a word that joins
Functions: joins two or more ideas together
establishes a relationship between ideas

The rally was cancelled <u>because</u> it was storming.

8. Interjection

Quick definition: word of expression
Function: used to express emotions

<u>Oh</u>, I forgot to tell you something.

Exercise 1   *Word Position and Part of Speech*

Each of the following sets contains three sentences. Each sentence of the set has the same word underlined, but the word functions as a different part of speech in each sentence. Indicate whether the underlined word is an adjective, noun, or verb. Check your answers with the Answer Key.

Example:

verb
a) Antoine would <u>love</u> to see you.

noun
b) <u>Love</u> makes the world go round.

adjective
c) The prime minister's <u>love</u> interest enthralled the public.

1. a) Sometimes I feel like an old <u>work</u> horse. _____

   b) Will you <u>work</u> this evening? _____

   c) Some <u>work</u> can be very rewarding. _____

2. a) Smith will <u>ranch</u> in Pleasant Valley. _____

   b) The <u>ranch</u> hand quit this morning. _____

   c) Jane Fonda's <u>ranch</u> was in Montana. _____

3. a) The <u>step</u> on the landing needs to be painted. _____

   b) She bought a new <u>step</u> ladder for the house. _____

   c) Please <u>step</u> over the mess. _____

4. a) Can you <u>post</u> this letter on your way out? _____

   b) The <u>post</u> office is closed on Sundays. _____

   c) The deck <u>post</u> is not very solidly installed. _____

5. a)   Do you <u>plant</u> a garden every spring? _____

   b)   The <u>plant</u> did not survive the early frost. _____

   c)   Our <u>plant</u> stand came from my grandmother's house. _____

6. a)   Will the carpenter <u>plane</u> the edge of the cupboard? _____

   b)   He lost his <u>plane</u> tickets at the airport. _____

   c)   The <u>plane</u> was being de-iced on the runway. _____

7. a)   What is the bank's <u>profit</u> margin? _____

   b)   Len might <u>profit</u> by the idea. _____

   c)   <u>Profit</u> comes with a price. _____

Exercise 2   Changing Word Function or Part of Speech

Write a sentence using each of the following words as the part of speech shown. Be prepared to share your answers. Your instructor might ask you to pair up with another learner from your class to do the checking.

1. a)   sailing (noun):

   _____

   b)   sailing (verb):

   _____

   c)   sailing (adjective):

   _____

2. a)   part (noun):

   _____

   b)   part (verb):

   _____

   c)   part (adjective):

   _____

3. a)   farm (noun):

   _____

   b)   farm (verb):

   _____

    c) farm (adjective):

_____

  4. a) rock (noun):

_____

    b) rock (verb):

_____

    c) rock (adjective):

_____

  5. a) tow (noun):

_____

    b) tow (verb):

_____

    c) tow (adjective):

_____

Exercise 3   Identification of Parts of Speech

The following sentences are fairly simple in their structure. Identify what part of speech each underlined word is. Write your answer above each underlined word. Your instructor may ask to see your work.

1. The <u>architect</u> studied the blueprints.

2. A <u>blue</u> flame <u>appeared</u> <u>above</u> the light.

3. <u>Yes</u>! <u>We</u> won <u>our</u> <u>first</u> game.

4. <u>Her</u> <u>paintings</u> are <u>stunning</u>.

5. Jimmy <u>rode</u> <u>his</u> bike <u>into</u> town.

6. <u>They</u> laughed, but he <u>was</u> <u>not</u> <u>happy</u> <u>about</u> it.

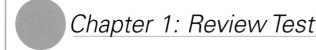

Chapter 1: Review Test

Identify the part of speech of each underlined word or phrase. Write your answer above each word or phrase.

1. Hermie <u>and</u> her brothers have <u>constructed</u> <u>their</u> own house <u>in the hills</u>.

2. One part of the problem <u>was</u> his <u>poor</u> attitude.

3. <u>Will</u> the injection cause swelling <u>at the site</u>?

4. <u>Wow</u>, that was a <u>huge</u> rat!

5. Mr. Rodriguez looked <u>everywhere</u> for his <u>missing</u> cat.

6. <u>Because</u> he was afraid <u>of contracting SARS</u>, he refused to board the plane.

7. <u>Their</u> <u>youngest</u> daughter <u>will be graduating</u> from the University of Toronto.

8. <u>Eating</u> <u>candy</u> <u>promotes</u> tooth decay.

9. The <u>postal</u> worker slowly handed <u>Mrs. Chikko</u> a small package wrapped in green paper.

10. I <u>find</u> <u>Japanese</u> architecture <u>very</u> interesting.

11. Walton <u>wanted</u> to study <u>interior</u> <u>design</u>, <u>but</u> he became interested <u>in computer graphics</u>.

12. <u>Those</u> children are far <u>too</u> <u>young</u> to be wearing makeup.

ESL POINTER

Parts of Speech and Word Order

The word order of statements in English is generally as follows:

subject   verb   object   manner   place   time

You will not necessarily need to use all components in every sentence you write in English. You will, however, need to provide or imply a subject for every English sentence you write.

subject   verb   object   time
Beta   bought   a car   yesterday.

subject   verb   manner   place

Kostya   stopped   suddenly   in the doorway.

Changing the word order in a sentence can drastically alter the intended meaning. Sometimes it can cause you to write a poor or confusing sentence.

subject   verb   object   time
The child   caught   a large trout   after school.

```
        subject      verb      object
The large trout   caught   the child   after school.
```

```
subject   verb      object              time
Lucia    drives    her car   on the weekends.
```

```
subject   object      verb              time
Lucia    her car    drives   on the weekends.
```

Often you can move the time or place element of the sentence to another point in the sentence without disrupting meaning.

Beta bought a car yesterday.

Yesterday Beta bought a car.

Kostya stopped suddenly in the doorway.

In the doorway Kostya stopped suddenly.

The child caught a large trout after school.

After school the child caught a large trout.

Lucia drives her car on the weekends.

On the weekends Lucia drives her car.

However, the position of the subject and the object is critical. The word order signals which part of the sentence is the subject and which is the object. The reader constructs meaning in English partly, but importantly, by the word order.

Adjectives are positioned in front of the nouns they modify.

The <u>young</u> pianist won the <u>national</u> competition.

Young is an adjective; it is placed before *pianist*, the noun it modifies. *National* is an adjective that modifies the noun *competition*.

<u>Regular</u> exercise maintains a <u>healthy</u> mind and body.

Regular is an adjective modifying *exercise*, and *healthy* is an adjective that modifies *mind and body*.

Adverbs usually come before or after a verb.

The students walked <u>proudly</u> to the podium.

The students <u>proudly</u> walked to the podium.

Proudly is an adverb: it can be placed before or after the verb *walked*, which it modifies. However, an adverb cannot be placed between a verb and its object.

The guest <u>respectfully</u> thanked his host.

(incorrect)
The guest thanked <u>respectfully</u> his host.

Do not split up the verb from its object. (The verb is *thanked;* the object is *host.*)

Frequency adverbs tell how often an action occurs. Some frequency adverbs like *always*, *usually*, and *often* are positioned before the verb.

Meike <u>usually</u> takes the train to her sister's.

I am <u>always</u> forgetting my car keys.

His relatives <u>often</u> eat at his restaurant.

Exercise 1   *Word Order*

Below you will see a series of words. Your task is to take each series of words and put them into an acceptable word order for statements. Rewrite each new sentence in the spaces provided. Check your answers with the Answer Key.

1. the arrived Japanese three in Canada spring students last.

2. midnight the Samir noise in usually after apartment dislikes.

3. accomplishments the celebrated the committee superior athlete's.

4. o'clock coffee will you we at the shop at meet seven?

5. paint often hardware mixes for the store Chan.

6. new the noticed the student in yesterday Amal cafeteria.

7. Africa her usually guests several includes from party.

8. in the the always wears goggles pool swimmer.

9. winter arrived Canada from in Anton and Germany during Blaz the.

10. morning usually our hot family porridge on a enjoys cold.

CHECKOUT

1. You can change the position of a word in a sentence, or you can change a word's form; when you do either, you might also be changing its part of speech.

2. It is important to know how parts of speech can function in sentences.

3. The reader constructs meaning in English partly but importantly by the word order.

4. Adjectives are positioned in front of the nouns they modify, whereas adverbs usually come before or after a verb. Adverbs cannot be placed between a verb and its object.

The Basic Sentence

Chapter Objectives

What will you have learned when you have completed this chapter?
You will be able to

1. recognize a basic English sentence.
2. identify the parts of a sentence.
3. find the subject and predicate of a sentence.
4. spot compound verbs.

Chapter 2: Self-Test

Read each group of words below. Write **YES** after each group of words that is a sentence. Write **NO** after each group of words that is not a sentence. Check your answers with the Answer Key at the back of the book.

1. Waiting by herself _____
2. By the old garage in the town _____
3. Lei plays the guitar well _____
4. Some children are afraid of the dark _____
5. Chris stopping to pick up a pizza for supper _____
6. Not all news reporting is honest _____
7. One of the pups is for sale _____
8. The idea was a good one _____
9. She sells Avon products _____
10. The first one to collect _____
11. Wanting the training for so long _____
12. She, stumbling on the hem of her new gown _____
13. I don't agree with the umpire's call on that play _____
14. Some plants are not hardy for this gardening zone _____
15. Legally speaking after some consideration of the facts _____

What Is a Basic English Sentence?

A *sentence* is a complete thought. It makes sense to a reader or listener. Every sentence needs a subject–verb set or a subject–verb–object set, but sentences can make sense without the modifiers (adjectives, adverbs, and prepositional phrases).

The committee met.

> This is a simple subject–verb or (S-V) set; it is a simple sentence.
> With modifiers:

adjective   prepositional phrase
The planning committee met on Thursday evening.

> You can remove the modifiers *planning* and *on Thursday evening*, and the sentence will still make sense.

His assistant pushed the button.

> This is a simple subject–verb–object set (S-V-O). In other words, something or someone (the subject) did something (verb) to someone or to a thing (object).
> With modifiers:

adjective   adjective   prepositional phrase
His nervous assistant pushed the wrong button on the control panel.

> The sentence has more detail in it with the addition of the modifiers (two adjectives and a prepositional phrase).

Exercise 1 *Identifying Sentences*

A sentence is a group of words that completes a whole thought and makes sense on its own. Read the word groups below. Write **YES** after each group of words that is a sentence. Check your answers with the Answer Key.

1. The security guard works on the weekends only _____

2. Drives an old Chevy truck _____

3. Elsie will not invest her money in that company _____

4. Coloured pens, glitter, glue, and cardboard cut-outs _____

5. The light at the head of the stairs _____

6. Francine's youngest daughter is 16 _____

7. The pulp mill is shutting down _____

8. Washing all the curtains in the apartment _____

9. At last he came to the end of the road _____

10. He owns a grocery store in Saint Hubert _____

11. For a short time during the afternoons _____

12. Mermaids sunbathing on the warm rocks at the shore's edge _____

13. Kobo will name his new cat "Smuckers" _____

14. Run for your life _____

15. Apparently, the supervisor was arrested for embezzling money _____

The Parts of a Sentence

English sentences must contain a *subject*—who or what is doing the action or who or what the sentence is about. The part of the sentence that contains the subject and its modifiers is called the *complete subject*. The second half of the sentence is called the *predicate*. It contains the verb and modifiers.

complete subject   predicate
The young bride smiled nervously at her family.

Sentences may contain more than one subject. Having more than one subject in a sentence is called a *compound subject*.

Waldo plays piano in the university band.

Waldo is the subject of the sentence.

Waldo and Antoinette play piano in the university band.

Waldo and Antoinette are the subjects of the sentence. This sentence has a compound subject.

The piano is old but in good condition.

The subject is *the piano*.

Exercise 2 Finding Subjects of Sentences

Read each sentence. First underline its complete subject. Then within each complete subject, identify the simple subject or compound subject. Check your answers with the Answer Key.

1. Shing and his neighbour are starting a small import business this spring.

2. My lawyer is a young woman of thirty.

3. He and the band practise downtown in a rented warehouse.

4. The medical student and the lab technician will consider the test results.

5. From the small bluff a lovely young deer gazed intently at the tourists.

6. A spokesperson for the lacrosse team commented on the fundraising campaign.

7. My uncle, grandfather, and brother are skilled carvers in the traditional way.

8. The disgruntled team captain refused to attend the press conference.

9. The venerable glassmaker and his enthusiastic apprentices design and produce some remarkable objects.

10. Antique dolls in pristine condition can command huge prices at auction.

11. The despicable miser and his money have left the country.

12. Numerous guests and their pets have all made reservations at our new hotel.

13. Thinly sliced cucumber and cream cheese on a fresh whole-wheat bagel will make a delicious lunch.

14. Mr. Alnoor and his two sons developed a new software program for the company.

15. The harpist, the cellist, and the pianist should perform with verve at tonight's concert.

Exercise 3   *Finding Subjects and Predicates*

Underline the complete subjects in the following sentences. Using a different coloured pen or pencil, underline the predicates. Check your answers with others.

1. In his school days, Ramon was an ambitious athlete.

2. Her favourite television program was cancelled this season.

3. Intelligence officers from the government caught the spy in the old railway station.

4. One of the actors fell sick on the night of the performance.

5. The campus security manager warned students about night attacks.

6. On a bright day in spring, the little swallow began to build its nest.

7. Without fresh air and good food, few children thrive.

8. I cannot remember how to play the card game.

9. A bundle of old clothes lay in the street.

10. The group of campers will explore the cave near the waterfall.

11. The magician's trick was not very impressive.

12. His ruthless business practices will be stopped by the courts.

13. Her sister's aunt watches the children during the work week.

14. You can open the can with this tool.

15. After many hours, the protestors took down their barricade.

Compound Verbs

Sometimes a sentence can contain more than one verb in the predicate. Remember that the predicate contains the verb or verbs along with objects and modifiers. A *compound verb* means more than one verb. Usually compound verbs show separate actions.

The inspector cleared his throat and spoke carefully into the microphone.

The inspector is the subject of the sentence. *Cleared his throat and spoke carefully into the microphone* is the predicate. The compound verb (two actions) is *cleared* and *spoke*.

After the long journey, the traveller placed his suitcase on the floor and flopped into bed.

After the long journey, the traveller is the complete subject. *Placed his suitcase on the floor and flopped into bed* is the predicate. The compound verb (two actions) is *placed* and *flopped*.

Exercise 4 *Predicates and Compound Verbs*

Read each sentence. Underline the predicate, and put brackets [ ] around each verb. Write **CV** after the sentence if it contains a compound verb. Check your answers with others.

1. With a good deal of hesitation, Mario got down on his knees and proposed to Jenna. _____

2. The head of state meets the delegates and welcomes them to Canada. _____

3. A sudden wind damaged some of the farm buildings and terrorized the cattle. _____

4. You apply to the Human Resources Department and wait for a response. _____

5. Jon and Armand designed the garden benches and supervised the construction of the gazebo. _____

6. Mr. and Mrs. Bendu own a store on the corner of my street and operate a furniture repair business, too. _____

7. The handler and his dog demonstrated bomb detection techniques and spoke to the crowd at the same time. _____

8. Werner finished high school in 1995 and then completed his training in aeronautical engineering at this university. _____

9. Without a doubt, Marcus plays hard at his sport and trains every summer in invitational race competitions. _____

10. The plumber inspected the drain under the bathroom sink and replaced the washer in the hot water faucet. _____

Chapter 2: Review Test

Part 1: Identifying Complete Sentences

Read each group of words. If the word group is a sentence, write **YES** in the space provided. If the word group is not a complete sentence, write **NO**.

1. Receiving a phone call after midnight startled the family. _____

2. At long last after five years of studying architecture a degree. _____

3. They cannot follow the instructions in their manual. _____

4. Pressing, folding, and cutting the lengths of cloth. _____

5. What a scream coming from the back alley! _____

6. On the campus near the student council office students gathering. _____

7. Without a heavy winter coat Ezra found the winter miserable. _____

8. The group will play cards and drink beer. _____

9. Amanda forgetting to get permission from her boss. _____

10. The plastic toolbox is too flimsy to hold these heavy tools. _____

Part 2: Identifying Complete Subjects and Predicates

Read each sentence. Underline its complete subject, and put brackets [ ] around its predicate.

1. During the weekend, Wasna lost the love of his life.

2. An African grey parrot can be easily trained to speak several words.

3. Norm and Tu became good friends over the semester.

4. The movers and the building manager have locked the elevator at the back entrance.

5. During the stampede, four horses and two drivers were injured seriously.

6. In my opinion, Nigel needs to work more on his studies.

7. Sometimes at night I think of the friends in my hometown.

8. Her salary increased by 3 percent this year.

9. The dog's bark is worse than his bite.

10. She is expressionless most of the time.

Part 3: Identifying Simple or Compound Subjects

Read each of the following sentences, and identify whether its subject is simple or compound. Write your answers in the spaces provided.

1. My duty is to my family. _____

2. Sequins and beads covered the dancer's costume. _____

3. Your doctor will recommend sleep and rest after the treatment. _____

4. The student nurses measured the drug and then calibrated the dosage. _____

5. The baseball manager and the player are arguing about the spring schedule. _____

6. Rice and beans are both complex carbohydrates. _____

7. The famous playwright and his dog visited this inn often in the winter of 1913. _____

8. Miniature lights, topiary, and paving stones were placed at the entrance to the restaurant. _____

9. Devane, Po, and Delia will work on the class project together. _____

10. Dust mites, animal dander, pollens, and moulds are the most common allergens. _____

Part 4: Identifying Simple or Compound Verbs

Read each sentence below. Underline the predicate in each sentence. Then, in the space provided, tell if each verb is simple or compound.

1. Misunderstanding leads to anger and disappointment. _____

2. The Hollywood actor owns 10 thoroughbreds and races them at this track. _____

3. A jewel sparkled from the depths of the bottle-green waters. _____

4. In a flurry of insults, Jalyn stormed across the room and slammed the door. _____

5. Some of these fruits and vegetables are grown locally. _____

6. The pizza delivery person tripped on the top stair and dropped the pizza boxes all over the landing. _____

7. The four astronauts checked the instruments, monitored their breathing, and made safety checks of the life support systems. _____

8. I walked along the shore and stopped at a small café for a cup of English breakfast tea. _____

9. The First Nations festival featured arts, songs, and stories from five Aboriginal peoples. _____

10. Mr. Chand likes to raise peaches in his backyard. _____

ESL POINTER

Inverting the Subject and Verb

In English, the subject and verb can change places or be inverted. You invert the subject and verb when you are forming questions and certain negative constructions.

Questions

Statement: Ana is a chemist.
(S-V order)

Question: Is Ana a chemist?
(V-S order)

Statement: Mrs. Hong loves cats.
(S-V order)

Question: Does Mrs. Hong love cats?
(auxiliary *Does,* V-S)

Negatives

Statement: Ana is a chemist.
(S-V order)

Negative: Not only is Ana a chemist, but she is also a musician.
(*Not only* V-S, S-V order)

Statement: Mrs. Hong loves cats.
Negative: Not only does Mrs. Hong love cats, but she also loves goldfish.
(*Not only* V-S, S-V order)

Exercise 1   Inverting S-V Order

Work in pairs. Write each of the following statements as questions and negatives. Rewrite your answers on the spaces provided. Notice the verb tense in each sentence: it will affect the auxiliary verbs.

Example: Chipo works at the computer store.
Question: Does Chipo work at the computer store?
Negative: Not only does Chipo work at the computer store, but he also skateboards in contests.

1. Bok-Soon studies business administration at Loell College.

Question:

_____

Negative:

_____

2. The dentist drills her teeth.

Question:

_____

Negative:

_____

3. My dog loves peanuts.

Question:

_____

Negative:

_____

4. Sarra spent time with Rami.

Question:

_____

Negative:

_____

5. The bulldog ate the squeaker out of the toy.

Question:

_____

Negative:

_____

6. Fen sliced the eggplant for the main dish.

Question:

_____

Negative:

_____

7. The pharmacist filled Lin's prescription.

Question:

_____

Negative:

_____

8. They changed the boundaries of her political riding.

Question:

_____

Negative:

_____

9. The ice cream cake melted on the back seat of the car.

Question:

_____

Negative:

_____

10. The cashier attends each training session.

Question:

_____

Negative:

_____

CHECKOUT

1. Every sentence needs a subject–verb set or a subject–verb–object set.

2. A sentence has more detail in it with the addition of modifiers.

3. The part of the sentence that contains the subject and its modifiers is called the complete subject.

4. The part of the sentence that is called the predicate contains the verb and modifiers of the verb.

5. A complete subject may have a simple subject or a compound subject.

6. Usually compound verbs show separate actions.

7. In English sentences, the subject and verb can sometimes change places or be inverted.

Four Sentence Types

Chapter Objectives

What will you have learned when you have completed this chapter?
You will be able to

1. tell whether a sentence is a statement, question, exclamation, or command.

2. agree that it's important to use the type of sentence that suits the purpose of your writing.

3. distinguish between fact and opinion in your writing.

4. form questions by changing the word order in a sentence.

Chapter 3: Self-Test

Part 1: Identifying Types of Sentences and Adding End Punctuation

Read the following sentences. Decide if the sentence is a statement, question, exclamation, or command. Write **S, Q, E,** or **C** after each sentence according to your decision. Add periods to the ends of statements and commands. Add question marks to the ends of questions. Add exclamation points to the ends of exclamations. Check your answers with the Answer Key at the back of the book.

1. Why did you say that to Mohammed _____

2. Stop telling me what to do _____

3. Buy some photo paper and print photos from your digital camera _____

4. I think the colour is too bright _____

5. Cecile, watch out for the ladder _____

6. What a poor listener Taki is _____

7. Would Rita like to come, too _____

8. Please pass the rice _____

9. Is that chocolate bar allowed on the Atkins diet _____

10. His little terrier chased the scruffy cat up a tree _____

11. Did you see Mike Myers's newest movie _____

12. Steve, try a little harder _____

13. Mark your answers in pencil _____

14. Did you renew your licence _____

15. The pilot was forced to make a landing in the meadow _____

Part 2: Changing Statements to Questions

Form questions using the following statements. Write your questions on the lines provided. Check your answers with the Answer Key.

> They played golf every Wednesday.
> statement
>
> Did they play golf every Wednesday?
> question

1. They enjoy learning English.

_____

2. This new book belongs to her.

_____

3. He drives to Hamilton once a week.

_____

4. The class met on the third floor.

_____

5. The store opened at nine.

_____

6. She often goes out of town.

_____

7. He wore an old coat to do the chores.

_____

Four Sentences Types

Statements, questions, commands, and exclamations make up the four basic types of English sentences. Which one you decide to use will depend on your purpose. Remember, though, that all sentences must begin with capital letters.

- *Statements* express facts or opinions. They end in periods.
- *Questions*, sometimes called *interrogative sentences*, ask for information. They end in question marks.
- *Commands*, sometimes called *imperatives*, give orders. Commands end in periods.
- *Exclamations* express surprise or emotion. They end in exclamation points.

Believe it or not, poisonous snakes do inhabit parts of Canada. (statement)

Did you know there are poisonous snakes existing today in Canada? (interrogative, or question)

Never pester a rattlesnake if you see one. (command)

A rattler can strike with lightning speed! (exclamation)

Statements: Fact or Opinion?

A *statement* is a kind of sentence that presents a fact or an opinion. Statements are the most common type of sentences found in written English. As a writer, you must think about whether your statements are expressions of fact or opinion. After all, it is important not to represent an opinion as a fact. *Facts* are provable, while *opinions* are not.

Arlo trains horses at the local race track. (fact)

Arlo is paid far too much for his work. (opinion)

Exercise 1 Finding Fact or Opinion

Write **F** after each statement that you think is a fact. Write **O** after every statement that you think is an opinion. Check your answers with the Answer Key.

1. Boys with knobby knees should not wear knee socks. _____

2. Restricted movies cannot be shown to children under the age of 18. _____

3. Algonquin National Park was designated in 1893 as Ontario's first provincial park. _____

4. The waterfalls in British Columbia are more spectacular than those in Nova Scotia. _____

5. Brothers are always a nuisance. _____

6. Children require at least eight hours of sleep per night. _____

7. Squirrels and chipmunks are pests that should be eliminated. _____

8. Eating low-fat and high-nutrition foods can help maintain good health. _____

9. No woman over the age of 30 should wear short skirts. _____

10. Canada produces the best hockey players in the world. _____

Commands

Commands are sentences stating that some action must be done. Commands can be direct and may have a harsh tone to them. You can soften commands by using *please* at their beginning or end.

Commands start with a present-tense action verb. Try to imagine you are speaking to a "you" person when you write a command. The subject of a command is understood to be "you" unless you name a particular person.

Pass the sugar for my coffee.

Please pass the sugar for my coffee.
Raissa, please pass the sugar for my coffee.

You will notice that the first command is direct, almost inconsiderate sounding, as if the speaker had no manners. The second example seems more acceptable because *please* softens it. The third example names a different subject than the *you* understood in most commands. *Raissa* is named as the subject, and a comma follows her name. A command starts with a capital letter and ends in a period.

Exclamations

Another type of sentence in English is called an exclamation. *Exclamation* comes from the root word *exclaim*, which means to express loudly or emotionally. You can expect that exclamations are used in writing to show emotion. They begin with capital letters and end in exclamation marks.

Stop teasing the dog!

We are working hard to stop crime in our neighbourhood!

The cat is getting out through the front door!

Watch out for the flying squirrel!

I am so fed up with my supervisor!

In all these examples you will notice emotion being expressed. In the first example, the speaker appears to be annoyed or angry about someone's action. In the second, the writer wants the reader to know there is strength in the neighbourhood's activities. In the next two sentences, you can see warning being given. The last example expresses someone's frustration.

Commands and Tone

A *command* may end with a period or an exclamation mark, depending on the feeling given to it by the writer. Understand that you can add an emotional feel to a sentence by the punctuation you choose. The tone is the attitude that you as a writer apply to your subject or topic. The tone will affect how your reader feels about the topic, too.

Please, have some consideration for people who are trying to study.

The command here has a particular tone. How would you characterize its tone?

Please be quiet in the library.

How would you characterize the tone of this command?

Shut up!

What about the tone of this last command?

As mentioned above, a command may end with a period or an exclamation mark, depending on the feeling the writer wishes to express by it.

Don't walk in the paint.

This command has a rather calm tone to it.

Don't walk in the paint!

Now the command expresses sharp warning and becomes an exclamation.

Exercise 2 Detecting Tone

Work in pairs. Read each sentence. Decide if the sentence is better expressed as a statement, command, or exclamation. Consider tone in making your decision. How might a listener or reader be affected by changing the tone in each sentence? Be prepared to share your answers.

1. How quiet this room is

2. Please open the door for me

3. What a peculiar walk he has

4. Something is burning

5. Please don't argue so much about it

6. Stop regretting the mistakes you have made in your life

7. Prepare for a bumpy landing

8. Please answer the question quickly

Questions

Most of the time a *question* is a sentence that asks for or invites information. You use questions when you want to know something. However, sometimes you wish to emphasize a point, or you want to make your reader stop to consider something. Sometimes you don't want an answer specifically: the answer seems obvious to you. This kind of question is used as a technique to engage the reader but not necessarily to ask for information. If a question is used for emphasis or persuasion, it is called a *rhetorical question.*

Rhetorical questions must be used appropriately. The answer to a rhetorical question may not be as obvious as you think. Use rhetorical questions sparingly.

Would you like to win some extra money? (asks for information)

Who wouldn't want to win some extra money? (rhetorical question used for emphasis)

Don't you hate it when people ask you too many questions? (rhetorical question used for persuasion)

Forming Questions

When you ask questions in English, you invert or change the word order a little bit. The *helping* or *auxiliary verb* is placed at the beginning of the sentence. Usually the subject of the sentence comes next, followed by the main or principal verb.

Canadian actors are not paid as well as their American counterparts. (statement)

Are Canadian actors not paid as well as their American counterparts? (question)

Hint

The auxiliary verb in the question should be in the same tense as the auxiliary verb in the statement. Notice that the statement above is in the present tense (auxiliary verb are*), so the question remains in the present tense (auxiliary verb* are*).*

Sometimes you need to add an auxiliary verb to form the question:

Some cowboys wear spurs. (statement)

Do some cowboys wear spurs? (question in the present tense with an auxiliary verb *do* added to the beginning of the sentence)

Exercise 3   Changing Statements to Questions

Change each of the following statements to questions. Write your answers in the spaces provided. Check your answers with others in the class.

1. A standard guitar usually has six strings.

_____

2. Pomegranates contain a lot of vitamin C.

_____

3. Carlos had never seen snow before he came to Canada.

_____

4. The students purchase their course texts from the campus bookstore.

_____

5. The decoration on the top of the chest is dated at AD 1400.

_____

6. Baby mice are born hairless.

_____

7. The sun faded our new drapes.

_____

8. Some insurance policies do not cover flood or water damage.

_____

9. Wallace Stegner wrote: "A writer is a man in search of an audience."

_____

10. The orchestra spends at least 30 minutes warming up.

_____

Exercise 4 Identifying Types of Sentences

Read the following sentences. Decide if the sentence is a statement, question, exclamation, or command. Write **S, Q, E,** or **C** after each sentence according to your decision. Add a period to the end of statements. Add a question mark to the end of questions. Add an exclamation point to the end of exclamations. Add a period (or exclamation point) to the end of commands. Check your answers with the Answer Key.

1. The cake Debra made for the party is really good   _____

2. The small animal in the pet store felt frightened by the passersby   _____

3. In a flash, the eagle swooped down on the salmon   _____

4. Stop making that terrible racket   _____

5. Would you prefer a table for one this evening, sir   _____

6. Eating melon between courses helps cleanse the palate   _____

7. Staple the ends of the bag together so the sand won't run out   _____

8. Masud works at his father's furniture store on the weekends   _____

9. How much will you earn on the construction crew   _____

10. Follow your heart instead of your head   _____

11. Please announce our engagement in the local paper   _____

12. Oh, the class picnic was a disaster   _____

13. Anthony likes to hunt and fish in the remote woods   _____

14. Where will Tanya be staying in Vancouver   _____

15. Please stop smoking as soon as you can   _____

16. Safia makes visits to the elderly in the hospital   _____

17. Some people don't mind the rain on the West Coast   _____

18. Were you ever in England   _____

19. To make good bread, you need good flour   _____

20. Close that window before the bird flies out   _____

21. The best restaurants often serve simple, fresh foods   _____

22. Oh dear, I've spilled my soup   _____

23. Has anyone seen my new squash racquet   _____

Exercise 5 *Writing Sentence Types*

Do your work on a separate sheet or use the computer. Your instructor may ask to see your sentence work, or you may be asked to correct answers in a small group.

Set 1: Write all the following sentences about hockey.

1. First write two statements.

2. Then write one question.

3. Then write one exclamation.

Set 2: Write all the following sentences about a hobby.

1. First write one question.

2. Then write three statements.

3. Then write one exclamation.

4. Then write one statement.

Set 3: Write all the following sentences about raising children.

1. First, write one exclamation.

2. Then write two statements.

Chapter 3: Review Test

Part 1: Sentences, Questions, Commands, and Exclamations

Identify each of the following sentences as a statement, question, command, or exclamation. Supply the correct end punctuation for each sentence.

1. A loathsome brown rat crept out from the wood shed   _____

2. Pay attention to what the lifeguard tells you   _____

3. Work the dough with your fingers for several minutes   _____

4. He made a childish remark about her behaviour   _____

5. Polar bears are being observed on the ice packs in parts of Nunavut   _____

6. The host made a vibrant speech and then fell off the podium   _____

7. Do you ride your bike to campus in the nice weather   _____

8. The president of the student council conveyed the information to the council   _____

9. Stop wasting my time   _____

10. The instructor asked the students to contrast the two theories   _____

11. That load is far too heavy for you to lift   _____

12. Please remind Kalid he is behind in his payments   _____

13. What specimens of native grasses did you collect for class   _____

14. Biochemistry is a relatively new field in the natural sciences   _____

15. Racism cannot be tolerated   _____

Part 2: Facts or Opinions?

Read each sentence and then write **F** after fact statements or **O** after opinion statements.

1. The Russian language is the most beautiful in the world. _____

2. The wedding took place on Saturday, May 25, 2002. _____

3. After a heavy rain, the roads are often slippery with car oil. _____

4. No one should be allowed to bring pets to campus. _____

5. Downloading music from the Internet is really a crime. _____

6. Professor Cho's lectures are really boring. _____

7. To be a parent should require a licence. _____

8. Devon has the cutest smile in town. _____

9. City planners are concerned about the traffic gridlock. _____

10. Cellphones must be turned off when students are using the library. _____

Part 3: Statements to Questions

Change each of the following statements into questions. Write the questions in the spaces provided.

1. They are not allowed to smoke anywhere on campus.

_____

2. Dutch cooking is really delicious.

_____

3. The surveyor pounded in the stake at the lot line.

_____

4. The producer always changes the set at the last minute.

_____

5. Two of the joggers witnessed the accident in the park.

_____

6. Zagir wants to study criminal justice at the university.

_____

7. The sale features special discounts for seniors.

_____

8. In Mexico, people celebrate the Day of the Dead in November.

_____

9. The agent listed the house on the Multiple Listing Service.

_____

10. The ski instructor prepares the site for his lessons.

_____

ESL POINTER

Asking Questions

When you ask questions in the English language, you can use one of several techniques. Asking questions in conversation may be different from asking questions in written form.

Tag Questions

Tag questions have to do with conversation. These are question phrases you can add or tag on to the end of a statement. You may use tag questions when you wish to start a conversation, get confirmation of something, or add emphasis.

Tag Questions						
do I?	does he?	does she?	does it?	do we?	do you?	do they?
did I?	did he?	did she?	did it?	did we?	did you?	did they?
don't I?	doesn't he?	doesn't she?	doesn't it?	don't we?	don't you?	don't they?
didn't I?	didn't he?	didn't she?	didn't it?	didn't we?	didn't you?	didn't they?
am I?	is he?	is she?	is it?	are we?	are you?	are they?
aren't I?	isn't he?	isn't she?	isn't it?	aren't we?	aren't you?	aren't they?
wasn't I?	wasn't he?	wasn't she?	wasn't it?	weren't we?	weren't you?	weren't they?
have I?	has he?	has she?	has it?	have we?	have you?	have they?
haven't I?	hasn't he?	hasn't she?	hasn't it?	haven't we?	haven't you?	haven't they?

Here are some examples of how tag questions are used:

I don't need to wait here, do I?

They won the contest, didn't they?

It's been a long, cold winter, hasn't it?

Lian has the chapter answers for anatomy class, hasn't she?

You were surprised by your fame, weren't you?

W5 plus How Questions

You might use a "question" word like *who, how, where, when, why,* or *what* (W5 plus How) at the beginning of your sentences in writing or in conversation.

To form some of your questions, use the word + an auxiliary verb + subject + the main verb:

Who was calling you last night?

How is your sister-in-law doing these days?

Where did Hans put the children's new shoes?

Why is Suki crying?

What were the birds eating?

Forming Standard Questions

To form questions in English you usually put the auxiliary verb at the beginning of the sentence, followed by the subject and then the main verb (aux + S + main).

Was Luc running from his past?

Have you visited the provincial museum?

Did the chipmunk eat all the peanuts?

Were the soldiers marching in the parade?

Had Orianna completed her degree in Finland?

Exercise 1 *Changing Statements to Questions*

Change each of the following statements to a question according to the instructions. Be prepared to share your answers.

1. July was an extremely dry and hot month. (Ask a tag question.)

   _____

2. Noel worked at this service station while he went to high school. (Ask a standard question.)

   _____

3. We can't make pudding without milk. (Ask a W5 plus How question.)

   _____

4. The little boy is tall for a three-year-old. (Ask a tag question that invites conversation.)

   _____

5. My bus leaves at three o'clock. (Ask a tag question that is looking for confirmation of information.)

   _____

6. Rafi graduated from a technical university in the United States. (Ask a standard question.)

   _____

7. The students do not know when their physics exam is scheduled. (Ask a W5 plus How question.)

   _____

CHECKOUT

1. Each of the four types of English sentences requires correct end punctuation.

2. The statement is a type of sentence that can express either fact or opinion.

3. Commands start with a present-tense action verb.

4. Tag questions have to do with conversation.

5. Some kinds of emotion can be expressed in exclamations.

6. The sentence tones you use as a writer can affect how a reader responds to the topic.

Sentence Patterns

Chapter Objectives
What will you have learned when you have completed this chapter?
You will be able to

1. identify the pattern of a sentence.
2. change the pattern of sentences.
3. make use of conjunctions to connect clauses.
4. tell conjunctive adverbs from conjunctions.
5. describe the types of clauses.
6. spot relative clauses.

Chapter 4: Self-Test

Part 1: Identifying Patterns

Identify each of the following sentences according to pattern by writing **1, 2, 3,** or **4** in the spaces provided. (Use 1 for simple sentences, 2 for compound, 3 for complex, and 4 for compound-complex.) Check your answers with the Answer Key.

1. Lenny is a hard-working student, but he often takes time to relax, too. _____

2. Nathaniel is a fastidious housekeeper who is constantly pestering his children to clean their rooms. _____

3. The officers stopped the speeding car and asked the driver several pointed questions. _____

4. Because of the fine weather, the family went for a walk near the woods. _____

5. Although his father was a carver, Keith finds it difficult to manipulate the tools in the correct manner, and he is often frustrated by his inability to work. _____

6. None of the members of the group would speak until one farmer got to his feet and began to address the government official. _____

7. Repair the damage to the tarp on the truck and then meet me out back. _____

8. The dancers moved in a slow circle while the drummers and singers accompanied their movements with rhythmic song. _____

9. Near the outcropping of rock at the frozen shore of the lake stood a magnificent snowy owl. _____

10. Breakfast will be served at seven; supper is served at six. _____

11. Wait here while I call my brother on my cellphone. _____

12. The horse that had escaped the fire was a valuable thoroughbred. _____

13. Putting posters up in the main hallways of the central campus building is not allowed. _____

14. Which of these brands of coffees do you prefer? _____

15. As the first of the fireworks exploded in the night sky, a surprising hush fell on the crowd and anticipation filled the air. _____

Part 2: Identifying Clauses

Underline each main clause in each of the following sentences.

1. The organist who plays in the band is an undercover agent for the police.

2. Whenever Eldon sees his supervisor, he pretends to be working.

3. The worst job that I ever had was being a line cook in a greasy spoon.

4. Quebec City is a special place to visit in the winter; the carnival is really exciting.

5. Four men got out of the car near the bank while one waited nervously.

Part 3: Constructing Patterns of Sentences

Add ideas to the following sentences as directed.

1. Shaina was afraid. (Add an idea to make the sentence into a pattern three as explained below.)

2. The door slammed. (Add an idea to make the sentence into a pattern two as explained below.)

3. Nola hesitated. She stared at him intently. (Join the ideas to make a pattern two sentence as explained below.)

4. The Halloween mask was grotesque. (Add other ideas to make a pattern four sentence as explained below.)

5. Going to parties is not his idea of fun. (Add another idea to make the sentence a pattern two as explained below. Use a semicolon correctly.)

Sentence Patterns

Sentence patterns are another way of thinking about sentence types. This textbook uses the term *pattern* like this:

A simple sentence is pattern one.
A compound sentence is pattern two.
A complex sentence is pattern three.
A compound-complex sentence is pattern four.

Using the pattern number will help you remember what sort of sentence you are reading, writing, and analyzing. What pattern of sentence you use will depend on your purpose in writing.

Self-Test: Pattern One Sentences

Try the following self-test to check out your knowledge of pattern one, simple sentences. Your instructor may want to see your work. Check your answers with the Answer Key.

Part 1: Identifying Sentences

Read each of the following groups of words. Put a checkmark beside each group of words that you think is a sentence.

 1. The huge rocks at the bottom of the riverbed. _____

 2. Several tourists were taking pictures of the totem poles. _____

 3. Suki's cat sleeping all day. _____

 4. Worm castings are added to the compost. _____

 5. In a minute after I arrange my DVDs. _____

 6. Stopping the baby from sucking his thumb is difficult. _____

 7. Peel the oranges and the pears for the fresh fruit salad. _____

 8. Mrs. Singh prepares her chutney from fresh ginger, raisins, apples, and spices. _____

 9. The twins are allergic to dust and pollen. _____

10. Worrying over her final driving test. _____

Part 2: Identifying Subjects and Predicates

Read each of the sentences below. Underline the complete subject of the sentence once. Underline the predicate of the sentence twice.

 1. Many cooks like to grow fresh herbs.

 2. During the festival a fiddler and a drummer played every day outside my shop window.

 3. His career in politics was finished in 2004.

 4. The small, sleek brown otter caught two little crabs for breakfast.

5. Our relatives will be at the terminal to meet us next week.

6. Were Ramone and Cecile engaged over the weekend?

7. Jasper National Park in Alberta contains the largest icefield in the Canadian Rocky Mountains.

8. Duncan spotted a small sailboat on the horizon.

9. Toby's children take ballet lessons at the community centre.

10. Brandon, Manitoba, has a major university.

Part 3: Identifying Pattern One Sentences

Read each of the following sentences. Write **S** after each sentence that is a simple or pattern one sentence.

1. The tourists and their guide stared in wonder at the large statue of a taco. _____

2. My dog, Spitz, knows 11 tricks, but my cat, Zoon, doesn't know a single one. _____

3. The newly elected government was erecting two bridges over the Red River. _____

4. Although Ezra is content with his new job, he does not like his salary. _____

5. Toronto's garbage strike was over in the summer of 2004. _____

6. Auntie fried the bacon, and then she poached some eggs. _____

7. Deep in the heart of the city a gang of Dobermans watched over a warehouse full of rare Dutch paintings. _____

8. Alex refused the offer; Dominic, on the other hand, accepted it. _____

9. Plagued by hungry mosquitoes, the campers took refuge in the small cabin. _____

10. The veterinarian is a strict vegetarian who gives lectures while she examines people's pets. _____

Pattern One: The Simple Sentence

A *sentence* is a word group that completes an idea or thought. In broad terms, a sentence is made up of two major parts:

- the *subject* (what the sentence is about)
- the *predicate* (tells about the subject)

complete subject   predicate
My pet rabbits   love to hide in the tall grass in their pen.

Here are more examples of subjects and predicates:

They inhabit the planet Earth.

This sentence contains only one idea. *They* is the subject of the sentence, and *inhabit the planet Earth* is the predicate.

Do you enjoy any sports?

This sentence contains only one idea. *You* is the subject and *do* and *enjoy any sports* is the predicate.

We worked in the garden and stopped for a cool drink.

In this one-idea sentence, *we* is the subject and *worked in the garden and stopped for a cool drink* is the predicate. Although you may have noticed two verbs in the sentence, you will recognize that there is only one subject and predicate set.

The fitness instructor attends Kelly College.

The subject of the sentence is *the fitness instructor*; the predicate of the sentence is *attends Kelly College.*

A pattern one sentence, then, is a *simple sentence* because it contains one subject and predicate set. A predicate must contain a verb, and a pattern one sentence must be complete in itself.

Hint

A pattern one sentence contains one idea (one subject–predicate set); therefore, it is considered to be a simple sentence. One idea = pattern one.

Here are a few more examples:

Roger has decided to work over the weekend in Hamilton.

Her favourite television program has been cancelled.

One of the cheapest restaurants in Montreal has the best food.

Our power went out during the heavy rainstorm.

The chief executive officer and his assistant defrauded the company of funds and then left for Mexico.

Look at the parts of each sentence. Then you can consider how many ideas each sentence has.

subject   predicate
Roger has decided to work over the weekend in Hamilton. (one subject–predicate set)

       subject   predicate
Her favourite television program has been cancelled. (one subject–predicate set)

        subject   predicate
One of the cheapest restaurants in Montreal has the best food. (one subject–predicate set)

  subject   predicate
Our power went out during the heavy rainstorm. (one subject–predicate set)

subject   predicate

The chief executive officer and his assistant defrauded the company of funds and then left for Mexico.

This last sentence also has only one subject and predicate set. Admittedly, the sentence may seem more complicated because two people (*the chief executive officer* and *his assistant*) are the subjects, and these two subjects completed two actions: *defrauded* and *left*. The sentence has two subjects and two verbs, so you might think, "Isn't that more than one idea?"

To help your thinking, consider the number of complete subject and predicate sets that appear in the sentence. Is there more than one?

You will see that the two subjects come together in the subject part of the sentence, and the two actions are positioned in the predicate part of the sentence. The pattern looks like this: SS-VV. Therefore, the sentence still contains only one subject–predicate set.

These examples show you that the most important condition for a simple sentence is that it contains only one subject and predicate set.

Exercise 1   *Identifying Pattern One Sentences*

The following are all sentences, but not every one is a pattern one sentence. Select the pattern one sentences and write **1** beside each. Check your answers with the Answer Key.

1. In the fall of 2005, Kimi visited her grandfather on a distant Japanese island. _____

2. The sale was over; Vitto had sold all his paintings. _____

3. The engineer of the train fell asleep at the switch. _____

4. Fancy material for the dress will cost about $250. _____

5. Mortified by her humiliating defeat, the tiny terrier roared at her shadow. _____

6. Will the university team decide on first-draft picks today, or will they postpone a decision until the new semester? _____

7. One of his children lives in a small town outside Barrie, Ontario; the other one lives in Windsor. _____

8. Paint the door trim gold. _____

9. Susanna and Reggie cleared the tables and then stacked the blueberry boxes. _____

10. The police reported a large adult cougar in the area and warned residents to keep children and small pets indoors. _____

11. Every piece of evidence pointed to the suspect. _____

12. Do you celebrate Valentine's Day in any special way? _____

13. Thick fog curled into the small port, but the fleet still left for a day of fishing. _____

14. I hate missing my bus when I sleep in on class days. _____

15. The new reporter stumbled on his words as he spoke to the fashion model. _____

Exercise 2 *Writing Pattern One Sentences*

Use each of the following words or phrases in an effective pattern one sentence. Your instructor may ask to see your work, or you may correct sentences in a small group.

1. at risk

2. her friend

3. one celebrity

4. shouted

5. under repair

6. after a workout

7. disappear

8. must have been lying

9. track

10. the realtor and her customer

11. in three minutes

12. Saskatoon

13. four clowns

14. a basket of bread

15. the score

16. three chickens

Exercise 3 *Identifying Pattern One Sentences*

Write **1** after each sentence that is a pattern one sentence. Check your answers with the Answer Key.

1. Lee was able to see Mr. Loukins about the fireplace in his new apartment. _____

2. After dinner, we will practise our tango lessons for Thursday's class. _____

3. Keely wanted one of her friends to take her to the opening of the film, but no one was able to go. _____

4. They have never tried to kayak in the ocean before. _____

5. With a flip of the switch, the lights of the new mall came to life. _____

6. Some monks will live in silence for the rest of their days. _____

7. Because the rookie was caught stealing, he was dismissed from the force. _____

8. Thanh and I love to go sightseeing in downtown Toronto, especially in the early evenings and late afternoons. _____

9. Which one of these brands of soap should I use on a cotton sweater? _____

10. He comes from a small mining town in northern Quebec. _____

11. The politician's advisor submitted her resignation and applied for a position with a different cabinet minister. _____

12. If you take the dog for a walk, be very careful not to run her too hard. _____

13. The guests sorted their gifts and then greeted their lively host. _____

14. Maxwell takes part in the rodeo every summer; his specialty is bronco-busting. _____

15. This recent survey says that Canadians tend to love to shop. _____

Self-Test: Pattern Two Sentences

Try the following self-test to check out your knowledge of pattern two, compound sentences. Your instructor may want to see your work. The answers are not found at the back of the book.

Part 1: Identifying Pattern Twos

Identify each of the following sentences as pattern two (compound) sentences by writing **2** in the spaces provided.

1. A Quebec photographer won a national award for nature photography, particularly for the shots of the Laurentian Mountains. _____

2. The leader of the opposition questioned the minister's motives in an insulting way, but the speaker of the house did not intervene. _____

3. The soccer park was recently upgraded for the competition, and the local community association felt proud of its contributions. _____

4. She presides over her garden like a queen over her estate. _____

5. The class called Willie a bookworm because he was always reading. _____

6. Strip off the old wax from the tabletop; then apply a thin layer of paste wax. _____

7. Friends invited me over for dinner on Saturday night, but I had to decline their kind invitation. _____

8. A winding path led up to a small, mushroom-shaped house deep in the fir forest. _____

9. Angry, his mother shouted at the man and shook her fist in a fury. _____

10. The baseball team practised on the field while fans whistled and cheered in the stands. _____

Part 2: Coordinating Conjunctions

Name four conjunctions that can be used to connect clauses in compound sentences.

1. _____

2. _____

3. _____

4. _____

Part 3: Changing Patterns

Change each of the pattern one (simple) sentences into pattern two (compound) sentences.

1. After a long day at the office, Ruben prefers to stay at home. (pattern one)

pattern two:

_____

_____

2. Please support Rashid as president of the student council. (pattern one)

pattern two:

_____

_____

3. The house guest overstayed her welcome. (pattern one)

pattern two:

_____

_____

4. The filmgoer enjoyed the foreign film. (pattern one)

pattern two:

_____

_____

5. It is easy to make strawberry freezer jam. (pattern one)

pattern two:

_____

_____

Pattern Two: The Compound Sentence

A pattern two sentence contains two subject–predicate sets (two ideas). Each subject–predicate set is complete, like a pattern one sentence. Therefore, a pattern two sentence, called a *compound sentence*, has two pattern one sentences in it. The two ideas are of equal importance in a pattern two sentence. Think: pattern one + pattern one = pattern two sentence.

The remote control was lost in the living room, but Bo found it yesterday.

Pattern one: The remote control was lost in the living room.

Pattern one: Bo found it yesterday.

The group of reporters met in front of the building, and the executive came out to greet them.

Pattern one: The group of reporters met in front of the building.

Pattern one: The executive came out to greet them.

Exercise 4   Identifying Pattern One inside Pattern Two Sentences

Read each of the following pattern two (compound) sentences. Underline each pattern one sentence you see within them. Check your answers with the Answer Key.

1. Several of the technicians were away for special training, but no one had been hired to replace them on the job.

2. Sometimes Rob stops for supper at fast-food outlets, and he loves to order the largest burger with extra cheese.

3. Some dogs have waterproof coats, and they can stay relatively dry even in heavy rain.

4. I was at a dance last Friday night, and I met a great new guy from New Zealand.

5. Please freeze this extra fish, and package up the salad for lunch tomorrow.

6. Health care workers walked off the job in Edmonton, and their union leader made an announcement about their complaints.

7. He was not sponsored in the race, but he ran anyway.

8. A backbencher from the provincial government apologized for his error, and he offered to resign his position on the committee.

9. The newest hybrid cars are becoming popular, but they remain too pricey for the average consumer.

10. Calgary firefighters were called to a house fire in the early morning, but they were unable to save the dwelling.

Clauses and Conjunctions in Pattern Two Sentences

Sometimes a pattern one or simple sentence is also called a main clause. A *clause* is a group of words with a subject and predicate. A *main clause* can stand alone. A pattern two sentence contains two main clauses. The two main clauses relate to each other and have equal value.

They advise their customers not to give out their credit card numbers over the phone, and they suggest being cautious about privacy using the Internet.

Pattern one sentence or main clause: They advise their customers not to give out their credit card numbers over the phone.
Pattern one sentence or main clause: They suggest being cautious about privacy using the Internet.

In pattern two sentences, the main clauses are connected by joiner words called *coordinating conjunctions*. The conjunctions show a relationship between the clauses. Coordinating conjunctions join ideas of equal value.

A comma is placed before the coordinating conjunction.

A semicolon (;) can also be used to join the two main clauses together in a pattern two sentence. The semicolon functions like the conjunction *and*.

Coordinating Conjunctions			
and	but	nor	or
so	for	yet	

    S-V set 1   S-V set 2
Kary was sorry, *and* she apologized.

There are two subject–predicate sets—two main clauses (fact 1: *Kary was sorry*; fact 2: *she apologized*).

    S-V set 1   S-V set 2
The cook was ill, *but* he came to work anyway.

There are two subject–predicate sets—two main clauses (fact 1: *the cook was ill*; fact 2: *he came to work anyway*).

S-V set 1   S-V set 2
You might try the ice cream cake, *or* you might enjoy the cherry torte.

There are two subject–predicate sets—two main clauses (fact 1: *you might try the ice cream cake*; fact 2: *you might enjoy the cherry torte*).

S-V set 1   S-V set 2
Philip is going to visit Spain this summer; he is learning Spanish for the trip.

There are two subject–predicate sets—two main clauses (fact 1: *Philip is going to visit Spain this summer*: fact 2: *he is learning Spanish*).

In each of these examples, notice the coordinating conjunctions (*joiners*) that connect the two subject–predicate sets. Notice that a semicolon (;) can join the two sets (two main clauses).

Here are a few more examples:

Jose was not pleased with the instructor's explanation, but he did not mention it.

Forget about your troubles, and take a walk with me.

The little boat washed up on the shore, for it had long been abandoned by its owner.

Every season PEI hosts a strongman competition; this year my brother is planning to enter the contest.

We could go on a picnic on Saturday, or we could make spaghetti at home.

He would not talk to the supervisor, nor would he talk to his friends.

The cat saw fledglings in the nest, so it waited in the bushes below.

Pat loved hiking, yet he had little time to enjoy his favourite activity.

Hint

Notice that you must place a comma in front of the coordinating conjunction in a pattern two sentence.

The Meaning of Different Conjunctions

Conjunctions are words that join. As you know, you would use one of the seven coordinating conjunctions (*and, but, for, so, yet, nor, or*) or a semicolon to join the two main clauses in a pattern two sentence. It is important for you to know that these conjunctions have different and subtle meanings.

1. **If you use the coordinating conjunction *and* in a pattern two sentence, it means you want to add another idea to the first idea.** You are not commenting on the first main clause; you are adding or reporting further information.
   The bull entered the ring, *and* he prodded the earth with his hooves.
   First main clause: The bull entered the ring.
   Second main clause: He prodded the earth with his hooves.

2. **If you use the coordinating conjunctions** *but* **or** *yet* **in a pattern two sentence, it means you are contrasting or contradicting the first idea.** The second main clause provides a contrast or change to the first main clause.

Helium is a relatively cheap gas to produce, *but* few industries have a use for it.

Helium is a relatively cheap gas to produce, *yet* few industries have a use for it.

First main clause: Helium is a relatively cheap gas to produce.

Second main clause: Few industries have a use for it.

The coordinating conjunctions *but* and *yet* show a change or contrast.

3. **If you use the coordinating conjunction** *for* **as the joiner in a pattern two sentence, it means you want to add a reason to the first clause.**

The picture was not flattering, for the child was making terrible faces at the camera.

First main clause: The picture was not flattering.

Second main clause: The child was making terrible faces at the camera.

The coordinating conjunction *for* provides a reason for the first clause.

4. **If you wish to use the coordinating conjunction** *so* **in your pattern two sentence, it means you want to talk about consequence in the second main clause.**

The door was jammed, so Nicky had to fix it.

First main clause: The door was jammed.

Second main clause: Nicky has to fix it.

The coordinating conjunction *so* shows what happened as a consequence of the first main clause.

5. **Using** *nor* **as a coordinating conjunction signifies a negative and means that you want to say "not either."**

The student did not want failure, nor did she want fame.

First main clause: The student did not want failure.

Second main clause: Nor did she want fame.

Notice the word-order change after *nor*—the main clause does not say *She did not want fame either,* but that is what it means. You will notice that the auxiliary or helping verb comes first, followed by the subject.

6. **If you use** *or* **as a coordinating conjunction in your pattern two sentence, it means you want to show a choice.**

The program has a damaged file, or the ISP is experiencing technical difficulties.

First main clause: The program has a damaged file.

Second main clause: The ISP is experiencing technical difficulties.

The coordinating conjunction *or* implies a choice—either main clause one or main clause two.

Exercise 5 *Identifying Conjunctions*

Underline each conjunction in each of the following sentences.

Then in the space provided, write **CHOICE** if the conjunction provides a choice. Write **REASON** if the conjunction indicates a reason. Write **CONSEQUENCE** if the conjunction shows a consequence. Write **ADD** if the conjunction adds a fact or information. Write **CONTRAST** if the conjunction shows a contrast. Write **NOT EITHER** if the conjunction shows a negative. Check your answers with the Answer Key.

1. The actor did not wish for stardom, nor did he want a huge salary. _____

2. Lolita was difficult to please, for she was young and easily bored. _____

3. The builder told the couple about the crumbling foundation, and he informed them of the delay. _____

4. No one was expected to clean house for the new priest, for he seemed energetic and anxious to do it himself. _____

5. The creature lived in the hole in the log, so our footsteps disturbed it. _____

6. Fifty people applied for the job, but only one was hired. _____

7. Gin and Fay will chop the wood, or they will help prepare the fireplace. _____

8. Millions of people visit Canadian national parks each year, yet few know the history of the parks. _____

9. Hockey practice starts at eight, and the coach wants us there on time. _____

10. He decorated the window, but he forgot to add the special checked sashes. _____

11. Can workers avoid injury in this occupation, or do they have to suffer later in life? _____

12. The duke has challenged you to a duel, but he can wait until Thursday. _____

13. The new cashier could not balance his cash, nor could he follow cashing out procedures. _____

14. They will invite you to their anniversary party, or they will leave you off their list. _____

15. The challenger wanted the larger club, for it was made of blasted oak. _____

Conjunctive Adverbs

These words look like true conjunctions, but they function differently. They work as sentence adverbs and help express a relationship between the ideas. When they relate independent clauses, they require a semicolon. Here are some common conjunctive adverbs.

> Conjunctive Adverbs
>
> | moreover | however | therefore |
> | furthermore | then | thus |
> | consequently | | |

True conjunctions are said to be fixed in their positions; they cannot be moved to other parts of the sentence. To determine whether a word is a true conjunction, or joiner, try moving it into different places in the clause. If the word can be shifted into various positions and the sentence still makes sense, then the word is not a conjunction. Remember: Conjunctions cannot be moved.

Ted wanted to take the training sessions on computer however he got his application in too late to join in. (Is however a true joiner?)

Try moving *however* to another part of the sentence.

Ted wanted to take the training sessions on computer; he got his application in too late to join in, however.

Because *however* can be moved around, it is not a true conjunction; it is a conjunctive adverb. Therefore, you have to use a semicolon to join the two main clauses.

Exercise 6 *Adding Punctuation to Pattern Two Sentences*

The following pattern two sentences have missing commas and semicolons. Put in the necessary punctuation. Be prepared to share your answers with the class.

1. We have a backup plan so we'll tell you about it in good time.

2. The video game did not feature anything new nor did it provide any extra levels of play.

3. Yung-Li was shocked to hear the news about her old boyfriend however she did not reveal her emotions to anyone.

4. You may order your purchases online or you may fax us.

5. Panda bears are believed to be connected with good luck but black cats are said to bring misfortune.

6. Her aunt does not want to be disturbed nor does she want to have anything more to eat tonight.

7. The technician separated the vials of blood into categories moreover she double checked the labels for safety's sake.

8. My neighbour's apple tree supplies the sweetest red apples furthermore it provides shade over part of their back patio.

9. Huge waves rolled onto the beach and high winds lashed the little huts.

10. Would you like me to cancel your reservations or would you prefer to go ahead with your trip?

11. Pass the cakes to Freddie but don't let him take too many!

12. Sara's rent will increase at the end of this month consequently she will visit her social worker to get extra financial help.

Self-Test: Pattern Three Sentences

Part 1: Identifying Pattern Three Sentences

Read each of the following sentences. In the spaces provided, write 3 after each pattern three sentence. Check your answers with the Answer Key.

1. Thinking through your problems may help you solve them. _____

2. Because she is often late for work, Cheryle received a reprimand. _____

3. Feeding the bears in the park is prohibited, but giving bread to the ducks is not. _____

4. The physiotherapist attached the ultrasound wand before she turned on the electricity. _____

5. When I hear that music, I want to cry. _____

6. Rubies and pearls were encrusted on the royal kitten's collar. _____

7. The police officer will give you a ticket now because you were speeding in the school zone. _____

8. Mr. Dhillon took a trip to India last week, and he really enjoyed seeing the old sights again. _____

9. May I offer you an aperitif before dinner, or would you prefer iced spring water? _____

10. Those loose ropes could cause problems for us when the boat pulls away from the dock. _____

Part 2: Clauses in Pattern Three Sentences

Underline the main clauses in the following sentences. Put brackets [ ] around subordinate clauses. Check your answers in the Answer Key.

1. Maxie wishes to apologize because she took your car.

2. When the dinner begins, tell us some of your favourite jokes.

3. Oda married Carla at the University of Regina when they were both physics students.

4. The paint that I bought for the dining room is a bright yellow rather than a creamy one.

5. Please disregard what the pilot says to you during the flight.

6. Most of the time the singer entertains on the cruise ship although he would prefer to be in Las Vegas.

7. No one suspected that the mild, wrinkled old woman was the bank robber.

8. If the announcer forgets how to pronounce your name, please assist him.

9. She has been the curator of a major museum in Toronto since she graduated with a master's degree in fine arts.

10. Before we light the birthday candles on our cake, let's all make a wish!

Pattern Three: The Complex Sentence

Complex sentences contain two or more ideas, but only one of these ideas is the main clause (main idea). The other idea or ideas in complex sentences depend on the main idea and cannot stand alone. They are, therefore, called *subordinate clauses* (*dependent ideas* or *fragments*). Remember that, although these ideas are dependent, they must contain a subject-verb set. The dependent ideas in complex sentences are joined to the main idea by *subordinate conjunctions* (joiners). The clauses relate by time, condition, or reason.

1. A clause is a word group that adds an idea.
2. All clauses contain subject and verb sets.
3. Clauses can function in different ways.

Here are some subordinate conjunctions that may be used in forming complex sentences:

        S V
because he was furious

      S   V
since George interrupted us

       S V
before I was there

Types of Clauses

There are basically two types of clauses: *main* and *subordinate*. A third type of clause is really a kind of subordinate clause. It is called a *relative* clause.

Main Clauses

Some English handbooks call clauses that can stand alone *main clauses*. Other books call main clauses *principal clauses*, and still others may refer to them as *independent clauses*. So, the terms *main clause, principal clause,* and *independent clause* may be used interchangeably. *Spotlight on Sentence and Paragraph Skills* refers to these clauses as *main*.

The thing to remember is that when main clauses stand alone, they are considered sentences. Here are some examples of main clauses:

He wrote a short story about their friendship.

Nadia works nights at the hospital.

She wore a yellow ribbon.

Subordinate Clauses

Some English handbooks refer to the second type of clause as a *subordinate clause*. Other books call them *dependent clauses*, and still others refer to them as *fragment clauses*. All three terms mean the same thing. *Spotlight on Sentence and Paragraph Skills* refers to these clauses as *subordinate clauses*.

It is most important to remember that when subordinate clauses stand alone they are considered to be a type of sentence error called a *fragment error*. Here are some examples of subordinate clauses:

since the dog is having puppies

that he received from his son

after the concert was over

In pattern three sentences, the clauses relate to one another in specific ways.

Subordinate Conjunctions

Conjunctions are words that act as joiners. They show how ideas relate to one another. Remember: conjunctions are joiner words.

Hint
The word conjunction has the word junction in it, and a junction is a place where things join.

Subordinate Conjunctions			
after	because	when	although
while	as if	unless	until
before	if	as	where

Here are some examples of subordinate conjunctions in pattern three sentences:

Sidney was away from work because he hurt his back. (*Because* is a conjunction; it joins the two ideas together and sets up a relationship between them.)

It rains a good deal in Victoria in March and April, although visitors do enjoy lovely summer months. (*Although* is a conjunction; it joins the two ideas together and sets up a contrast between them.)

Relationships and Subordinate Conjunctions

Conjunctions express a relationship between ideas or clauses. In pattern three sentences, subordinate conjunctions indicate causes, effects, comparisons, contradictions, conditions, or time.

Subordinate Conjunctions				
Cause and Effect	Comparison	Contradiction	Condition	Time
because	as though	although	if	whenever
since	as if	even though	unless	when
so that		though	when	before
				while
				as
				as soon as
				after
				until *or* till
				once

Here are some examples of how subordinate conjunctions function:

Because the children were tired, they were unable to watch the late movie. (*Because* indicates a reason or causal relationship.)

Mr. Brooks left early even though he had spent the weekend in bed. (*Even though* indicates a contradiction.)

Although he had not done the work, George left early because he had an appointment. (*Although* indicates a contradiction.)

While Adolf slept, Skippy warmed herself in the sun. (*While* indicates time or simultaneous action.)

I will not be coming to the party since I have not been invited. (*Since* indicates a reason or causal relationship.)

After he completed the play, he got drunk. (*After* indicates a time relationship.)

Rhonda played tennis while her husband coached soccer. (*While* indicates time or simultaneous action.)

The dancer felt emotionally exhausted because she had lost the competition. (*Because* indicates a reason or causal relationship.)

Unless you apologize to me, I will never forgive you. (*Unless* sets a condition.)

Relative Clauses

Relative clauses are a kind of subordinate clause that must be placed beside the words they modify. They begin with special pronouns called *relative pronouns* (*who, whoever, that, which, whose*) if the pronoun is acting as the subject of the clause. If *that* begins the clause but is not the subject of the clause, it is considered a conjunction.

The tiger that was rare was shipped to the zoo in Calgary. (*That was rare* is a relative clause modifying *tiger*. *That* is the subject of the clause.)

The little boy who was missing has been found safe. (*Who was missing* is a relative clause modifying *boy*. *Who* is the subject of the clause.)

Some of the seed that was in the small bag has spilled all over the floor. (*That was in the small bag* is a relative clause modifying *seed*. *That* is the subject of the clause.)

The contest that was advertised on local television is sponsored by WorkRite. (*That was advertised on local television* is a relative clause modifying *contest*. *That* is the subject of the clause.)

He knew the man who was singing. (*Who was singing* is a relative clause. It modifies *man* and tells which man is being discussed. *Who* is the subject of the relative clause.)

The lamp that sits in the hallway was broken yesterday. (*That sits in the hallway* is a relative clause modifying *lamp*. *That* is the subject of the relative clause.)

Notice that sometimes relative clauses can split the main clause in two.

The drug that was banned was manufactured in Europe. (*The drug was manufactured in Europe* is the main clause. *That was banned* is a relative clause, modifying *drug*. The relative clause splits the main clause in two.)

When referring to people, try to use the relative pronoun *who* rather than *that*.

The woman that sewed the dress is famous. (incorrect)

The woman who sewed the dress is famous. (correct: *who sewed the dress* refers to a person, so use *who* in reference)

Exercise 7   Identifying Types of Clauses

Underline the main clauses. Put the subordinate clauses in brackets [ ]. Check your answer with the Answer Key.

1. When the paint factory allowed effluent into the stream, thousands of salmon fingerlings died.

2. The diamonds glittered as they lay in the snow.

3. Do not hesitate to call me if you have concerns.

4. After you add the eggs, stir the dumpling dough rapidly.

5. The heat from the July sun is not good for lettuce because the leaves wilt easily.

6. The school district is promoting a new reading program for kindergarten classes by outlining its complete literacy offerings in its current brochure.

7. His website features pink poodles, dancing popcorn, and a blinking robot when you click the "enter" button.

8. The light that comes in from the street disturbs my sleep.

9. The bartender who runs this place is an old friend of the duke's.

10. She studied the map, which confused her even more.

Exercise 8 *Adding Clauses to Make Complex Sentences*

These are subordinate clauses. Add a main clause to make each of the sentences complex. Underline each subject once. Underline the verbs twice. Be prepared to share your answers.

1. since the boys were late

2. although the weather has changed

3. if you have your wish

4. when an election is called

5. which was almost extinguished

6. who was a hard worker

7. because the days are longer

8. after the bullfight was over

Exercise 9 *Group Activity: Combining Ideas for Complex Sentences*

Work in groups of three to five. Using the conjunction indicated, combine the two ideas together to form a complex sentence; rewrite your sentences on the lines provided. Be prepared to share your responses.

1. Adult male bears can weigh up to 400 kilograms each. They are among the world's largest animals.

(because)

_____

_____

2. The beluga whale averages 3 metres in length and 320 kilograms in weight. The largest grow to 5 metres and 550 kilograms or more.

(although)

_____

_____

3. Outfitters are experienced Inuit hunters. Their ancestors have matched wits with the bear for centuries.

(whose)

_____

_____

4. Polar bears live basically on seal. They hunt the seal out on the sea ice.

(which)

_____

_____

Exercise 10   Complex Sentences with Relative Clauses

Write a new sentence by joining the two sentences using *that*, *which*, or *whereas* as joiners. Be prepared to share your answers.

1. Every atom has electrons. Electrons are very small particles of an atom.

2. Lightning is one form of static electricity. Lightning can become very dangerous.

3. Static electricity often causes "shocks." This electricity is "standing still."

4. We had supper in the banquet room. There were beautifully set tables.

5. The trees were laden with fruit. The trees were sprayed to protect them from insects.

6. Dogwood is found throughout British Columbia. It is the floral emblem of this province.

Exercise 11   Group Activity: Clauses in Complex Sentences

Work in a group of three to five people. Read the following complex sentences. Tell if the ideas relate by time, reason, or condition. Be prepared to share your answers.

1. Some animals can detect danger because they can identify unusual scents in the air.
   _____

2. Whenever our child gets a cold, we keep him at home for a few days to prevent the spread of infection. _____

3. Once Joanne found out about the job offer, she began to celebrate with her friends.
   _____

4. Weary from the long car trip, Lou sat back in his easy chair while he enjoyed a cool beer. _____

5. Dealing with illness is very difficult because most people feel helpless in that situation. _____

6. The Toronto director of the film lost patience because several of the sound crew were late almost every day. _____

7. If I speak too loudly in the theatre, please tell me so. _____

8. Since Meagan won her scholarship, she has been working very hard at her studies. _____

9. Sometimes when Kyle is alone, he loves to watch 1950s Hollywood movies. _____

10. The students will meet the dean after the session is over. _____

Pattern Four: Compound-Complex Sentences

A pattern four sentence is not as common as the other three patterns. A pattern four sentence contains both coordinate and subordinate conjunctions and clauses. Think of a pattern four sentence as a pattern two sentence plus the addition of one subordinate clause or more.

As Mr. Fatwah listened to the endless complaints of his friend, he propped up his head on his elbows, and then he yawned.

As Mr. Fatwah listened to the endless complaints of his friend is a subordinate clause, beginning with the subordinate conjunction *as*.

He propped up his head on his elbows, and then he yawned is a pattern two sentence containing two main clauses joined by the coordinating conjunction *and*.

Therefore, the sentence is like a pattern two sentence with an additional subordinate clause—in other words, a pattern four, compound-complex sentence.

Exercise 12 *Analyzing Pattern Four Sentences*

Read each of the pattern four sentences below. Place brackets around each subordinate clause. Underline all main clauses. Circle all conjunctions. Be prepared to share your answers.

1. After Erin practised field hockey, she went out with her friends, but she did not have any alcohol because she felt too exhausted.

2. Since Ton left Japan, he has been very busy with his new studies and he rarely has time to email me any more.

3. The fields were covered in slow-moving water that had come with the floods; consequently, the new wetland was becoming a habitat for wild fowl that normally overwintered elsewhere.

4. One of the contractors was hired by the former city councillor who was his brother; therefore, many citizens believed that corruption in hiring practices had been at work.

5. The medical students listened as the neurologist explained the nature of the spinal cord injury; then she queried them on their knowledge.

Exercise 13   *Identifying Pattern Four Sentences*

Read each of the sentences below. Write **4** after every pattern four (compound-complex) sentence. Check your answers with the Answer Key.

1. Paying extra money for the service did not seem to be worth it to Yoshi. _____

2. These peaches have a lot of flavour, so you can make delicious chutney from them if you use them within a day. _____

3. Regarding your recent application, we must inform you that the positions have been filled, and we have contacted the successful candidates. _____

4. Because I've never been in a car rally, I really don't know what to expect. _____

5. The town will hold a strawberry festival since the crop is so important to its region. _____

6. The impact of jogging on the asphalt streets produced shin splints, swollen ankles, and a sore back. _____

7. Tighter security measures at borders make international travel somewhat more difficult today for business people who must fly between continents. _____

Chapter 4: Review Test

Part 1: Identifying Clauses

Indicate whether the clause is a subordinate clause or an independent clause. Write **SUB** above subordinate clauses; write **MAIN** above independent clauses.

1. Since Roxane was a girl, she loved to enter contests.

2. Many of the horticulture students were advised to avoid the use of pesticides even though these chemicals are readily available.

3. Disney Corporation had bought the rights to marketing the RCMP because the full dress uniform is so attractive to tourists.

4. At the airport Arlene greeted her sister who had just arrived from Ireland.

5. Some birds such as the Northern Flicker do not like to nest too close to human habitation as these particular birds are rather reclusive.

6. The painter who works at the studio gave me a lift home.

7. Beyond the gate a soldier waited while the prisoners crept along the wall.

8. I told him that he was wrong to lie to her.

9. Yellow and green were chosen as the new school colours because the old scheme was rather dull.

10. Teddy bears became famous at the turn of the twentieth century when the Western world seemed fascinated by all kinds of toys.

Part 2: Identifying Sentence Patterns

Identify each sentence as pattern 1, 2, 3, or 4. Write the numbers in the spaces provided.

1. He became a botanist after he visited the rain forests in Patagonia. _____

2. Ari played the game for a while, and then he watched television because he felt bored on that rainy afternoon. _____

3. Spelling counts on your assigned essays, and grammar and punctuation are important, too. _____

4. The yellow flowers were blooming all over the field next to the railway tracks, but no one could figure out who had planted them. _____

5. Since he was 19, Richard has been working on oil rigs all over the world. _____

6. Paco worried about his future in the electronics business. _____

7. After you lift the handle, push the little blue button to your left, and a light will appear on the main control panel. _____

8. The thief stopped to catch his breath and tie his shoelace. _____

9. Near the fish pond next to the hydrangeas, you will find a pretty place to sit. _____

10. If I pretend to laugh at your jokes, will you be happy? _____

ESL POINTER

Working with Sentence Patterns

Word Order and Pattern One Sentences

Pattern one sentences usually have one of five structures:

Subject–Verb combination:
Soo-jin sleeps in.
Kenzo is talking to you.
The girl will play at the concert.
Jorge and his wife retire early every evening.
(You may have more than one subject.)

Her kitten eats and plays a lot.
(You may have more than one verb in the predicate part of the sentence.)

Subject–Verb–Object combination:
I enjoy her company.
The assistant ordered coffee.
She's arranging flowers.

Subject–Linking Verb–Adjective combination:
The secretary is tall.
Those plums are sour.
Koko appears angry.

Subject–Verb–Adverb combination:
She speaks quickly.
The sparks were everywhere.
The ships are over there.

Subject–Linking Verb–Noun combination:
Her son is a dentist.
Those children are little devils.
Eva's husband is a counsellor.

Exercise 1   Identifying Pattern One Structures

Read the following pattern one sentences. After each sentence, write **S-V, S-V-O, S-LV-ADJ, S-V-ADV,** or **S-LV-N** to show the structure combination. Check your answers with the Answer Key.

1. Duc exercises here.

2. The carpenter measures the porch door.

3. Several students were eating lunch by the fish ponds.

4. His best suit was expensive.

5. Mei becomes a registered nurse this semester.

6. Those coconuts taste sour.

7. The architect plans carefully.

8. Korin's joke was ridiculous.

9. Her father is a music teacher.

10. Those men are supervisors at the nuclear plant.

11. He forgets his glasses.

12. The news spread everywhere.

13. Takashi speaks four languages.

14. I spilled my tea on the new white tablecloth.

15. The light becomes intense with more heat.

Exercise 2 *Writing Pattern One Sentences*

Use each of the following words or phrases in an effective pattern one sentence. Use each of the five structures S-V, S-V-O, S-LV-ADJ, S-V-ADV, or S-LV-N. Be prepared to share your answers. Your instructor may ask to see your sentences.

1. dinner

2. becomes

3. in broad daylight

4. watches

5. experienced

6. Tito and Helen

7. the storm

8. puzzle

9. in the middle

10. 12 hot dogs

11. splash

12. private

13. complains

14. the inspector

Exercise 3 Writing Sentences

Using the following target words, write sentences in the patterns specified. Your instructor may ask you to hand in your work, or student pairs may mark each other's sentences.

1. ducks (pattern two sentence)

2. hastily (pattern one sentence)

3. vegetarian (pattern four sentence)

4. natural (pattern three sentence)

5. park (pattern one sentence)

6. swindle (pattern three sentence)

7. volunteer (pattern four sentence)

8. valid (pattern two sentence)

9. rumour (pattern three sentence)

10. patience (pattern one sentence)

11. obviously (pattern two sentence)

12. invisible (pattern four sentence)

13. swamp (pattern three sentence)

14. contest (pattern one sentence)

15. trade (pattern two sentence)

CHECKOUT

1. This textbook uses the term *pattern* like this:

   A simple sentence is pattern one.
   A compound sentence is pattern two.
   A complex sentence is pattern three.
   A compound-complex sentence is pattern four.

2. A coordinating conjunction (*and, but, for, so, yet, nor, or*) is used to join two pattern-one sentences in a compound sentence.

3. Conjunctive adverbs may look like conjunctions, but they function to relate ideas in the sentences.

4. When a main/principal/independent clause stands alone it is a simple sentence.

5. When a dependent/subordinate clause stands alone it is a sentence fragment error.

6. A subordinate conjunction is used to join dependent ideas to the main idea in a complex sentence.

Noun and Pronoun Usage

Chapter Objectives

What will you have learned when you have completed this chapter?
You will be able to

1. distinguish between different types of nouns.

2. identify the noun subjects and objects in sentences.

3. form the possessive case of nouns.

4. form the plurals of English nouns.

5. recognize three pronoun cases.

6. apply the correct pronoun cases in sentences.

7. identify and correct pronoun agreement errors in sentences.

Chapter 5: Self-Test

Part 1: Types of Nouns

Tell if the underlined words are concrete, abstract, collective, common, or proper nouns.

1. A <u>herd</u> of young <u>elk</u> were browsing in the new <u>grass</u> next to the golf <u>course</u>.

2. <u>Sumi</u> says she has <u>faith</u> in our <u>ability</u> to make good <u>choices</u>.

3. The <u>Mount Rose Bakery</u> makes delicious chocolate <u>biscotti</u>.

Part 2: Attributive Nouns

Underline all the attributive nouns in the following sentences.

1. They are building a new town hall next to the community centre.

2. What furniture store sells leather chairs?

3. At the meeting, we discussed employee benefits for the new salespeople.

4. Nanaimo bars, one of my favourite desserts, are so fattening.

5. From the terrace, Ivan and Mary Rose are watching the Spanish dancers.

Part 3: Functions of Nouns

Underline all the nouns in the following sentences. Tell whether each underlined noun is functioning as a subject, object, or subject complement.

1. Bernice and her husband operate a fishing camp in northern Saskatchewan.

2. The lieutenant was the supervisor during the rescue mission.

3. The gang of thieves holed up in the mountains.

4. Four candidates for the parts were seasoned actors.

5. We set out candles on the beach during a memorial for our friend.

Part 4: Possessives

Form the possessives for the following nouns.

1. the bouquet of the bride: _____

2. the sweater belonging to Ross: _____

3. the cage of the monkey: _____

4. the policy of the company: _____

5. the toys of the children: _____

Part 5: Noun Plurals

Provide the plurals for the following nouns.

1. fox: _____

2. tooth: _____

3. wrench: _____

4. tray: _____

5. kiss: _____

6. volcano: _____

7. person: _____

8. lunch: _____

9. sample: _____

10. candy: _____

Part 6: Pronoun Cases

Select the correct pronoun case in each of the following sentences.

1. _____ (Who/Whom) was first over the finish line?

2. _____ (Him/His) barking all night disturbs my sleep.

3. Zachary and (I/me/myself) _____ play in a band on the weekends.

4. The chief investigator (who/whom) _____ the agency had hired was a drunkard.

5. It was actually (she/her) _____ (who/whom) rode the motorcycle.

Part 7: Pronoun Agreement

Correct the errors in pronoun agreement in each of the following sentences.

1. Everybody should remember to bring their backpack on the hike.

2. Few of those boards is useful for the tree house.

3. One of the students want to arrange the ski trip.

4. The government must be accountable, and they should do their duty to the people.

5. When the last person leaves the building, you should lock the steel doors.

Types of Nouns

Nouns name things, either concrete or abstract. You will often see three words, *a, an,* or *the,* used with nouns. These words are called *articles. The* is called a *definite article* because it refers to a specific noun.

The boy began to cry. (*The* names a specific noun, *boy*.)

A and *an* are called *indefinite articles* because they do not name specific nouns. Instead, they refer to a noun in a general sense.

A dog can make a fun and excellent pet. (The article *a* indicates that the writer is referring to the noun *dog* in a general way—as a class of things.)

An egg contains 5 grams of fat and 6.3 grams of protein. (The article *an* indicates the writer is speaking about eggs in general, not a specific one.)

Concrete nouns refer to items (people, places, or things) that are tangible. These are things we can see, hear, touch, feel, or taste. *Abstract nouns* refer to ideas or emotions; these are intangible.

Concrete Nouns	Abstract Nouns
rug	thought
cookie	faith
desk	anger
paper	permission
Amanda	error
glue	kingdom

Exercise 1 *Finding Concrete and Abstract Nouns*

Work in pairs. Read the following passage. First, underline all nouns. Then select the concrete nouns, the nouns that refer to things in the physical world. Write each one under the heading **CONCRETE**. Then select the abstract nouns, the nouns that refer to feelings, emotions, or ideas. Write each abstract noun under the heading **ABSTRACT**. Some words may occur more than once in the passage; however, list them only once. Be prepared to share your answers with the rest of the class.

Horses are an important part of Canadian history. People depended on horses many years ago just as they rely on cars and trucks today. When Canada was being settled, there were few roads for anyone to use. The best way to get around was by horse or by horse and carriage. Even then, roads were little more than muddy paths full of potholes and rocks. Farmers relied heavily on their horses to pull machinery for the fields and to help clear the land. Horses were the farmers' only form of transportation. In towns and villages, horses were used to make deliveries and to move goods around the community. Despite all the hardships of early life in Canada, the country prospered because of the contribution of these animals.

Concrete Nouns   Abstract Nouns

_____   _____

_____   _____

_____   _____

_____   _____

_____   _____

_____   _____

_____   _____

Collective Nouns

Collective nouns are nouns that name a group. A collective noun is usually considered to be singular (one), although there are cases in which a collective noun is plural (more than one).

Collective Nouns		
army	herd	family
class	crowd	audience
administration	team	orchestra

The context of the sentence will determine if the collective noun is singular or plural.

The staff have left for their holidays. (plural: The staff is not acting as a team; different staff members will go on different holidays.)

The staff has made its decision. (singular: the group acts as one to make a single decision)

The jury are arguing about the new evidence. (plural: the jury members have differing opinions)

The jury has reached a verdict. (singular: the jury acts as a unit)

Common Nouns and Proper Nouns

Common nouns refer to the everyday or generic names of things. *Proper nouns* are the specific name of things, places, or people. Brand names are proper nouns, too.

Common Nouns	Proper Nouns
writer	L.R. Wright
city	Richmond
language	Italian
squirrel	Richardson's ground squirrel
day	Friday

Exercise 2   *Adding Proper Nouns*

Add an example of a proper noun or a common noun in each of the blanks below. Be prepared to share your answers.

Common	Proper
1. a town	_____
2. a river	_____
3. _____	Rocky Mountains
4. _____	Okanagan Valley

5. a bay   _____

6. an island   _____

7. a restaurant   _____

8. _____   Sears

9. a park   _____

10. _____   Pacific

11. _____   Trans-Canada

12. a drink   _____

13. a singer   _____

14. _____   Prince Edward Island

15. _____   Pakistan

Exercise 3   Finding Proper Nouns and Abstract Nouns

For each of the following sentences, underline every proper noun and write "abstract" above every abstract noun. Check your answers with the Answer Key.

1. With delight, the child played with the antique trains given to him by Uncle MacIntosh.

2. Ramjit works at the service station at the corner of Main Street and Commercial Avenue.

3. Her hope was to enter the Academy of Fine Arts in Montreal to study baroque music.

4. In his frustration, Nazim spilled his can of Coke all over the seat of his new Mazda.

5. What solution do you have for the problem given on page 89 of *Introductory Physics* by I.M. Moved?

6. His apartment is on the sixteenth floor of Habour Towers.

7. Happiness came to Fang Yin in the form of a dream.

8. The freeway near Hull was jammed with rush-hour traffic.

9. Our new community has a shopping mall, six churches, one mosque, one temple, three pharmacies, five restaurants, a small hospital, and a 7-Eleven.

10. Justin's fame was that he could hum any melody exactly as he had heard it.

11. Suzette pulled a Kleenex out of her purse and with sadness dabbed at her eyes.

12. His doubt caused him to lose so much sleep that Mrs. Guptah, his supervisor, became concerned.

13. "Cigarettes can ruin your health" the poster from Health Canada warned.

14. Samson is my dog and Delilah is my cat.

15. Miss Soto had the fright of her life when she lost her wallet in the MediaSport Technology Building.

Attributive Nouns

Sometimes nouns can be used like adjectives; in other words, they add a quality to the nouns they modify or describe. These are called *attributive nouns*, and they may be common or proper. Nationalities, for example, can be used as attributive nouns (use their adjective forms).

Canadian wine
night owl
worker benefits
bean bag
English muffin

Exercise 4 *Attributive Nouns*

Use each of the following nouns as attributive nouns. Create a sentence for each. Your instructor may ask to see your sentences or have you share them with the class.

Example:

Noun: club
Sentence: My aunt forgot her club card at home when we went to the grocery store.
(*Club* is an attributive noun in the sentence because it modifies *card.*)

1. French

2. chocolate

3. blood

4. life

5. office

6. red

7. coffee

8. Japanese

9. water

10. glass

Exercise 5 Identifying Types of Nouns

Work in pairs. Underline all nouns and tell what type of noun each is. Write your answers after the sentences. Check your answers with the Answer Key.

Example: We ordered a large *Hawaiian pizza* for *Sunday dinner.*

Hawaiian (proper/attributive)
pizza (common/concrete)
Sunday (proper/attributive)
dinner (common/concrete)

1. The recreation director welcomed the English passengers aboard the Jamaican cruise.

2. His idea was to call Premier Wrangler in his office.

3. Pamela prepared an outline for her report about the Pacific dolphin.

4. California sea lions can be taught many tricks.

5. Ling prefers Chinese tea with her breakfast.

Functions of Nouns

Nouns have work to do in sentences. They can function as subjects, objects, and subject complements.

• The *subject* of the sentence is the person or thing that does the action; if the sentence does not contain an action verb, then the subject is what the sentence is all about.

• An *object* receives the action of the verb; it is to whom or to what the action is being done. Nouns can also be objects of prepositions.

• A *subject complement* completes information about the subject. A subject complement can be a noun, telling what the subject is. It can also be an adjective that describes the subject. A subject complement comes after a linking verb and completes the sentence. A *linking verb* tells the state of being of a subject; it often links to a word describing a sensation. Some linking verbs of sensation are *feel, look, smell, sound,* and *taste.* State of being verbs include *act, appear,* forms of *to be, become, continue, grow, prove, sound, remain, seem, sit,* and *turn.*

The next chapter on verbs will provide you with more detailed information.

Noun subject: Kites are fun to fly. (*Kites* is what the sentence is all about.)

Noun object: Riko built a kite for his son. (*Kite* is the object of the verb *built.* To determine an object, ask yourself: "Built what?")

Objects can be direct or indirect. A *direct object* is the one that directly receives the action. An *indirect object* receives the direct object.

Bobo passed the cookies. (*Bobo* is the subject—he did the action. *Cookies* is the object. They are what Bobo passed. Therefore, *cookies* is a direct object.)

Bobo passed <u>Monique</u> the <u>cookies</u>. (*Monique* is the indirect object. She received *the cookies*, the direct object. She is not the direct object because she is not what got passed; Bobo passed the cookies, not Monique.)

Noun object of the preposition: Riko and his son built another kite for a <u>race</u>.

In a later chapter, you will learn more about prepositions. For the time being, think of *prepositions* as small words that start word groups called *phrases*. Prepositions are words of direction such as *to, at, in, on, beside, beyond, out, of,* and *for*. *Prepositional phrases* begin with a preposition and end in a noun (or sometimes a pronoun).

In the sentence above, *for a race* is a prepositional phrase. *For* is a preposition. Notice that the phrase ends in a noun—*race*. In this phrase, *race* is called the object of the preposition because it answers "what." In other words, "For what?"—"For a race." Notice that there is more than one subject because both *Riko* and *his son* did the action in the sentence.

Subject complement: Annika is a <u>lawyer</u> for the government of the Yukon. (*Lawyer* is a subject complement in this sentence. It completes the sentence and tells what Annika is. Notice the linking verb *is*. Remember that subject complements follow linking verbs.)

Exercise 6   *Functions of Nouns*

Underline each noun; then tell what function it has. Check your answers with the Answer Key.

1. The petty dictator entertained his guests with boring stories.

2. One character in the book is an important chef at a grand hotel.

3. Santoso is taking notes of the meeting of the Conservation Society.

4. Allen is the chief steward in his union.

5. Strangely enough, the fielder threw the ball to the first baseman.

6. UPS delivered two packages to the tenth floor of the office tower.

7. Danh won a free trip to the British Isles.

8. Helen and Vi were the first reporters on the scene.

Note

A special verbal called a gerund *can also be a noun. (You will find more about gerunds in Chapter 8: Verbals.) A gerund ends in* -ing. *Gerunds often name an activity.*

smoking   swimming   writing   singing   baking

Canoeing is relaxing for most people. (*Canoeing* is a gerund and is the subject of the sentence.)

John enjoys canoeing on the summer weekends. (*Canoeing* is a gerund and is the object of the verb enjoys: "Enjoys" what?)

Writing can be hard work. (*Writing* is a gerund and is the subject of the sentence.)

My cousin loves writing. (*Writing* is a gerund and is the object of the verb loves: "Loves" what?)

Exercise 7 Finding Subjects, Objects, and Subject Complements

Read each of the following sentences. Indicate the subject of the sentence, the object of the verb or preposition, and the subject complement. Be prepared to share your answers.

Example:

subject   object   object of prep   object of prep
A red <u>squirrel</u> hoards its <u>treasures</u> in an old oak <u>tree</u> in the <u>backyard</u>.

1. The computer technician organizes the computer software for the entire staff.

2. Waking up too early irritates Sal.

3. The young server brought hot beverages to our table.

4. A huge snake was dangling from the tree limb.

5. Her English professor comes from Sweden.

6. The spiteful witch cackles over her bubbling cauldron.

7. A small child was whining inside the hot bus.

8. The magnificent dragonfly drifted aimlessly in the summer breeze.

9. His disabled son is playing soccer this summer.

10. Three girls were eating dinner on the patio outside the student council office.

11. Mitsu warned her boyfriend about the dark alley behind the shops.

12. The butler served iced tea in crystal pitchers.

13. The jug of milk leaked all over the inside of the fridge.

14. Has the provincial government cut the budget of colleges?

Apostrophe Use and Possessive Cases of Nouns

Possessive case means the form of a noun or pronoun used to show that someone or something owns or possesses something else. To show the possessive case of nouns, use an *apostrophe*; it looks like this: '.

It is easiest to learn about possessives if you consider the root word first. For example, suppose you want to make a sign to advertise that you have some men's clothing to sell at a garage sale.

Begin with the root word:

men

Make the root word possessive by adding an apostrophe and an *-s* after it:

men's

Your sign would then read:

men's clothing for sale

As another example, suppose you wish to show that a girl owns a bicycle. Begin with the root word:

girl

Make the root word possessive:

girl's

Your possessive word group would look like this:

girl's bicycle

However, if three girls shared the same bicycle, your root word would change. Add the new root word.

girls

Put the apostrophe after the root word.

girls'

Your new word group would look like this:

girls' bicycle

Now your meaning is that several girls are using the same bicycle: it is commonly owned among them.

In all cases of noun possession, notice that the root word is found to the immediate left of the apostrophe. Therefore, you would never write *childrens' toys* because there is no such root word as *childrens*.

Exercise 8 *Group Activity: Recognizing the Meaning of Possessives*

Work in a group of two to three. Together decide what the following examples of possessives mean. You may write out your answers or prepare them orally. Your instructor will ask you to share your answers with other groups.

1. the boy's decision

2. the boys' decision

3. the boy's decisions

4. the boys' decisions

5. the class's assignments

6. the classes' assignments

7. the Smiths' car

8. the Joneses' car

9. workers' compensation

10. dogs' kennel

Exercise 9 *Forming Possessives*

Write the correct possessive case for each of the following. Check your answers with the Answer Key.

1. the news of tomorrow: _____

2. the nest of two birds: _____

3. the cat belonging to the Toor family: _____

4. the slippers belonging to the woman: _____

5. the plays of Shakespeare: _____

6. a wallet belonging to one man: _____

7. the affairs of the nation: _____

8. the car belonging to Bob and Ami: _____

9. the ideas of the committees: _____

10. the skill of the surgeon: _____

11. the calls of the geese: _____

12. the novels of Charles Dickens: _____

13. the soup of the day: _____

14. the feelings of Joan: _____

Plurals of Nouns

Nouns can be singular (one) or plural (more than one). In the English language, there are different ways to form noun plurals. Some plurals do not follow any specific rule but have become part of English usage and spelling over the years.

If you want more practice with or information about spelling plural forms than is provided in this chapter, you may want to consult a spelling reference book or look up English spelling on the Internet. You can also access good resources in your campus or community library.

Regular Plural Forms of Nouns

You can form the plural of most English nouns by adding -s or -es to the root word. Add -es if you need to pronounce /ez/ at the end of the word. Without the -es, the plural would be too difficult to pronounce. The -es really adds another syllable in these cases. A *syllable* is a word part with a sounded vowel.

Singular Form	Plural Form
road	roads (one syllable)
cheese	cheeses (chee/zez) (extra syllable added)
bear	bears (one syllable)
tax	taxes (tak/zez) (extra syllable added)
index	indexes (in/dek/zez) (extra syllable added)

Irregular Plural Forms of Nouns

Some English nouns do not change form from the singular to the plural.

sheep	sheep
deer	deer
corps	corps

Some nouns ending in *f* or *fe* change spelling in the plural form. The *f* changes to *v* and -es is added. The -es is not pronounced as /ez/ in these plurals because no extra syllable is needed to help with pronunciation.

knife	knives
scarf	scarves
wolf	wolves

Some common English nouns end in *o*. Add -es when you are forming their plural. The -es is not pronounced as /ez/ in these plurals because no extra syllable is needed to help with pronunciation.

hero	heroes
tomato	tomatoes
potato	potatoes

Less common nouns ending in *o* have only -s in their plural forms. Musical terms ending in *o* generally have -s in the plural.

alto	altos
soprano	sopranos
avocado	avocados

If a noun ends in *y* and has a consonant before the *y*, change the *y* to *i* and add -es to form the plural. The -ies is pronounced /eeze/.

party	parties
assembly	assemblies
body	bodies

Some nouns have quite unusual forms. You will have to remember them because there are few spelling guidelines.

mouse	mice
foot	feet
man	men
dice	die

Exercise 10 *Forming Plurals*

Change each of the following nouns to their plural forms. Check your answers with the Answer Key.

1. rodeo: _____

2. tray: _____

3. bubble: _____

4. flurry: _____

5. wife: _____

6. solo: _____

7. turkey: _____

8. elf: _____

9. church: _____

10. risk: _____

11. box: _____

12. wave: _____

13. bunch: _____

14. worry: _____

15. key: _____

16. half: _____

17. child: _____

18. species: _____

19. fence: _____

20. policy: _____

Pronoun Usage

Pronouns are words that take the place of nouns. They can function as subjects and objects in sentences just the same as nouns do.

Martha finished her salad. (*Martha* is a noun and is the subject of the sentence.)

She finished it. (*She* is a pronoun that stands for the subject *Martha*, and *it* is a pronoun substituted for the object *salad*.)

Here are some examples of pronouns:

I   he   she   it   we   you   they

Exercise 11   *Recognizing Pronouns*

First, underline the complete subject noun or nouns in each of the following sentences. The complete subject includes the noun, articles such as *the* or *a*, and all words that describe the noun. Above the underlined nouns, write the pronoun that can take the place of each noun. Check your answers with the Answer Key.

Example:

He
Bonzo was watching TV.

1. The glistening sea lay before us like a velvet spread.

2. Alf and Shorty branded the cows out in the back pasture.

3. The clock just exploded.

4. Benny and Klaudia went to the only drive-in movie theatre in Ontario.

5. Collin is an excellent hockey player.

6. Hot chocolate tastes scrumptious on a wintry evening.

7. The students and their coach practised for Saturday's soccer game.

8. Luke baked a fluffy lemon chiffon pie.

9. Boris, come over here, please.

Pronoun Cases

Pronouns have different forms called *cases*. The case you use in pronouns depends on whether a pronoun is being used as a subject or an object or if it is being used to show ownership or possession.

Pronoun Cases

Subjective	Objective	Possessive
I	me	my, mine
he	him	his
she	her	her, hers
it	it	its
we	us	our, ours
you	you	your, yours
they	them	their, theirs
who	whom	whose

Hints

1. *Use the subjective case of a pronoun after a linking verb.*
2. *Use a possessive case in front of a gerund (a verbal acting as a noun but ending in* -ing.*)*
3. *If you are using the comparative word* than, *consider the meaning of the sentence you have constructed in order to decide whether to use the subjective or the objective case.*

   Hasid is taller than he. *(What you are really saying here is that Hasid is taller than he is.)*

   He loves her more than me. *(What you are saying here is that he loves her more than he loves you.)*

Pronoun Usage in Three Cases

To <u>whom</u> does <u>she</u> wish to speak? (*Whom* is the objective case. It is the object of the preposition *to*. *She* is the subject of the sentence.)

<u>They</u> were concerned that <u>their</u> son would not receive <u>his</u> scholarship. (*They* is the subject of the sentence. *Their* and *his* are in the possessive case.)

<u>It</u> is <u>she</u> <u>who</u> won the contest. (*It* is the subject of the sentence. *She* is the subject complement. It is in the subjective case after a linking verb *is*. *Who* is the subject of the clause *who won the contest*; therefore, you must use the subjective case.)

Exercise 12 Pronoun Cases

Work in pairs. Provide the correct pronoun case in each of the following sentences.

1. To _____ (who, whom) do I give my application form?

2. Between you and _____ (me, I), you are right.

3. Janine, Mari, and _____ (I, me) bought Lukas lunch.

4. The college president wanted to help _____ (us, we) students.

5. They asked Tony and _____ (me, I) to build the new set for the production.

6. Suzie's aunt found out it was _____ (me, I) _____ (who, whom) lied.

7. Chris is taller than _____ (I, me).

8. He is the person for _____ (who, whom) the parcel was delivered.

9. _____ (Who, Whom) called the meeting today?

10. Chief Malarky welcomes all of _____ (us, we) new recruits.

11. _____ (We, Us) parents want more say in the school system.

12. _____ (Them, Their) relatives are extremely boring.

13. We wrote to _____ (them, their) to ask for permission.

14. _____ (His, Him) borrowing electrical tools annoys me.

15. Thomas offered Frans and _____ (I, me) a ride home.

Reflexive Pronouns

Reflexive pronouns have the ending *self*; they refer to the subject.

Rodeo riders give themselves terrible injuries in a dangerous sport. (*Rodeo riders* is the subject of the sentence.)

Lasha gave the speech herself when the guest speaker cancelled. (*Lasha* is the subject of the sentence.)

Hint

Do not use reflexive pronouns as subject or objects of sentences.

Ren and myself took a trip to Niagara Falls. (incorrect in subjective case)

Ren and I took a trip to Niagara Falls. (correct)

The company sent Ren and myself to Niagara Falls. (incorrect in objective case)

The company sent Ren and me to Niagara Falls. (correct)

Ourself is incorrect; the reflexive form is always plural—ourselves. Yourself *refers to a singular subject.* Yourselves *refers to a plural subject.*

Exercise 13   *Correct Pronoun Usage*

Work in pairs. Find the error in each pronoun usage; then together correct the error. Be prepared to share your answers.

1. Him and Derek play on the university hockey team.

2. The toll booth operator gave the message to the driver and I.

3. The small dog had lost it's leg in a car accident.

4. Frankly, it is her whom needs to arrange the schedules.

5. Him complaining all the time really irritates his wife.

6. The clerk gave Rocko and myself two free tickets to the dance.

7. Karli is angrier than him over the incident in the subway.

8. Whose been sleeping in my bed?

9. Her roommate couldn't decide whom she should go out with.

10. Fredericka and myself will be greeting the guests at the main entry.

11. The principal spoke to we parents about the new math program.

12. You interfering in her private affairs doesn't help the situation at all.

13. He provided an explanation to Miguel and I.

14. Us students should complain about rising tuition fees.

15. The tutor provided instruction for two international students and myself.

Pronoun Agreement

Pronouns must agree with the nouns they refer to in sentences. The noun the pronoun refers to is called its *antecedent*. A pronoun must refer to the same number and gender as its antecedent; this is called *pronoun agreement*. If the pronoun is the subject of the sentence, then you must use the verb that matches.

The onlookers were astonished to see the princess wink at them as she went by.

The antecedent of the pronoun *them* is the *onlookers*. Because *onlookers* is a plural noun, the pronoun must also be plural.

The antecedent of the pronoun *she* is *princess*. Because *princess* is a singular noun referring to a female, the pronoun must match the form.

Everything seems to be going wrong today!

Everything is the subject pronoun. It is considered singular. *Seems* is the verb that matches.

Getting pronoun agreement straight can sometimes be tricky because of certain pronouns called *indefinite pronouns*. They are indefinite because they do not refer to a specified noun. Most indefinite pronouns are singular and should refer to a singular noun.

Singular Indefinite Pronouns				
everyone	everybody	everything	anyone	anybody
anything	someone	somebody	something	no one
nobody	nothing	one	another	either
each	little	much	other	

Plural Indefinite Pronouns				
both	few	many	several	others

Depending on the context of the sentence, the following can be singular or plural:

somebody
few
one
none

<u>Somebody</u> has stolen my purse, and I want <u>him</u> or <u>her</u> caught. (refers to a singular *somebody*)

<u>Few</u> of those cans of paint are still useful. (refers to a plural *cans*)

<u>One</u> of the beaches is closed. (refers to a single *beach*)

<u>None</u> of this tomato tastes good. (refers to a single *tomato*)

<u>None</u> of these tomatoes taste good. (refers to several *tomatoes*)

Gender and Pronoun Use

Indefinite pronouns do not refer to any particular person or thing. Sometimes it is difficult to decide whether to use a masculine or feminine pronoun. The tradition has been to use the third person masculine pronoun as a generic pronoun, like this:

Everyone ought to take his own lecture notes.

Sometimes it becomes quite ridiculous to try to stick to the third person masculine when the sentence clearly demands you write it otherwise. Look at the following example, apparently written by a political group:

Everyone will be able to decide for himself whether to have an abortion or not.

However, over the past several decades this practice has been called into question by feminists and others who claim such writing excludes a good many readers. It is not inclusive language.

A more accurate way of writing the sentences using inclusive language is as follows:

Everyone ought to take his or her own lecture notes.

or

Everyone ought to take her or his own lecture notes.

Another difficulty might arise when you use an indefinite pronoun in one part of the sentence and you wish to use a pronoun that includes both genders in another part of the sentence.

Everybody in the room knew where his or her children were that night.

The sentence is correct but sounds awkward. Clearly, *people in the room* represents both genders.

Everybody in the room knew where their children were that night.

The sentence is technically incorrect because *everybody* is singular and *their* is plural. However, the sentence reads more smoothly. Obviously, *everybody in the room* refers to "all people." You will have to check with your instructor to see if he or she will accept the use of *their* with indefinite pronouns in special cases.

You may use a plural pronoun in some cases to avoid awkward structure or to stay away from choosing a gender where none is implied.

Who has the time to prepare their families' dinners and still go to school full time?

Exercise 14   *Pronoun Agreement*

The following sentences contain some errors in pronoun agreement. Find the errors and repair them. Check with the Answer Key.

1. Squirrels and chipmunks are related and its habits are similar.

2. The police officer was stopping traffic along the highway, and they were asking drivers questions.

3. Has everyone given their consent to have their pictures taken on Friday?

4. Some of the printer cartridges has dried up.

5. Jana dislikes films that depict violence because it tends to oversimplify situations.

6. The young soccer coach gave me a book to read, and they will improve my winning psychology.

7. Few workers spend time developing his safety knowledge on the job.

8. Many of those books smells musty.

9. A person usually doesn't want to show how they feel.

10. The curriculum committee have filed their report.

Exercise 15   *Review*

Find all errors in noun or pronoun usage in the following passage. Underline the errors and then repair them by writing the correct answer above the error. Be prepared to share your answers.

Edgar Wongs' dog, Rufus, was a real handful. Him chewing the furniture was his worst habit. Rufus also loved to chew the families' shoes. As a matter of fact, Edgar was spending most of his money replacing item's that Rufus had ruined. Edgars wife, Laura, was more patient than him. She claimed that Rufus would outgrow his bad habits'. Edgar wanting to send Rufus to canine obedience school irritated Laura. "Its too expensive," Laura claimed. "After all that money, the dog might still not listen to you or I." "The lessons real value," retorted Edgar, "may simply be us escaping Rufus for a few nights' every week. Maybe we can concentrate Rufuses' energy on finding new friends while you and me find relief!"

Chapter 5: Review Test

Part 1: Recognizing Nouns

Tell if the underlined words are concrete, abstract, collective, common, or proper nouns.

1. A <u>flock</u> of <u>sheep</u> had escaped from their pen during the <u>night</u>.
2. <u>Toto</u> imagines a <u>world</u> without <u>pain</u> or <u>fear</u>.
3. The <u>McIntosh Curling Club</u> has <u>equipment</u> to rent to the <u>public</u>.

Part 2: Attributive Nouns

Underline all the attributive nouns in the following sentences.

1. They make hero sandwiches with lots of French mustard.
2. Who wants to play some Chinese checkers after English class?
3. The lavender soap made the bathroom fragrant.
4. Her aunt's maple chest came from a Quebec farm.
5. Our coffee maker blew its circuit yesterday morning.

Part 3: Functions of Nouns

Underline all nouns. Tell whether each underlined noun is functioning as a subject, object, or subject complement in each of the following sentences.

1. Sol and his wife own a shoe factory in Winnipeg.
2. The young doctor was the assistant during the brain surgery.
3. The army of ants invaded the picnic basket on the grass.
4. Four hamsters were pets for the grade four children.
5. You must deliver this package to Moscow.

Part 4: Possessives

Form the possessives for the following nouns.

1. the wings of the dove: _____

2. the router belonging to Yves: _____

3. the mistakes of the president: _____

4. the rights of the individual: _____

5. the flight of the geese: _____

Part 5: Noun Plurals

Provide the plurals for the following nouns.

1. watch: _____

2. banjo: _____

3. jeans: _____

4. life: _____

5. risk: _____

6. salmon: _____

7. clerk: _____

8. philosophy: _____

9. trout: _____

10. hoof: _____

Part 6: Pronoun Cases

Select the correct pronoun case in each of the following sentences.

1. _____ (Who/Whom) was the driver of the winning car?

2. _____ (Him/His) challenging me is quite upsetting.

3. Roderick and (I/me/myself) _____ enjoy going to antique sales.

4. The translator (who/whom) _____ the company hired was a cheat.

5. It really was (he/him) _____ (who/whom) brought the bicycle into the restaurant.

Part 7: Pronoun Agreement

Correct the errors in pronoun agreement in each of the following sentences.

1. Everybody should practise their yodelling on the top of this hill.

2. Few of those biscuits is edible after being left in the freezer too long.

3. One of the parents wish to speak to the principal.

4. The law must be fair, and they should serve every person.

5. When the first individual steps up to the microphone, you should speak clearly.

ESL POINTER

Count and Non-count Nouns

One of the difficulties in using English-language nouns comes in deciding which are count nouns and which are non-count nouns. *Count nouns* refer to persons, places, things, or ideas that can be calculated or counted because they are seen as separate units. *Non-count nouns* are not calculable. Non-count nouns should not be made plural.

Count Nouns	Non-Count Nouns	
pencils	dirt	magic
dresses	offspring	cash
films	rice	anger
strategies	clergy	furniture
birds	machinery	help
saucers	leisure	courage
	peace	luck
	cattle	merchandise
	wealth	wisdom

Hints for Using Non-count Nouns

1. You can pluralize the containers, the weights, or the shapes commonly associated with non-count nouns.

bags of flour	jugs of milk	bars of soap
bits of advice	bunches of spinach	litres of oil

2. In the case of naming species or types, you may see a non-count noun in a plural form.

fish (non-count)	fishes (species or types of fish)
lettuce (non-count)	lettuces (varieties or types of lettuce)
grass (non-count)	grasses (varieties or types of grass)
fruit (non-count)	fruits (varieties or types of fruit)

We bought fish at the market.

How many different fishes do you have in your aquarium?

This lettuce is terribly wilted.

This salad mix is made up of 10 different lettuces.

Roscoe hates cutting the grass.

These tropical grasses will not survive at temperatures lower than 10 degrees Celsius.

Please buy some fresh fruit at the farmers' market.

In his country families enjoy exotic fruits at every meal.

3. Sports are viewed as non-count nouns.

   soccer   baseball   basketball   tennis

4. Professions are viewed as non-count nouns.

   engineering   nursing   law   physics

5. Meat from animals is viewed as non-count nouns.

   beef   lamb   ham   venison

Exercise 1 *Choosing Count or Non-count Nouns*

Repair the error in each of the following sentences. Be prepared to share your answers.

1. The datas from the research is inconclusive.

2. Lamb are a Canadian barbeque favourite.

3. The majorities of landowners is rich.

4. Badmintons is a great indoor game for the winter.

5. My uncle and I used a lot of lumbers to build the new front porch.

6. The Malaysian tourists loved the sceneries along the St. Lawrence River.

7. For such a young child, she possesses a lot of wisdoms.

8. I want to give you some important pieces of informations.

9. Do you want mustards on your hot dog?

10. Agosto is preparing spaghettis for the banquet tonight.

Demonstrative Pronouns

Demonstrative pronouns point out particular nouns. They modify the nouns they are placed next to. Sometimes they are called *determiners* because they determine or indicate which noun is being pointed out.

Singular forms:

this   that

Plural forms:

these   those

This and *that* point out nouns that are nearby. *That* and *those* point out nouns that are farther away.

A demonstrative pronoun must agree in number with the noun it modifies:

This tie looks ridiculous with my new suit.

Those ties on the rack are even worse!

Exercise 2   *Demonstrative Pronoun Agreement*

Choose the demonstrative pronoun that best fits each sentence. Check your answers with the Answer Key.

1. (Those/This) children take the school bus each morning.

2. (This/These) cups have chips in them, so I want a discount.

3. Botan loves (these/this) type of pizza.

4. Some experts report that (these/this) terriers have problems with their skin.

5. (Those/This) magazine advertises a lot of women's fashions.

6. Helmut wanted me to give you (these/this) order of fresh vegetables.

7. My accountant says I will have to do better selling (this/these) products.

8. Wasps always pester you when you are holding (this/these) sort of sticky drink.

9. (These/Those) pastries I have here in this box are for our dessert at lunch.

10. Do you know (these/those) brothers standing over there by the desk?

CHECKOUT

1. There are collective, proper, and attributive nouns.

2. In sentences, nouns can function as subjects, objects, and subject complements.

3. A gerund is a verbal ending in *-ing* that functions as a noun.

4. Which pronoun case you use depends on whether the pronoun is being used as a subject or an object or if it is being used to show ownership or possession.

5. Reflexive pronouns refer to the subject of the sentence, and so are not used as subjects or objects.

6. A pronoun must refer to the same number and gender as its antecedent.

7. Non-count nouns should not be pluralized.

Verbs

Chapter Objectives

What will you have learned when you have completed this chapter?
You will be able to

1. distinguish between the three kinds of verbs.
2. identify auxiliary verbs.
3. recognize the function of auxiliary verbs.
4. identify verb phrases.
5. recognize types of verb tenses.
6. use various verb tenses.
7. identify the main forms of regular and irregular verbs.
8. apply the correct verb forms in sentences.

Chapter 6: Self-Test

Part 1: Identifying Types of Verbs

Each sentence contains an underlined verb. Tell if the underlined verb is an action, linking, or auxiliary verb. Check your answers with the Answer Key at the back of the book.

1. Every Valentine's Day, she <u>buys</u> me some chocolates.
2. Jayden <u>is</u> the project manager for the city of Hamilton.
3. <u>Do</u> they <u>want</u> more information about the missing dog?
4. One of the customers <u>has tried</u> on every pair of shoes in her size!
5. Agatha <u>becomes</u> very ill if she <u>eats</u> peanuts.
6. The owner of the small art gallery <u>invited</u> members of the community to a special show.
7. We <u>are throwing</u> an office party for Marion who <u>is leaving</u> the firm.

Part 2: Recognizing Transitive and Intransitive Verbs

Tell if the underlined verb is transitive or intransitive by writing **T** or **INT**.

1. The hunters <u>bought</u> their ammunition at Canadian Tire.

2. My friend Gerda <u>speaks</u> quietly because she is shy.

3. Yesterday the team <u>ran</u> for two hours to get ready for the tournament tomorrow.

4. We <u>buttered</u> our toast with cream cheese.

5. Toti will <u>remain</u> in the room while the supervisor discusses her evaluation.

Part 3: Auxiliary Verbs and Their Functions

Underline the auxiliary verbs in each of the following sentences. If they primarily add emphasis to the main verb, write **E**. If they support the main verb in indicating time, write **T**. If they are a modal auxiliary verb, write **M**.

1. They absolutely do not want to arrange a meeting.

2. Primates like chimpanzees can communicate effectively with facial expressions.

3. The microscope had been adjusted to its maximum strength.

4. Trina was admiring the vase in the store window.

5. Were the fishery workers laid off because of the decline in the fishing industry?

6. Will Kalle join us in a glass of wine with dinner?

7. According to our professor, we must reference our notes based on MLA guidelines.

Part 4: Identifying Verb Phrases

Underline the verb phrases in each of the following sentences.

1. The sergeant-at-arms is calling for a change of the guards.

2. They should be expecting an increase in pay since the contract settlement.

3. I must remember to recharge my cellphone.

4. Have you ever seen the beautiful ballet *Swan Lake*?

5. Fen has been acting in a play with the Five Nations Community College Theatre Society.

6. Were you and Feenie staring at the new handsome student in English class?

7. I must have been saving my energy for the race on Saturday.

Part 5: Identifying Verb Tenses

Underline the verbs or verb phrases in each of the following sentences. Write down the tense after each sentence.

1. Finally, the court will be able to hear your case next week. _____

2. The group must have planned the event carefully. _____

3. We are trying to establish our own small company. _____

4. Her parents will be staying with her for a month. _____

5. Were the soldiers successfully completing the latest campaign? _____

6. Patricia did give a memorable speech at the graduation ceremony. _____

7. Wire-haired terriers are becoming more popular in North America. _____

8. Bob will work overtime at the plant because of the winter storm. _____

9. Was Alexa interfering with the police investigation? _____

10. Our expert in foreign glass had made an important discovery in Egypt. _____

Part 6: Adding Correct Forms of Verbs

Add the correct form of each main verb shown in parenthesis.

1. He always _____ a shower after work. (take)

2. Lou _____ his time when he does a job. (take)

3. Would you _____ a bicycle to class if you could? (ride)

4. When Auntie Mee _____ (fall), she _____ her arm. (break)

5. Has the child _____ the rules just a little? (bend)

6. Nobody had _____ his or her research paper for sociology class. (begin)

7. Have you _____ about my marriage proposal? (think)

Part 7: Forms of Tenses

Read each of the following sentences. Tell if the underlined verb is simple, progressive, perfect, or perfect progressive. Also tell if the verb is in the present, past, or future.

1. The sheepdog had been chasing the coyote for at least 15 minutes by the time we arrived.

2. The grocery store is having an excellent sale on mangoes by the case.

3. The spectacular fireworks brightened the night sky above the small cove.

4. The crossing guard must not have been paying attention to the two small boys.

5. She always pretends she is not hungry.

6. My cousin has left the university to work in Hong Kong.

7. Mr. Endo will be pleased that we know how to speak Japanese.

Kinds of Verbs

Broadly speaking, the English language has three types of verbs: action, linking, and auxiliary. Sometimes verbs appear alone or in groups. A group of verbs that function together is called a *verb phrase*.

Action verbs show actions people can do, like *jump, hum, yell,* or *listen.*

Mr. Turnowski works hard all day at his recycling business. (*Works* is an action verb; it tells what Mr. Turnowksi does.)

Jan reads many Canadian novels from the early twentieth century. (*Reads* is an action verb; it tells what Jan does.)

Linking verbs do not show action. Instead, they tell the state of the subject and link the subject to the rest of the sentence.

The new president of the club is very pleasant. (*Is* is a linking verb; it links the subject to what he or she is—*pleasant.*)

Those bananas become brown in the fridge. (*Become* is a linking verb; it links the subject, *bananas,* to *brown* to tell the state of the subject.)

Auxiliary verbs are sometimes called *helping verbs*. You will find auxiliary verbs with main verbs in verb phrases. Auxiliary verbs support the main verb. They also help in the formation of questions and of negatives.

Most of the business students are taking their economics exams today. (*Are taking* is a verb phrase. *Are* is the auxiliary verb. *Taking* is the main action verb.)

Raymond should be driving more carefully. (*Should be driving* is a verb phrase. *Should* and *be* are the auxiliary verbs. *Driving* is the main verb.)

Are you applying for the position of assistant director? (*Are* is the auxiliary verb. *Applying* is the main verb. Notice that to form a question, you place the auxiliary verb at the beginning of the sentence.)

Action Verbs

An *action verb* is a word that tells what action the subject is doing. Some experts classify verbs such as *remember, believe,* and *love* as non-action verbs because they do not represent a physical action. Instead, they express something people do emotionally or mentally. However, you can classify them as action verbs, although it is important to recognize that the action may not be physically apparent.

Since sentences can have more than one action verb, read each sentence carefully as you analyze it for grammatical structure and meaning. Look for *compound verbs* (two or more verbs functioning separately).

Adalia speaks clearly as a TV announcer. (action is physical)

The technician repaired the monitor and replaced the fan belt in the CPU. (Notice the compound action verb.)

His old mother worries about him. (action is not physical)

She thinks about her new car all the time! (action is not physical)

Exercise 1 *Recognizing Action Verbs*

Underline all the action verbs in each of the following sentences. Check your answers with the Answer Key.

1. Scary movies really frighten my children.

2. Mr. and Mrs. Hoek opened a little card shop next to the bank.

3. The rushing waters engulfed the little fallen fledgling.

4. Sometimes we brew our own beer during the winter months and drink it in the summer.

5. The warden of the prison ordered an evacuation of the inmates.

6. Most roses grow well in full sunshine and well-drained soil.

7. The priest blessed the young couple, and the guests applauded.

8. One of the real estate agents wants to take your photograph for his album because he thinks you are beautiful.

9. Every week Jorge writes letters home to his girlfriend and reports on the news.

10. Hugo and Bert enter the squash tournament every year.

Transitive and Intransitive Verbs

Action verbs can be either transitive or intransitive. *Transitive verbs* take objects, whereas *intransitive verbs* do not; however, some verbs can be transitive or intransitive depending on how they are used.

TRANSITIVE

The police officer warned the driver about the landslide. (*Warned* is a transitive verb because it takes the object *driver*. Think: "Warned who?")

Lorna calculated the balance in her chequing account. (*Calculated* is a transitive verb because it takes the object *balance*. Think: "Calculated what?")

INTRANSITIVE

She stands firm on her decision. (*Stands* is intransitive. It does not take an object. Think: "Stands what or who?" Since the answer does not make sense, the verb cannot take an object.)

Baby weeps over his spilled juice. (*Weeps* is intransitive. It does not take an object. Think: "Weeps what or who?" Since the answer does not make sense, the verb cannot take an object.)

Here are some examples of how the same verb can be transitive or intransitive, depending on the sentence:

Transitive	Intransitive
She plays the oboe.	She plays in the backyard.
Malcolm runs the drill press.	Malcolm runs in the city marathon.
Glen collapsed the folding table.	Glen collapsed after the competition.

Exercise 2 *Identifying Intransitive and Transitive Verbs*

First, underline all the verbs in each sentence. Then write **T** above the verb if the verb is transitive. Write **IN** above the verb if the verb is intransitive. Check your answers with the Answer Key.

1. The manager of the planning agency ordered several maps of the region.

2. Goofus refused to answer any questions from reporters.

3. Several of the contractors spoke at the meeting, but no one responded.

4. City council voted on the new proposed development.

5. Amy vacations in the south of France each year; however, she's becoming bored by it.

6. My father broke his promise to me, and I will never forgive him.

7. The gardener pruned the rhododendrons and the witch hazel.

8. My nephew threw a party for his boss when Mr. Dodger got a promotion.

9. One fellow pretended to be the president of the United States.

10. The chef prepared cheese soufflé for the business luncheon.

11. The consultant concentrated on her notes during the presentation and did not look at the audience at all.

12. The accused appealed to the jury's sympathy, but they remained grim.

Linking Verbs

These verbs do not show action; instead they link the parts of the sentence together. In fact, they connect the subject to its subject complement.

Stanislaw Lem is the famous Ukrainian science fiction writer who wrote *Solaris.* (The linking verb *is* connects the subject *Stanislaw Lem* with the subject complement *writer*.)

Following is a list of common linking verbs. Remember that linking verbs do not show action and do not take objects.

Related to the verb *be*:

am   is   are   was   were

Gus is a competitive snooker player when he is pushed a little.

Several of the women are trained physiotherapists.

Sadeem was a heavyweight boxer.

Related to the senses:

look   sound   smell   feel   taste

We felt tired today after we moved from our apartment.

That sounds terrible!

The machinist looks busy right now; I'll talk to him later.

That cream cake tastes delectable.

The water smells fishy even though it is supposed to be fresh.

Related to the state of being:

appear   seem   become   grow   turn   prove   remain

They appear upset by the incident.

Eddie seems confused about the arrangement, so please speak to him about it.

Hint

- Linking verbs do not take objects.
- Linking verbs are followed by subject complements that complete sentences.

Exercise 3   *Constructing Sentences with Linking Verbs*

Work in pairs. Write sentences for each of the following. Be prepared to share your answers.

1. Use *become* as a linking verb in a sentence of at least five words. Use *fascinated* in your subject complement.

2. Use *sound* as a linking verb in a sentence of at least five words. Use *ridiculous* in your subject complement.

3. Use *were* as a linking verb in a sentence of at least five words. Use *researchers* in your subject complement.

4. Use *looks* as a linking verb in a sentence of at least five words. Use *attractive* in your subject complement.

5. Use *appeared* as a linking verb in a sentence of at least five words. Use *useless* in your subject complement.

Auxiliary Verbs

Auxiliary verbs, sometimes called *helping verbs*, are grouped with main verbs to support them in verb phrases. *Be, do,* and *have* are the three main verbs that you will use to form most auxiliaries. Auxiliaries are used to express time or tense.

The Main Auxiliary Verbs

be: am, is, are, was, were, been

do: do, does, did, done

have: has, have, had

Hint

Do *can also add emphasis to the main verb.*

> I do really love you!

> She does want a new car from that dealership.

> Micki did try to telephone the police from his cellphone, but he could not get through.

Here are some examples of auxiliaries in verb phrases:

I am reading one of Farley Mowat's books.

(*Am reading* is the verb phrase. *Am* is used as the auxiliary verb here. It is telling about the present, so it is in present tense.)

Yesterday Hedda did decide to marry her childhood sweetheart.

(*Did decide* is the verb phrase. *Did* is used as the auxiliary verb. It shows past tense.)

The bus driver has stopped to check one of the tires on the bus.

(*Has stopped* is the verb phrase. *Has* is the auxiliary verb. It is in the present tense.)

Another group of auxiliary verbs, called *modal auxiliary verbs*, helps to express obligation, possibility, or intent.

Modal Auxiliary Verbs

can	may	will	used to
could	might	should	ought to
would	must	shall	

Hints

- Use can *when you wish to indicate that someone or something has the ability to do something.*
  Joshua is a long-distance runner and can run a long time without getting winded. (*Can* indicates he has the ability to do so.)
- Use may *when you wish to indicate permission.*
  May I sit with you during the concert? (*May* points out that the speaker is asking for permission.)

Exercise 4 *Identifying Auxiliary Verbs*

Underline the auxiliary verbs in each of the following sentences. Check your answer with the Answer Key.

1. The pianist may perform at Regis Theatre Centre this evening, so would you like to accompany me?

2. The children will plant pumpkin seeds in our garden this spring.

3. Darla has roasted a small chicken for supper, and her brother has prepared a chilled wine punch.

4. Mr. Levy, the new vice-president, might join you later after he delivers his speech.

5. Tomas might borrow some money to pay off his loan, but he will discuss the idea with his parents first.

6. Their youngest son has passed his courses at the college.

7. Because Tuan became ill, Akim will complete the negotiations for the ferry workers' union.

8. Fortunately, the administration has responded positively.

9. Did Allison prepare the customers for the news, or did she ask you to do it?

10. Raspberry sorbet will make a refreshing dessert tonight.

11. Mr. Campos and Mrs. Shaffer do regard you with a lot of respect.

12. May I use the computer terminal near the reference desk?

13. We must call the locksmith to repair the lock on the patio door before a burglar discovers the easy entry.

14. If the owner of the dry-cleaning shop were a responsible individual, he would reimburse us for the ruined sweater.

15. They were placing an order over the Internet when the power went out all over the city.

Verb Phrases

Some textbooks refer to *verb phrases* as the verb, its modifiers, and its complements. Others refer to verb phrases as the auxiliary and main verbs grouped together in a sentence. *Spotlight on Sentence and Paragraph Skills* will use the second definition: A verb phrase consists of an auxiliary verb and a main verb. You may recall that auxiliary verbs can support meaning in a number of ways. Two important purposes are to tell when the action takes place (the tense) and to set a condition on the action verb (modal auxiliaries).

Helen is working with Morris on the new project.

The verb phrase is *is working*. *Is* is a linking verb used in the present tense; it shows that the action is occurring in the present. *Working* is the main verb.

The students might have supported the proposal if they had known about it.

The verb phrase is *might have supported*. The auxiliary verbs are *might have*. They set a condition or possibility. *Supported* is the main verb. *Had known* is a second verb phrase. *Had* is the auxiliary.

Those reports were missing from the vice-president's office.

The verb phrase is *were missing*. *Were* is an auxiliary verb in the past tense.

Exercise 5   *Identifying Verb Phrases*

Work in pairs. Underline the verb phrase in each of the following sentences. Decide if the linking verb expresses a time or possibility.

1. Roberto might have been waiting for us this evening.

2. The football player was developing a sore shoulder after he had been tackled.

3. Some dancers are choosing to stay with the Canadian dance company, although many had been tempted by the American offer.

4. We will be announcing our engagement in the newspaper.

5. Can the military develop many of its own policies today?

6. Skilled workers have been leaving the country to go to Asia.

Exercise 6   *Constructing Sentences with Verb Phrases*

Put each of the following verbs into verb phrases and then into your own sentences. Be prepared to share your sentences with others.

1. blaming

2. does

3. interrupted

4. may

5. would

6. frowned

7. celebrating

8. clear

Verb Tense

Tense is a way of referring to time—past, present, and future. By changing its form, a verb indicates the time of an action or condition. Sometimes you can look to the auxiliary verb to help you identify the tense.

Exercise 7　Identifying Time of Verbs

Underline the verb or verb phrase in each sentence. Then write **PRESENT, PAST,** or **FUTURE** after each one. Check your answers with the Answer Key.

1. I will be marking papers until midnight. _____

2. Some of the trees were cracking in the powerful wind. _____

3. One of the officers is arresting the panhandler. _____

4. Will we speak to the temporary supervisor? _____

5. No one at the mall had received their candy shipments. _____

6. Plants do grow well in our south-facing front garden. _____

7. The biker at the park has slipped on the trail. _____

8. Nicholas will wait until Saturday for his car. _____

9. Several of the teens were smoking outside the store. _____

10. Many people did protest the ferry fare increases. _____

11. Had you forgotten about the dental appointment? _____

12. In time, we will forgive you for your unkind words. _____

13. Those red pears are ripening nicely on the window sill. _____

14. The campers were moving out of the restricted area. _____

15. Jadwiga is expecting her baby in March. _____

Tenses can have different forms: simple, perfect, progressive, and perfect progressive. *Spotlight on Sentence and Paragraph Skills* refers to these forms as *tenses*. You may see progressive tense referred to as *continuous tense* in some books. They mean the same thing.

Review the chart below. Think about how these verb forms, or tenses, are different.

Time	Tense	Example
present	simple	Snow falls in winter.
		Purpose: provides a fact or truth

present	simple	He eats at noon. Purpose: expresses a habit
past	simple	Kim drove a truck. Purpose: expresses a completed action
future	simple	He will meet us at 5. Purpose: shows action is to follow
present	perfect	We have begun the process. Purpose: an action that began in the past and is still affecting the present
past	perfect	Sue had read the article. Purpose: an action that took place over time and was completed in the past
future	perfect	He will have opened the kit before he builds the model. Purpose: a future action that will be completed before another action
present	progressive	I am thinking about it. Purpose: continuing action that happens in the present
past	progressive	Lisle was fishing all day yesterday. Purpose: action continued over a period of time in the past
future	progressive	They will be singing in the choir. Purpose: continuing action that will take place in the future
present	perfect progressive	She has been living with him for five years. Purpose: stresses the ongoing nature of an action that began in the past
past	perfect progressive	They had been listening to the television when the screen went black. Purpose: an action continuing in the past that was interrupted by another action
future	perfect progressive	Petra will have been analyzing her data for more than three years. Purpose: stresses an ongoing action that will continue into the future

Exercise 8   Identifying Tenses

Tell what verb tense you see in each of the following sentences. Check your answers with the Answer Key.

1. Mr. Migneault was bargaining with a fat man in a porkpie hat. _____

2. The recreational trailer slid down the small hill into the grassy picnic area. _____

3. CBC will have been broadcasting the Stanley Cup playoffs for five weeks now. _____

4. The generous tycoon is promising to leave the university $15 million. _____

5. The goalie's mask has been slipping off his face for the whole game. _____

6. Will she brew some peppermint tea to go with our lunch? _____

7. I have waited a long time to say this to you. _____

8. Will Mortimer have exceeded his credit limit at the bank? _____

9. Walter and Taki take the kayak out on the lake in the early morning. _____

10. The students have been studying their English for two semesters. _____

11. Will you be planning to come on the trip to the mountains with us? _____

12. The dog and the cat were fighting over the piece of sausage. _____

13. Roger had not understood the passage in the novel. _____

14. The little watch had been working for almost 50 years. _____

15. Fumie has supplied us with a very funny answer. _____

Exercise 9 *Transforming Tenses*

Change the tenses as indicated by the directions given in each set of parentheses. Check your answers with the Answer Key.

1. Maybe they will find out about us. (change to simple past)

2. George entered to win the horseshoe throwing contest. (change to present progressive)

3. The choir did give a lovely performance at the church on Saturday. (change to past progressive)

4. No one cycled on the new bike path since the flooding of some sections. (change to future perfect progressive)

5. Layer cakes had been a favourite at birthday parties in the 1950s. (change to simple past)

6. Were you mowing the lawn for your in-laws? (change to present progressive)

7. Several of the witnesses refused to give testimony. (change to past perfect progressive)

8. Children from several classes planted a garden along the south wall of the school. (change to present progressive)

Exercise 10 Group Activity: Constructing Sentences with Tenses

Work in groups of three. Using the following verbs, construct sentences together according to the tense listed for each. Be prepared to share your answers with the rest of the class.

1. *enjoy* in the future perfect progressive tense.

2. *escort* in the simple past tense.

3. *hesitate* in the past perfect tense.

4. *scratch* in the simple future tense.

5. *creep* in the present progressive tense.

6. *freeze* in the future perfect tense.

7. *practise* in the present perfect progressive tense.

8. *design* in the past progressive tense.

9. *write* in the simple present tense.

10. *suffer* in the present perfect tense.

Forms of Verbs

The main parts of an English verb are the *base form* (seen in the present tense below), the *simple past*, and the *past participle*. The past participle is used to make perfect tenses.

We have released the eagle back into the wild.

(*Have released* is in the present perfect tense. *Released* is the past participle.)

The service station staff had organized a fundraising event for cancer.

(*Had organized* is in the past perfect tense. *Organized* is the past participle.)

She had taken a room for the weekend at the Maki Maki Hotel on the beach.

(*Had taken* is in the past perfect tense. *Taken* is the past participle.)

The English language contains regular and irregular verb forms. Since there are no hard and fast rules as to how the past participle is formed, you will have to do your best to remember as many of them as you can. Notice that you add *-s* or *-es* to the base form of the verb when you are working with a third person singular subject (*he, she,* or *it*).

They watch their diets carefully.

He watches his diet carefully.

Regular Verbs

Present	Past	Past Participle *(has, had, have)*
review(s)	reviewed	reviewed
cough(s)	coughed	coughed
cry (cries)	cried	cried
wonder(s)	wondered	wondered
play(s)	played	played
snore(s)	snored	snored

Irregular Verbs

Present	Simple Past	Past Participle *(has, have, had)*
bear	bore	borne *or* born
beat	beat	beaten
bleed(s)	bled	bled
begin	began	begun
bid (offer)	bid	bid
bid (order)	bade	bidden
bind	bound	bound
bite	bit	bitten
break	broke	broken
bring	brought	brought
burst	burst	burst
buy	bought	bought
catch	caught	caught
choose	chose	chosen
creep	crept	crept
dive	dived *or* dove	dived
draw	drew	drawn
dream	dreamt *or* dreamed	dreamed *or* dreamt
drink	drank	drunk
drive	drove	driven

eat	ate	eaten
fall	fell	fallen
feed	fed	fed
feel	felt	felt
fight	fought	fought
find	found	found
flee	fled	fled
fly	flew	flown
forbid	forbade *or* forbad	forbidden
forget	forgot	forgotten
forsake	forsook	forsaken
freeze	froze	frozen
give	gave	given

Unusual Verbs

Present	Simple Past	Past Participle *(has, have, had)*
grind	ground	ground
hurt	hurt	hurt
kneel	kneeled *or* knelt	kneeled *or* knelt
leap	leapt *or* leaped	leapt *or* leaped
light	lighted *or* lit	lighted *or* lit
lose	lost	lost
mistake	mistook	mistaken
seek	sought	sought
speed	sped *or* speeded	sped *or* speeded
stride	strode	stridden
strew	strewed	strewn
strive	strove *or* strived	striven *or* strived
thrive	thrived *or* throve	thriven *or* thrived

Exercise 11 Using Correct Verb Form

Fill in the correct form of the base verb to suit each sentence below. Be sure to read each sentence carefully. Use the preceding tables as a reference. Check your answers with the Answer Key.

Example: Since the weather has turned cold, I have bought a new coat to <u>wear</u>.

1. To my surprise, Amund _____ his car last Thursday. (sell)

2. My mother has _____ in a choir for the past two years. (sing)

3. Jonas had _____ many articles for the newspaper. (write)

5. Water _____ at 0 degrees Celsius. (freeze)

6. Has he ever _____ the train to Calgary before? (ride)

7. Yesterday while running, I accidentally _____ my new jacket. (tear)

8. A foreign boat _____ in the harbour last week. (sink)

9. Has the new infant _____ at all during the past week? (grow)

10. Every morning, Bernard _____ for work at exactly the same time. (leave)

11. Raoul and Tracy _____ to meet you at 11 after class. (promise)

12. We have _____ to them about the fridge. (speak)

13. Each day I _____ breakfast by myself. (eat)

14. Have you ever _____ your promise to one of your kids? (break)

15. Since we were at the same meeting last month, Bob _____ me when we met in the street. (know)

16. Who has _____ my favourite hammer from my toolkit? (take)

17. Oh, no! The customer _____ the wrong order! (eat)

18. Last spring the river that runs through the city _____ 2 metres in one week. (rise)

19. Yesterday I _____ in until 10 (sleep) and _____ (miss) my psychology class.

20. The architect and her assistant have _____ up the new plans for the hockey arena. (draw)

Exercise 12   More Practice with Verb Forms

Work in pairs. Fill in the correct form of each base verb to suit each sentence below. Be sure to read each sentence carefully. Use the tables above as a reference.

1. I had never _____ such large ships as when I visited Vancouver. (see)

2. Many of our trees _____ down in last night's storm. (blew)

3. We _____ beer and pretzels for the party. (bring)

4. After leaving the podium, the speaker of the house _____ a flower from a bunch proffered by one of the pages. (choose)

5. After we got our approval and building permit, we _____ to build our house. (begin)

6. Ranger _____ a very fast Gardner Douglas T70 Spyder. (drive)

7. Last winter my grandmother _____ on the snowy steps (fall) and _____ (break) her hip.

8. Every year Jing and Xue _____ their cousin a birthday card. (give)

9. Have you ever _____ to one of the Greek islands? (go)

10. My uncle is from the Caribbean, but I haven't _____ him for a very long time. (see)

11. The accident victim _____ several kilometres to get help for others involved in the crash. (run)

12. To amuse themselves, the boys _____ rocks at tin cans. (throw)

13. The tiny child _____ tired of the game (grow) and _____ to sleep in the hammock. (go)

14. Last week after a heated argument, the couple _____ out the old rug. (throw)

15. I am worried because I don't know whether she _____ the bill or not. (pay)

16. During the fire drill, someone _____ my purse and laptop. (steal)

17. Daphne has _____ horses since she was little. (ride)

18. The boy has _____ the pigs the supper leftovers. (feed)

19. A new baby often _____ cold easily. (catch)

20. My dad _____ three glasses of milk at lunch every single day. (drink)

21. Last summer Werner _____ his motorcycle (fix) and _____ it to work. (ride)

22. Carmer always _____ very frankly. (speak)

23. The old man _____ very carefully over the slippery roads. (drive)

24. Have you _____ her brother? (meet)

25. Mrs. Lum _____ piano in the basement of her home. (teach)

26. The cats _____ over the fish last evening. (fight)

27. Bo has _____ the children's gifts. (hide)

28. Have the workers _____ for more pay? (strike)

29. She _____ on the bus every day. (stand)

30. Has he _____ behind in his work? (fall)

Exercise 13   Constructing Sentences with Different Verb Forms

Use each of the following verb forms in effective sentences. Follow the directions provided. Be prepared to share your answers.

1. Use the past participle of *draw* in a complex sentence.

2. Use the simple past of *choose* in a simple sentence.

3. Use the present of *grind* in a simple sentence with *Elza* as the subject.

4. Use the simple past of *bite* in a compound sentence.

5. Use the past participle of *freeze* in a simple sentence having a compound subject.

6. Use the present of *catch* in a compound sentence with *Lonnie* as the subject.

7. Use the past participle of *fight* in a complex sentence using a pronoun as subject.

8. Use the simple past of *lose* in a simple sentence containing a compound subject.

9. Use the present tense of *fly* in a complex sentence that includes the names of two Canadian cities.

10. Use the simple past of *begin* in a simple sentence with a pronoun subject.

Exercise 14 Editing Verb Errors

The following passage contains verb errors. Find the errors and correct them. Check your answers with the Answer Key that follows.

Sheila had called and wrote several letters to the telephone company about her bill. Once again, Sheila dialled the customer service department; a voice tells her that "a representative would be with you in a moment." She begun waiting on the line, listening to some recorded music which is very boring. It seemed as if they has taken more time than necessary. What the company done to satisfy Sheila's claim was not acceptable to her. The company believed it had strove to meet all customer demands, but Sheila seen only bad service. As far as she was concerned, the new phone company had broke most of its advertised promises. Sheila hanged up the phone in sheer disgust and pledging to switch her account to another phone company.

Answer Key

Sheila had called and wrote (written) several letters to the telephone company about her bill. Once again, Sheila dialled the customer service department; a voice tells (told) her that "a representative would (will) be with you in a moment." She begun (began) waiting on the line, listening to some recorded music which is (was) very boring. It seemed as if they has taken (were taking) more time than necessary. What the company done (had done) to satisfy Sheila's claim was not acceptable to her. The company believed it had strove (strived or striven) to meet all customer demands, but Sheila seen (had seen) only bad service. As far as she was concerned, the new phone company had broke (broken) most of its advertised promises. Sheila hanged (hung) up the phone in sheer disgust and pledging (pledged) to switch her account to another phone company.

Chapter 6: Review Test

Part 1: Identifying Types of Verbs

Each sentence contains an underlined verb. Tell if the underlined verb is an action, linking, or auxiliary verb.

1. A vinyl suitcase <u>stood</u> in the doorway of the motel room.

2. <u>Had</u> the meat inspector <u>noticed</u> the infraction?

3. <u>Were</u> the patients <u>developing</u> salmonella from the tuna noodle casserole?

4. Remarkably, the athlete <u>jumped</u> out of the way of the oncoming sled.

5. That problem <u>sounds</u> very serious indeed.

6. <u>Was</u> he <u>reading</u> the newspaper all morning?

7. Emile's students <u>were</u> <u>planning</u> a field trip to Swanson's Bog.

Part 2: Recognizing Transitive and Intransitive Verbs

Tell if the underlined verb is transitive or intransitive by writing **T** or **INT** above it.

1. Has Mr. Atkin <u>interpreted</u> the data for the committee report?

2. Several of my neighbours were <u>complaining</u> about the smoke from his barbeque.

3. Do most teenagers <u>like</u> to sleep in every morning?

4. Sammy <u>likes</u> orange and onion sandwiches for his lunch.

5. We <u>happen</u> to know your new boyfriend, Sasha, is a heartbreaker.

6. Since it is so hot outside, should we <u>order</u> a cold citrus drink?

Part 3: Auxiliary Verbs and their Functions

Underline the auxiliary verbs in each of the following sentences. If they primarily add emphasis to the main verb, write **E**. If they support the main verb in indicating time, write **T**. If they are a modal auxiliary verb, write **M**.

1. Dogzilla, his new pug puppy, has dug up everything in the back garden.

2. Stethoscopes have been used by doctors for almost 200 years.

3. Roscoe's ex-wife does not talk to him at all.

4. We were listening to tapes of his earliest interviews on radio.

5. Are the candidates speaking tonight at the debate?

6. His lawyer will fax you the important documents by noon of October 23.

7. The contractor might order the lumber from a mill in Chicoutimi, Quebec.

Part Identifying Verb Phrases

Underline the verb phrases in each of the following sentences.

1. They should have been avoiding the icy roads that fateful night.

2. Are Stella and Dudley offering us their cottage for the weekend?

3. She may have been watching too much television lately.

4. Must I always remind you to take out the garbage?

5. The sponsor has been asking the star for a special interview.

6. Professor Fenwright might extend the deadline for our physics reports.

7. No doubt they will be arguing over the money again tonight.

Part 5: Identifying Verb Tenses

Underline the verbs or verb phrases in each of the following sentences. Tell the tense after each sentence.

1. The crush of the waves must have been a powerful force of the tsunami. _____

2. Were the cyclists waiting to talk with the organizer of the race? _____

3. The shark is heading off in the direction of that small lagoon. _____

4. She will dress the baby in this cute outfit for his first birthday party. _____

5. His idea of a practical joke had gone too far. _____

6. The memorial garden had been opened a full year before the family knew of it. _____

7. Moe is rinsing off the dust on his new Mazda truck. _____

8. Someone should have told me about the accident this morning. _____

9. Lord Gulliver Cadbury had owned a large estate in the county for 50 years. _____

10. The foreign journalist is preparing to leave the war-torn country today. _____

Part 6: Adding Correct Forms of Verbs

Add the correct form of each main verb shown in parentheses.

1. Have the children _____ their vegetables yet? (eat)

2. Gomer has _____ a small aircraft across the straits before. (fly)

3. The magazine _____ too much money. (cost)

4. When I _____ (cough) so much yesterday, I _____ my rib. (hurt)

5. Have they _____ to their parents about it? (speak)

6. Somebody _____ his or her car into the stop sign last night. (drive)

7. The goose _____, so be careful when you enter the pen. (bite)

Part 7: Types of Tenses

Read each of the following sentences. Tell if the underlined verb is simple, progressive, perfect, or perfect progressive. Also tell if the verb is in the present, past, or future.

1. After a long journey, the traveller <u>slept</u> on the bench in the train station.

2. <u>Will</u> the dance instructor <u>be</u> <u>teaching</u> us some hot salsa steps tonight?

3. Musical snobs <u>had</u> always <u>hung out</u> at this coffee shop.

4. Professor Fungus carefully <u>arranges</u> all PowerPoint presentations for his students.

5. Although Maggie <u>has</u> not <u>mentioned</u> it, I know she <u>wants</u> to be invited to your party.

6. <u>Had</u> he <u>been competing</u> for the championship when he <u>was</u> that young?

7. Mrs. Norland <u>hated</u> wearing a hat when she <u>visited</u> the Duchess of Yewsbury.

ESL POINTER

Modal Auxiliaries

Modal auxiliaries enhance main verbs in a number of ways. Most of them help express possibility or obligation.

These are the most common modal auxiliary verbs used in the English language:

can   could   will   would   may   might   must   should

The game may be delayed if it rains.

Ivana might go out with Mitch if he asks her.

These express possibility:

may   might   could   would

Would is generally used when some condition is named in another part of the sentence.

Carlos would paint the bathroom if you suggested it.

Her students could study a little harder, don't you agree?

If my sister had the money, she would take her family to Disneyland.

These auxiliaries express obligation:

must   should

Must indicates an urgent responsibility.

The child must be picked up by five when the daycare closes.

Should points out an obligation or duty, but it does not necessarily have strong urgency.

The dentist says you should floss your teeth at least once a day.

Will can be used to indicate a future time, but it can also show determination.

With hard work and dedication, I will win the championship.

Can is used to express ability to do something.

Jojo can swim really well for such a young girl.

Hint

Use the base form of the verb with modal auxiliaries.

<u>can</u> disagree (base form of the verb)
<u>might</u> intrude (base form of the verb)
<u>should</u> memorize (base form of the verb)

Exercise 1   *Working with Modal Auxiliaries*

Work in pairs. Construct sentences together according to the instructions. Be prepared to share your work.

1. Use *frighten* with a modal auxiliary that indicates possibility.

2. Use *throw* with a modal auxiliary that indicates ability.

3. Use *complain* with a modal auxiliary that indicates obligation.

4. Use *load* with a modal auxiliary that indicates possibility.

5. Use *build* with a modal auxiliary that indicates determination.

6. Use *seek* with a modal auxiliary that indicates obligation.

7. Use *draw* with a modal auxiliary that indicates ability.

8. Use *collect* with a modal auxiliary that indicates determination.

9. Use *attach* with a modal auxiliary that indicates possibility.

10. Use *serve* with a modal auxiliary that indicates obligation.

11. Use *practise* with a modal auxiliary that indicates obligation.

12. Use *remove* with a modal auxiliary that indicates determination.

13. Use *announce* with a modal auxiliary that indicates possibility.

14. Use *avoid* with a modal auxiliary that indicates obligation.

15. Use *cycle* with a modal auxiliary that indicates ability.

Exercise 2   *Changing Modals*

Change each of the modal auxiliary verbs in the following sentences according to the instructions. Check your answer with the Answer Key.

1. The landlady might raise the rent in my apartment building. (Change the modal auxiliary to one that indicates ability.)

2. I will confess to the lie I told you. (Change the modal auxiliary to one that indicates obligation.)

3. The paddlers must set off tomorrow if the weather is calmer. (Change the modal auxiliary to one that indicates possibility.)

4. Miss Ramos will be hired as the new vice-chair of academic operations. (Change the modal auxiliary to one that indicates possibility.)

5. When my cheque arrives at the bank, I will take Yvette out to dinner. (Change the modal auxiliary to one that indicates ability.)

6. The firefighters can protect themselves from serious injury by taking advanced training. (Change the modal auxiliary to one that indicates obligation.)

7. Her children will perform at the concert at the university tonight. (Change the modal auxiliary to one that indicates possibility.)

8. If anything goes wrong with the plan, Alric might telephone us. (Change the modal auxiliary to one that indicates determination.)

9. These cookies will be baked at 350 degrees for 18 minutes. (Change the modal auxiliary to one that indicates obligation.)

10. Come-by-Chance, Newfoundland, must be one of the most interesting place names in Canada. (Change the modal auxiliary to one that indicates possibility.)

11. With a new excellent coach and money from a private donor to practise and compete, Violet will ski in the 2010 Olympics at Whistler, British Columbia. (Change the modal auxiliary to one that indicates possibility.)

12. If you wake up early in the morning, you might assist with breakfast preparation for the guests. (Change the modal auxiliary to one that indicates obligation.)

CHECKOUT

1. The English language has three types of verbs: action, linking, and auxiliary.

2. Action verbs can be either transitive or intransitive.

3. You can use a modal auxiliary verb to set a condition on the action verb.

4. A verb phrase consists of an auxiliary verb and a main verb.

5. Tense is a way of referring to time—past, present, and future.

6. Tenses can have different forms: simple, perfect, progressive, and perfect progressive.

7. In English there are regular and irregular verb forms.

8. By changing its form, a verb indicates time of an action or condition.

Modifiers

Chapter Objectives
What will you have learned when you have completed this chapter?
You will be able to

1. include adjectives to add detail and colour to your writing.

2. compare things using positive, comparative, and superlative forms.

3. use adverbs to describe verbs, adjectives, or other adverbs.

4. increase your grammatical power with small words called prepositions.

5. work with prepositional phrases.

6. spot sentences containing misused prepositions.

7. find idiomatic prepositions.

Chapter 7: Self-Test

Complete the following self-test on modifiers. Check your answers with the Answer Key at the back of the book.

Part 1: Adjectives and Adverbs

Read each of the following sentences. In the spaces provided, tell if the underlined words are adjectives or adverbs.

1. <u>Suddenly</u> the schoolchildren were excited by the arrival of the <u>new</u> student. _____

2. A <u>fierce</u> roar came out of the <u>tiny</u> terrier. _____

3. He decided to buy all the <u>fresh</u> <u>coconut</u> buns arranged <u>so</u> <u>attractively</u> in the <u>glass</u> case. _____

4. The family moved <u>far</u> <u>away</u> from their <u>troubled</u> country. _____

5. His restaurant <u>usually</u> closes around midnight. _____

6. Mrs. Tan sat <u>silently</u> in the corner of the <u>crowded</u> hall. _____

7. I spoke <u>gently</u> to the <u>upset</u> protestor. _____

8. Chang is <u>quite</u> <u>worried</u> about passing his <u>English</u> course. _____

9. All the <u>glazed</u> doughnuts looked <u>stale</u> and <u>unappealing</u>. _____

10. You have worked <u>very</u> <u>hard</u> on your <u>physiology</u> report. _____

Part 2: Prepositional Phrases

Read each of the sentences below. Use brackets **[ ]** to indicate prepositional phrases.

1. We slowly paddled our canoe in the still waters of Moose Lake.

2. Go practise your flute in the back room.

3. Without a care in the world, the puppies gambolled in the grassy field.

4. Sometimes in the evening they go for a relaxing stroll along the beach.

5. Where will you store your bicycle during the harsh months of winter?

Part 3: Comparative Adjectives

Add the correct comparative in each of the following sentences.

1. Of all the girls in the world, I believe she is the _____ (lovely).

2. Raymond says that, between the two novels, this one is the _____ (good).

3. The flowers of the lilac are _____ than those of the hazel. (pretty)

4. We did not understand which brand of soap was the _____ in the store. (good)

5. My cousin's daughters are _____ than she is. (tall)

6. The weather this evening will be _____ than yesterday. (cool)

7. A small meal is _____ when you feel exhausted. (good)

8. Try pulling the line a little _____. (tight)

9. His cooking is the _____ of any I've ever tasted! (bad)

10. That paint appears _____ when it is wet. (bright)

Adjectives

Adjectives are words that describe nouns. They tell what kind or what sort of noun. They help to define nouns by pointing out characteristics.

the <u>tall</u>, <u>lean</u> <u>young</u> man

The three underlined words are adjectives. They all describe the word *man*.

Adjectives add detail and colour to your writing. They help the reader "see" something being described, whether it is a person, situation, place, or thing.

a ruthless, aging dictator
a dingy, filthy room
an ingenious invention
a secretive, romantic meeting

Exercise 1   *Identifying Adjectives*

Underline all the adjectives in the following sentences. Check your answers with the Answer Key.

1. A sudden storm caused extensive damage to the maple tree in the park.

2. An electrical short in an old iron was the cause of the house fire down the street.

3. Yesterday I called the new plumber to come to fix the leaky faucet.

4. My neighbour is cantankerous at the best of times.

5. Bleach is a caustic substance found in many kitchen cupboards.

6. His argument was so compelling that we all agreed with him.

7. The toasted tomato sandwiches tasted scrumptious.

8. The scraggy brush was very dense near the railway tracks.

9. The pet was confined to the dark basement of the family house.

10. This vanishing cream eliminates ugly wrinkles.

11. Mr. Castillo's carefree attitude is refreshing.

12. In a peaceful part of the forest the young stag settled in for an undisturbed rest.

13. The short, sharp blade of this knife is effective for cutting mangoes.

14. The serpentine front of the antique oak chest of drawers made it very valuable.

15. The civil war was devastating to the tiny African country.

Comparisons and Adjectives

Adjectives can be used to compare two or more things. The three forms of adjectives used in making comparisons are called the *positive, comparative,* and *superlative.*

You may find yourself wanting to describe something as having more of a quality than another thing does. For instance, if you are discussing two restaurants and you say "Hobby's is a better restaurant than Yolanda's," you are making a comparison between two things. One is good, but the other is better. This form of the adjective is called the *comparative.* If, however, you want to say that another restaurant is the top one in the city, you might say, "I've been to a lot of restaurants in town, but I think Joey's is the best." The first is good; the second is better, but the third is the best of all. You have just used the *superlative* form of the adjective. Consider the forms of comparison:

Forms of Comparison			
	Positive (one item)	Comparative (two items)	Superlative (more than two items)
Regular formation:	sad	sadder	saddest
Irregular formation:	bad	worse	worst
With multi-syllabic adjectives:	unfortunate	more unfortunate	most unfortunate

By looking over the examples, you can see three ways of forming adjective comparisons. Spend some time practising with the forms of comparison. You will see that you can master them.

Exercise 2 *Working with Forms of Comparison*

Work in pairs and together agree which is the appropriate adjective. Fill each space with an answer.

1. I use Frilly-Dilly soap, but my sister-in-law says Hurray soap is _____. (form of good)

2. Marshall wanted to show his friend that the car he had purchased was the _____. (form of expensive)

3. Josef has the _____ luck of anyone I have ever met. (form of good)

4. The model was the _____ Ivan had ever seen. (form of pretty)

5. The lilac bushes are _____ today than yesterday. (form of dry)

6. The rookie is a _____ player than most of the older ones on his team. (form of skillful)

7. Dana is the _____ (form of old) girl in the family, and she is the _____. (form of extravagant)

8. We believe it is _____ to be gentle with animals than to treat them badly. (form of kind)

9. The young parent was the _____ one in the room when his daughter won the poetry contest in the grade six class. (form of proud)

10. Travis told us about the _____ incident he had experienced in his life when he was lost at sea. (form of terrifying)

11. Bo bought the _____ of the two sweaters for her baby. (form of cute)

12. Some northern cities are the _____ in the world. (form of isolate)

13. The soup at Sally's is far _____ than this thin gruel. (form of thick)

14. Ari is the _____ student in our English class. (form of proficient)

15. I think the _____ solution to your problem is to do nothing at all. (form of simple)

16. Do you think he makes the _____ coffee in the building? (form of bad)

17. Riding a bike in traffic is _____ than taking the bus. (form of difficult)

18. The basketball team had the _____ record in their league. (form of poor)

19. The dietitian will tell you which foods are the _____ of all. (form of nutritious)

20. The prospector had struck the _____ vein of gold in his life. (form of rich)

Adverbs

Adverbs describe verbs, adjectives, or other adverbs. When adverbs describe verbs, they tell how, when, or where an action is or was done.

She will clear the tables quickly for the next customers. (*Quickly* is an adverb. It tells how the subject will clear the tables. It modifies the verb *will clear*.)

When adverbs describe adjectives, they tend to heighten or intensify the qualities of the adjectives.

adv   adj
very polite

adv   adj
too weary

adv   adj
extremely upset

adv   adj
happily married

When adverbs describe other adverbs, they tend to heighten or intensify the qualities of how something was done.

Wendy works quite well under stress. (*Quite* is an adverb that describes the adverb *well*. *Quite* expresses how well the subject works.)

Adverbs Working Singly

An adverb is also an important sort of modifier in your writing. Like other modifiers, it adds detail. It provides information about why, how, where, when, or how much.

adv   v
Haley suddenly screamed.

Here *suddenly* is an adverb; it describes the verb *screamed*. The adverb tells when Haley screamed.

adv   v
Skip was perfectly prepared for the winter.

Here *perfectly* is an adverb; it describes the adjective *prepared*. The adverb tells how prepared Skip was.

adv   v
The guest is very impatient.

In this sentence *very* is an adverb; it describes the adjective *impatient. Very* tells how impatient the guest is.

Here are more examples of adverbs working singly:

Rosa is always late.
Her older sister is never upset with her children.
Sometimes we walk along the shore.
The residents of the town scarcely understood what the mayor was saying.
How often do you shop in the city?
Bridget's family frequently visits her in the summer.
Occasionally Mr. Potter has a pint of beer.
She seldom speaks to her neighbours.
Such a bird is rarely seen in these parts.
Do you usually expect him to call you?
The prisoner hardly paid attention to the judge.
Stanley hardly ever used his dirt bike on the weekends.

Adverb Forms

You will notice that most of the time adverbs end in the *-ly* suffix. Here are some typical adverbs:

surely	quickly	happily	certainly
finally	rapidly	coldly	nervously
only	frankly	immediately	usually
silently	extremely	truly	basically

However, some adverbs do not end in *-ly*. Here is a list of these common adverbs:

often	just	never	almost
not	quite	there	now
ever	soon	rather	also
somewhat	seldom	much	less
more	too	so	here
always	then	very	always

Exercise 3 Recognizing Adverbs

Read each of the sentences that follow. Underline all the adverbs. Check your answers with the Answer Key.

1. Apparently, the courier was quite lost on his new route.

2. On the weekends, Mel regularly visits his father at the nursing home.

3. Finally, Arlene spoke calmly to the angry tenant.

4. The sailboat appeared to float effortlessly on the peaceful ocean.

5. The leafy vegetables should be coarsely chopped and quickly stir-fried.

6. The archaeologists unexpectedly discovered an ancient text deep in the cave of the desert mountain.

7. During the campaign, Estella was certainly brilliant in the debate.

8. Yesterday the children were happily painting the back fence a bright green.

9. Indeed, many of the speakers were strongly opposed to the motion.

10. Krystal was concentrating so deeply that she did not hear me enter the study room.

11. Today we went about our unfinished business efficiently.

12. Wynn kissed the baby tenderly and softly closed the bedroom door.

13. The colt awkwardly frolicked on the grassy field.

14. Suddenly, Arnold swept his arm backward and clumsily knocked over Mrs. Piettla's favourite vase of flowers.

15. The artist painstakingly daubed vivid points of colour as he hummed cheerfully to himself.

Exercise 4 Identifying Adverbs

Read each of the sentences that follow. Underline all the adverbs. Check your answers with the Answer Key.

1. After a few drinks, we found ourselves merrily singing around the piano.

2. She is equally disturbed by the ugly rumour.

3. Lucy is rather short but is apparently good at basketball.

4. Mr. Lucas is constantly worrying about his huge property taxes.

5. The thief quietly entered the hotel room and systematically rummaged through the guests' luggage.

6. Randolph stood approximately 3 metres from the crowd before he began speaking calmly.

7. We were just leaving when the alarm rang sharply.

8. Are you quite sure you must leave tomorrow?

9. The boisterous children were playing together contentedly.

10. Our boss was busily directing us toward the meeting room.

11. Apparently, the husband was considerably older than his wife.

12. She strained intently as she listened at the outer door.

13. Because I was quite late, I had to eat my supper unceremoniously in my room.

14. Guadalupe stared coldly at her supervisor, and then with a sweeping motion she pushed her chair backward and smirked crookedly at him.

15. The guests were visibly upset by the minor earthquake that had rumbled through the resort town.

16. We were definitely opposed when the chairperson wildly preached her point of view.

17. Quite often the nanny will cheerfully take the children to the community centre.

18. I almost forgot my car keys when I got extremely busy today.

Exercise 5 Adverbs for Sentence Construction

Choose 30 of the following list of adverbs. Create 10 sentences, each containing three adverbs. Your instructor may ask you to hand in your work for checking.

afresh	airily	suddenly	amusingly
conversely	together	aloud	interestingly
agog	alike	constantly	anew
quite	visibly	also	just
consequently	almost	merrily	apart
agreeably	inward	altogether	knowingly
shortly	alone	exceedingly	apparently
ahead	freely	always	late/later
rudely	aloft	directly	contentedly

approximately	behind	frankly	officially
today	firmly	noisily	charmingly
asunder	below	extremely	ordinarily
yesterday	now	too	cheerfully
aback	beneath	busily	originally
tomorrow	nowadays	rather	chiefly
really	beside	attractively	collectively
backward	consistently	often	considerably
last	occasionally	carelessly	understandably
badly	beyond	oddly	quickly
finally	obviously	certainly	surely
barely	heartily	openly	gladly
lastly	boldly	cheaply	

Exercise 6   *Group Activity: Identifying Adverbs and Adjectives*

Form a group of three to five people. Read the sentences that follow. Then underline all the adjectives and put the adverbs in brackets [ ].

1. A brown, speckled bird squawked sharply from the blackberry bushes and flapped its wings menacingly at passersby.

2. Norma very much enjoyed the skiing vacation early in the new year.

3. Stephen nodded agreeably as Tony explained the secret plan.

4. Occasionally, the family eats at restaurants; usually, they prefer the taste of home-made food.

5. One police officer told me that I was driving too carelessly through a school zone.

6. The wildlife officer cautiously approached the sedated bear as it lay limply beneath the tree.

7. The landscaper stubbornly refused to cut the huge Gary oak trees which stood in a part of the housing development.

8. Some computer experts argue that sustained computer use will ultimately make humans into slower thinkers.

9. Although Warren has a flexible schedule, he is often late for meetings.

10. The dean of the community college was working toward agreeable solutions to some of the college's rather difficult problems.

11. Let me know soon if you are planning to come to the company party.

12. The explorer seemed oddly disturbed by the message he received yesterday.

13. We moved the car seat forward in order to make my sister more comfortable.

14. They are selling DVDs very cheaply because the store is trying earnestly to attract new customers.

15. A tiny hummingbird hovered effortlessly as it drank deeply at the bright red feeder.

Exercise 7 *Identifying Adjectives and Adverbs*

Read each of the following sentences. Circle all the adjectives and underline all the adverbs. Be prepared to share your answers.

1. We respectfully submitted our resignation last week to our overbearing supervisor.

2. The water appeared green to us as we flew high above it in the space shuttle.

3. My cousin rents water skis to tourists and contentedly runs a small boat rental business at the lakeside resort.

4. Auntie Mag was waiting anxiously for the expensive parcel.

5. The rocks, bleached a bright white from the blistering sun, provided a comfortable perch for snakes and lizards.

6. He recently bought a spacious rancher in the western part of the city.

7. A bitter winter wind gusted fiercely down the empty residential street.

8. Conveniently, we arranged our car loan at the friendly dealership.

9. A rusty yellow van was running noisily beneath my bedroom window.

10. The young mother felt too exhausted by the Christmas shopping.

11. Tomorrow Marlene will provide clerical assistance to the sportscasters at the racing event.

12. I felt frightened as a clammy hand pressed hard on my shoulder.

13. Surprisingly, Helima loves to solve all mechanical problems around the house.

14. Mrs. Lou gave an angry response to her neighbour who was apparently trying to eavesdrop.

15. Although the sale was successful, the organizers were constantly bothered by city bylaws.

Prepositions

You will often notice that a small word can have a lot of grammatical power. Certain small words that are used to connect a noun or pronoun to another word in a sentence and to show detail are called *prepositions*. They show direction in time or space.

The following is a list of some common prepositions. Learn to recognize them. Notice that they provide a direction in time or space.

Common Prepositions					
about	above	across	after	against	along
among	around	at	before	behind	below
beneath	beside	between	by	down	during
except	for	from	in	inside	into
like	near	of	on	over	past
through	to	toward	until	up	upon
with	without				

To show that a preposition can change the meaning of a sentence, select one from the list below and use it to complete one of the sentences that follow. Use a different preposition in each sentence.

around
toward
over
under
behind
behind
from
through
into
onto

1. The dog ran _____ the little shed.

2. The dog ran _____ the little shed.

3. The dog ran _____ the little shed.

4. The dog ran _____ the little shed.

5. The dog ran _____ the little shed.

6. The dog ran _____ the little shed.

7. The dog ran _____ the little shed.

8. The dog ran _____ the little shed.

Here are some possible answers.

1. The dog ran around the little shed.

2. The dog ran under the little shed.

3. The dog ran toward the little shed.

4. The dog ran behind the little shed.

5. The dog ran from the little shed.

6. The dog ran through the little shed.

7. The dog ran into the little shed.

8. The dog ran over the little shed.

9. The dog ran behind the little shed.

Each one of these sentences has a different meaning. The difference in the preposition makes the difference in meaning.

Exercise 8 Prepositions

From the list of prepositions above, choose one to fill in the blank in each of the following sentences. Try not to use the same preposition twice. Check your answers with the Answer Key.

1. The plane flew _____ the bridge.

2. Water flows _____ the bridge.

3. Cars are moving _____ the bridge.

4. The woman is standing _____ the bridge.

5. The man is leaning _____ the bridge.

6. John is climbing _____ the steps.

7. The child is coming _____ the steps.

8. The car is _____ two trucks.

9. The lunch will start _____ noon.

10. The flower pot was placed _____ the front steps.

Prepositional Phrases

Notice that a preposition is usually not used alone in a sentence. It is the first word in a group of words that work together to change or modify the meaning. This group of words is called a *prepositional phrase*.

Hint

Prepositional phrases add interesting detail to the meaning of sentences.

The last word in a prepositional phrase must be a noun or pronoun. This noun or pronoun in a prepositional phrase is called the object of the preposition.

across the street

Across is the preposition; *street* is the object of the preposition.

Exercise 9   Objects of Prepositions

In the following phrases, underline the preposition. Draw an arrow to the noun or pronoun that is the object of the preposition. Be prepared to share your answers.

Example: <u>under</u> the rug

1. on paper

2. without help

3. after Christmas

4. in the cool stream

5. across the crowded street

6. during the Easter break

7. on the untidy desk

8. after much hard work

9. for the poor people

10. with his friends

11. toward the motel

12. before a happy holiday

13. from the rocky coast

14. near the high school

15. among the bushes

16. with a good meal

Exercise 10 *More Objects of Prepositions*

Underline the prepositions in the following sentence. Draw an arrow to the object of each preposition. Check your answer with the Answer Key.

1. The road to the house is long and winding.

2. The old cat became too hot in the sun.

3. The scholar of the month was given a trip to Ottawa.

4. Her husband made repairs to the large family van.

5. I was talking to the woman in the blue suit.

6. The editor of the paper was sued by the city councillor.

7. An officer from the RCMP visited the criminal justice class.

8. In the afternoon the children built a fort from old boards.

9. The tips were divided among the staff.

10. The temperature rose during the day.

Prepositions—Misused

In the preceding exercises you learned that a preposition does not usually work alone. It must have a noun or pronoun as its object. A common mistake is to use a preposition without an object. Phrasal verbs and idiomatic expressions are the exception.

Incorrect:	I wish I had of gone.
	(the preposition *of* has no object)
Correct:	I wish I had gone.
Incorrect:	I am kind of lonesome.
	(the preposition *of* has no object)
Correct:	I am very lonesome.

Another mistake is to use two prepositions when one will do.

Incorrect:	My hat blew off of my head.
	(only one preposition should be used)
Correct:	My hat blew off my head.

Exercise 11 *Prepositions Misused*

In the following sentences you will see prepositions misused. Write the sentences correctly. You may have to write an entire new sentence with the same meaning. Check your answers with the Answer Key.

1. Yes, I am sort of tired.

2. They worked kind of hard.

3. I bought it off from him.

4. Let's get it over with.

5. We will start wearing slacks as of today.

6. I bought it from off someone.

7. Where is he at?

8. I don't think she knows where she is going to.

9. The paper blew out of the window.

10. Look out through the window at the snow.

Adjective or Adverb Prepositional Phrases

Prepositional phrases can modify nouns, and when they do they are called *adjective* or *adjectival prepositional phrases*.

The basin of water has frozen. (*Of water* modifies *basin*, a noun. *Of water* is an adjective prepositional phrase.)

The woman in the red hat loves to gamble. (*In the red hat* modifies *woman*, a noun. *In the red hat* is an adjective prepositional phrase.)

My cousin from Singapore writes me long emails. (*From Singapore* modifies *cousin*, a noun. *From Singapore* is an adjective prepositional phrase.)

Prepositional phrases can also act as adverbs. They can modify verbs, adjectives, or other adverbs.

The musician played the accordion with gusto. (*With gusto* modifies *played*, a verb. Therefore the prepositional phrase is an adverb or adverbial prepositional phrase.)

Their friend works hard at the fish plant. (*At the fish plant* modifies *works*, a verb.)

Wen is sad about the loss. (*About the loss* modifies *sad*, an adjective.)

We found this ring among the stones. (*Among the stones* works like an adverb because it describes where we found the ring; therefore, it is called an adverb prepositional phrase.)

Here are a few more examples:

The racer in the blue-striped jersey won the race. (adjective prepositional phrase)

Will he leave his position in a hurry? (adverb prepositional phrase)

A box of onions fell <u>into the path</u> <u>of an oncoming cyclist</u>. (adverb prepositional phrase and adjective prepositional phrase)

Exercise 12   Identifying Types of Prepositional Phrases

Underline the prepositional phrases. Write **ADJ** above adjective prepositional phrases. Write **ADV** above adverb prepositional phrases. Check your answers with the Answer Key.

1. Marek and Hans hid the boat under the bridge.

2. At night we can spot many sparkling stars in the sky.

3. The baby with the big brown eyes was staring at the bright lights of the toy.

4. Go through the doors and follow the stairs to the right of the entrance.

5. The cowboy with the 10-gallon hat won the bucking contest.

6. After surgery, she did not understand the doctor's advice about her diet.

7. For two weeks, Amir was sick at home with the flu.

8. Inside the submarine, the crew was preparing for war.

9. Under the porch, we found an old blue bottle full of strange stones.

10. The early ferry arrived on time for a change.

11. The politician gave a speech about world poverty to the conference delegates.

12. Outside the theatre the rain fell on the waiting patrons.

13. The technician and the controller will stop work at seven o'clock and go for supper.

14. The load of wash was ruined by the dye from her orange pyjamas.

15. About midnight, the campers heard an eerie howling from the dark woods.

Chapter 7: Review Test

Part 1: Finding Adjectives

Underline all the adjectives in the following sentences.

1. The rusty abandoned car was sitting in an oily pool.

2. The brilliant scientist developed a devious plan for the company.

3. We felt bored with the new Hollywood movie.

4. She is a British engineer who is teaching at a western Canadian university.

5. Sun is a broad-minded individual who strongly disagrees with you.

6. They wish to purchase a two-storey house.

7. This fish is far too bony.

8. Our long ride to the farm was bumpy and hot.

9. One brave passenger attempted to rescue the drowning man.

10. The congested traffic came to a halt at rush hour.

11. We bought a defective toaster at the bargain store.

12. The cookies that we bought tasted buttery and sweet.

13. One financial expert gave us a favourable report.

14. The open door let in the cold autumn wind.

15. Some people enjoy chilled wine with their evening meals.

Part 2: Finding Adverbs

Put brackets around all adverbs in the following sentences.

1. Amy quit her rather new job quite suddenly last month.

2. He began to speak so excitedly that the emergency team were unable to understand him clearly.

3. The chef rarely prepares his soufflés on a very humid day.

4. Unfortunately, four of the crew were unexpectedly lost at sea during the terrible storm.

5. The English glass factory located here in the countryside skillfully produces crystal glasses of nearly perfect quality.

6. We hardly expected development to continue so rapidly, especially during the rainy months.

7. The report discussed the issues fairly, yet many community members remained extremely dissatisfied with it.

8. Heather was exercising so vigorously that she pulled a muscle in her left leg.

9. The feral cat gradually accepted his new owners, and accordingly, he became fairly affectionate toward them.

10. The craftsperson lovingly applied a thin layer of lacquer to the tabletop as she focused intently on her task.

Part 3: Finding Prepositional Phrases

Underline all the prepositional phrases in the following sentences.

1. Near the bridge is an old, rusty baby carriage from the 1950s.

2. Leave the parcel for my cousin under the first step.

3. About three o'clock I'm calling my lawyer about the matter.

4. After the rain, the trees seem greener and the clouds in the sky disappear.

5. Mr. Rattu is in his office from eight until five.

6. With delight, we watched the snow geese through the binoculars.

7. Milo leaned the shovel against the fence as he wiped his brow with an old rag.

8. On Tuesday we will have lunch with my cousin from Saint John.

9. Paolo went around the building about two hours ago.

10. Lucy accompanied her daughter to the hospital for her check-up.

11. You can see her car on the road across the parking lot

12. Mimi and George walked slowly along the road to the lake.

13. With a flurry, Antonio left for work without his glasses.

14. The mouse peeked through the hole at the fat, waiting cat.

15. The car slid over the bank and into the icy waters.

16. On each work day, the banker closed the bank at exactly three-thirty.

17. His little boy plays games on the veranda by himself.

18. The students will meet with their advisor about their courses.

19. Marvin and Lionel are a new comedy team on the new television network.

20. No one could see the figure in the darkness.

Part 4: Adjective or Adverb Prepositional Phrases

Underline all the prepositional phrases in the following sentences. Tell what type of prepositional phrase—adjective or adverb—each is. Write **ADJ** or **ADV** above each phrase.

1. The road near the ferry terminal is covered with thick snow.

2. The woman with the yellow bouquet was the president of the club.

3. Marcel and Roger were worried about their jobs at SaskTel.

4. None of the students completed the research assignment on information technology.

5. A game of cards can be fun with the right players.

6. The buckle on my saddle has been broken by the fall.

7. The witness on the stand could not remember the man with the large scar.

8. A heart of red velvet was pinned to the picture of the missing child.

9. Farley connected the two pieces of water pipe with tape.

10. Near the barn beside the high rocks grew a fragrant wild rose.

ESL POINTER

Idioms and Prepositions

Idioms are expressions whose meaning does not follow literally from their words. They mean more than their words and are found in common usage. You may find idioms troublesome because there are no clear rules to guide you.

Prepositions can be idiomatic as well. Idiomatic prepositional phrases are perhaps the most difficult feature of the English language to remember. You will find it valuable to spend extra time learning these phrases. Since you cannot use rules to help you, you must learn by practice and application.

Read the following. You should know that the list is not complete. Check off the expressions that are unfamiliar to you. You may want to add more idiomatic prepositions as you come across them.

Idiomatic Prepositions

abhorrence of	beneficial to
abhorrent to	buy from
abide by a decision	confer with (talk to)
abide with a person	confide in
abound in	conform to
abound with	consist in (exists in)
accompanied by (a person)	consist of (made up of)
accompanied with (something)	correspond to/with (agrees with)
acquit of	correspond with (write letters)
adapt to (adjust to)	credit for
adapted for (made for)	deal in (goods and services)
adapted from a work	deal with (people)
agree to a proposal	depend on
agree with someone	dependent on
angry at (thing or condition)	independent of
angry with	different from (not *than* or *to*)
attend to (listen)	disappointed in or with
attend upon (wait on)	dispense with

employed at (a salary)	part with (give up)
employ for (a purpose)	plan to
employed in, on (a business)	profit by
enter into	in regard to
enter in a record	with regard to
enter at a given point	as regards
exception to (a statement)	retroactive to (not from)
familiarize with	speak to (tell someone something)
foreign to	speak with (discuss with)
identical with	wait for (a person, event, etc.)
inferior/superior to	wait on a person (serve)
part from (leave)	

It is also important for you to know that context often determines which preposition is to follow which word. Look at these examples:

Ernest is troubled about his relationship with his girlfriend. (a situation that causes worry)

My grandmother has been troubled with arthritis all her adult life. (a situation of an illness or ailment)

The ticket agent is having trouble with a passenger. (a situation of conflict)

I am having trouble with the operating system on my computer. (difficulty)

Several police were called to the trouble at Greenwood Place. (a location where there is trouble)

When the power went out, there was trouble on the construction site. (located at a specific place)

Her niece is always getting into trouble at school. (difficulties with the authorities)

Exercise 1 Working with Idiomatic Prepositions

Choose 10 or more idiomatic prepositions from the preceding lists and write an effective sentence with each one. Your instructor may ask to see your sentences or may ask you to work with a partner from class.

Exercise 2 Writing Sentences with Prepositional Phrases

Add prepositional phrases that provide the details asked for in the following. You may check your answers with another student from your class, or your instructor may ask you to hand in the practice for checking. Pay attention to the position of the prepositional phrases in each sentence. Use correct punctuation, spelling, and capitalization.

1. The alarm rang (when?) (where?).

2. The jar (of what?) spoiled (where?).

3. The graduate (of what?) found employment (where?).

4. Norby spoke (how? when?).

5. (When?) the dog howled (how?) (where?).

6. The young cook made the sandwiches (with what?) and placed them (where?) (for how long?).

7. The scholar sat (where?) and read (how?).

Exercise 3   Using Prepositions

From the list of prepositions in this chapter, choose one to fill in the blank in each of the following sentences. Try not to use the same preposition twice.

1. The plane flew _____ the bridge.

2. Water flows _____ the bridge.

3. Cars are moving _____ the bridge.

4. The woman is standing _____ the bridge.

5. The man is leaning _____ the bridge.

6. Mrs. Cheema is climbing _____ the steps.

7. The child is coming _____ the steps.

8. The car is _____ two trucks.

9. The lunch will start _____ noon.

10. The flower pot was placed _____ the front steps.

11. The anthropologist found the map _____ a rock _____ the old mansion.

Exercise 4   Group Activity: Using Prepositional Phrases

Choose three to five group members. Write 10 sentences together, using as many prepositional phrases in each sentence as you can. Use the pages on prepositional phrases to help you construct your sentences. Make sure the sentences make sense.

Be prepared to share your answers with the rest of the class. One group member may record the sentences for the group, and another may report the sentences to the class.

Common Mistakes with Idiomatic Prepositions

Listed below for your reference is a group of common errors. Review the list and consider which ones you ought to practise.

Common Prepositional Errors

Error	Correct Expression
comply to	comply with
according with	according to
in accordance to	in accordance with
jealous to	jealous of
conform in	conform with
superior than	superior to
on the way	in the way

CHECKOUT

1. Adjectives are words that describe nouns.

2. The three forms of adjectives used in making comparisons are called the positive, comparative, and superlative.

3. Adverbs describe verbs, adjectives, or other adverbs.

4. A phrase that begins with a preposition is called a prepositional phrase.

5. The last word in a prepositional phrase must be a noun or pronoun and is called the object of the preposition.

6. Prepositional phrases that modify nouns are called adjective prepositional phrases.

7. Adverb prepositional phrases act as adverbs and modify verbs, adjectives, or other adverbs.

8. Idiomatic prepositional phrases are expressions whose meaning does not follow literally from their words.

Verbals

Chapter Objectives

What will you have learned when you have completed this chapter?
You will be able to

1. recognize the three types of verbals in English.

2. identify how a verbal functions in a sentence.

3. apply the possessive case of a noun or pronoun in front of a gerund.

4. identify and repair split infinitives.

5. identify and repair dangling participles.

4. construct sentences using verbals correctly.

Chapter 8: Self-Test

Part 1: Identifying Gerunds and their Functions

Underline the gerund or gerund phrase in each sentence. Tell if each functions as subject, object, or subject complement. Check your answers with the Answer Key.

1. Touring around the countryside is Omar's special weekend activity.

2. Reena hates practising the piano.

3. My parrot's favourite activity is singing.

4. Playing baseball can be inexpensive fun for the entire family.

5. His grandmother loves telling stories of the old country.

Part 2: Identifying Infinitives and their Functions

Underline the infinitive or infinitive phrase in each of the following sentences. Tell if the infinitive is functioning as the subject, object, or subject complement.

1. To wait is all we can do.

2. The housekeeper loves to hum as she works.

3. Many of the elders began to worry when they saw how the young people behaved.

4. His ambition is to draw.

5. To please her employer was Emma's biggest challenge.

Part 3: Identifying Participles and their Functions

The participles or participial phrases are underlined in each sentence. Tell what noun or pronoun the participle or participial phrase modifies.

1. <u>Stretching</u>, the kitten rose to sniff the toy mouse.

2. I saw Dottie <u>rushing off</u> to catch her bus.

3. One of the criminals, <u>feared</u> for his unpredictability, was sentenced to 50 years.

4. <u>Crashing</u> against the rocks, the waves created a thunderous crescendo.

5. This music, <u>soothing</u> to the soul, is putting me to sleep.

6. Her <u>adopted</u> daughter has graduated from the University of Windsor.

Part 4: Correcting Errors with Verbals

Read each of the following sentences. Find the error connected with the verbal and correct the error.

1. Yoni pushing you to complete the project may provide you with motivation.

2. After teaching the dog tricks all afternoon, the cat became jealous.

3. Sheena running too hard and too long may injure her ankles over time.

4. Regaining her strength, the suitcase was shifted into another position.

5. His younger sister wanted to eagerly and with passion act in the college play.

6. Stalling, the car made Mr. Brooks angry.

What Is a Verbal?

A *verbal* is an expression formed from a verb. Although a verbal looks like a verb, it functions differently. In English, three verbals are commonly used: gerunds, infinitives, and participles.

Gerunds

A *gerund* is a type of verbal because it is formed from a verb; it ends in *-ing*, but it functions like a noun. It can function as the subject, object, or subject complement in a sentence.

Cheating is discouraged.

Cheating is the subject of the sentence; it is a gerund because it ends in *-ing*. It is a noun because it refers to the act of cheating.

Exercising was important to Peggy.

Exercising is a gerund and is the subject of the sentence (like a noun).

Gerunds can be placed in phrases. These gerunds or gerund phrases can also be the subjects of sentences.

Cheating on exams is prohibited.

Cheating on exams is a gerund phrase functioning as the subject of the sentence.

Exercising on her bike was important to Peggy.

Exercising on her bike is a gerund phrase that functions as the subject of the sentence. To determine if the following underlined words are gerunds, consider how they function in the sentence. If the verbal functions as a subject, object, or subject complement, then it is a gerund.

Writing music is his passion. (*Writing music* functions as the subject of the sentence and is therefore a gerund phrase.)

His passion is writing music. (*Writing music* is acting as the subject complement and as a noun. It completes the sentence by stating that *writing music* is the activity.)

Alphonse enjoys writing music. (*Writing music* is the object of the verb *enjoys*.)

USING THE POSSESSIVE CASE WITH GERUNDS

Since a gerund functions in the same way as a noun, it requires the possessive case in front of it. A common mistake in spoken English is to use the incorrect pronoun or noun form in front of the gerund. In written English, however, you must use the correct possessive case.

Incorrect: Him owning a company at age 20 is truly amazing.

Correct: His owning a company at age 20 is truly amazing.

Owning is a gerund. You must use the possessive case of the pronoun, which is *his*. *His owning a company at age 20* is the subject of the sentence. It is the amazing fact that the speaker is talking about.

Exercise 1 Finding Gerunds

For each of the following sentences, decide if the underlined words are gerunds or not. Careful: some underlined words are verbs and not gerunds. Check your answers with the Answer Key.

1. The weather forecaster is <u>predicting record high temperatures</u> for today.

2. One of the harbour seals relishes <u>basking in the sun</u> on our dock.

3. If you rent a power boat, then <u>your speeding</u> could be a problem on this placid lake.

4. <u>Worrying about her sick mother</u> occupies most of Nuri's time.

5. <u>Orval's constant lying</u> became a serious issue in his relationship with my sister.

6. <u>Feeding the animals</u> in the zoo is strictly forbidden.

7. The police <u>are investigating</u> the mysterious disappearance of a pair of blood-stained cowboy boots.

8. <u>Skiing off the main runs</u> has its potential dangers.

9. Zora continues <u>her smoking</u>, despite her doctor's orders to stop.

10. With a huge roar, a torrent of water <u>was rushing</u> down the mountainside.

Exercise 2   *Using Gerunds in Sentences*

Work in pairs. Use each gerund in an effective sentence. Be prepared to say how the gerund is functioning in your sentence. Also be prepared to share your answers.

1. coughing

2. surprising

3. biting

4. hearing

5. weaving

6. listening

7. reading

8. driving

9. teaching

10. breathing

Exercise 3   *Possessive Cases and Gerunds*

Read each of the sentences below. Some contain errors with the possessive case and the gerund. Make repairs to the incorrect sentences. Check your answers with the Answer Key.

1. Velma believes you running for office is entirely silly.

2. Without his glasses, the counsellor was not seeing the student frowning.

3. She was not aware of the municipality warning posted outside the gate.

4. Them blocking your promotion at the firm was unwarranted.

5. Us kneading the dough made the bread soft and luscious.

6. The diplomat describing the attack in the airport was fascinating.

7. The school board requires the parents signing the release forms.

8. I don't like Frederico cheating on his wife.

9. Him understanding the directions is critical.

10. The registrar has approved you transferring to another program.

Infinitives

Another type of verbal is called an *infinitive*. It is also a verbal because it is formed from a verb. An infinitive is made up of a base verb and the word *to*.

> to sing
> to ride
> to run
> to study

Infinitive phrases are made up of infinitives and their modifiers.

Mr. Koga wanted to sing loudly.

To sing loudly is an infinitive phrase. *To sing* is the infinitive. *Loudly* is an adverb modifying *to sing*.

They wanted to ride the shaggy, grey donkey.

To ride the shaggy grey donkey is an infinitive phrase. *To ride* is the infinitive. *Donkey* is the object of the action expressed in the infinitive *to ride*. *Shaggy* and *grey* are adjectives describing the donkey.

FUNCTIONS OF INFINITIVES

Infinitives are somewhat tricky to work with because they can have several functions. One common function is to act as the subject of a sentence.

To win was the most important thing in the coach's life. (*To win* is an infinitive that functions as the subject of the sentence.)

To delay would be costly. (*To delay* is the subject of the sentence. It is an infinitive.)

Infinitives can also function as the object of a verb.

Mr. Knightly wants to dance. (*To dance* is an infinitive; it is the object of the verb *wants*: You might ask: "Wants what?" The answer is "to dance.")

We decided to complain. (*To complain* is an infinitive. It is the object of the verb *decided*—decided what?)

Infinitives can also function as the subject complement in sentences.

Her desire is to sing. (*To sing* is an infinitive, acting as the subject complement after the linking verb *is*.)

The company's aim was to please. (*To please* is an infinitive, acting as the subject complement after the linking verb *was*.)

Exercise 4 *Identifying Infinitives and Infinitive Phrases*

Read each of the following sentences. Underline the infinitives or infinitive phrases in each sentence. Check your answers with the Answer Key.

1. After the long ceremony, the bride began to cry.

2. He only wishes to help you to get ahead in life.

3. My cat, Spooky, seems to be afraid of her own shadow.

4. Lady Drippley will buzz the butler to let you in.

5. However, she will not attempt to swim the lake this year.

6. Her greatest desire is to sing in the opera.

7. One of the rumours continues to plague him.

8. To gain the agent's attention was Linley's aim.

9. To do is to act.

10. Mike gets to shake the hand of the prime minister.

Exercise 5 *Identifying Functions of Infinitives*

Work in pairs. For each of the following sentences, decide whether the infinitives or infinitive phrases function as subject, object, or subject complement. Be prepared to share your answers.

1. To challenge was the teenager's main objective.

2. My friend chooses to lock the doors of her car when she is driving.

3. To mourn the loss of a loved one is a natural thing.

4. I want to thank you for the lovely dinner.

5. To wear a bright colour was forbidden in the strict society.

6. The ice cream cake started to melt in the hot sun.

7. Upon his arrival, the sea captain agreed to meet his new relatives.

8. Joey intends to introduce his partner to the committee.

9. Whenever the noise begins to irritate me, I aim to block it out.

10. To accuse him of the crime seems to be wrong.

Exercise 6 *Constructing Sentences with Infinitives*

Use each of the infinitives as subjects, objects, or subject complements in your own effective sentences. Be prepared to explain how each infinitive functions in each sentence.

1. to laugh

2. to succeed

3. to arrange

4. to hover

5. to own

6. to scheme

7. to plan

8. to substitute

9. to scatter

10. to wrestle

SPLIT INFINITIVES

Causing some debate is a common error in English called a *split infinitive*. You split an infinitive if you place another word, usually an adverb, between the *to* and the base form of the verb. Some people believe that a single adverb splitting the infinitive is acceptable, but many experts still insist that splitting infinitives is bad grammar.

Incorrect: Tibor decided to not go on the camping trip.
(The infinitve *to go* has been split up by the adverb *not*.)

Correct: Tibor decided not to go on the camping trip.
(The infinitive is left intact.)

Think of eliminating ambiguity when you are deciding whether to split an infinitive or not. Consider the following sentences:
1. We are learning to constantly check our grammar in English.
2. We are constantly learning to check our grammar in English.
3. Constantly, we are learning to check our grammar in English.
4. We are learning to check our grammar in English constantly.

Can you perceive the differences in meaning between the sentences?

Sentence 1 indicates that it is the checking that is constant, but in sentence 2, it is the learning. In sentence 3, *constantly* is an adverb modifying the entire sentence, and in sentence 4, *learning to check our grammar in English* is the constant activity.

In order to decide which one you would use, you must first decide which meaning you intend.

Hint

Sometimes you might find it difficult not to split the infinitive without creating a grammatical "mud pie."

Correct: The company has been <u>asked to more than triple</u> its production.

Incorrect: The company has been <u>asked more than to triple</u> its production.

(What else has it been asked?)

Incorrect: The company has been <u>asked to triple more than</u> its production.

(What other thing besides production must be tripled?)

Although you may see split infinitives in writing or hear them in people's speech, you should avoid using them in your academic work whenever possible. If you must split an infinitive, do not use a string of words between *to* and the base verb.

Participles

Another verbal, called a *participle*, ends in *-ing* or *-ed*; it is used as an adjective.

> a babbling baby
> a frosted cake
> the sparkling light
> some travelling salespeople

A present participle with an *-ing* ending describes a present condition or situation. A past participle ends in *-ed* and refers to something that has already occurred.

> a borrowed book
> some breathing exercises
> the cracked dish
> that irritating noise
> an attempted robbery
> a missing person

Deciding whether to use an *-ing* or *-ed* ending will depend on the meaning you intend. For example, the difference in meaning between *a frightened student* and *a frightening student* is huge.

By using participles you can make smoother, more effective sentences; at the same time, you can vary your sentence style.

Somewhat awkward: The robbery that Olfred attempted was a disaster.

Improved with participle: Olfred's attempted robbery was a disaster.

Exercise 7   Group Activity: Using Participles to Improve Sentences

Work in a group of three to five people. Together improve each of the following sentences by using participles wherever effective. Be prepared to share your answers.

1. She lightened her hair, and it suited her.

2. The toast popped, but the toast was cool.

3. The valve that had been repaired worked more smoothly.

4. The manager had been embarrassed, and he apologized to the customer.

5. A spider that jumps is commonly found in British Columbia.

6. The pudding was scorched, and it tasted terrible.

7. Most fruits that have been preserved carefully contain vitamins and minerals but are low in fat and sodium.

8. The dog was whining, so I took the dog for a walk.

9. The students collected the songs of the Irish immigrants; they put the songs on a special CD that is available at the university bookstore.

10. Her car was running; it was creating exhaust fumes in the house.

Participial Phrases

Often you will see participles working together with modifiers, nouns, or pronouns. Such word groups are called *participial phrases*. Participial phrases function as adjectives.

Fearing the worst, Aaron drew in his breath. (*Fearing the worst* is a participial phrase describing *Aaron*.)

The hiker saw a light burning in the forest. (*Burning in the forest* is a participial phrase. It describes *light*.)

One protestor removed from the site was charged with obstruction. (*Removed from the site* is a participial phrase. It describes *protestor*.)

Exercise 8   Identifying Participles and Participial Phrases

Underline the participles and participial phrases in the following sentences. Check your answers with the Answer Key.

1. Watching the stars through a telescope, Ajax spotted an alien spacecraft hurtling toward Earth.

2. Frowning, the professor read my history paper.

3. The roasted coffee beans smelled delicious.

4. Presenting the young man with a medal, the lieutenant-governor of Canada stood on a decorated podium.

5. Jerked chicken and flaming kebobs are on Bob's special barbeque menu.

6. Standing his ground, the soldier looked the enemy in the eye.

7. Preparing the nest, the parent chickadees used gathered moss and twigs in frenzied activity.

8. Kicking the mound with his foot, the pitcher scowled at the approaching manager.

9. Absorbed in his mathematics problem, Philby did not notice the advancing darkness that was surrounding the little library.

10. Roaming the meadows, Alicia found the tracks of a small deer.

Exercise 9 Constructing Sentences with Participial Phrases

With a partner, construct sentences using the participles and participial phrases given below. Be prepared to share your answers.

1. turning on one foot

2. crushed

3. tampering with the blueprints

4. protecting

5. examined by a judge

6. rattling his chain

7. rotted

8. noticing his smile

9. burned

10. switching sides

Exercise 10 Identifying Differences between Participles and Gerunds

Underline the participles, participial phrases, gerunds, and gerund phrases in each of the following sentences. Then identify the underlined part accordingly. Careful: Some words ending in -ing or -ed could be verbs! Check your answers with the Answer Key.

1. Volunteering has become Mr. O'Dwyer's main activity every day.

2. Having no place to park, the young lawyer was late for court.

3. The prodigy, taught from age three by a famous composer, was a respected musician in Alberta during the 1970s.

4. During the American Civil War, a bugler's main role was rallying the troops to battle.

5. The whimpering puppy attracted our attention as we walked near the stepping stones to the wharf.

6. Rainbows created during or just after local showers are best seen with polarized sunglasses.

7. Planning ahead for a party can save lots of stress and embarrassment.

8. After surviving a near death experience, my uncle Jay very much valued every aspect of his life.

9. Laughing all the way to the bank, Monardo cashed in on his invention of a moulded television planner.

10. Her immune system, having been compromised by the drug, seemed a compelling concern to her physician.

11. The burned house looked especially forlorn in the deepening shadows.

12. Hunting is not my idea of sport.

13. Speeding in a school zone is against the law.

14. Her favourite pastime was baking cookies for the children.

15. We can get harnessed energy through using solar panels in our homes.

Exercise 11   Identifying Phrases

Work in pairs. Different types of phrases have been underlined in each sentence. Tell whether the phrase is participial, gerundial, or infinitive. Careful: some verbs may end in -*ing* or -*ed*!

1. <u>To be the head of the company</u> was Fong's ambition.

2. <u>Playing tennis</u> can be hard work if you wish <u>to compete nationally</u>.

3. <u>Constructing some birdhouses for her backyard</u> helped Mona learn about basic carpentry.

4. <u>Dated 1892</u>, an old diary lay inside the abandoned cabin.

5. <u>To solve the problem</u> required courage and conviction.

6. <u>Conserving water</u> should be everyone's goal.

7. In the play <u>the character's forgetting the punch lines to jokes</u> is just like my dad.

8. <u>Rearing children</u> and <u>providing them with a good life</u> can be trying.

9. Her relatives from Saskatchewan called her on the weekend <u>to complain</u> about her brother's cattle.

10. <u>Blaming someone else</u> is easy on the conscience.

Dangling Participles

Participles function like adjectives. They are placed next to the nouns they modify. A common error is made when a participial phrase modifies the wrong noun. This error is called a *dangling participle* because the participle is not attached to a logical modifier, and thus seems to dangle.

Sporting a new jacket with a white tie, the dinner was made more formal.

The participial phrase *sporting a new jacket with a white tie* modifies the noun *dinner*, but the meaning is ridiculous. The writer needs to recast the sentence.

Improved: Sporting a new jacket with a white tie, Mr. Alonzo seemed to make the dinner more formal.

Now the participial phrase modifies *Mr. Alonzo*, which is a more logical connection.

Exercise 12   Repairing Dangling Participles

Each of the following sentences contains a dangling participle error. Find the errors and repair them. Be prepared to share your answers.

1. Munching on a sandwich, the letter was intently read.

2. Balancing on one foot and juggling small squashes, the party was made a success.

3. Whistling down the street, the dog started chasing me.

4. Studying late into the night, the loud stereo annoyed me.

5. Walking at a quick pace, the house appeared on the left.

6. Crossing the dance floor, her shoe caught on the edge of the carpet.

7. Talking on the phone, the cat was able to sneak into the hamster cage.

8. Peeling the mounds of onions, the room became oppressive.

9. Driving through Toronto, the CN Tower dominates the landscape.

10. Frustrated by the news, approaching the traffic jam was not a good idea.

Exercise 13 *Repairing Errors*

The following sentences contain errors in infinitive, participle, or gerund use. Read each sentence, spot the error, and repair it. Some sentences do not contain any errors. Be prepared to share your answers.

1. Randy drinking all the time created serious family life problems.

2. You'll have to rely on the program turning itself off and on.

3. After letting me drive, the car ran out of gas.

4. Without hesitation, the assistant began to aggressively and repeatedly berate me for my poor performance.

5. Knowing only a few tricks, the animal trainer dismissed the rehearsal.

6. The wedding planner began to expensively and elaborately decorate the head table.

7. With it's whining, the fly irritated the sleeping camper.

8. Jin was ejected from the meeting because he continued to persistently and rudely at every opportunity interrupt the speaker.

9. Morgan finding the time to help the new resident move in was a generous thing to do.

10. Relaxing, the sun made me feel good.

Chapter 8: Review Test

Part 1: Identifying Gerunds and Functions

Underline the gerund or gerund phrase. Tell if each functions as subject, object, or subject complement in each sentence.

1. Playing golf on the professional circuit is Jeff's ambition.

2. The toddler loves mashing his dinner on the wall.

3. My soccer coach's favourite exercise is swimming.

4. Tide pooling is an entertaining way for young children to explore marine wildlife.

5. Their chairperson loves organizing community events for teenagers.

Part 2: Identifying Infinitives and Their Functions

Underline the infinitive or infinitive phrases in each of the following sentences. Tell if the infinitive is functioning as the subject, object, or subject complement.

1. The lighthouse keeper loves to keep busy in the winter.

2. To lie would be a sin.

3. Enid's special talent is to drum.

4. The parents began to attend all the school meetings actively and with good intentions.

5. To understand calculus is my aspiration.

Part 3: Identifying Participles and Their Functions

Underline the participles or participial phrases in the following sentences. Then tell which noun or pronoun each modifies.

1. Several of the bystanders injured by the blast have been waiting for medical assistance.

2. We spotted the biologist gathering her specimens by the pond.

3. Yawning, the child scribbled on her drawing pad.

4. This leaking boat is about to sink.

5. Heaving a sigh of relief, Zelda welcomed the news.

6. His continued good health was a blessing to us.

Part 4: Correcting Errors with Verbals

Read each of the following sentences. Find the error connected with the verbal, and correct the error.

1. Gino working overtime causes his wife some worry.

2. After pushing the button, the machine jammed.

3. Sylvia spreading that gossip might cause some damage to his reputation.

4. Bowing to cheers and hoots, the concert ended.

5. What she really wanted to discuss was him cheating on her.

6. The director began to tenderly and quietly calm the young actor.

ESL POINTER

Participle Use

Use participles to add variety and interest to your sentence style. Often you can combine two short, related sentences into one participial phrase.

We had spent all our money at the casino. We had to find an ATM to get more.

Combined using a participial phrase:

Having spent all our money at the casino, we had to find an ATM to get more.

Hint

Use a comma after the participle phrase if it begins the sentence.

Exercise 1   Group Activity: Combining Ideas Using Participles

Form a group of three to five people. Work together to combine the pairs of ideas by using a participial phrase. Be prepared to share your answers. Remember to use a comma after the participial phrase.

1. The badger left its den. It was searching for food after a long winter.

2. Demi remained calm. She reported the accident.

3. The coach used to teach at the University of Toronto. His experience will make an excellent addition to our college.

4. One study researched the benefits of humour. It found that laughter relieved stress and built trust.

5. Hugh MacLennan won the Governor General's Literary Award five times. His work was acclaimed the world over.

6. The colt paced. It waited for its mother. The colt could sense her nearby.

7. Milla worked in a shoe factory for many years. She became allergic to the chemical dyes used in the leather.

Participle Usage Hint

Participles may end in *-ing* or *-ed* and function as adjectives. However, sometimes students do not know the correct participle form to choose.

Incorrect: Crossed the street, the young woman was hit by a motorcycle.
Correct: Crossing the street, the young woman was hit by a motorcycle.

Often you use *-ing* or the present participle form when the participle begins a sentence.

Exercise 2   Correcting Participle Use

Work in pairs. Read the following sentences, and together correct the participle usage errors. Supply commas where they are needed. Be prepared to share your answers.

1. Mrs. Quong tiring after so much reading went to bed early.

2. Walked to the museum the group of students felt refreshed.

3. The dog biting by his fleas fussed in the corner of the room.

4. Yelled he reached the finish line of the race.

5. The teaching assistant knew how to tutor helped many of the new students.

6. Fallen behind the smallest child began to cry.

7. Smiled the clerk assisted me.

8. The road flooding by the sudden rains was washed away.

9. Nodded the officer urged us to move our vehicle along.

10. Waken the infant screamed for its parent.

CHECKOUT

1. If a verbal functions as a subject, object, or subject complement, then it is a gerund.

2. Generally, when a gerund is preceded by a noun or pronoun, the noun or pronoun must be in the possessive case.

3. An infinitive is a verbal that may function as subject, object, or subject complement in a sentence.

4. You should avoid splitting infinitives in your academic writing whenever possible.

5. Another verbal, called a participle, ends in -*ing* or -*ed*; it is used as an adjective.

6. By using participles you can make smoother, more effective sentences and at the same time vary your sentence style.

7. Participles function like adjectives and are placed next to the nouns they modify.

8. Dangling participles are not considered acceptable in written English.

Subject–Verb Agreement

Chapter Objectives

What will you have learned when you have completed this chapter?
You will be able to

1. apply eleven rules of subject–verb agreement.

2. recognize common errors in subject–verb agreement in sentences.

3. repair common errors in subject–verb agreement in sentences.

Chapter 9: Self-Test

Part 1: Identifying Subjects of Sentences

Underline the subject or subjects of each of the following sentences. Check your answers with the Answer Key.

1. Neither the bell nor the alarm could wake Turner from his sleep.

2. Basketball, hockey, and football are outstanding spectator sports to watch on widescreen plasma television.

3. Either of you is welcome to take the extra time off.

4. The construction noise disrupted not only the residents but also the animals.

5. Leaving a relationship after 10 years must be extremely difficult for him.

6. Placing the tip of the sword on his shoulder, the queen pronounced him "Sir Steadfast."

7. Cellphones or laptops are not allowed in the provincial museum exhibits area.

8. Although Yan wants to be a chef, she must attend a reputable cooking school.

9. The Aboriginal women, highly respected for their weaving skills, received a special award from the minister of culture.

10. Dancing and swimming are good anaerobic exercises that promote muscle strengthening and coordination.

11. A nest box for tree swallows sits at the top of a tall post at the bird sanctuary and attracts many families of swallows throughout the season.

12. Feeling rather sad, Sue left the party early.

Part 2: Subject–Verb Errors

Find the subject–verb errors in each of the following sentences. Correct the errors. Check your answers with the Answer Key.

1. Either of the requirements of the bylaw sound very complicated.

2. Each of Choo's pet rabbits have escaped from the hutch.

3. Neither of the reporters ever ask embarrassing questions of the prime minister.

4. The king of the two countries or his representative are signing a trade agreement with France.

5. Alice is the only one of the contestants who travel by train to the competition.

6. Four hundred dollars are the cost of repairing the broken window.

7. Either the peanuts or the chocolate in the candy bar are mouldy.

8. One gang of children play ball hockey every summer afternoon.

9. Neither rain nor snow stop Mr. Vargas from taking his daily walk.

10. Only a few students likes writing reports.

11. Some of the cherries is spoiled.

12. Their terrible arguments is the main cause of their break-up.

13. None of those digital photos is worth saving to your hard drive.

14. Behind the mountain and deep in the woods are Professor Evil's haunted castle.

15. Here is the coffee and sausage roll you ordered.

What is Subject–Verb Agreement?

A difficulty for most writers in the English language is ensuring that verbs in sentences agree in number and in person with their subjects. Sometimes you can spot an error easily, as in this sentence: *The small boy have forgotten his telephone number.*

Of course, the sentence should read like this: *The small boy has forgotten his telephone number.* *Has* is the auxiliary you have to use with the subject *the small boy.*

However (and unfortunately), not all errors in matching subjects and verbs are as evident to you as a writer, particularly when you are mostly concerned with getting the meaning on the page. Therefore, you will have to pay extra attention to grammatical elements when you are editing and revising your work.

Subject–verb agreement means that subjects and verbs match. As mentioned above, mistakes occur when the two main elements of sentences—the subject and the verb—do not agree.

Hint

- Number *means whether the subject is singular or plural.*
- Grammatical person *means the forms that designate people or things. In English, you will see three persons. Review the chart below.*

Person	Number	Forms	Examples
First	singular	I	I go to bed early.
First	plural	we	We expect rain today.
Second	singular	you	You meet him often. (Only one person is designated here.)
Second	plural	you	As students, you study for exams. (The subject *you* includes a number of people.)
Third	singular	he	He gets sleepy on the train.
Third	singular	she	She arrives at eight.
Third	singular	it	It breaks easily.
Third	plural	they	They love bagels.

Having some basic guidelines for subject–verb agreement can assist you enormously when you edit for grammatical mistakes in your writing.

Rules for Subject and Verb Agreement

RULE 1

Phrases, particularly prepositional phrases, can come between a subject and its verb or verbs. Do not choose the noun or pronoun in the prepositional phrase as the subject.

Incorrect: Stacks of paper covers his desk.
(*Of paper* is a prepositional phrase. *Paper* has been misidentified as the subject of the sentence in order to write *paper covers.*)

Correct: Stacks of paper cover his desk.
(*Stacks* is the subject of the sentence, so *cover* agrees with *stacks.*)

RULE 2

Inverted word order can put the subject at the end or toward the end of a sentence. Be sure you locate the subject correctly in order to match it.

Incorrect: In the lounge upstairs is some toasters for students to use.
(*In the lounge upstairs* is a prepositional phrase. The writer might have thought *lounge* and *is* sound better together, but *lounge* is inside the phrase and is not part of the subject or verb.)

Correct: In the lounge upstairs are some toasters for students to use.
(*Toasters* is the subject of the sentence, so *are* agrees with *toasters.*)

Hint

Analyze sentences carefully when they begin with there is, there are, here is, *or* here are. *The subject may come at the end of this type of structure.*

Incorrect: Here is some special toppings for your pizza.
(*Here* is not the subject of the sentence. Undoubtedly, you will have heard some people make this error in spoken English; it is rather common. For written English, however, this error is not acceptable.)

Correct: Here are some special toppings for your pizza.

(Since *toppings* is the subject of the sentence, you must use *are* as the verb.)

RULE 3

Compound subjects are plural and require a plural verb.

The director and the technicians work together to stage productions.

Director and *technicians* make a compound subject (more than one). The compound subject designates a plural. *Work* is a plural verb.

Hints

- *Don't confuse plurals in nouns with plurals in verbs. In other words, regular noun plurals take* -s *or* -es *as an ending. However,* -s *as an ending on a base verb means it matches a third person singular subject: he, she,* or it. *In fact, a plural verb never has* -s *or* -es *added to the base verb.* Are *and* were, *for example, are plural verbs and agree with plural subjects, as in the following:*
  We are glad you are here.
  The birds were singing in the birdbath.
- *The expressions* as well as, in addition to, *and* along with *can come after the subject, but they are not part of the subject. Therefore, you might think subjects are made compound because of these expressions, but they are not.*
  Noreen, along with Vito and Erica, arranges the equipment for the speaker.
  (*The subject of the sentence is* Noreen; *the verb* arranges *is therefore singular to match the singular subject*.)
  My neighbour, as well as my boss, is coming to the party.
  (*The subject is* neighbour; *therefore, the verb is singular*—is coming.)

RULE 4

These indefinite pronouns—*each, neither, either, another, everyone, someone, everybody, somebody, anyone, anybody, no one, nobody*—are singular. They require a singular verb.

>   Each of those cartons of milk is empty.
>   Neither is interested in running for student council.
>   Either was a good choice.
>   Anybody who works there is invited.
>   Everybody listens to the news.
>   No one has been held responsible.

RULE 5

Some indefinite pronouns—*none, any, all, more, most, some*—can be either plural or singular depending on the context, that is, the meaning, of the sentence.

Some of the fish were rotten. (refers to a number of fish)
Some of the fish was rotten. (refers to a single fish)
None of the books were any good. (refers to several books)
None of the book was any good. (refers to a single book)

Hint

Sometimes none *may be singular when it seems to mean* no one *or* not one.

None of the chairs is extremely valuable.

In this sentence, none *means not a single one of the chairs.*
None *can also suggest more than one person or thing. In these cases,* none *takes a plural verb.*

None of the chairs are worthless because they are all antique.

In this sentence, none *means not any of the chairs.*

In order to have correct subject and verb agreement, you must begin by correctly identifying the verbs in your sentences. The next exercise will give you practice in finding subjects in sentences.

Exercise 1 Identifying Subjects

Read each sentence and underline its simple or compound subjects. Remember that compound and complex sentences have more than one subject–verb set. Verbals like infinitives and gerunds can also be the subjects of sentences. Check your answers with the Answer Key.

1. Romeo, along with Juliet, is a tragic figure in Shakespeare.

2. Many antique cups and saucers are tremendously expensive to purchase for a collection, but Chenoa loves to purchase them anyway.

3. None of the lectures was inspiring.

4. Because the players and the coach were fighting on the field, the referee ejected them from the game.

5. There are some issues that the union, as well as members, wants to discuss with management.

6. About 10 years ago there was a terrible flood in the small village, and about eighty people died.

7. A beautiful basket of bronze sunflowers sat on the railing of the fence.

8. At the back of the cathedral stood a statue of a saint from the twelfth century.

9. To make special ethnic dishes usually involves the whole family.

10. Having diabetes has been made more manageable with modern medicine and technology.

11. A small herd of deer lives on my property and eats all my garden vegetables unless I fence the garden area.

12. No one wishes to contradict you, but some of us have an opposing opinion.

13. There are many reasons why McLooney, in addition to his sons, wants a change in local government.

14. Located in the main lobby just below these stairs is a huge snack bar.

15. Organically grown fruits and vegetables, along with natural fruit juice, are available from the downtown supermarket.

16. Most of the crackers were too stale to serve to our guests, but some of the cheese was still fresh.

17. Nobody takes the time to smell the roses!

Exercise 2   Group Activity: Correcting Subject–Verb Agreement Errors

Work in small groups. Together decide what the subject–verb agreement error is in each of the following sentences, and then repair it. Be prepared to share your answers.

1. The Atkins diet, as well as the South Beach diet and the Zone diet, claim the benefits of eating more protein and fats and fewer refined carbohydrates.

2. Bertram and his brother plays snooker every Tuesday evening at the club.

3. Koi and goldfish of the common carp family is now being kept as outdoor pets in backyard ponds and streams.

4. There was some serious reporting mistakes in the newspaper article.

5. Lack of money for students often lead to dropping out of school.

6. Some of the European traders is responsible for bringing dreadful diseases to the Aboriginal peoples of North America.

7. These are a collection of his 1960s rock and roll albums.

8. At the edge of the forest were a crowd of spectators waiting to see Tiger Woods.

9. Coach Munez, along with her assistant, were in the 2004 Olympic games held in Athens, Greece.

10. Each of these sweaters were hand-knitted by Selma's great aunt.

11. None of the banana were good to eat.

12. Looking in the university paper and reading the job board outside the student employment office is what Howard plans to do.

13. The issue of increased library fees need to be discussed in a public forum.

14. There are a number of overdue bills to consider.

15. His arm, in addition to his knee, continue to bother him after his injury.

More Rules for Subject–Verb Agreement

RULE 6

Compound subjects joined by *or* or *nor* may indicate plural or singular subjects.

Werner or Morgan was born in Germany. (*Werner* and *Morgan* are the singular subjects.)

A student card or a receipt is necessary for proof of registration. (*Card* and *receipt* are the singular subjects.)

Neither bleach nor stain remover is recommended for the fabric. (*Bleach* and *stain remover* are the singular subjects.)

Either beaches or parks need extra provincial funding this year. (*Beaches* or *parks* are the plural subjects.)

Hint

Either... or, neither... nor, not only... but also *are seen as pairs of words; they are called* correlative conjunctions *because of their close relationship to each other. In many sentences, each part of the pairs refers to a subject. Make sure that each refers to the same sort of grammatical unit or part of speech.*

Either Francine or her sister Eloise is hoping to buy a ticket.

Both Francine *and* Eloise *are subjects, but* or *indicates that only one at a time is being indicated. Therefore, you must use the singular verb* is.

Neither tigers nor bears have been kept in these cages.

Both tigers *and* bears *are plural subjects; therefore, you must use the plural verb* have.

Not only Mr. Franks but also his boss rides the bus each day.

Mr. Franks *and* his boss *are the singular subjects; each is being indicated separately in the sentence. Therefore, you must use the singular verb* rides.

RULE 7

In special cases where singular subjects are mixed with plural subjects, make the verb agree with the last subject in the sequence.

The teaching assistants or the professor teaches Saturday classes.

The subjects are mixed in number: *assistants* is plural while *professor* is singular. *Teaches* agrees with the last subject, *professor*.

A security guard or two students walk you to your car.

The subjects are mixed in number: *guard* is singular, but *students* is plural. *Walk* agrees with the last subject in the sequence, *students*.

Either the dogs or the cat was up all night.

The subjects are mixed in number: *dogs* is plural, but *cat* is singular. *Was* agrees with the last subject in the sequence, *cat*.

RULE 8

The verb agrees with the subject, not the subject complement (after a linking verb).

The dessert was strawberry meringues.

Dessert is the singular subject. *Was* is a singular verb. *Strawberry meringues* is the subject complement.

RULE 9

Collective nouns take a singular subject when they refer to a unit as a whole, but they are plural when they refer to parts or members of a unit.

Half of the pizza was eaten. (*Half* refers to a single pizza.)

Half of the pizzas were eaten. (*Half* refers to more than one pizza.)

The committee has called for a vote. (*Committee* is a collective noun acting as a whole; it takes the singular auxiliary verb *has*.)

The committee have been arguing over the points of the policy. (*Committee* refers to individual members of the group. Therefore, it takes a plural verb.)

Jasmine was awake, but her family was sleeping. (*Family* is a collective noun seen as a unit here; it takes the singular auxiliary verb *was*.)

RULE 10

Money amounts, measures of distance, and time take a singular verb.

Two hundred dollars is too much to pay for that printer.

Two hundred dollars is the subject; it is expressed as a money amount in the sentence. Therefore, it takes the singular verb *is*.

Five kilometres is a long way to walk.

Five kilometres is expressed as a measure of distance; therefore it takes the singular verb *is*.

RULE 11

Verbs within adjective clauses must agree with the subject that the clause modifies.

A pesticide that harms insects has been commonly sold in hardware stores.

That is the subject of the clause *that harms insects*. *That* refers to a singular noun—*a pesticide*. Therefore, the verb *harms* must be singular, too.

Pesticides that harm insects have been commonly sold in hardware stores.

That is the subject of the clause *that harm insects*. *That* refers to a plural noun—*pesticides*. Therefore, the verb *harm* must be plural, too.

RULE 12

Some expressions require special attention. Agreement with the following expressions depends on the number of the word or phrase to which the expressions refer.

> one of the...
> a number of
> one of those...
> the number of
> only one of...

> Tula is one of those people who are always late.
> Tula is one of the people who are always late.
> Tula is the only one of those people who is always late.

In the first and second sentences, *who* refers to *people*; therefore, *are* is the verb.
In the third sentence, *only one* implies a singular; therefore, *is* is the verb.

A number of people are always late.

(*A number* is generally plural.)

The number of late people is appalling.

(*The number* is generally singular.)

Exercise 3 *Identifying the Subject of Sentences*

Read each sentence and underline its simple or compound subjects. Remember that compound and complex sentences have more than one subject–verb set. Verbals like infinitives and gerunds can also be the subjects of sentences. Check your answers with the Answer Key.

1. Gretta is the only one of the singers who prefers to be in the back row.

2. Mr. Loo, Mrs. Singh, and Ms. Wong are recent immigrants.

3. Either the cellphone, the licorice, or the calculator was stolen from my desk.

4. A number of situations call for clear thinking and fast action.

5. Being correct all the time is not the most important thing in the world.

6. Because the bright sun and the slippery roads made driving conditions hazardous, the family had to curtail their plans.

7. The tellers or the manager is implicated in the robbery.

8. Buying clothes for your children at garage sales can save money.

9. Either Ulrich or his cousin plays for the Calgary Flames.

10. The ingredient that works best is Epsom salts.

11. Angelina maintains that neither chocolate nor peanut butter is high in fat.

12. Having a small stature is one criterion for being a jockey.

13. The chickens or the rooster enjoys scratching around the pen.

14. Her favourite subject is computer graphics.

15. The majority of the student body was opposed to the new dress code.

Exercise 4 *Subject–Verb Agreement Errors*

Work with another person in class to complete this exercise. Read each of the following sentences, and decide if its subject agrees with its verb. If the sentence is correct, write **OK** after it. If the sentence contains a subject–verb agreement error, repair the error. Write your answers above the sentence. Be prepared to share your answers.

1. The first of the psychology experiments reveal interesting new ideas.

2. Five hundred dollars are a lot to pay for a dog.

3. The results of the English test was posted outside the office door.

4. The bus driver, as well as two passengers, were injured in the accident.

5. One of the children in Mr. Louis's class paints wonderful landscapes.

6. Mason is one of those people who always wants to win.

7. The notice mentioned that the board of governors meet every Tuesday.

8. On the other side of this curtain is a new Honda and a motorboat.

9. Creating exotic interiors are her special hobby.

10. One of my students have been absent for more than three classes.

11. A number of unopened cards were lying on the hall table.

12. A ludicrous group of practical jokers has put airplane glue on the supervisor's chair seat.

13. Neither they nor I are to blame for all the accounting errors in the department.

14. The standard of living of Canadian people are relatively high.

15. Abdul is one of the most gifted violinists that has ever played at our college.

Exercise 5 Identifying Subject–Verb Agreement Type

Read each sentence and identify the type of subject–verb agreement error it contains. Write the number of the rule beside each sentence. Then correct the errors in the sentences. Check your answers with the Answer Key.

Incorrect: Here's the litre of milk, jar of mustard, and bag of buns.

Correct: Here are the litre of milk, jar of mustard, and bag of buns.

1. The watchman and the new employee has discovered a burglar in the computer room.

2. Only one of those packages are ready to be shipped.

3. Neither Conrad nor Blake know the identity of their benefactor.

4. Everybody on the middle management teams are happy with the new arrangement in administration.

5. The staff feel excited about the employee contest.

6. The report said a flash of brilliant colours were spotted in the midnight sky.

7. Near the California lilac hedge on the busy intersection sit a large raccoon.

8. The consumers or their lawyer are going to speak to the television journalist on Monday.

9. Products that contains trans fats should be avoided.

10. Diseases of small rodents are the topic of today's lecture.

11. Four thousand dollars were too high a price to pay for the ring.

12. Garnett or Angelo disagree with your particular position on the matter.

13. Conducting stem-cell research studies are creating controversy in the medical community.

14. He claims that Alexander the Great or Napoleon are considered the world's greatest general.

15. We discovered the administration were firm in its decision.

Exercise 6 Correcting Subject–Verb Agreement Errors

Work in pairs. Find all the subject–verb agreement errors in the following sentences, and correct each one.

1. At the turn of the century, a crowd of people were considered an illegal gathering.

2. Everybody in the room were holding their breath.

3. A small box of chocolates cost a lot of money these days.

4. Neither Pepe nor his brother Miguel know the combination of the safe.

5. The saltwater crocodile, the American alligator, and the Black Caimin belongs to the class Reptilia.

6. During the student protest, one of the rabble-rousers are instigating the crowd to riot.

7. Robin Goodfellow or Puck are a mischievous fairy from English folklore.

8. Erected in 1990 at the new city hall was a statue of the soft drink baron I.M. Burpee.

9. DNA and the human fingerprint is said to be unique.

10. The soap opera star, along with her entourage, sign copies of her new novel *My Secret Secrets*.

11. The select cast of the Broadway musical meet at the White House for an informal dinner.

12. The administration want all the students at the university to pay a fee for Saturday library use.

13. None of the children was ready for the nap; they were laughing and shouting.

14. Charlotte is one of those dancers who does their warm-up exercises one hour before a performance.

15. Under the pile of old shields in the turret room of the castle the mice makes their home.

Exercise 7 Repairing Subject–Verb Agreement Errors

Read the following sentences and consider if any contain subject–verb agreement problems. If there is an error, correct it. If the sentence appears to be correct, write **OK**. Check your answers with the Answer Key.

1. Over the hill and through the small town flow a small salmon-spawning stream.

2. Being of a rather careless nature are one of Jayne's biggest faults.

3. After standing outside the music store for several minutes, a crowd of young musicians was beginning to play.

4. Some of the films at the festival were extremely provocative.

5. The conductor, the orchestra, and the audience is going to pay tribute to the recently deceased composer.

6. To laugh at her mistakes are unkind.

7. Everybody on board the plane were placed in danger when the passenger threatened the attendant.

8. None of the colours being selected for the interiors of the new townhouses was appropriate; they all seemed too bright.

9. Each of the cyclists attempt to pass the other participants on the track.

10. That planes can fly attest to engineering inventiveness.

11. Avoiding too much processed fat in the diet is a sensible measure in protecting good health.

12. Sometimes nobody in the ranks want to do the job.

13. A bulging bag of groceries and two small children in car seats was filling the back seat of the station wagon.

14. Either Bentley or his sister Emily have the key to my aunt's house.

15. Several of the world's top golfers were playing in the invitational tournament held at Thousand Oaks.

16. Digging weeds and hauling dirt in the garden has made my back ache.

17. A number of coins were missing from the collection.

18. Neither the scientist nor his capable assistant was responsible for the accident.

19. To stay in shape and to earn her degree in nursing were her goals.

20. Some of the shipment of apples were spoiled in transport.

21. Ten hours are a long time to study yesterday.

22. Some of the shrubs or one potted plant are being donated to the church.

23. Bing told the audience that the songs he sang in the war was his favourite.

Exercise 8 Editing for Subject–Verb Agreement Errors

Find the subject–verb agreement errors in the following paragraph, and repair each one. You will have nine subject–verb agreement errors in total. Be prepared to share your answers.

Brewer and Kelvin were brothers who received an invitation to attend their first high school reunion in 15 years. They both were feeling somewhat anxious about the event because it is the first time that either one of them have seen any of their old friends from high school. The group of students that the brothers knew back in the 1980s were now spread out across Canada. Some of the group was professional people who had gone on to university while others had started their own businesses. Because Brew and Kel had taken over the family farm when their dad had died, they felt unsure of how everybody in their old group were going to view the brothers' "profession." Perhaps their old high school class were going to look on Brew and Kel a little unfavourably. After all, going to university or college and getting a "professional" job was what everyone do seem to expect these days. After talking it over, the brothers began to feel real pride in their choices in life. Each of the brothers were happy in their roles and had earned a good living at farming. After a long discussion, the brothers decided that they would attend; having fun, eating good food, and meeting old friends was just too much to miss!

Exercise 9 Editing for Subject–Verb Agreement Errors

Find the subject–verb agreement errors in the following paragraph, and repair each error. Check your answer with the Answer Key at the back of the book.

Ken enjoys the outdoors, but he notices that in the fall there seem to be a swarm of wasps everywhere he goes. Although none of the wasps has stung him, Ken remain curious about them. Some of the female wasps appears a bit more aggressive than others, especially as the season come to a close. Ken knows that wasps is a social insect, so he often searches for the nest. A group of guards remain at the entrance of the nest to protect the queen inside. Neither the guards nor the queen appear to notice Ken. Disturbing the nest or killing the wasps are unthinkable. Ken, along with his children, enjoy cautiously watching the activities of wasps. Over the years, the family have learned many curious facts about them, and nobody in the family have been stung yet.

Chapter 9: Review Test

Part 1: Identifying Subjects of Sentences

Underline the subject or subjects of each of the following sentences.

1. Since Chevonne speaks so clearly, she might be elected class valedictorian.
2. Inviting the new employee to lunch, Carter smiled warmly.
3. Stuffing the chicken with herbs and lemon slices will make the meat more aromatic.
4. The eviction notice alarmed not only the homeowner but also her neighbours.
5. Either of them is available for an interview.
6. Stretching in the morning sunshine, the kitten yawned lazily.
7. Accounting and marketing are good courses that encourage creative problem solving.
8. Neither higher pay nor better working conditions could lure Quincy from his current job.
9. The inventor, praised for his ideas, obtained a Canada Council grant.
10. Motorboats or motorbikes are not allowed in the quiet lakeside park.
11. A lounge for international students is located near the cafeteria on the third floor of the Montroe Building.
12. Pizza, sandwiches, and California wraps have been ordered for the participants of the table tennis competition.

Part 2: Subject–Verb Errors

Find the subject–verb errors in each of the following sentences. Correct the errors.

1. The pig is the only one of the animals that enjoy being by itself in the petting zoo.

2. The flowers in the bouquet or the bridal ornament are missing from the car.

3. Either of the main dishes on the menu seem expensive.

4. Only a few parents likes meeting the teacher.

5. Neither of the runners ever win at track and field events.

6. Two hundred dollars are a lot to pay for this used couch.

7. Each of Myron's friends have supported him through his medical training.

8. Some of the apple pie are uncooked.

9. Neither discussion nor threats stops Boris from smoking.

10. Christine from the French company or representatives of the German firm intends to merge their interests this fall.

11. Down the steep slope and into the swampy water slide the river otter.

12. Her ineffective work habits is the main reason for her dismissal.

13. None of those printers is working this afternoon; they all appear to be out of order.

14. One gang of children play ball hockey every summer afternoon.

15. Here is the coffee and sausage roll you ordered.

ESL POINTER

More about Indefinite Pronouns as Quantifiers

Indefinite pronouns such as *each, every, both, few, none, some, all, most, many,* and *more* are often called *quantifiers* because they have to do with amounts. As mentioned earlier, some of these quantifiers can be singular, plural, or either, depending on the meaning expressed in the sentence.

HINT 1 When you use a quantifier to modify a non-count noun, use a singular verb.

Incorrect: Most furniture have been imported to Canada.
Correct: Most furniture has been imported to Canada.

HINT 2 When you use *all, many, most, some, few,* or *both* as quantifiers to modify a count noun, use a plural verb.

Incorrect: Some students leaves the library at 10 each night.
Correct: Some students leave the library at 10 each night.

Exercise 1   Group Activity: Finding Agreement Errors with Quantifiers

Work in a group of three to five people. Find the errors in the following sentences, and correct them together. Be prepared to share your answers with the rest of the class.

1. More equipment are needed at the disaster site after the earthquake.

2. Both species has a similar habitat.

3. Most information about the tuition increases have been broadcast over student radio.

4. All clothing have been purchased from a factory near Shanghai.

5. Some fruit in the produce department are too expensive for the average family.

6. Most foliage on the delicate bamboo were damaged by the sudden frost.

7. Many chemical sensitivities triggers an allergic attack in the young patients.

8. The couple found that every enjoyment have come through doing simple things together.

9. Many scientific discoveries was made by chance and observation.

10. More intelligence are needed to ask the right questions about the exploration of space.

11. Both of the men is truly sorry for the offensive language.

12. Most Canadian literature have been about isolation and wilderness.

13. Many attempts was made to rescue the kittens from the flood.

14. All courage come from conscience and hope.

15. Most of the deer has fled the woods.

Exercise 2   *Sentences and Quantifiers*

Work in pairs. Use each of the following expressions as subjects in sentences you construct with your partner. Be prepared to edit another pair's sentences before the class discusses everyone's work.

1. few liars

2. most anger

3. many principles

4. both projects

5. more trouble

6. some news

7. all advice

8. most wildlife

9. some education

10. all problems

CHECKOUT

1. Having some basic guidelines for subject–verb agreement can assist you enormously when you edit for grammatical mistakes in your writing.

2. *None* may be singular when it seems to mean *no one* or *not one*.

3. Indefinite pronouns such as *each, every, both, few, none, some, all, most, many,* and *more* are often called quantifiers because they have to do with amounts.

Sentence Style

The next chapters aim to help you improve your sentences. *Sentence style* has to do with how you express yourself in writing. It is also about how you use language, grammar, punctuation, and vocabulary. Generally speaking, effective writing is clear and concise.

Achieving good sentence style involves considering a number of features together. These chapters will encourage you to

- write a variety of sentences.
- vary the length of sentences.
- choose the appropriate tone.
- avoid clichés.
- avoid choppiness.
- be accurate in language use.
- avoid empty expressions (wordiness).
- avoid repetition.
- choose effective words.

Common sentence errors can really disrupt meaning for readers. As an academic writer, you want to eliminate major mistakes in sentences.

chapter 10

Eliminating Sentence Faults

Chapter Objectives

What will you have learned when you have completed this chapter?
You will be able to

1. recognize four common sentence faults.

2. repair run-on sentence faults.

3. repair comma splice errors.

4. repair sentence fragment faults.

5. repair errors in parallelism in sentences.

Chapter 10: Self-Test

Part 1: Recognizing Sentence Faults

Identify the sentence fault in each of the following sentences. Write **F** for fragment, **RO** for run-on, **CS** for comma splice, or **P** for parallelism. Check your answers with the Answer Key at the back of the book.

1. The tired parent stopping to take a break for a few minutes. _____

2. Pandas are a much revered animal in China, they are the symbol of the World Wildlife Fund. _____

3. Alistair didn't want to write the long report for his boss or sitting in on the extensive meeting. _____

4. When you're new to a city, public transportation can be a problem, the system may be difficult to figure out unless you're a long-time resident. _____

5. Dancing and to sing are Nella's passions. _____

6. Without hesitation and with confidence, the contestant at the back of the stage. _____

7. Thank you for holding your call is important to us. _____

8. Walter was learning to rope a calf he slipped and broke his wrist. _____

Part 2: Repairing Parallelism Faults

Fix each of the following parallelism faults. Check your answers with the Answer Key.

1. Downloading the new software from the Internet and to configure it with his other programs took Charlie four hours yesterday.

2. The new building on campus is bright, spacious, and has lounge spaces for students.

3. Spending time with your children is interesting and a challenge.

4. Meredith is not only appreciated as generous but also as humorous.

5. The company dislikes the complaints more than the customers.

6. Bryce walked to the mall but not his work.

7. The clerk has been talking to the customer for 20 minutes and demonstrated the power of the paper shredder.

8. My cousin likes to read widely, deeply, and in an intense manner.

Part 3: Repairing Different Types of Sentence Faults

Each of the following sentences is a sentence fault: a fragment, comma splice, or run-on. Fix each of the faults, then check your answers with the Answer Key.

1. Wrapping the small gift, smiling to herself, and humming to a tune on the radio.

2. Wind and solar power are two natural sources of energy they do not deplete or pollute the earth or its atmosphere.

3. Gerald fighting off a cold and the flu before his exams.

4. The drainage of wetlands around developing cities has had a destructive influence on bird populations, water fowl have fewer and fewer places to feed and to nest.

5. Because the concert was not a success.

6. How many single Canadians actually visit bars, how many really meet new people there?

7. Stacie's planning of the student elections the most successful ever.

Part 4: Parallelism Faults

Repair the parallelism fault in each of the following sentences.

1. In order to meet the nursing qualifications in the province, you must possess the following: Bachelor of Science degree from a reputable university, ability to speak and write English fluently, and to have demonstrated clinical experience.

2. Neither the German shepherd dog nor to stop the burglar the alarm worked.

3. Luke was better in physics than graphic art.

4. "Tiger oak" is the term used to describe maple wood that has striped grains, and it has some mottling, too.

5. Svettla paid more for the two rattan chairs than her husband.

What Is a Sentence Fault?

Some errors in English composition are more serious than others. The *sentence fault* is considered the most serious, since it disrupts or confuses meaning for the reader. Common sentence faults, or errors, are the run-on sentence, the comma splice, and the sentence fragment. Errors in parallelism are also considered a type of sentence fault. All four of these errors seriously impair meaning in sentences, so you must try to eliminate them from your writing.

Run-on Sentence Fault

A *run-on* sentence fault is sometimes referred to as a *fused sentence*. It is an error because it is really two or more sentences written together as one sentence without correct punctuation or conjunctions.

Incorrect: The client was thrilled with the new advertising brochure he particularly liked the new brightly coloured logo on the cover.

Correct 1: The client was thrilled with the new advertising brochure since he particularly liked the new brightly coloured logo on the cover.

Correct 2: The client was thrilled with the new advertising brochure; he particularly liked the new brightly coloured logo on the cover.

Correct 3: The client was thrilled with the new advertising brochure. He particularly liked the new brightly coloured logo on the cover.

The first sentence is a run-on fault because there are two sentences fused together. The three correct examples show that the fault can be eliminated by adding a conjunction, *since* (correct 1), inserting a semicolon (correct 2), or making two separate sentences (correct 3).

Exercise 1 *Finding Run-on Faults*

Read each of the following sentences. If the sentence is a run-on, write **RO** after it. If the sentence is correct, write **OK** after it. Check your answers with the Answer Key.

1. The storm over Porcupine Lake caused extreme damage to the campgrounds the province will contribute $2 million toward the clean-up. _____

2. Being careful of health hazards, Patsy always cooks ground beef until it is well done. _____

3. Logan loves speeding down the freeway late at night with all the windows down in his car and the stereo blasting his friends worry that he'll have a dreadful accident some day. _____

4. Examining and reporting on the financial transactions of the federal government and overseeing the issue of government cheques are the main responsibilities of Auditor General Sheila Fraser. _____

5. At McMahon Stadium in Calgary during the weekend, the players' association organized and staged a country and western festival to raise money for the children's hospital. _____

6. Bud and Joey are restoring their dad's Dodge Charger they're planning to race the car competitively next summer. _____

7. A report showed that, during the mad cow crisis of 2003, the meatpackers' profits tripled. _____

8. Mr. Anoke who owns Everfresh Seafoods is buying two large vessels he plans to convert the ships to enable them to freeze scallops while at sea. _____

9. Lola plays the guitar, writers her own songs, and performs each year at the Festival for Folks in rural Ontario. _____

10. The Manitoba Health Authority concluded that it needed to issue public warnings West Nile virus, spread by mosquito bites to birds and humans, was becoming a risk. _____

11. Job growth has slipped in Canada in recent years the minister of employment maintains otherwise. _____

12. Beer advertising has been restricted in Russia when authorities began to see a link between beer's rising popularity and alcoholism. _____

Exercise 2 *Repairing Run-on Sentence Faults*

Work in pairs. Repair the run-on errors you found in Exercise 1 above. Be prepared to share your answers.

Comma Splices

Remember that a run-on sentence is a sentence fault because it contains two or more sentences not joined correctly. Another form of the run-on fault is called a *comma splice*, in which two sentences appear to be joined by a comma. However, a comma cannot join two complete sentences. To join two sentences, you must use the correct punctuation marks, either a semicolon or a colon, or you must choose an appropriate conjunction. You may also choose to write two separate sentences.

Incorrect: The German singer gave a powerful performance of the aria, his robust voice resonated throughout the small auditorium.

Correct 1: The German singer gave a powerful performance of the aria. His robust voice resonated throughout the small auditorium.

Correct 2: The German singer gave a powerful performance of the aria; his robust voice resonated throughout the small auditorium.

Correct 3: While the German singer gave a powerful performance of the aria, his robust voice resonated throughout the small auditorium.

Correct 1 breaks the sentence into two separate ones. Correct 2 joins the two sentences with a semicolon, and correct 3 uses the subordinate conjunction *while* to begin the sentence with a subordinate clause. The comma after the subordinate clause is correct. You may also find other ways to correct the comma-splice error.

You may recall that conjunctive adverbs such as *therefore, consequently, moreover, however, then, thus, otherwise,* and *furthermore* are not conjunctions. Chapter 4 discusses conjunctive adverbs in detail. For purposes of eliminating run-on sentences and comma splices, you must keep in mind that conjunctive adverbs are weak connectors that require the use of semicolons.

Incorrect: Filmore went to college for four years then he took time off to travel.
(This is a run-on sentence fault. *Then* is a conjunctive adverb, not a conjunction.)

Incorrect: Filmore went to college for four years, then he took time off to travel.
(This is a comma splice. A comma cannot join two sentences.)

Correct: Filmore went to college for four years; then he took time off to travel.
Correct: Filmore went to college for four years, and then he took time off to travel.
(This is a compound sentence. Notice the comma before *and,* the coordinating conjunction.)

Correct: Filmore went to college for four years. Then he took time off to travel.
(One sentence has been made into two separate sentences.)

Exercise 3 *Repairing Comma Splices*

Some of the following sentences contain comma splices. Some do not. Write **OK** after any correct sentences you see. Write **CS** after those with comma-splice faults. Repair the faults. Be prepared to share your answers.

1. The tennis champion from Britain met her American opponent only once at a media gathering, the American seemed upset at the time. _____

2. Donnie wants to apprentice, but the shop isn't hiring right now. _____

3. Oprah Winfrey's latest contract is for $600 million, it is the largest sum a talk-show hosted has ever received. _____

4. A composer may work with an orchestra when he or she is composing; the work becomes enriched by such a process. _____

5. The military will return to Canada's Arctic, the soldiers will learn new skills for fighting in extreme conditions. _____

6. El Niño is expected to return in the next few years it will bring changes in temperature and weather. _____

7. Mrs. Jack enjoys preparing traditional foods from her culture for family and friends from her grandmother she learned how to smoke fish. _____

8. Woodbine Beach on Lake Ontario is a popular recreation spot, however, swimmers must be careful in the unpredictable waters of the lake. _____

9. Because of the high cost of oil and gas, car sales slumped in 2004–2005, but some shrewd consumers benefitted from year-end bargains due to the overstock. _____

10. Donald Duck finally got a star on the famed Hollywood Hall of Fame created in 1958, the Walk stretches for 17 blocks along both sides of Hollywood Boulevard. _____

11. The new Coyotes are armoured vehicles used by the Canadian military; each has been equipped with state-of-the-art detection devices, including radar, infrared, and laser range finders. _____

12. Alka wants to become a marine biologist she plans to work in Australia, researching the Great Barrier Reef. _____

13. The cousins took a long trip to Sicily together, searching for their roots. _____

Repairing Comma Splice and Run-on Faults

Now you know that a run-on sentence is a fault because two complete ideas have been connected without proper punctuation or a proper connector, or conjunction, and that a comma splice is two sentences incorrectly joined by a comma. Remember: Conjunctive adverbs such as *however, then,* and *moreover* require the use of a semicolon to connect two main or independent clauses.

Incorrect:

1. Consuelo moved to the centre of the stage then she began to read her poems.
2. Sol was angry over the incident moreover he wrote a letter of complaint.
3. The lawyers met with the judge in chambers they discussed the selection of the jury.
4. The shop closes early today therefore we will have to arrange to get the car out by five.
5. Several of the contestants were thrilled about the prizes, one was disappointed with the case of Ragu sauce.

Can you spot the errors? How can you repair each run-on sentence or comma splice? Try to repair each fault in three ways. Use a semicolon, too. Use scrap paper to do your corrections. Then check the suggested answers that follow.

Suggested corrections:

1. a) Consuelo moved to the centre of the stage; then, she began to read her poems.
   b) Consuelo moved to the centre of the stage, and then she began to read her poems.
   c) After Consuelo moved to the centre of the stage, she began to read her poems.
   d) Consuelo moved to the centre of the stage. She began to read her poems.

2. a) Sol was angry over the incident; moreover, he wrote a letter of complaint.
   b) Sol was angry over the incident, and he wrote a letter of complaint.
   c) Sol wrote a letter of complaint because he was angry over the incident.
   d) Sol was angry over the incident. He wrote a letter of complaint.

3. a) The lawyers met with the judge in chambers; they discussed the selection of the jury.
   b) The lawyers met with the judge in chambers to discuss the selection of the jury.
   c) The lawyers met with the judge in chambers where they discussed the selection of the jury.
   d) The lawyers met with the judge in chambers. They discussed the selection of the jury.

4. a) The shop closes early today; therefore, we will have to arrange to get the car out by five.
   b) The shop closes early today. Therefore, we will have to arrange to get the car out by five.
   c) The shop closes early today, and therefore, we will have to arrange to get the car out by five.

5. a) Several of the contestants were thrilled about the prizes; one was disappointed with the case of Ragu sauce.
    b) Several of the contestants were thrilled about the prizes, but one was disappointed with the case of Ragu sauce.
    c) Several of the contestants were thrilled about the prizes; however, one was disappointed with the case of Ragu sauce.

Exercise 4   Finding Run-ons and Comma Splices

The following sentences may contain run-on errors or comma splices. The sentences may also be correct as given. Write **RO** if the sentence fault is a run-on. Then correct the run-on. Write **CS** if the sentence fault is a comma splice. Then correct the comma splice. Write **OK** if the sentence is correct as given. Check your answers with the Answer Key.

1. He gave his old car to Helena, unfortunately she cannot afford to pay for insurance. _____

2. Amaro is going to take a course at Lewison College in technology, but he is not sure which specific program to take. _____

3. Because of the dangerous wildfire, the Ministry of Forests ordered an evacuation of the area after three days of rain, the alerts were lifted people were allowed to return home. _____

4. No one realized the mistake everyone was too busy looking after business. _____

5. Some webpages are really difficult to navigate, often the side bars are distracting and the colours are too busy. _____

6. Gay cruises have become lucrative for cruise lines last year major companies reported a 26 percent increase in ticket sales. _____

7. Clara could not afford the proposed rent increase since she had only a small pension to live on. _____

8. Where was Izo when I needed him, was he with the inspector on the roof? _____

9. Were the children planning to attend the play, or will they stay at the daycare centre? _____

10. I am not certain how the thief entered the building the police suspect that he or she gained entry through the unlocked window. _____

11. We could clearly see water marks from condensation in the ceiling, and moreover, we thought we could detect a faint smell of mildew in the closets. _____

12. An HIV-positive man is facing criminal charges because apparently he did not inform his sex partners he had a moral and legal obligation to do so. _____

Sentence Fragments

As mentioned earlier, a *sentence fragment* is a fault or error in academic writing. A sentence fragment means that the words do not make up a true sentence because they do not form a complete thought.

Incorrect 1: Because Ilene was away from work.
Incorrect 2: Fearing the worst from his enemies.
Incorrect 3: The girl waiting at the bus stop.

These examples all start with capital letters and end in periods, but they are not sentences—they are fragments, or pieces of sentences. Incorrect 1 is a subordinate clause beginning with the subordinate conjunction *because*. The main clause is missing. Incorrect 2 is a participial phrase, and has no subject or verb. In Incorrect 3, the fragment requires an auxiliary verb, for example, to make a complete sentence.

Correct 1:   Because Ilene was away from work, she lost pay.

Correct 2:   Fearing the worst from his enemies, the politician retreated from the cameras.
Johnnie is fearing the worst from his enemies.

Correct 3:   The girl was waiting at the bus stop.
The girl waiting at the bus stop is a friend of mine.

Hints for Repairing Fragments

- Add a subject or verb (whichever is missing).
- Add the fragment before or after the sentence, whichever makes sense.
- Recast the fragment by adding grammatical elements to make it a complete sentence.

Exercise 5 Finding and Repairing Fragments

Read each of the following sentences. Some may not be complete sentences, despite the fact that they begin with capital letters and end in periods or question marks. If the word group is a fragment, write **FRAG** after it. Then make it a complete sentence. Be prepared to share your answers.

1. Leaving class early is not a recommended practice. _____

2. The new government allowing more generous and flexible student loans. _____

3. Failing to raise money for his independent film. _____

4. Since the trailer was bogged down in the soft ground of the meadow. _____

5. The Toronto Blue Jays having recently fired their manager. _____

6. Bill C–27, the Public Safety Act, may suspend due process in the legal system for the sake of national security. _____

7. Greenhouse gas emissions from cars and trucks contributing enormously to air pollution. _____

8. Her favourite books chosen from the bestsellers list. _____

9. Jody, preparing for an argument with her boyfriend, wrote down her points. _____

10. Some books of trivia often hilarious and weirdly informative. _____

Exercise 6   Editing Fragments, Run-ons, and Comma Splices

Work in pairs. Read the following paragraph. Circle all errors you spot, and correct each error. The class will discuss answers together.

Many people are turning to making their own wines and beer. Because the cost of these spirits is rising so rapidly at the liquor store. Some individuals begin by making a simple red or white wine from kits available at specialty stores, these kits are relatively inexpensive they come with detailed instructions. After trying a few batches of wine and finding success. A person may move on to experimenting with making beer. Perhaps a Canadian lager at first. Bottling beer requires more precision than bottling wine. Because the beer must be bottled and capped when the beer is "just ripe" and not before. Some novice brewers get anxious and drink the beer before it has settled then the beer tastes slightly "off." However, if brewers are patient. They will find some great successes which they can share with their friends, everyone can take part in enjoying the fruits of their labours and for much less money than usual.

Exercise 7   Editing Fragments, Run-ons, and Comma Splices

Work in pairs. Read the paragraph. Circle all the errors you spot, and correct each one. The class will discuss answers together.

The Canadian film industry has been steadily growing over the past 20 years. Bringing movies to the big screen is an elaborate enterprise governments at different levels, along with new public policy, are involved. Producers have a complicated job, they are involved with preparation, shooting, and activities after post production. Must also work with distributors to market, promote, and distribute a film after it is finished. Of course more theatres must be built or refurbished, otherwise, film producers have a limited number of places. Where they can exhibit their creative products. Although Canadian films are receiving critical claim. They do not do well at the Canadian box office. With only about 2 percent of the total Canadian market.

Parallelism

Correct sentence *parallelism* means that structures are in balance in all parts of the sentence. The writer uses the same pattern of words, phrases, or clauses to show that ideas are of equal importance. *Faulty parallelism* is a type of sentence fault because parts of the sentence are not in balance. Ideas lack clarity. As a result, the reader experiences an interruption in the flow of expressed ideas.

Faulty Parallelism: Ramona managed the office more than her family.

Does this sentence mean that Ramona did more managing than her family did?

Improved: Ramona managed the office better than she managed her family.

Guidelines for Eliminating Faulty Parallelism

1. Use equal grammatical elements with coordinating conjunctions *and, but, or, for, nor, yet,* and *so.*

   Incorrect: Jacqueline was enthusiastic, charitable, and a good friend to everyone.
   Correct: Jacqueline was <u>enthusiastic</u>, <u>charitable</u>, and <u>friendly</u>.
   (All underlined elements should be equal; they should all be adjectives.)

2. Balance equal grammatical elements around *correlative conjunctions*, particularly *either... or, neither... nor,* and *not only... but also.* For example, whatever grammatical element follows *not only* should also follow *but also.*

   Incorrect: Her company is not only recognized as profitable but also as efficient.
   Correct: Her company is recognized not only as profitable but also as efficient.

3. Balance comparisons logically.

   Incorrect: The research showed that women hate shopping more than men.
   Correct: The report showed that women hate shopping more than men do.
   (Add the auxiliary *do* to set up the comparison with the verb *hate*. Otherwise, the comparison is set up between *shopping* and *men*.)

4. Repeat prepositions and articles in order to add clarity to comparisons.

Incorrect: The community centre hired a clown and accountant.
Correct: The community centre hired a clown and an accountant.
(Otherwise, it sounds as if the community hired only one person instead of two.)

Incorrect: We found better restaurants in Vancouver than Victoria.
Correct: We found better restaurants in Vancouver than in Victoria.

4. Provide equal elements after a colon that introduces a list.

Incorrect: Our supplies for the fishing trip contained these items: a box of matches, three battery-operated lanterns, some dried foods, and we also found a fish knife that was sharp.
Correct: Our supplies for the fishing trip contained these items: a box of matches, three battery-operated lanterns, some dried foods, and a sharp fish knife.

Exercise 8   Group Activity: Correcting Parallelism Faults

Form a small group of three to five. Together, correct all parallelism faults in the following sentences. Rewrite your sentences. Be prepared to share your answers with the rest of the class.

1. Our pizza is not only equal but is superior to theirs also.

2. The report made the following recommendations: to increase access for disabled students, to allow weekend use of computer labs, and having cheaper bus passes for students.

3. The student survey showed that boys own more pets than girls.

4. The government agency hired an investigator and plumber.

5. Suneet not only likes chutneys but also pickles.

6. The sea monster was large, hated humans, and ate them for lunch.

7. Working part time, raising two children, and to volunteer as a literacy tutor took most of Jen's time.

8. Horatio is handsome, rich, and a jerk.

9. Not only did the student study colour theory, but also the properties of oil paint.

10. I find the traffic far worse in Montreal than Toronto.

11. Her understanding of the situation is not only as confused as mine but as incomplete also.

12. Either you pay at the gates or they make you pay at the terminal itself.

13. To manage a senior hockey team, to do woodwork, and being a peer counsellor at the hospital helped Tobias adjust to his retirement.

Exercise 9 Repairing Parallelism Faults

Each of the following sentences contains a parallelism fault. Find each fault and repair it. Rewrite your sentences on separate paper. Check your answers with the Answer Key.

1. Working with children is stimulating, challenging, and has its rewards.

2. Not being able to speak the language causes confusion, is frustrating, and it's embarrassing.

3. To prevent crime, attending to victims of accidents and crimes, and how to apprehend safely those suspected of crime are a police officer's responsibilities.

4. Being sound of mind and physically strong, the elderly man was able to live quite happily by himself.

5. Three of the issues the committee will have to deal with right away are as follows: camp maintenance, how to get staff for the camp, and promoting camp.

6. His doctor advised him to eat less, exercise more, and no smoking at all.

7. For many people, attending AA meetings is first embarrassing, possibly even humiliating, then helpful, and finally it is a success.

8. A high level of motivation, experience in problem-solving, and you should not be concerned about your every decision are necessary if you hope to run a successful business.

9. Influential factors in any nation's economic regression are these: bad management of natural resources, policies regarding national debt might be unwise, and the unions' inflationary demands.

10. Although the first applicant seemed scared and showed shyness, the second was a composed person and outgoing.

11. Not only did we see smoke, but we noticed flames, also.

12. She looked for work in the want ads of *The Ottawa Citizen* and the employment pages of the university's student paper.

Exercise 10 Correcting Sentence Faults

Read the paragraph. Correct each sentence error. To make the task a little easier for you, parts that contain errors have been underlined. Be prepared to share your answers.

Studying takes practice. <u>Because studying is a learned skill</u>. Many adult students return

to school <u>wanting to succeed very badly, they are unsure of how to apply skills effectively</u>.

<u>Tend to cram for exams, to take too many notes, and mismanagement</u> of their time <u>is a</u>

Part 2: Repairing Parallelism Faults

Fix each of the following parallelism faults.

1. The manager spoke to the planner but not her assistant.
2. A woodpecker had been hammering on the house and causes a fair bit of damage.
3. My cousin enjoys sewing more than my aunt.
4. Mrs. Ajani is not only seen as hard-working but also as efficient.
5. Watching too much television is boring and a time-waster.
6. Lifting the heavy load from the truck and to carry it to the office caused Manny to hurt his back.
7. The condo is small, modern, and has privacy.
8. Flame retardant has been found in breast milk and wild salmon.

Part 3: Repairing Different Types of Sentence Faults

Each of the sentences is a sentence fault: a fragment, comma splice, or run-on. Fix each of the following sentence faults.

1. Will was an air cadet in 1986 he joined the Canadian Forces in 1995.
2. Stephen feeling rather bitter about the whole affair.
3. Self-defence classes for girls will be held every week registration begins this Saturday.
4. The powwow included First Nations dancers from all across North America the 200 competitors participated in a variety of dance categories.
5. Water quality concerns many Canadians, some people want stricter regulations.
6. Kaspar bought a small sailboat he enjoys sailing it on weekend and summer holidays.
7. Jamaica's High Commissioner to Canada gave a speech on August 1, Emancipation Day. The day Jamaica won its independence.

Part 4: Repairing Parallelism Faults

Repair the parallelism fault in each of the following sentences.

1. The African grey parrot is shy, wary, and has intelligence.
2. We should design our homes to help us not only manage but also for reducing stress.
3. Karla is talented in drawing, in sculpting, and photography.
4. Teddy told me either the peach ice cream or for the dessert the blueberry pie is delicious.
5. Ancient Roman baths had different pools and exercise rooms, and they even had slaves to give olive oil massages.

ESL POINTER

Correlatives and Sentence Parallelism

Earlier in the chapter you worked with correlative conjunctions in connection with parallelism in sentences. Remember that *correlatives* are pairs of words used together but not right next to each other in sentences.

The main correlative conjunctions are as follows:

not only... but also

both... and

neither... nor

not... but

either... or

The placement of the correlatives is somewhat tricky. To ensure correct parallelism in your sentences, balance the parts of the correlative by placing each one next to the same grammatical element.

The restaurant serves <u>not only</u> fresh lobster <u>but also</u> local game.

Not only is placed in front of the object *lobster*, modified by the adjective *fresh*. Therefore, you must place *but also* in front of a parallel adjective noun construction—*local game*.

<u>Both</u> fire <u>and</u> water were considered essential elements of life in Greek mythology.

Both is placed before a noun, *fire*; *and* is placed in front of another noun, *water*.

The child <u>neither</u> smiled at us <u>nor</u> waved in our direction.

Each part of the correlative is placed in front of a past-tense verb.

She prefers <u>not</u> reading <u>but</u> sleeping.

Each part of the correlative is placed in front of a gerund.

<u>Either</u> he was trying to get her attention, <u>or</u> he was acting like a fool.

Each part of the correlative is followed by a main clause.

Exercise 1   Identifying Correlatives and Elements

Work in pairs. Underline the correlative conjunctions in each sentence. Then identify what grammatical element comes after each part of each correlative pair. Be prepared to share your answers.

1. Gerard has rejected either gambling or smoking.

2. Mrs. Hina has neither emailed nor telephoned her estranged sister in more than 10 years.

3. Both terriers and foxes have keen hunting instincts.

4. The driver turned neither left nor right but remained in the intersection when the light turned green.

5. The Rutherford Mall sells not only hand-crafted leather products but also imported art glass.

6. Tamra wanted either to leave her job or to quit her university classes.

7. Mr. and Mrs. Dharma considered buying both a boat and a trailer but decided the prices were too high.

8. Not courage but determination will conquer world hunger.

9. Her friend Ram neither studies very hard nor attends classes regularly.

10. The camera not only captures an image but also represents an impression.

Exercise 2 *Constructing Sentences with Correlatives*

Complete the following exercise. Write your answers in the spaces provided. Then be prepared to work in a group as part of a peer editing exercise—an activity in which your classmates view, analyze, and comment on your written work.

1. Combine the two sentences using the correlatives *not only... but also*.

    Ali loved restoring interesting antique furniture.

    Ali enjoyed researching the provenance of each piece.

    _____

    _____

2. Combine the two sentences using the correlatives *neither... nor*.

    The puppet play could not stop the small child's crying.

    The quiet song could not stop the small child's crying.

    _____

    _____

3. Combine the three sentences using the correlatives *either... or*.

    The cause of the crash is uncertain.

    The driver fell asleep at the wheel.

    The tow truck driver crossed the centre line on the highway.

    _____

    _____

4. Combine the two sentences using the correlatives *not... but*.

    When tested, the cows were infected with West Nile virus.

The horse was infected with West Nile virus.

_____

_____

5. Combine the three sentences using the correlatives *both... and*.

The quilters are sewing quilt blocks for a large work.

The project is to support research in breast cancer.

The quilters are selling raffle tickets for the finished work.

_____

_____

6. Combine the two sentences using the correlatives *either... or*.

The grain elevator was torn down because of its condition.

The grain elevator was torn down due to financial reasons.

_____

_____

7. Combine the two sentences using the correlatives *not only... but also*.

Caring for a pet develops a child's sense of responsibility.

It promotes understanding for the needs of others.

_____

_____

CHECKOUT

1. A sentence fault that disrupts or confuses meaning for the reader is considered a serious error.

2. There are four common sentence faults:
   - run-on sentence faults
   - comma splice errors
   - sentence fragment faults
   - errors in parallelism in sentences

3. A comma cannot join two complete sentences.

4. Conjunctive adverbs like *however*, *then*, and *moreover* require semicolons to connect main clauses.

5. Correlatives require careful placement in sentences.

Improving Sentence Style

Chapter Objectives

What will you have learned when you have completed this chapter?
You will be able to

1. improve your sentence style by thinking about how you construct sentences.

2. adapt your writing form and style to the requirements of different conventions.

3. put modifiers into the correct position in a sentence.

4. distinguish passive and active voice.

5. write concisely by choosing words that are precise and effective.

6. develop your writing style by varying sentence length and pattern.

Chapter 11: Self-Test

Try the self-test that follows to help you examine sentence style and to warm up to using the power of modifiers in your writing. First, try this test yourself. Then get together with a group of three to five people to discuss possible answers. Be prepared to share your answers and to provide good reasons for them.

Part 1: Writing Situations

Name two writing situations in which adjectives are really important.

Situation 1:

_____

Situation 2:

_____

Part 2: Adverb Use

Name two adverbs you might use to describe how someone ate a pizza. Use those adverbs in a sentence and copy it below.

_____

_____

Part 3: Types of Writing

Name two types of writing that benefit from effective and carefully chosen modifiers.

1. _____

2. _____

Part 4: Examining Sentence Style

Find a sentence from a newspaper, magazine, or Internet article to give to a member of your group. This sentence should contain lots of adjectives, adverbs, and prepositional phrases. Ask the group member to find the modifiers in the sentence and to talk about their effectiveness. Work in pairs. Each pair should then report their discussions and observations to the group.

Part 5: Modifiers and Your Vocabulary

Add a modifier to the following sentences according to the directions. Write each sentence in the space provided. Be prepared to share your sentences with the group.

1. The (adjective) (adjective) (adjective) woman spoke (adverb) (adverb) (prepositional phrase).

_____

_____

2. (prepositional phrase) a (adjective) chef was (adverb) slicing a (adjective) (adjective) pepper and then tossing it (adverb) (prepositional phrase).

_____

_____

3. A (adjective) (adjective) friend lost his (adjective) ring when he was swimming (prepositional phrase) (prepositional phrase).

_____

_____

4. (prepositional phrase) my (adjective) (adjective) cat hissed (adverb) and then sprinted (adverb) (prepositional phrase).

_____

_____

5. We shop (adverb) (prepositional phrase) and spend (adjective) money (prepositional phrase).

_____

_____

Part 6: Adding Adjectives

Add as many adjectives as possible to each of the following nouns. Write your answers on a separate piece of paper. Be prepared to share your answers.

1. vacation

2. headache

3. puppy

4. goalie

5. nightmare

Part 7: Misplaced Modifiers

The following sentences contain misplaced modifiers. Reorganize or rewrite each sentence to repair these errors.

1. Installed properly, Edna found the email program worked well.

_____

_____

2. On Green Island, closure of ferry services forced some travellers to find beds with friends.

_____

_____

3. These docile birds can be distressed by people who let their dogs run loose, drive off-road recreational vehicles, or hike while playing loud music.

_____

_____

Part 8: Passive to Active Voice

Change each of the following passive-voice constructions to active voice. Rewrite each sentence in the space provided.

1. Carlos was hounded by the bill collector.

_____

_____

2. The complaints of the team were brought forward by the manager.

_____

_____

3. It has been reported that four teenagers were seen leaving the scene of the crime.

_____

_____

Part 9: Wordiness

Remove the wordiness in each of the following sentences. Rewrite each sentence in the space provided.

1. As far as I am concerned and in my opinion, I think his argument was weak, ineffective, and not very convincing at all.

_____

_____

2. The fact of the strike had the effect of impacting on the public in a number of ways.

_____

_____

3. Mike has an expectation to win that competition in sailing he plans to enter next weekend.

_____

_____

Part 10: Vagueness in Sentences

Eliminate the vagueness in each of the following sentences. Rewrite each sentence in the spaces provided.

1. The problem with all of this is that they won't go along with it.

_____

_____

2. There are a lot of people out there who want change.

_____

_____

3. The government should do more for disadvantaged people.

_____

_____

After your group has discussed all the answers, review your own answers in order to assess your sentence style.

Thinking about Your Writing Style

Writing style involves many factors—your purpose in writing, your choice of words to express your ideas, your arrangement of those words, the audience for your writing, your knowledge of some basic writing rules, and your acquaintance with the rules of English grammar and mechanics.

Developing good writing style begins with awareness. Paying attention to how other writers craft their sentences may be the first step. Next, you will improve your sentence style by thinking about how you construct your own sentences. You make stylistic choices as you write, even though you may not realize it. Making choices that add greater clarity and concision will result in more effective writing.

Writing style involves choices in words, purpose, sentence length, variety, organization, and structure. Selection will depend on different writing contexts. For example, you do not make the same style choices when you write to a friend as you do when you communicate with a government official. Similarly, as an academic writer, you learn sets of rules and guidelines that help you develop different writing styles for different academic disciplines. Your business professor will look for a writing form and style that meet the conventions of writing for business, whereas an instructor in history or sociology will look for another set of conventions.

Knowing the basic rules is vital. If you wish to vary sentence organization or structure, for instance, you should apply what you know about simple, compound, complex, and compound-complex sentence patterns. Reorganizing or rewriting includes editing, and editing academic writing rests on grammatical conventions.

Some writers claim that "good writing is lean." Repetition and puffed-up language, like unnecessary fat, are eliminated. Complex ideas do not require overly complicated sentences. Instead, complicated thought depends on careful sentence construction and your full attention.

Avoiding Misplaced Modifiers

Correct placement of modifiers is critical in English. If you put an adjective, adverb, participle, prepositional phrase, or any other modifier into the wrong position in a sentence, you can bet the results will be confusing, amusing, or irritating to your reader.

The city has a museum for tourists with mummified remains.

As a bird that grew up in the rainforests of South America, I knew my macaw had special needs.

Lying in the bottom of the dusty old chest, Alma found her grandmother's diary.

As you read over the sentences you have written, think about what they are saying, the sentence sense. Misplaced modifiers can make sentences illogical or ambiguous. They can destroy sentence sense.

You should place the following modifiers near the word or words they modify.

only   simply   just   almost   even   hardly   nearly   merely

If incorrectly placed in sentences, these modifiers can create confusion for a reader. James Thurber provided an interesting example of the problem placement of *only* in his sentence *He only died last week.* What is the meaning of Thurber's sentence? Can you change the meaning by moving *only* to a different position in his sentence?

Here are some examples of problem word placement:

The twins caught <u>only</u> a cold on the trip.

<u>Only</u> the twins caught a cold on the trip.

Milos apologized <u>even</u> to me.

<u>Even</u> Milos apologized to me.

The supervisor said he <u>simply</u> couldn't understand my report.

The supervisor <u>simply</u> said he couldn't understand my report.

<u>Hardly</u> a single person touched the noodle salad at the buffet.

A single person <u>hardly</u> touched the noodle salad at the buffet.

Pia has <u>just</u> announced her engagement to Silas.

<u>Just</u> Pia has announced her engagement to Silas.

Breezer was <u>merely</u> a boy when he inherited billions from his grandfather.

Breezer was a boy when he inherited <u>merely</u> billions from his grandfather.

The bride spent <u>almost</u> $1600 on her wedding gown.

The bride <u>almost</u> spent $1600 on her wedding gown.

The quarterback completed <u>nearly</u> 220 passes in the 2004 regular season.

The quarterback <u>nearly</u> completed 220 passes in the 2004 regular season.

Exercise 1 *Misplaced Modifiers*

Rewrite the following sentences to eliminate confusion stemming from misplaced modifiers. Check your answers with the Answer Key at the back of the book.

1. During the last holiday our family almost ate 3 kilograms of chocolates.

2. The student nearly irritated every student in our economics class.

3. Mr. Mazur spotted a deer while he was having coffee in his vegetable patch.

4. A man with a small brown dog who had lost his glasses asked us for help.

5. Tonia is writing a research report about Jean-Paul Sartre in her philosophy class.

6. When it is autumn, almost remove the plant from the garden and store it in the greenhouse.

7. A tall yellow vase sat in the hallway that Claude had purchased.

8. You will only need to cook one casserole for the dinner.

9. I bought fresh flowers at the store which I gave to a dear friend.

10. Jen saw a destitute old lady walking down the street in raggedy clothes.

11. Although smaller than expected, parents who did turn out for the rally were very angry.

12. Kora-Lee nearly wrote all of her term paper yesterday.

13. I saw a church as I walked up the hill with a white steeple.

14. Talking excitedly with her friend, the puppy in the pet store window was adored by Peggy.

15. The player ignored the referee who blew his whistle simply.

Using Passive or Active Voice

Passive and *active voice* refer to the placement of the verb in the sentence. In *active voice*, the subject or agent does the action. In *passive voice*, the subject receives the action. Passive voice in a sentence means one of two things: that a verb is placed before a subject or that the subject or agent of the action is not named specifically.

Active voice: Roberto climbed the stairs to the apartment.

Passive voice: The stairs to the apartment were climbed by Roberto.

In the second sentence, notice how far away from the action the subject is. *Stairs* is the subject of the sentence, but the stairs did not perform the action—Roberto did.

In some cases, by not mentioning the subject you are failing to place responsibility for the action:

It was decided to do away with student grants under $500.

Who did the deciding? Who was responsible for the decision?

The proposal was accepted to begin development of the park.

Who accepted the proposal? Who was responsible?

Reasons to Use the Active Voice

1. Your active-voice sentences will focus on subjects or agents.

2. Your active-voice sentences will make action more direct.

3. Your active-voice sentences will assign responsibility.

4. Your active-voice sentences will develop clarity and concision.

5. Using active-voice sentences is a preferred writing style in academic writing.

Reasons to Use the Passive Voice

1. Your passive-voice sentences will focus on the actions or events, not the agents.
   The assassination of the president shocked the nation.

2. Your passive-voice sentences will emphasize receivers of actions.
   Millions of consumers are persuaded to buy useless products.

3. You do not know the agent of the action.
   The car was struck on the passenger side.

4. The agent of the action is unimportant.
   Next week's meeting has been cancelled.

5. You are writing a scientific report that focuses on procedures. How things are carried out is more important than who carried them out.
The beaker was cooled to –2 degrees Celsius.

Exercise 2 *Identifying Active or Passive Voice*

Identify whether each sentence has an active or passive voice construction. Check your answers with the Answer Key.

1. Action must be taken to curb greenhouse gas emissions.

2. Increasing greenhouse gases in the atmosphere will lead to frequent, intense heat waves.

3. The World Health Organization estimates that climate change was responsible for 150 000 deaths in 2000.

4. In July 1995 a severe heat wave caused the deaths of 500 people in Chicago.

5. In 2003 a terrible heat wave, the worst in 150 years, was blamed for killing 14 000 people in France.

6. A heat-health alert system has now been established in Toronto as a result of climate change impact.

7. Environment Canada monitors several climatic factors and alerts key city officials of the risk to populations.

8. A Heat Alert is issued by Toronto's Medical Officer of Health upon advice received from Environment Canada.

9. A Heat Emergency is issued by Toronto's mayor when risk of heat mortality reaches 90 percent.

10. Greenhouse gas emissions can be eased by individuals' using less energy and reducing waste.

Exercise 3 *Changing Passive to Active Voice*

Change each of the following passive voice constructions to active voice. You may have to supply some subjects. Check your answers with the Answer Key.

1. A gift of a pearl brooch was given to Maude.

2. Sugar beets are raised in southern Manitoba.

3. A rare salamander was found among the rocks on the eastern coast of the island.

4. The children's school supplies were sorted by grade and district.

5. The registration for advanced physics was completed at noon by Ethan on the Internet.

6. The boxes were packed by the movers and were labelled carefully.

7. Soon after sunrise a male moose was spotted by three of the hunters.

8. Only one of the campers was fined $250 for not having a permit.

9. The point was raised by Hasim that student parking permits were entirely too pricey.

10. A hollow was made and lined with thick reeds and down; then five light-green eggs were laid.

Exercise 4   *Group Activity: Active or Passive Voice*

Work in a small group of three to five people. Read the following sentences. Decide if each sentence is constructed using active or passive voice. If the sentence has passive voice, decide if it is appropriate. If it is, give the reason. If it is not appropriate, change the passive to active voice. Be prepared to share your answers.

1. French is spoken in many parts of Canada.

2. Helmut deserves to be elected as student council president.

3. Plans were made by both sides to get back to the bargaining table on Monday.

4. Some police officers were removed from duty while the investigation was underway.

5. The project was scaled back when partial funding was cut by the sponsor.

6. A blood test to detect the presence of cancer has been developed by Canadian and American researchers.

7. Buyers can often purchase single pieces or whole albums by sampling online what they might like to purchase.

8. A special medal was awarded to Darcy for his heroism in saving an elderly woman from drowning.

9. The patient was admitted to hospital at 4:42 a.m. on July 12.

10. "These blueberries were picked at the peak of their perfection," the sign in the produce department read.

Being Concise

You may be one of those people who believe that good writing should sound "lofty." You may also think that pumping up the word count is all there is to writing term papers. However, quite the opposite is true.

Concise means saying what you have to say using as few words as possible. Your words should be precise and effective. Your instructors or professors will not be pleased or impressed by inflated language in your writing. In fact, they will downright shun that practice and discourage it in their students' writing.

Puffed-up or verbose writing is sometimes called "purple prose." *The New Dictionary of Cultural Literacy*, Third Edition, defines purple prose as "writing full of ornate or flowery language." This writing is self-conscious and pretentious—so much so that it can be hilarious to read. It is full of bad clichés, poor or inappropriate comparisons, and unsuitable words. Purple prose is also wordy. You will see lots of purple prose in fiction, particularly romance writing, but you will also come across it in academic writing.

The 2004 Purple Prose Winner of San Jose State University's 23rd Bulwer-Lytton contest wrote this "winning" sentence:

She resolved to end the love affair with Ramon tonight... summarily, like Martha Stewart ripping the sand vein out of a shrimp's tail... though the term "love affair" now struck her as a ridiculous euphemism... not unlike "sand vein," which is after all an intestine, not a vein... and that tarry substance inside certainly isn't sand... and that brought her back to Ramon.

Here is the runner-up's winning sentence:

The notion that they would no longer be a couple dashed Helen's hopes and scrambled her thoughts not unlike the time her sleeve caught the edge of the open egg carton and the contents hit the floor like fragile things hitting cold tiles, more pitiable because they were the expensive organic brown eggs from free-range chickens, and one of them clearly had double yolks entwined in one sac just the way Helen and Richard used to be.

What do you notice about these sentences? Can you find inappropriate comparisons? Can you spot the "word padding"?

Making your writing "leaner and cleaner" means you will have to work at getting rid of unnecessary words and eliminating vagueness. You will have to revise sentences, even when you would rather just settle for what you wrote in your first draft. You will need to leave behind some bad habits and bring a new perspective and awareness to your writing as you edit. The following sections will help you become a better editor of your sentences as you give them a more concise writing style.

Eliminating Wordiness

Wordiness means having unnecessary words. Although a small amount of repetition can create emphasis in your writing, too much results in poor style. *Redundancy* is, as Fowler says in *Fowler's Modern English Usage*, "saying the same thing twice." Here are some examples:

> a short, brief encounter
> He felt anger and was upset, too.
> a tiny, little, wee baby
> I am definitely and certainly afraid.
> an enormous, giant spider
> The prince was banned and never allowed to return.

It can be difficult to get rid of verbosity in your writing style if you are unaware that it is a problem. Thinking about what constitutes wordiness will help you when you write and edit your own sentences.

Read the following sentence, looking for unnecessary words and repetition:

Because of the fact that it was revealed to me that Mr. Buster may have been the person to whom I should have spoken in regard to obtaining an appointment for the potential employment I was looking for, I, unfortunately, missed the date to which a deadline had been assigned.

What is this sentence saying? Can you express it in simpler terms by removing the wordiness?

Plague Words

Plague words are those that add padding without contributing ideas, much like overpacked products. Below is a list of common plague words and expressions. The right side of the list gives a more concise way of expressing these ideas.

Review the list and think about your writing. How many of these plague words do you use? Try to eliminate them. Try to trim down your expressions to make them concise.

Common Plague Words/Expressions	Concise Expressions
to have a harmful effect on	to be harmful
a surprising and unexpected result	an unexpected result
mutual agreement	agreement
to have an expectation	to expect

to have a hope	to hope
to have an understanding	to understand
consensus of opinion	consensus
at this point in time	currently
for the reason that	because
in a situation in which	when
for all intents and purposes	(delete)
future plans	plans
important essentials	essentials
the end result	the result
very unique	unique
large in size	large
a majority of	most
make an assumption	assume
on the whole	(delete)
all of a sudden	suddenly
last but not least	finally
the manner in which	the way
a considerable amount of	much
came to the realization	realized
on top of all of this	(delete or use *moreover*)
every single one	each one or each
is aware of the fact	knows
study in depth	study
symbolically represents	symbolizes or represents
totally obvious	obvious or clear
first and foremost	first
in conclusion, I wish to say...	in conclusion

Exercise 5 *Getting Rid of Wordiness*

Work in pairs for this exercise. Read each of the following sentences and then rewrite them to eliminate wordiness. Be prepared to share your answers.

1. The antique quilt of a bright colour and heavy in weight was displayed for all to see in the museum as an artefact of historical significance.

2. It is possible that the extensive and lengthy court proceedings will be so long as to go on for at least or at a minimum of eight months.

3. We wish to draw your attention to the fact that your account is presently overdue and that we have not received your last payment in full by the due date.

4. It is a true fact that all amphibians like frogs, salamanders, and others require and have a need for water and all forms of moisture.

5. In spite of the fact that in the course of the evening the guests made a decision to depart early, the hostess made the final decision that essentially every single one of them should still have dessert before it came such time for their departure.

6. The loud siren will, by and large, provide advance warning to all citizens who are residents of the small city community.

7. By virtue of having extremely valuable paintings locked in the underground vault of his basement, the earl came to the realization that he needed additional, extra security devices to protect his property from theft or robbery.

Avoiding Vagueness

Someone once said that the worst English word was *nice*. Read these sentences to get a glimpse of why the person may have believed that *nice* was not nice at all:

> We had a nice time at Roger's party.
> The meal at the seafood restaurant was very nice.
> This nice resort is a nice place to visit.
> Mathilde is nice to her family.

Can you tell exactly what *nice* means in each of these sentences? Does the word provide you with any useful details? The main problem with *nice* is that it does not have a specific meaning. In fact, it is completely inexact. Using such words in your writing leads to vagueness.

If someone says "You're being too vague in this sentence," the person means your writing is not communicating clearly. The reader is having difficulty understanding precisely what you are saying. Perhaps what you are saying is too general, or perhaps the words you have chosen to express your ideas are vague. Of course, a writer may have a problem with vagueness because he or she may lack an extensive writing vocabulary. However, vague writing is usually due to a writer's inattention to details. Taking time to select precise words will help eliminate vagueness from your writing. Start considering which words are important concept words, because they contain the specific information you want to convey.

You can eliminate vagueness by writing concisely and precisely. The previous section discussed being concise in your writing. If you want to write precisely, you must spend time choosing the most effective, appropriate, and exact words and phrases possible.

Here are some examples of vague writing:

> I found the town unfriendly.
> Although she is a great person, she is not good at organizing.
> Your work needs improving.
> The policy created a problem in the later part of the year.
> There was some confusion on the point.

What makes these sentences vague?

In the first sentence, it is not clear what the writer is saying. How can a town be "unfriendly"? Obviously, the writer is talking about people in the town, but he or she does not mention specifically who in the town is unfriendly. Besides being vague, the statement is making an overgeneralization because not everyone in the town can be unfriendly.

In the next sentence, *Although she is a great person, she is not good at organizing*, the writing is vague on two counts. Can you spot the vagueness? First, the writer uses two value-laden words, *great* and *good*. You do not know what the writer means by these terms because they are an evaluation only the writer will understand. Second, you do not know what *organizing* means—the term is too broad. *Organizing* can refer to people, objects, systems, and so forth.

In the next sentence, *Your work needs improving*, the writer gives no details about what needs improvement (or why). If a boss said these words, an employee would be upset not only because the boss seems to be criticizing the work, but also because he or she does not give directions for improvement. The writing is vague because the words are too general—they provide no useful details for the reader.

The statement, *The policy created a problem in the later part of the year*, is also vague. First, it does not name the person who is responsible for the policy. Policies cannot act on their own. Next, the policy is not named and the problem and its date are not specified.

In the last sentence, *There was some confusion on the point*, the writer is not telling the reader what the confusion was, nor is he or she specifying the point. Note, too, that the writer starts with *There was*, which is not the best beginning to a concise sentence.

Vague Pronoun Usage

Check your sentences to be sure that pronouns have clear antecedents. If the pronoun has no antecedent, or can refer to more than one antecedent, then sentence meaning falters.

Marion told Georgiana that she was late.

Who was late? A reader cannot tell if it is Marion or Georgiana.

In my opinion, they are charging too much for school supplies.

Who is *they*? The pronoun has no antecedent (the noun it relates to).

Although the bird hit the door, it was not harmed.

What was not harmed—the bird or the door?

Vagueness and *This*

Most of the time, starting a sentence with *this* leads to vagueness. Why? Many beginning academic writers forget to place a noun or reference after *this*.

Reading the owner's manual before using a new piece of equipment is recommended by all manufacturers. However, most people are too busy or too lazy to do so. This can lead to confusion.

What leads to confusion—the fact that people are busy, are lazy, or haven't read the owner's manual?

Drinking and driving can lead to serious accidents, damage to property, and serious injuries to drivers and passengers. This is of great concern to most people.

What specifically is causing the concern? What is the antecedent for *this*?

TIPS ON HOW TO AVOID VAGUENESS

1. After you have written a sentence, go back over it and ask this: "Am I being concise here? Are any of the words I've used unnecessary?"

2. Which word is too general? Can you think of another word that might be more exact?

3. Have you started sentences with *there is*, *there are*, or *this*?

4. Have you given your reader specific details by using concept words and concise terms?

5. Have you made clear and effective word selections?

Exercise 6   *Eliminating Vagueness*

Read each of the following sentences. Decide if the sentence is vague in meaning or contains vague elements. Write down what makes each sentence vague, and why. Be prepared to share your answers with the class.

1. Because the board was upset by the decision, this caused delay.

2. If you put the flowerpot in the window, it will look lovely.

3. They should outlaw television violence.

4. The driver took me to Nathan's address, but he was not home.

5. The competition is getting tougher.

6. My parents' beliefs are outdated.

7. Divorce is on the rise.

8. I believe they should do more to get people working.

9. Dogs make nice house pets.

10. Last week the weather was great.

11. The movie critics trashed the movie.

12. There were disagreements at the meeting.

13. I called the service desk, but they didn't answer.

14. This will cause a loss of pay.

15. Samuel explained it to Thomas before he left the office for the day.

Exercise 7 Editing for Vagueness

Read the following short paragraph. Imagine that it is part of a student's essay. Underline the parts that seem vague to you. What would this student need to do to remove the vagueness and improve the writing? Be prepared to share your answer. Your instructor may have you work on this exercise with other members of the class.

Personally, I did not believe that the hero of the story was believable. He was not the kind of guy you'd expect to meet. The things he did were not average. I mean, who would do what he did in this situation? I think most people would not find him to be a believable character, either. Maybe he was just confused.

Exercise 8 Removing Vagueness or Wordiness

Rewrite each sentence to make the meaning more exact. Be prepared to share your answers.

1. The committee is indecisive.

2. After all is said and done, Christine's car is a mess.

3. At this point in time that museum is a big waste of time.

4. I believe the city has used the land inappropriately, in my opinion.

5. There is a consensus of opinion that everyone agrees taking Mr. Fuji's course is a good thing.

6. The childcare centre needs some revisions.

7. For all intents and purposes, there should be more laws against drunk driving and tougher penalties for this.

8. His family's house is the nicest because of the fact that they've done renovations.

9. There is an expectation that this will stop in due time.

10. Molly called Sheena to give her the news she had been hired for the position.

11. After all is said and done, there is some need for us to help support the notion that was put forward by Delbert during yesterday's meeting.

Combining Sentences for Variety

You can develop your writing style by varying sentence length and pattern. For example, you may try writing one or two short sentences followed by a longer one. You may also look over your writing to analyze what sentence patterns you tend to use the most—simple, compound, complex, or compound-complex. Then you might try writing different sentence patterns from the ones you are in the habit of using.

A good method of increasing your sentence variety is to combine sentences. You can merge two or three simple sentences into a compound or a complex sentence.

Simple sentences: Major was my sheepdog. My father bought him for me. I was seven at the time.

Combined 1: My father bought Major, my sheepdog, for me when I was seven.

Combined 2: Major, bought for me by my father when I was seven, was my sheepdog.

Combined 3: Major, my sheepdog, was bought for me by my father when I was seven.

Combined 4: When I was seven, my father bought me Major, a sheepdog.

How you combine the sentences will depend on what meaning you want to construct. In sentence 1, *father* is the subject and focus of the sentence. In sentences 2 and 3, *Major* is the subject. In sentence 4, *I* is the subject. You will have to decide which idea should be the main focus of the sentence.

Tips for Sentence Combining

1. **Use an appositive.** An *appositive* is a phrase that provides more detail about the noun that precedes it.

   Sentence 1, *My father bought Major, my sheepdog, for me when I was seven,* contains an appositive, *my sheepdog.* It tells what or who Major is.

2. **Use adjectives or adverbs to express an idea.**

   The counsellor has a lot of popularity. She has kindness. She was nominated for a college award.

   Improved: The kind and popular counsellor was nominated for a college award.

3. **Do not stack too many nouns into adjective positions when you combine ideas.** Your sentence will sound awkward.

   The policy had to do with air pollution. It was brought into law in 1992. The policy was national and popular environmentally.

   Awkward: In 1992 the national environmentally popular air pollution policy became law.

4. **Use active voice where appropriate.**

   Bylaw 57 was passed by municipal council. The date of the bylaw's passing was January 26, 2005.

   Improved: Municipal council passed bylaw 57 on January 26, 2005.

5. **Use adjective clauses.** *Adjective clauses* modify nouns or pronouns and begin with the relative pronouns *who, whom, whose, that,* or *which.* They are also referred to as *relative clauses.*

   The customer spoke to Mrs. Chung. The customer arrived at 9:00 a.m. Mrs. Chung shook his hand.

   Improved: Mrs. Chung spoke to the customer who arrived at 9:00 a.m. and shook his hand.

Tips for Using *That* and *Which*

1. *Which* refers to things.

   The book which he bought was published in Toronto.

2. *That* refers to things, but it can also be used to refer to a class or type of person.

The book that he bought was published in Toronto.

He is the type of person that always wants to be on time.

3. Most experts suggest using *that* in a *restrictive clause* (one essential to identifying the noun).

The message that notifies faculty about safety is important.

That notifies faculty about safety is essential in defining which message is important.

4. Most experts suggest using *which* in a *non-restrictive clause*.

President Pomp's message, which has an interesting opening paragraph, is important.

Which has an interesting opening paragraph is not essential for defining the noun *message* because *President Pomp's* already defines it.

5. Use *participial phrases*.

The photographer struggled to take the baby's picture. He used a squeaky duck to try to make the baby smile.

Improved: Struggling to take the baby's picture, the photographer used a squeaky duck to make the baby smile.

6. Choose a *coordinating* or *subordinating conjunction* that expresses the kind of relationship you want between ideas.

The sailors came ashore. They headed downtown. They wanted a good time.

Improved using a coordinating conjunction: The sailors came ashore <u>and</u> headed downtown, wanting a good time.

Improved using a subordinating conjunction: <u>After</u> they came ashore, the sailors headed downtown for a good time.

<u>Because</u> they wanted a good time, the sailors came ashore and headed downtown.

Exercise 9   *Combining Sentences*

Work in pairs or a small group. Combine the following sentences according to the instructions. Be prepared to share your sentences with others in the class.

1. Using an appositive, combine the ideas into one sentence.

Keith was the assistant principal. He sent the parents a message about the field trip.

_____

_____

2. Using *which* to begin a non-restrictive clause, combine the ideas into one sentence.

The pizza was cold. The pizza was greasy. Barb ordered the pizza. It came from Pronto's.

_____

_____

3. Combine the ideas into a complex sentence.

   The actor was embarrassed. The actor has misread the lines during first rehearsal.

   _____

   _____

4. Combine the sentences into one sentence, using adjectives.

   Several tourists were Canadians. They were exasperated. They could not find a money exchange service in the small town. The town was in Spain.

   _____

   _____

5. Changing the ideas into active voice, combine the sentences into one.

   The food guidelines were accepted by the Canadian Nutrition Association. The guidelines suggested that raw foods such as nuts be included in the daily diet.

   _____

   _____

6. Using a participial phrase, combine the ideas into one sentence.

   Toyota makes 10 kinds of diesel engines. Toyota is developing a hybrid engine that consists of diesel or gas and an electric motor.

   _____

   _____

7. Select an appropriate coordinating or subordinating conjunction and combine the ideas into a single sentence. Be prepared to explain your choice.

   A massive blackout occurred in August 2003. Fifty million people in eastern North America were without power in their homes and at work.

   _____

   _____

8. Use *that* to begin a restrictive clause as you combine the ideas into a single sentence.

   The famous designer uses only natural fabrics in her clothing line. The fabrics are specially dyed with organic materials.

   _____

   _____

Guidelines for Improving Sentence Style

Consider sentence logic.
Avoid clichés and slang.
Convey your message as simply and directly as possible.
Eliminate wordiness and repetition.
Eliminate vagueness.
Combine sentences or ideas to vary sentence style.

Chapter 11: Review Test

Part 1: Misplaced Modifiers

Correct the misplaced-modifier errors in each of the following sentences. Rewrite your sentences in the spaces provided.

1. Whining near the garbage can, I looked into the alley and noticed a lost puppy.

_____

_____

2. The manager of the department only wants to help the new customers.

_____

_____

3. Locked in the tomb for one thousand years, the archaeologist discovered the ruined artefacts of the ancient king.

_____

_____

4. My brother almost drove 1000 kilometres to see his latest girlfriend.

_____

_____

5. After the heavy meal, Darrin promised to wash all the greasy pots and pans.

_____

_____

Part 2: Active or Passive Voice

Identify whether the sentences are in active or passive voice.

1. Hockey sticks are made in Quebec.

2. Many days were passed at the park by lovers of all ages.

3. If you send this order to Ramon, he will reply by early next week.

4. A suspect was seen running from the jewellery store.

5. The unusual orchid was identified by the famous Romanian botanist.

Part 3: Being Concise

Make the sentences below more precise by finding the purple prose and plague words, and then recasting the sentences to make meaning more concise.

1. The message was really extremely important and needed to be answered immediately and without delay.

   _____

   _____

2. It is felt virtually by the entire committee that the present procedure is faulty due to the fact that it is, with all due respect, cumbersome and rather awkward for a majority of the clerks to handle effectively and with efficiency.

   _____

   _____

3. At this point in time, our company is unable to comply with your request due to unforeseen interruptions in services that ship our goods.

   _____

   _____

Part 4: Eliminating Vagueness

Eliminate the vagueness in the following sentences. Some sentences contain problems with pronoun vagueness. Rewrite your sentences in the spaces provided.

1. Chris told Danny that he was late; this upset him.

   _____

   _____

2. One of the manufacturers went out of business and therefore the specialized parts for the weaving machines became difficult to obtain. This caused job loss.

_____

_____

3. They ought to do something about the noise from the airport.

_____

_____

4. Honzo told Shen that he had been hired by the government.

_____

_____

5. Mrs. Miles wants you to make some improvements in this document.

_____

_____

Part 5: Sentence Combining

Combine the sentences into a single sentence according to the instructions given. Write your sentences in the spaces provided.

1. Mr. and Mrs. Nguyen are the co-presidents of our condo association. They have organized several improvements to the outside of our building.

   Combine the two sentences into a single sentence by using an appositive.

   _____

   _____

2. The city councillor voted against the development of some parkland. The councillor was an advocate for green space in an urban environment.

   Using a subordinate conjunction, combine the sentences.

   _____

   _____

3. Connor felt silly. He had just noticed an oddity: he was wearing two different shoes.

Using a participial phrase, combine the sentences into a single sentence.

_____

_____

ESL POINTER

Positions of Modifiers

To make your sentence style more interesting, you can add description. However, it is important to know where to place modifiers. In English, adjectives, adverbs, prepositional phrases, and other modifiers can be placed in various positions in sentences. You must also know where to use commas in two categories of adjective constructions.

Hints for Using Coordinate Adjectives

- **In English, adjectives usually come before the noun.**
  the small roadside café

  a solitary, happy moment

  the broken, elegant porcelain vase

- **When you use adjectives in English, place commas between each one if each separately describes the noun.** These adjectives are called *coordinate adjectives* because they are equal.

  Think of the word *and* when you see a comma in a string of adjectives. If you can successfully use *and*, then you can insert commas.

- **Check that the adjectives can be switched around with no loss in meaning.**
  The rough, worn fence had been built many years ago.

  Say: *the rough and worn fence*.

  Switch the adjectives around. Does the sentence still make sense?

  The worn, rough fence had been built many years ago.

  The following adjectives can be switched around as well:

  Caterina felt a rapid, sharp, and throbbing pain in her leg.

  Caterina felt a throbbing, sharp, and rapid pain in her leg.

  Caterina felt a sharp, rapid, and throbbing pain in her leg.

  Caterina felt a throbbing, rapid, and sharp pain in her leg.

- **Place a comma before the *and*.** Many experts say that the comma in front of *and* adds clarity.

Hints for Using Cumulative Adjectives

Another category called *cumulative adjectives* can also be placed in a string. However, they appear in a specific order. Together the order makes up the whole meaning.

- **Cumulative adjectives cannot be switched around.**

  the yellow finch fledgling

  Not: the finch yellow fledgling

  executive committee agendas

  Not: committee executive agendas

  dangerous chemical pesticides

  Not: chemical dangerous pesticides

- **No commas are used between cumulative adjectives.**

  a modern elementary school

  Not: a modern, elementary school

  Not: an elementary, modern school

Hint for Using Predicate Adjectives

Predicate adjectives appear in the predicate of a sentence. They come after linking verbs.

  is tired

  was awake

  will be afraid

Hints for Using Adverbs

- **Adverbs should be placed close to the verb, either before it or after it.**

  worked enthusiastically

  enthusiastically worked

  frequently met

  met frequently

- **Sometimes adverbs can be placed in front of adjectives, if they intensify their meaning.**

  quite relaxed

  very frightened

  too close

Hints for Using Prepositional Phrases

- **Prepositional phrases can be placed at the beginning of a sentence, at the end of a sentence, or next to the word they modify.**

  Under the stairs was a lost wallet.

  The burglar ran *up the alley*.

  The soldier *in full uniform* waited *for the bus from Moncton*.

- **Place a comma after the prepositional phrase if it introduces what follows.**

  On the other hand, most of the students work hard.

  Despite her headache, Bing kept working.

  With a broad smile, Tony introduced himself.

Exercise 1   Adjectives and Commas

Underline the adjectives in each of the following sentences. Decide if the adjectives are coordinate or cumulative. Add commas between modifiers wherever necessary. Check your answers with the Answer Key at the back of the book.

1. A former heavyweight champion of the world was Muhammad Ali.

2. The young man made a firm final offer on the purchase of the downtown condo.

3. During the weekend, the committee worked toward a sensible satisfying outcome.

4. Leaving the field, the disgraced disqualified player bowed to the crowd.

5. The tractor knocked over the rotting wooden shed.

6. Our little community purchased an expensive fire truck.

7. In a recent political poll, the federal Liberals seemed to be gaining in popularity.

8. The pilot of the disabled plane was directed to an approved flight path.

9. One of the costly waterfront properties burned to the ground in the wild fire.

10. Cyril won a free trip to the fabulous sunny coast of Mexico.

Exercise 2   Adding Modifiers

Add modifiers as specified to each of the following sentences. You may work in pairs. Check each other's answers. If you are in doubt, ask your instructor.

1. The nurse spoke with the patient. (Add one string of cumulative adjectives.)

_____

_____

2. The students rehearsed for the play. (Add one string of coordinate adjectives.)

_____

_____

3. Our cat napped. (Add two prepositional phrases.)

_____

_____

4. Her parents were arriving. (Add one adverb and one adjective.)

_____

_____

5. The students evaluated the course. (Add one adverb and one prepositional phrase.)

_____

_____

6. Aiko and her friend study. (Add one coordinate adjective string, two adverbs, and one prepositional phrase.)

_____

_____

7. Alexis parked her car. (Add two prepositional phrases, one adverb, and two adjectives.)

_____

_____

CHECKOUT

1. Correct placement of modifiers is critical in English.

2. A problem with vagueness in writing may stem from a lack of writing vocabulary, but most often it is due to the writer's inattention to details.

3. Develop sentence style by combining ideas and getting rid of wordiness.

4. No commas are used between cumulative adjectives.

5. Sometimes adverbs can be placed in front of adjectives, if they intensify their meaning.

Building a Writing Vocabulary

Chapter Objectives

What will you have learned when you have completed this chapter?
You will be able to

1. invent ways of building your writing vocabulary.
2. prepare to build a writing vocabulary suitable for each academic course.
3. agree that building vocabulary in writing takes attention and application.
4. deal with problematic expressions.
5. develop strategies to alter your writing patterns and styles.

Chapter 12: Self-Test

Try this little self-test. Its purpose is to check your word power. Do the best you can, and don't worry: this isn't a "big exam." Don't use a dictionary or thesaurus! Find out what you can do without using these. After completing the self-test, bring it to class. You will check your answers with others from the class.

Limit yourself to 20 minutes to do the self-test.

1. Write down as many words you can think of that mean the same as *big*.

a) _____

b) _____

c) _____

d) _____

e) _____

f) _____

g) _____

h) _____

2. Replace each of the underlined words with new words that mean the same.

a) The movie made me feel <u>bad</u>. _____

b) They built a <u>nice</u> house. _____

c) My uncle was <u>cheap</u> with his money. _____

d) It <u>angers</u> me when you do that. _____

e) Rufus is a <u>good</u> dog. _____

f) The child was <u>afraid</u> of the dark. _____

g) We <u>walked</u> along the beach. _____

h) The bird <u>flew high</u> over the rocks. _____

i) Joanne is a <u>good</u> friend. _____

j) Ivan <u>laughed</u> at the joke. _____

k) The food tastes <u>bad</u>. _____

l) Her brother is a <u>messy</u> person. _____

m) I guessed that the job would be finished <u>soon</u>. _____

n) The old man told a <u>funny</u> story. _____

o) Tony is a <u>careless</u> driver. _____

What your score means:
- 34–46: Quite a champ! Your word power is strong. Just a bit of practice is needed.
- 30–33: Nicely done! Your power is good, but practice will help.
- 28–32: A fair swing! Your power is satisfactory, but you need practice.
- Below 28: Practise! You'll improve your word power with more work.

Building New Habits

In his best-selling book *The Seven Habits of Highly Effective People: Powerful Lessons in Personal Change*, Stephen R. Covey has this to say about habits: "Power is the faculty or capacity to act, the strength and potency to accomplish something. It is the vital energy to make choices and decisions. It also includes the capacity to overcome deeply embedded habits and to cultivate higher, more effective ones."

Bad habits are hard to break. Even more difficult is building better or more useful ones. As the saying goes, "Bad habits are like a comfortable bed: easy to get into, but hard to get out of." Developing a new habit often means you have to give up old ones. Your language usage is built on habit, too. You need first to pay attention to your language habits before deciding about change.

Exercise 1   Group Activity: Speech Habits

Getting Organized

Get together in a group with five members in it. Decide who will take which of the following roles: Clock Watcher, Collector and Town Crier, Discussion Pilot, Summarizer, and Presenter.

The Clock Watcher's job is to time the group as they write.

The Collector and Town Crier's job is to collect all the papers and read out to the group what its members have written.

The Discussion Pilot will lead the discussion. He or she will keep the conversation flowing in the right direction.

The Summarizer will organize the main points of the discussion and write them down.

The Presenter will tell the rest of the class what the main points of the discussion were.

What to Do

The group takes five minutes to write down any speech habits they think they have that are <u>irritating</u> to themselves or others.

The Clock Watcher times the group, but he or she also takes notes. The Collector collects the irritating-habits comments.

The group then takes another five minutes to write down speech habits they think they have that are <u>effective</u>. The Clock Watcher times the group, but he or she also takes notes.

The Collector collects the effective-habits comments. The Collector and Town Crier read out the irritating-habits comments to the group.

The Discussion Pilot leads the group in a 10-minute discussion about irritating speech habits. He or she should try to get people to talk about what makes a speech habit irritating and which irritating speech habits the group has in common. The Clock Watcher times the discussion, but he or she also takes part. The Summarizer takes notes, trying to capture the main points of the discussion. He or she may want to end up with a list of irritating speech habits the group says it has.

The Collector and Town Crier read out the effective habit comments to the group.

The Discussion Pilot leads the group in a 10-minute discussion about effective speech habits. He or she should try to get people to talk about what makes a speech habit effective and which effective speech habits the group has in common. The Clock Watcher times the discussion, but he or she also takes part. The Summarizer takes notes, trying to capture the main points of the discussion. He or she may want to end up with a list of effective speech habits the group says it has.

The Presenter gives the class the irritating and effective speech habits the group has discussed. He or she can do this in a list form. The instructor may then have a discussion of the whole.

Exercise 2 *Inventory of Vocabulary and Writing Habits*

Now turn your attention to writing habits. The exercise you just did in paying attention to speech habits—both good and bad—should also help when you consider some of the vocabulary habits you use in writing.

Take a few minutes to think about your writing vocabulary. Do the following inventory of vocabulary and writing habits. Check the items that you feel are appropriate to you.

1. True Most of the Time
2. True Some of the Time
3. Rarely True
4. Never True
5. N.A. Doesn't Apply to Me

Beside each of the following statements, write the number of the item from the list above that seems to apply to you. Remember: Think about you as a writer.

1. When I am writing and I cannot think of the precise word I want to use, I usually give up. _____
2. When I am stuck for a word, I rarely use a thesaurus. _____
3. When I don't know a word, I don't usually look it up. _____
4. When I am writing, I don't have a lot of effective and different words at my disposal. _____
5. I don't pick up a lot of new words from television and use them in my writing. _____
6. I seldom try to use new words in my writing. _____
7. When I see a new word I like in my reading, I don't try to use it in my writing. _____
8. My writing doesn't contain lots of modifiers. _____
9. I am never satisfied with how I write. _____
10. I am not satisfied with my word power in writing. _____

11. I am unaware of the word choices I make when I am writing. _____
12. I never buy books to develop my writing and vocabulary. _____
13. When I am writing, I never find it difficult to find the exact words to fit what I am trying to say. _____
14. I never force myself to use new words when I am writing. _____
15. Reading is not an important method of improving my writing. _____

Total: _____

Scoring and Your Results

First, total the numbers of all the items you have entered.

Put your total in the space provided.

Check your results with the information given next.

The Results

- If your score was 15–30: You are a confident writer who uses many good strategies for building your writing word power.
- If your score was 30–40: You have some confidence in your writing and sometimes you use strategies for building your writing word power.
- If your score was 40–50: You do not have much confidence in your writing and do not build many strategies for writing word power.
- If your score was 50–60: You have no confidence in your writing and do not use strategies for building word power.

You may notice in the inventory that some strategies are implied:

- Items 1, 2, and 3 imply that you ought to persevere in your word searches. When you cannot find a precise word, use a thesaurus, dictionary, or reference book to help you. You may also want to ask others.
- Items 4, 9, 10, and 13 have to do with your confidence as a writer. If your answers to these items were in the True Most of the Time or True Some of the Time range, then you lack confidence in yourself as a writer. In order to gain the conviction you need, you must change some of your habits to the "higher, more effective ones" to which Covey refers.
- Items 5, 12, and 15 help you consider the sources of your new words. Television may provide viewers with some information; however, television's aim is not to develop writers. Reading is a critical source of new words and ideas. Don't forget that when you are a writer, you are a reader, too.
- Items 1, 6, 7, 8, 11, and 14 have to do with attitude toward writing. Using new words, choosing words and ideas from reading and applying them to writing, adding colour words, and being aware of word choices are all effective strategies good writers use when they write.

Be aware of your writing and vocabulary habits. Change some. After all, American writer John Irving says "Good habits are worth being fanatical about."

Strategies for Adding New Words

It will come as no surprise to hear that building new words into your writing vocabulary requires a conscious effort. It takes attention and application.

Imagine that learning new words is like meeting people at a party. You find yourself paying attention to the people there. After all, you go to parties, generally speaking, for the people who will be there. You look forward to seeing old friends and maybe making some new ones. You don't say to yourself, "That's it! I don't ever want to meet anyone new in my life. I don't want any new friends. I have enough." When you are learning new vocabulary for writing, try to adopt an open attitude.

When you are reading or listening, you often see or hear words you don't know. After all, no one, not even the most educated or skilled among us, knows the meaning of all English words. But instead of saying, "I don't know that word. Skip it," it is important that you pay attention to it.

Let's return to the party. Here you are arriving on the scene, looking around at the people. You don't stop and say, "I don't know her. Skip her. I don't know him. Skip him." You want to gain new friendships and knowledge about people, culture, and the world, just as you want to add new words to your vocabulary.

Some Tips for Adding New Words

Attention

Paying attention to new words is not as difficult as you may think. If you are listening to someone and the person uses a word you do not recognize, ask the person what the word means if you feel comfortable doing that. If you feel embarrassed asking, then quickly jot the word down before you forget it.

Before going to sleep that night, look up the unfamiliar word in a dictionary. Think about the word meaning. Reread the definitions. Taking about two full minutes to do this will force you to pay attention.

Keep your slips of paper with the unfamiliar words written on them. Just toss them into a small box or drawer somewhere.

If you are reading and you come across a word you don't know, circle it (if you can) or jot it down. Look up the circled words after you have finished reading. Then go back and quickly reread the sections with the circled words. Has your comprehension improved by knowing what the words mean?

If there are too many words to look up or if you do not have access to a dictionary, try to figure out what the circled words mean by looking at the sentences around them. Specialists call this reading strategy *using context clues*, or using the surroundings to get at the meaning.

Application

Once you have paid attention to some new words, you should try to use them. How do you apply new words to your speaking and writing? Here are some tips:

Ask yourself: Is this new word used fairly frequently? Is it such a specialized word that it is used only in specific situations? For example, if you are taking a course in psychology, you will come across new terms that are part of the vocabulary of psychology.

These must be learned because they represent concepts in the body of psychological theory and knowledge. Your professor will expect you to be familiar with the terms and to understand the thinking underlying them. Unless you become a practising psychologist, however, these words are unlikely to become part of your speech and writing outside the psychology classroom.

In other words, every discipline, whether it be psychology, biology, physics, accounting, medicine, education, or mathematics, has its own specialized vocabulary. These terms must be learned in your courses.

For your purposes, you are thinking more broadly about adding new words to your vocabulary. You are thinking about developing new ways to express yourself—new ways to say what you want to say with an expanded repertoire of words to help you do that. Choose wisely when adding to this repertoire in speech and writing. Some words may be quite appropriate, while others may not.

After you have selected a word for application, write it down somewhere, along with its definition. Some people keep a special notebook of new words they are trying to acquire. Others keep a file on their computer for that purpose.

Each day (or at least once a week), choose one or two words from the list of collected words. Write them down somewhere handy. Perhaps use a slip of paper, write the words on it, and then put the paper into your wallet, or purse, or knapsack.

Remind yourself to look at the words once or twice, maybe at lunch or at coffee with a friend.

Some other time in the day, look for an opportunity to use the new word. Maybe you will be with someone on the phone, and you will get a chance to use the new word. Try using it then. Maybe you will be writing a term paper when you see an appropriate spot for the new word. Try using it then.

The more often you use the new word in your speech or writing, the more likely it will become part of your language habits. With such practice, using the word will seem natural to you.

Building a Writing Vocabulary

Effective Use of Modifiers

You may recall what a *modifier* is. Common modifiers—adjectives, adverbs, and prepositional phrases—are critical to English because they add detail and colour to ideas. Without them, your language would be boring indeed. Let's consider some examples:

EXAMPLE 1

"The Heart of Darkness" is a short work by Joseph Conrad, a Polish-born writer who emigrated to Great Britain. Here is a sentence from the story, written about 1898:

We had a glimpse of the towering multitude of trees, of the immense matted jungle, with the blazing little ball of the sun hanging over it—all perfectly still—and then the white shutter came down again, smoothly as if sliding in greased grooves.

Take out the main adjectives, adverbs, and prepositional phrases to see how the sentence will look and read:

We had a glimpse—all still—and then the shutter came down as if sliding.

What a difference there is between the two sentences! The first sentence gives the reader small but significant details. The writer is describing a lush, forested place—the prepositional phrases *of the towering multitude of trees* and *of the immense matted jungle* provide the feel of the place. Your senses become engaged when you read the phrase *with the little blazing ball of the sun hanging over it.* As a reader, you can picture the sun, and you can feel its heat when you imagine Conrad's words. The phrase *all perfectly still* appeals to your sense of hearing. Visual details of a *white shutter* that moves *smoothly as if sliding in greased grooves* tell you what to pay attention to in the human landscape.

Without these details, you would know very little about where you are and what you are watching. Conrad's details combine to provide a feeling (or mood) for you as a reader. You feel the languid heat of the jungle and some of its startling features when you read Conrad's sentence.

EXAMPLE 2

Canadian writer Gabrielle Roy was born in 1909 in Manitoba to Québécois parents. She died in 1983. The following sentence is taken from "The Well of Dunrea," a short story first published in 1957.

Papa, when he clambered out of his wagonette and hitched his mare Dolly to the edge of the well of Dunrea, beheld a ravishing landscape: scattered in the greenery lay a score of half-hidden little white houses with thatched roofs; there were as many outbuildings, equally clean, whitewashed every spring; and besides all this, beehives, dovecots, lean-tos of leaves and branches where in the heat of the day the cows came for shelter; throughout the village there wandered freely flocks of white geese which filled it with their amusing clatter.

Of course, Roy's sentence is an exceptionally long one, filled with many details. Her style is generally much leaner than this; however, the sentence illustrates the power of modifiers. Try removing some of the main ones:

Papa clambered out and hitched his mare, beheld a landscape: scattered lay outbuildings, beehives, dovecots, and lean-tos; flocks wandered.

Roy's original sentence conveys the orderliness and prosperity of the settlement. She uses the adjective *ravishing* to describe the landscape. This word is crucial, for it gives you a sense of wonder mixed with contentment. Papa's horse, Dolly, has a friendly name, innocent and childlike. Roy describes the houses as *half-hidden* and *whitewashed* with *thatched roofs.* These modifiers help identify who the settlers might be: they are people who possess skill and industry. The scene appears to be a rather happy one; even the geese *wandered freely* and *filled* the village with *amusing chatter.* Overall, then, Roy has created a mood by using specific, carefully chosen modifiers in her sentence.

Modifiers are words that can convey powerful detail to the basic parts of a sentence. All writers recognize how valuable such words can be.

Exercise 3 *Recognizing Modifiers*

Choose something like a magazine or a textbook from home or the library. You might use a favourite site on the Internet that has lots of text; a movie review site, for example.

Select one paragraph at random. Choose one of the longest sentences of the paragraph. Write out the sentence, or if you are on the Internet, copy that paragraph and print it. Then do the following:

Underline all the adjectives in the sentence you selected.

Circle all the adverbs.

Put all prepositional phrases into parentheses, like this ( ).

Sit back and look at the sentence with your markings.

What makes the sentence effective? Are the modifiers clear and convincing? Are there carefully chosen modifiers that add lots of interest to the sentence? How have these modifiers improved the sentence?

Working with Adjectives

Adjectives describe nouns. They tell what kind of noun you are discussing—its shape, size, texture, shade, number, and so forth. They express what kinds or sorts of things you are reading or writing about, how some things look, or how many things you are considering (quantity). Adjectives, then, confer detail or colour to nouns.

table	a large, round, antique table
nurse	an efficient, pleasant nurse
game	a complicated, time-consuming game
idea	an exciting, sparkling idea

Do you see how the adjectives give the nouns deeper meaning and interest? Without them, English would be very dull indeed.

Exercise 4   *Group Activity: Adding Adjectives*

The exercise that follows will introduce you to the thesaurus. Here's what to do:

1. Work in a group with two or three others. You can do the exercise together or separately. Then discuss your answers in the group.
2. Using your thesaurus, find at least two adjectives that could be used to describe each of the following nouns. Do not use adjectives you normally use; instead, find interesting and appropriate adjectives that are new to you.

Model: a motivated, eager student

a/an _____, _____ party

the _____, _____ child

their _____, _____ king

a/an _____, _____ shopper

his _____, _____ house

my _____, _____ party

a/an _____, _____ story

her _____, _____ attitude

a/an _____, _____ accident

the _____, _____ movie

a _____, _____ criminal

the _____, _____ missile

a /an _____, _____ door

their _____, _____ living room

our _____, _____ habits

a _____, _____ cup of coffee

Exercise 5 *Adding Adjectives to Describe Places*

Add at least two adjectives (and one or two more if you wish) that could be used to describe the following places. Use your thesaurus. Write your answers in the spaces provided. Be prepared to share your answers with others in a group.

Model: Freemont College: enormous, exciting

the mountains: _____, _____

a large Canadian city: _____, _____

a shopping centre: _____, _____

your campus: _____, _____

a hospital: _____, _____

a beach: _____, _____

a movie theatre: _____, _____

a fast-food restaurant: _____, _____

a community centre: _____, _____

a gym: _____, _____

Exercise 6 Adding Adjectives to Describe Situations

Add at least two adjectives (and one or two more if you wish) that could be used to describe the following situations. You should consider how you or someone else might feel in the situation. Use your thesaurus. Write your answers in the spaces provided. Be prepared to share your answers with others in a group.

Model: a walk in the park: relaxing, refreshing

a store sale: _____, _____

a rave: _____, _____

a dentist's office: _____, _____

a dog at the beach: _____, _____

a mouse in the house: _____, _____

your wedding day: _____, _____

a blind date: _____, _____

a country auction: _____, _____

fishing on the lake: _____, _____

a traffic jam: _____, _____

an examination room at college: _____, _____

a banquet: _____, _____

a hockey play-off game: _____, _____

camping with family and friends: _____, _____

riding a horse: _____, _____

being on a motorcycle: _____, _____

a first kiss: _____, _____

a surprise party: _____, _____

a moonlight walk: _____, _____

a hiking accident: _____, _____

a new driver at the driving test: _____, _____

buying a special gift: _____, _____

celebrating someone's birthday _____, _____

studying late at night: _____, _____

giving a pet a bath: _____, _____

Exercise 7 Adding Adjectives to Describe People

Before you begin this exercise, you will need to be somewhat familiar with the notion of stereotypes. Without realizing it, you could be heavily influenced by the generalized way you are thinking about people. In other words, your perspective about particular groups of people may be driven by your stereotypes of them.

Thinking about a group of people in one set way or imagining that all people of a particular group are the same is called *stereotyping*. Stereotypes surround race, gender, occupation, sexual orientation, and so forth. Their constructions are based on incomplete or faulty information and overgeneralization. For example, some people build their view of a whole nation of people on the basis of having met only one person of that nationality. Stereotyping leads to false information and assumptions.

Sometimes stereotyping is a useful tool in certain situations. The media use stereotypes in their advertising. Viewers recognize a stereotype along with certain qualities that attach to it, and such an association can be a positive thing. For example, think of the stereotype of "the doctor" you see on television. Is the doctor wearing a white lab coat? Is the doctor a male? Is the doctor older and slightly greying? Is he smiling? Does the stereotyped image of "the doctor" fill you with trust? All these constructions lead to a particular stereotype—that doctors are middle-aged, confident, trustworthy, distinguished-looking men who wear white uniforms.

Be aware of stereotypes as you add adjectives to the people nouns below. Add at least two adjectives (and one or two more if you wish) that could be used to describe the following people. Use your thesaurus. Write your answers in the spaces provided. Be prepared to share your answers with others in a group. In your group, you should also discuss possible stereotypes that emerge.

Model: a pilot: calm, commanding

a cowboy: _____, _____

a Hollywood star: _____, _____

your instructor: _____, _____

your boss: _____, _____

your grandmother: _____, _____

a hot dog vendor: _____, _____

an undertaker: _____, _____

a recent college graduate: _____, _____

a nurse: _____, _____

a plastic surgeon: _____, _____

a mechanic: _____, _____

a young mother: _____, _____

a priest: _____, _____

a musician: _____, _____

an animal trainer: _____, _____

a plumber: _____, _____

an opera star: _____, _____

a farmer: _____, _____

an artist: _____, _____

you: _____, _____

Exercise 8   Adding Adjectives to Describe Animals

Add at least two adjectives (and one or two more if you wish) that could be used to describe the following animals. Use your thesaurus. Write your answers in the spaces provided. Be aware that cultural associations are made with certain animals. Be prepared to share your answers with others in a group.

Model: a kitten: helpless, wide-eyed

a snake: _____, _____

a porcupine: _____, _____

a garden spider: _____, _____

a seagull at the beach: _____, _____

a raven: _____, _____

a grizzly bear: _____, _____

an octopus: _____, _____

a goldfish: _____, _____

a hamster: _____, _____

a rat: _____, _____

a fox: _____, _____

a newly born calf: _____, _____

a whale: _____, _____

a street dog: _____, _____

a race horse: _____, _____

an eagle: _____, _____

a wolf: _____, _____

Exercise 9 Stereotypes

If you want to do some extra work with stereotypes, you may decide to watch films, movies, or television, looking for examples. Much has been written on the subject. Here are some titles that may interest you. See if your college or university has these books in its holdings:

Friedman, Lester. *Unspeakable Images: Ethnicity and the American Cinema.* Urbana: University of Illinois Press, 1991.

Toplin, Robert. *Hollywood as Mirror: Changing Views of "Outsider" and "Enemies" in American Movies.* Westport: Greenwood, 1993.

Null, Cary. *Black Hollywood: From 1970 to Today.* Secaucus: Carol, 1993.

O'Reilly, Evelyn M. and Stuart Bruchey (Eds.). *Decoding the Cultural Stereotypes about Aging: New Perspectives on Aging Talk and Aging Issues.* Garland Studies on the Elderly in America. Garland Pub., 1997.

Martin, Terry L. and Kenneth J. Doka. *Men Don't Cry... Women Do: Transcending Gender Stereotypes of Grief.* Philadelphia: Brunner-Routledge, 1997.

Stangor, Charles. (Ed.). *Stereotypes and Prejudice: Essential Readings (Key Readings in Social Psychology).* New York: Psychology Press, 2000.

Dealing with Problematic Expressions

Trite expressions are phrases repeated so often in writing or speech that they have lost their original sparkle and become boring. Sometimes trite expressions are referred to as *hackneyed* expressions (which is another way of saying "worn-out"). You should avoid using four types of expressions—clichés, jargon, slang, and euphemisms—because they make academic writing unclear and dull.

The word *cliché* comes from the French; it means a commonplace word, phrase, or opinion that has been tired out from overexposure in speech and writing. Clichés abound in English, and many have become an accepted part of the language.

You have heard someone say *no beating around the bush*, or *read my lips*, or *get on his high horse*. These are all clichés that have become part of everyday speech.

Jargon has to do with specialized language, often associated with particular occupations. Most groups have special terms connected with work or with special interests. Computer technologists, engineers, teachers, doctors, nurses, police officers, business people, government officials, and almost every other professional group you can think of has its own language of specialized terms and shortened expressions. To an outsider jargon is difficult to understand, but to a member of the group it functions as a kind of communication shorthand.

Slang, on the other hand, has to do with informal, usually spoken language. Sometimes a group wants to distinguish itself by using language that is different from standard language and from that of other groups. Slang is often trendy and relies on its freshness for impact. Like clothing fashions, particular slang expressions become popular for a time, but after reaching their peak, they seem to disappear.

Finally, a *euphemism* is a milder way of saying something that may be too harsh or direct otherwise. Euphemisms seem to make some ideas more socially acceptable. They are also commonly adopted and overused. To increase your understanding of these four types of expression, read the following sections.

Clichés

Clichés are expressions you hear or read every day. Every writer or speaker probably uses some clichés without realizing it. Any overused words or expressions can become a cliché—even trendy expressions that stay around too long will lose their impact. However, some clichés are adopted by users over time, and thus they seem acceptable to standard practice.

Consider an example. *A blanket of snow*, an original expression at one time, became a cliché but did not fall out of use. Most people would likely use this metaphor to describe a snowfall; after all, the expression works well and has few useful alternatives. *A covering of snow* is ineffective and *a mantle of snow* is strained. *A blanket of snow* seems an apt description: snow is being compared to a blanket. Users have come to adopt the expression, and along with its acceptance comes a way of seeing the world. *A blanket of snow* frames your thinking about snow—it is like that cozy piece of cloth that wraps you warmly and securely. Whenever you think of snow or see it, you might begin to view it only in those *blanket* terms.

Many other clichés, however, completely disappear from use over time. The loss of these clichés may have to do with cultural change more than anything else. As cultures change, people's language adapts—some language expressions are retained while others are discarded.

Writers must pay particular attention to avoid the use of clichés. The reasons are simple: First, most writers work at making their sentences interesting. They want their writing to be fresh to readers. Clichés can make writing boring, like old recycled items. Furthermore, writers should strive for clarity, particularly in academic writing. Clichés do not make writing clear. Instead, these expressions tend to bog it down. Finally, readers can be irritated by reading clichés since these phrases do not add anything much to the content. You do not wish to lose your reader, especially someone who is evaluating what you have to say in writing.

The immediate thing to do is to eliminate as many clichés from your academic writing as possible. Here are some common clichés that students and other writers use. Avoid using these in your writing.

Common Clichés

Cliché	Alternative Expression
studies show	name the specific study or delete
over the hill	getting older
sad but true	a sad fact
window of opportunity	a chance
easy as pie	simple
under the weather	not well
missed the boat	missed an opportunity
a heart of gold	kind
a drop in the bucket	a small amount
too close for comfort	close
a shot in the dark	a chance
pushing his or her luck	taking a risk
thick as a brick	stupid
add insult to injury	make things worse
all the bells and whistles	with all possible gadgets
at the end of the day	after all
a piece of cake	easy
white as snow	white
will give the shirt off his back	generous
in the nick of time	in time
around the clock	24 hours
bite the bullet	accept the outcome of your actions
face the music	recognize what you have done

Sentence Clichés

If you can't beat them, join them.
Rome wasn't built in a day.
Nobody's perfect.
Take each day as it comes.
Look on the bright side.
Live and learn.

> Don't worry; be happy!
>
> Time heals all wounds.
>
> The more things change, the more they stay the same.
>
> When the going gets tough, the tough get going.
>
> I was laughing on the outside but crying on the inside.
>
> Love hurts.
>
> Haste makes waste.
>
> Experience makes us stronger.
>
> Don't judge a book by its cover.

Jargon

Jargon is the term used to describe the specialized language used by people in a particular profession, occupation, or interest group. These expressions can become overused on the job and, in a sense, they too can become trite. Jargon often enters the mainstream language. Think about all the jargon that has come into everyday English from various fields:

telecommunications and computing: *digital, cell, cross-over cable, glitch, bug, virus, boot, hard boot, click, multi-task, email, hacker*
business: *buyout, blip, head hunter, ethical investment*
government: *cap, restraint, outsourcing, shore up*

Many more examples of jargon are so specialized that only those working in the field recognize them. For this reason, student writers should avoid using jargon in their essays and term papers unless the assignment includes a specialized, technical vocabulary.

Jargon is considered non-standard English. If student writers use jargon in their written work, the writing will usually fail to communicate clearly. Your professor or instructor will discourage the use of jargon unless there is a specific need to use a term or set of terms.

If you must use a special term (or jargon), use quotation marks around it. Depending on the style of your paper, you may use italics instead. You must also explain what the term means, particularly if it is specialized. If you are in doubt about whether the use of specific jargon will be acceptable in your writing assignments, ask your instructor or professor.

Slang

Slang is informal English made up of words or expressions that generally come from speech. It should not be included in academic papers unless there is a specific reason to do so. Slang is associated with social groups. Particular people use slang in order to distinguish themselves from other groups.

Slang and specific cultures are closely tied. Linguists and sociologists have documented many slang cultures. They have studied biker slang, gay slang, cool slang, military slang, music slang, drug slang, gamer slang, hip-hop slang, street slang, computer slang, police slang, and many more. Each group possesses its own terms and its own manner of speaking.

Slang is a kind of language fashion. For a time, certain words and expressions become a style within a group. Then after more and more people begin to use the term outside the group, the slang begins to fade from use within the original group because the slang no longer differentiates the group from any other. Even children are attracted to language that is different from their parents'.

Language can delineate generations or age groups. Slang your parents used—perhaps expressions such as *hip, far out, groovy, or right on*—might seem ridiculous to you now, but in the 1960s such expressions were considered "cool." Some expressions you used when you were younger may no longer be part of your speech. You abandoned a lot of your slang as your groups and interests changed.

Of course, some slang expressions do become part of mainstream English and eventually become accepted as standard English. For example, the expression *traffic jam* came first from slang and then made its way into everyday usage. Here are some other instances:

- *Chintzy* is an accepted word in English but originally came from slang. It means showy but cheap. It is still commonly used in speech.

- *Booze* is a word used for alcohol. It is considered slang but continues to be used in everyday speech.

- *Gut*, meaning the intestine of an animal, was not a slang word originally. However, slang usage shifted its meaning to other applications. Today you speak of *gut reactions*, meaning a basic instinct, or a *gut issue*, the basic issue. You also speak of having *guts* or courage.

You may find that the context of a writing assignment allows for some slang usage. For example, if you were to write a narrative piece about your exploits in a local rock band, you may include some slang as part of the assignment, simply because it furnishes the piece with the needed colour and details to make it seem real to the reader. If the writing assignment allows for informal language usage and tone, then slang may seem quite appropriate.

In general, however, when writing formal, academic papers avoid using slang expressions. Although some instructors and professors may accept some slang in written assignments, many do not. It is really up to you to find out if your instructor will accept slang usage in your papers.

Euphemisms

A *euphemism* is a milder expression used to replace one that might be viewed as more harsh or unpleasant if it was stated directly. In other words, euphemisms help soften the meaning and the message.

Euphemisms have a history of usage. The Victorians were particularly sympathetic to euphemistic speech, mostly because it was considered taboo to discuss openly matters of sex and the human body. Such talk was said to be indelicate. For example, it was considered impolite to use the word *leg* because it referred to a specific body part. Instead,

Victorians used *limb*. Some people took on the responsibility of making English "delicate." Thomas Bowdler is famous for editing out passages in Shakespeare deemed by him to be indecent to the "common reader." In 1818 Dr. Bowdler published *The Family Shakespeare*, a book far more suitable in his estimation for family reading. The term *bowdlerize* comes from the famous doctor's activity of censoring passages. Today euphemisms still surround us, not particularly for delicacy's sake, but rather for the power they have to soft-pedal a message.

News broadcasts, newspaper articles, television interviews, letters from officials, government press releases, sales promotion materials, and popular magazines contain the greatest number of euphemisms. Think of how the advertising industry employs euphemisms.

Advertisers know how to sell their products: language is their medium. A commercial, for example, would not say "This cream will stop you from looking so old." The product would not sell because the language is too direct, and some people might find the directness offensive. However, if the manufacturer and the advertiser claim "This cream will make you look younger," more consumers will be attracted to purchasing it. The message has been toned down. Advertising is very skilled at deploying the most effective euphemisms in the right contexts. After all, you don't have to strain your imagination too much when you think of some products that would be very difficult to sell without a softer message. Bad news or hard facts have to be bundled in soft packages.

Here are some euphemisms for you to consider:

- *Experiencing an economic downturn* is a euphemism a government official might use. What does this mean in everyday English?

- *Fudging his answers* and *fudging the numbers* are common euphemisms you encounter in connection with politics or accounting. What do they mean?

- The military uses the euphemism *friendly fire*. What does it mean?

 1. *Experiencing an economic downturn* means you are short of cash. You are running out of money.

 2. *Fudging his answers* means equivocating—not saying anything directly, being deliberately ambiguous. *Fudging the numbers* is a gentle way of saying inaccurate accounting practices.

 3. *Friendly fire* is a euphemism the military uses to describe bombing or firing from its own side, resulting in injury or death to its own forces.

Exercise 10 *Group Activity: Euphemisms*

Work in a group of three to five people. Each member of the group should take about 20 minutes to complete the exercise. Add as many euphemisms to each standard term as you can. Remember: Euphemisms are gentler expressions substituted for harsher ones.

Discuss your answers in the group, and then review them using the Answer Key that follows the exercise.

Standard Term

drunk	death	prisoner
old	wrong	unemployed
steal	problem	break-in
addict or addiction	sick	poor
brothel	fat	power failure
dead	fire (from work)	kill or murder
cheap	to be jailed	old person's home
garbage dump	bombing	ugly
used	a poor nation	victim
toilet	a lie	tip (as a noun)

Answer Key

Standard Term	Common Euphemisms
drunk	intoxicated; tipsy; inebriated; pickled; soused; tight
old	mature; distinguished; senior; seasoned; ripe; elderly, venerable; advanced in years
steal	appropriate (v); lift; borrow; salvage; purloin; remove; take possession of
addict (addiction)	substance abuser; substance abuse; chemical dependency; chemically dependent
brothel	massage parlour; a pleasure establishment
dead	departed; deceased; late; lost; gone; passed; defunct
cheap	economical; frugal; penny-wise; thrifty; budget-conscious
garbage dump	landfill; recycling station; reclamation site
used	pre-owned; previously owned; refurbished; second hand; antique; collectible
toilet	washroom; powder room; the men's or women's room; bathroom; WC
death	demise; end; afterlife; final destination; better world; gone to meet The Maker
wrong	inappropriate; inaccurate; mistaken; unsound; erroneous; amiss
problem	issue; challenge; complication; difficulty; dilemma
sick	indisposed; under the weather; ill; ailing; unwell; declining health; confined; bed-ridden
fat	overweight; chubby
fire (from work)	lay off; dismiss; downsize; let go; streamline; displace; release
to be jailed	imprisoned; incarcerated; detained; secured
bombing	air support; supply air support
a poor nation	undeveloped nation; developing nation; third-world nation; emerging nation
a lie	a fib; a fabrication; a mental reservation; an inaccuracy; an untruth; a stretching of the truth
prisoner	inmate; detainee; convict

unemployed	between jobs; out of work; inactive; without active employment
break-in	breach of security; trespass
poor	underprivileged; low-income; modest income; working class; lower income group; needy
power failure	interruption of service
kill or murder	put down; put away; put to sleep; finish someone off; liquidate
old person's home	retirement home; rest home; nursing home; centre for retirement
ugly	unattractive; unsightly; unseemly
victim	casualty; unfortunate person; sufferer; scapegoat
tip (as a noun)	gratuity; gift; fee for service

Other Examples of Euphemisms

dearly departed

a little bundle of joy

sensitive viewers

your better half

coarse language

adult entertainment

fixer-upper

a human shield

impaired driving

confidential source

underachiever

surveillance

Can you give the standard English for each of the euphemisms listed above? Who uses each one? Can you give reasons why an individual or group would use them?

Certainly most people may use euphemisms in certain contexts, particularly sensitive ones. People in the media use them frequently, and new euphemisms are added or introduced constantly. While euphemisms may be socially acceptable manners of expression, try to avoid using them in academic writing.

For further practice in recognizing euphemisms, try the following exercise.

Exercise 11   Euphemisms

Watch or listen to a newscast this evening. Pay attention to the language the broadcaster is using. Find two or more euphemisms he or she uses. Try to capture the context in which the euphemism was used: Was it a press release from government? Was it a report on the economy? Was it a local story?

Write down these euphemisms and their contexts. Bring your answers to class, and be prepared to share your answers with others.

Exercise 12   *Eliminating Clichés, Jargon, Euphemisms, and Slang*

Each of the following sentences contains examples of problematic expressions. Read each sentence. Underline and label clichés, jargon, euphemisms, and slang. Rewrite each sentence using standard English. Be prepared to share your answers in a class session.

1. First and foremost, Jamal was really over the hill to enter the skateboarding gig, even though he is a really cool guy.

2. I thought it was awesome, brilliant even, when Nadia told off her old man and gave him a piece of her mind.

3. Like I feel really bummed out that someone ripped off your books, man, but, hey, that's the way the cookie crumbles, right?

4. We deeply regret to inform you, Mrs. Wong, that your beloved feathered friend, Bobo, has bitten the dust.

5. It's no big thing if you don't want to party with us, but stay cool and we'll catch you later.

6. Thurston had to reinstall his operating system because he kept getting a blue screen.

7. Wow, was my brother steamed when he found out his new girl had ditched him!

8. Let it be known to one and all that due to circumstances beyond our control, there will be an interruption of service.

9. Stavros thought the test was gruelling, a real nail biter, but all my buddies said it was a piece of cake!

10. She stared at him with eyes as cold as ice, but he must be as thick as a brick because he didn't even notice.

11. We're going to have to migrate those files over to the new system, stat!

12. Carla is going to stick to her guns this time and pay off her student loan; basically what she owes is just a drop in the bucket compared to my whopping amount.

13. In the nick of time, he grabbed his gear and got out of there.

Chapter 12: Review Test

Identify each of the following as a cliché, jargon, slang, or a euphemism by writing **C**, **J**, **S**, or **E**.

1. Hernando was a very cool guy. _____

2. He'll have to relay the CPEC to those nodes. _____

3. Let us assure you every bodily convenience will be provided to our clients. _____

4. They were as drunk as skunks. _____

5. With a little more consciousness-raising, we could up our profile. _____

6. The room was as silent as a graveyard. _____

7. Outsourcing will result in renewed employment to that economic region. _____

8. What's up? _____

9. The bride was as pretty as a picture. _____

10. Dear Uncle Flugel passed on to a better place yesterday. _____

11. Jojo had to use the facilities. _____

12. Not a single particle of doubt remained in his troubled mind. _____

13. The elderly gentleman was cautious in his gastronomic escapades. _____

ESL POINTER

Building Your Sentences

Adding to your writing vocabulary requires a conscious effort on your part to make a change. Most adult writers find it difficult to alter their writing patterns and styles.

The following passage contains simple sentences and unexciting language. Rewrite it according to the instructions given within the passage. Your instructor may ask to see your work, or you may share it with the rest of the class.

The cat spent most of its days sleeping. (Add two new adjectives.) It was very lazy. (Add a comparison, but do not add a cliché.) One day it decided to move. (Expand the sentence with a prepositional phrase and add a new idea of some sort.) It had seen a mouse. (Add a new, more interesting verb.) It hunted. (Construct a pattern 4 sentence to convey the hunt. Use at least one adverb.) It soon became bored. (Construct a pattern 2 sentence, and use at least two adjectives.) It gave up. (Add a sentence that contains a description of how the cat felt. Add two adjectives and one prepositional phrase.) It went back to its bed to sleep. (Add two new ideas; use a semicolon to join the ideas.)

CHECKOUT

1. Building your vocabulary in writing takes attention and application.

2. Sometimes you can figure out what words mean by looking at the sentences around them; in other words, by using context clues.

3. Some people keep a special notebook of new words they are trying to acquire. Others keep a file on their computer for that purpose.

4. Using a thesaurus, you can find modifiers that add powerful detail to the basic parts of a sentence.

5. Be wary of clichés, jargon, slang, and euphemisms.

part 3

Mechanics

English *mechanics* has to do with the general rules for using capital letters and punctuation marks. Although marks such as commas, semicolons, and apostrophes may seem like small details that don't really matter in your writing, they are critical because they help signify meaning. Punctuation marks point out to your reader where sentences are to be separated and what ideas fit together. Punctuation marks help make meaning clear.

This section introduces you to the rules of capitalization and to the uses of commas, semicolons, quotation marks, and apostrophes. Try reading, practising, applying, and remembering these detailed ideas.

chapter 13

Capitalization

Chapter Objectives

What will you have learned when you have completed this chapter?
You will be able to

1. recognize the function of capital letters.

2. apply the suggested rules of capitalization.

3. edit sentences for correct application of the rules of capitalization.

Chapter 13: Self-Test

Part 1: Applying Seven General Rules of Capitalization

Insert capital letters wherever they are needed in the sentences below. Check your answers with the Answer Key.

1. certainly we serve valley farms vanilla, strawberry, and chocolate frozen yogurt made from fresh fruit grown in the annapolis valley and from milk from ontario.

2. the english class took a tour of the perksy library on the grounds of the university of passmore.

3. Before october 9, 2005, ellie must have work done on her ford mustang.

4. i really enjoy chopped Spanish peanuts on the sundaes i purchase from dairy queen.

5. andy, do you know if bingo's pizza place puts greek olives on their special pizza?

6. the trip to hamilton, ontario, on january 15, 2004, made thomas so tired that he missed two days of teaching at george johnson elementary school.

7. the royal bank of canada accepted my cheque from the bank of hong kong.

8. our instructor of japanese told us to purchase the book *haiku from the heart.*

9. has wallace ever worked with an apple computer before he took his course at the alberta institute of technology?

10. on august 15, 2004, the twins, barney and bernie, received a huge carton from the big brick furniture store on fourth street.

11. mr. gervais read an excellent book for gardeners called *special plants for the canadian garden,* published in toronto, ontario, in 2002.

12. dave, please prepare the hall by sweeping the floor, washing the dishes, and stacking the chairs.

13. he owned three businesses: a restaurant, a hotel, and a dry cleaning store in sidney, n.s.

14. buy some Kleenex, pepsi, old dutch popcorn, and island farms butter.

15. the journalist who is studying german interviewed mrs ludlum at the canadian embassy in zurich, switzerland.

Part 2: Applying Seven Special Case Rules for Capitalization

1. gary's specialist, dr. chung, wants gary to come to westside hospital for some tests.

2. their family wants to travel to sri lanka in april for the buddhist new year.

3. through pats (pacific animal therapy society), sharlene takes her scottish terrier to visit the elderly.

4. armand's email read: "the meeting was too long for my tastes!"

5. the header for the chapter was "seven rules for spanish punctuation."

6. the stone age refers to an early time in the development of human cultures, before the use of metals.

7. uncle arthur plays the hawaiian guitar with great style and enthusiasm.

8. before the rally at miracle stadium, several olympic contestants spoke with president bush.

9. the title of the section should be as follows: "medicinal flowers of ontario."

10. the song "like a virgin" was playing on the radio when my husband arlo proposed to me.

11. the cruise ship, *caribbean cool*, was docked in the inner harbour last week, so many residents of victoria were able to tour the facilities on board.

12. the dragon boat festival held every summer in vancouver, b.c., attracts thousands of visitors.

13. professor hector elmez will give a lecture tonight entitled "costs of the spanish civil war."

14. ms. buckley, my neighbour, purchased a 2005 red toyota solara.

15. on mother's day, they purchased the perfume called sensi by giorgio armani, a box of godiva chocolates, and a large bouquet of roses called fragrant cloud to give to their beloved mother.

Seven General Rules of Capitalization

Use capital letters in the following seven situations.

1. At the beginnings of sentences and when using the pronoun *I*
   The youngest elf did not enjoy doing the work in the princess's garden.
   I must admit I was surprised.

2. For proper nouns (nouns naming particular people, places, or things). Days of the week and months of the year should always be capitalized. Include all parts of the title of a building, bridge, street, avenue, boulevard, or monument.
   The Lion's Gate Bridge is undergoing reconstruction.
   The Eiffel Tower is in Paris, France.
   For his work in physics, Anthony J. Leggett won the 2003 Nobel Prize.
   Sean went to Ryerson University on Victoria Street in Toronto, Ontario.

3. For geographical names, as in rivers, mountains, or valleys
   The Mackenzie River, Canada's longest river, ends at the Arctic Ocean.

4. For brand names of products
   We bought a case of Coke and some Que Pasa burritos to snack on while we studied.

5. In titles of books, short stories, films, plays, and poems. Do not capitalize unimportant words like *a, an, the, to, for,* and *at* unless one begins the title. (Make sure to underline or italicize the titles of books, movies, plays, television programs, newspapers, and magazines.)
   My son's favourite book was Dr. Seuss's *Green Eggs and Ham.*
   My mother loved watching *Coronation Street* every day on television.
   My sister and I have a subscription to *Canadian Gardening* magazine.

6. For names of countries, languages, nationalities, and religions
   Joel is a Catholic who comes from Portugal; his wife is a Muslim from Pakistan.

7. For names of boats, trains, ships, aircraft, and spacecraft
   James T. Kirk was the captain of the *Starship Enterprise.*
   The *Bluenose II* is a famous schooner from Nova Scotia.
   In 1883 a French railway company began running the *Orient Express,* which travelled from Paris to Istanbul.

Exercise 1 Applying the First Seven Rules of Capitalization

Insert capital letters wherever you think they are needed in the following expressions. Check your answers with the Answer Key.

1. montreal, quebec

2. kraft marshmallows

3. irish coffee

4. my friend peter

5. kelley's bar on broad street

6. the park building on first avenue

7. the author ann rice

8. the film *pirates of the caribbean*

9. councillor monica shempsky

10. the poet phyllis webb

11. the province of prince edward island

12. the new territory of nunavat

13. moose jaw, saskatchewan

14. the television show *space cops*

15. blue sky valley

16. short story writer alice munro

17. the cookbook *vegetarian snacks*

18. the village of pemberton, b.c.

19. the canadian tire store

20. teachers credit union

Exercise 2 Capital Letters

Place capital letters where they are needed in the following sentences. Underline wherever necessary. Check your answers with the Answer Key.

1. enid read the book the understanding of hope by philip renner.

2. does the red river flow through manitoba?

4. clark kent bought a small condo in ottawa, ontario.

5. moira's children enjoyed watching the movie the princess and the pea.

6. louise works in squamish, b.c., but her husband works in toronto, on.

7. such a long journey is a lovely book that kaitlin will enjoy.

8. the rocky mountains are found in alberta and british columbia.

9. baldev will call ontario hydro to have the temporary power connected.

10. on saturday we bought a large pepsi and a mccain's pizza and watched the movie the hitchhiker's guide to the galaxy.

11. the college of the west offers a course in breaking quarter horses and in learning the trade of the farrier.

13. the cafeteria offers dasani and perrier water but does not sell carbonated soft drinks such as sprite, dr. pepper, or mountain dew.

14. herbert's favourite mystery novel is the spy who came in from the cold.

15. disney's movie the lion king was popular with children.

Exercise 3   Capital Letters

Work in pairs. Insert capital letters and underlining as needed in the following sentences. Be prepared to share your answers.

1. everyone in their family enjoys the tv program law and order.

2. have you seen the children's copy of alice in wonderland?

3. ranjit's three teenagers enjoy eating mcdonald's food.

4. the play the importance of being earnest is a satirical comedy.

5. a fine russian wolfhound won first prize at the 2005 westminster dog show.

6. near the goldstream river we spotted a pair of american bald eagles.

7. mrs. chin, the daycare teacher, bought play-doh and crayola crayons for her class.

8. the wild pacific salmon is a different species from the salmon of the north atlantic ocean.

9. i will buy you a turkish coffee after our game of chinese checkers.

10. donna will meet us in the lobby of park pacific mall so that we can see the lord of the rings at the new silver screen cinema centre.

11. "the best rum in the world is jamaican!" exclaimed teddy.

12. would you prefer asian noodle salad or greek salad for our luncheon meeting next monday?

13. according to mr. kendrick, our plane to tobago will be with air canada.

14. ronnie purchased a new digital konica camera and a japanese tripod.

15. my favourite treat is english toffee with brazil nuts.

16. many viewers enjoy watching programs like national geographic.

17. penny's favourite film is the last of the mohicans.

18. simon fraser university in burnaby, b.c., is built on the top of a small mountain.

19. the tourists enjoy seeing the canadian elk in jasper national park in alberta.

20. lars ordered the software, norton anti-virus, over the internet.

Seven Other Rules for Capitalization

Use capital letters in the following seven situations.

1. for titles of people, either professional or kinship, and in nouns of address
   Uncle Rufus won the hot dog eating contest.
   The faculty representative spoke to Dean Rathwell on Thursday.
   A *noun of address* is a proper noun that a writer or speaker is directly addressing in a sentence:

      (*Uncle* is a noun of address.)
   Would you like more tea, Uncle?
   Cousin Jib, have you opened the garage door yet?

2. for holidays and festivals
   The family went to some shoe sales on Boxing Day.
   Labour Day is celebrated in many countries all over the world.

3. for acronyms
   Acronyms are labels formed from the first letters of words of titles or names. Often acronyms are pronounceable, such as SARS, but sometimes they are not, such as IBM, for example.
   The Women's Television Network, or WTN, began its operation in 1995.
   The Canadian Radio-television and Telecommunications Commission, or CRTC, monitors Canadian content on our radio and television networks.

4. to represent shouting (and sometimes give emphasis) in email messaging
   The email read, "The remark he made was very insulting; I felt VERY ANGRY, and I want him TO APOLOGIZE."

   (for emphasis)
   The guests should be escorted to the dinner AFTER the speeches.
   Using capital letters for emphasis is NOT recommended in academic writing.

5. to politicize an issue, group, or idea
   Sometimes groups can co-opt particular terms by capitalizing them as they would a product. As a reader, you begin to read the capitalized terms in a new way, as if they were commodities. Do not use capitals in this way in your academic writing, but do pay attention to how various groups use capital letters to serve their own interests.

   The People
   Big Government

6. for headers
   A *header* is the title of a section in a report, article, or paper. Capitalize only the important words of the header, just as you would in a title of a book, film, movie, or play.

   Four Methods of Backfilling

7. to refer to significant events, eras, or epochs in human history or the history of the earth

   the Bronze Age
   the Paleozoic Age
   World War II

Exercise 4   *Using Seven More Rules of Capitalization*

Insert capital letters according to the rules of capitalization given in the section above. Check your answers with the Answer Key.

1. would you please tell officer bailey i will see her at five after i speak with superintendent burbles?

2. chief engineer patterson spoke to mayor simpson about the city strike.

3. would you buy a new chevrolet from tim brown chevrolet, aunt arthie?

4. the reporter from the *globe and mail* spoke to alderman dawson about the fire in bixby's department store.

5. the golden age of greece refers to a time of great stability and culture when democracy was born.

6. sister monique, a carmelite nun from Saskatchewan, wrote a powerful article on various child-rearing practices among first nations peoples.

7. the parent spoke to principal brown about her son's progress in school.

8. many children are fascinated by how stone age people lived.

9. every march japan holds the doll festival called hinamatsuri.

10. king arthur and the knights of the round table were said to live in the age of chivalry.

11. in june el salvador celebrates a special holiday called school teachers' day.

12. mothers against drunk driving, or madd, began as a grassroots movement.

13. the section was titled "the klondike gold rush of 1897."

14. mannfred named his rowboat *lily of the valley* after his favourite flower.

15. Why don't you consider using david austin roses, mother, in your english country garden?

Chapter 13: Review Test

Part 1: Applying Seven General Rules of Capitalization

1. they bought bic pens and scotch tape from office depot last friday evening.

2. our french class visited queen's university during the month of june.

3. twyla left the canadian armed forces on september 8, 2005.

4. fay really loves the swiss chocolate that she buys from zellers.

5. marshall, do you know if we get french fries with our polish sausages?

6. his journey up the fraser river was documented in a book titled *wild waters*.

7. the credit union of saskatchewan met with its chief officers on june 12, 2004.

8. mr nells is our swedish professor who studies the life cycle of the milbert's tortoiseshell butterfly.

9. jens worked for new brunswick power and used fluid mechanix as his main software.

10. we called the sears store on branch street to have our new panasonic home theatre system delivered to our home address in woodstock, ontario.

11. my sisters simone and dawn loved the movie *finding nemo*.

12. klaus, please buy some starbucks coffee and krispy kreme doughnuts for the staff meeting.

13. mrs. trowley went on a trip to spain, portugal, and italy.

14. at the bottom of my desk drawer, i found a smashed mars bar and a small box of kleenex.

15. one of the early explorers of the canadian north died near the bering sea.

Part 2: Applying Seven Special Case Rules for Capitalization

1. their pediatrician, dr. hanah safir, was featured in the tv show *famous people*.

2. on halloween we love to give out planter's peanuts and old dutch potato chips.

3. groundhog day comes around every february in Canada.

4. rakesh sent an angry email that read, "don't you ever speak to me again!"

5. the header for the section is as follows: invertebrates of southern alberta.

6. the age of the dinosaurs happened about 250 million years ago.

7. please forgive me, uncle seth, i neglected to give you some news from your friend, dr. lukas.

8. the family celebrates both the jewish holiday of hanukkah and the christian holiday of christmas.

9. kala loves to have a bit of jamaican rum in her columbian coffee.

10. on board the ship *pacific princess* passengers can enjoy the swinging music of freddy don and his cruisers.

11. no one expected to receive a whole box of ibm computer paper free with the purchase of an z12 ibm notebook.

12. the ballet company of montreal will perform *swan lake* next april.

13. dean neela singh opened the new wing of holy mercy hospital named after its benefactor, mr. logan smiley.

14. his son bought a new mini-cooper at british car imports down on fairfield street.

15. on father's day, we bought dad a new toro lawnmower, a subscription to *golf digest*, and a membership to pine hills golf course.

ESL POINTER

Capitalization and Nouns of Address

As mentioned earlier in this chapter, a *noun of address* refers to the person that the speaker or writer is addressing. Nouns of address are proper nouns. They often indicate kinship relationships such as uncle, aunt, and cousin. They may include the professional title of the person (or animal) being addressed. In such cases, the titles along with the person's name must be capitalized.

Exercise 1 Using Nouns of Address

Work in pairs. Follow the instructions given to develop sentences together. Use capital letters according to the rules discussed in this chapter.

1. Make up a sentence using *Auntie Lise* as a noun of address. Use the name of a Canadian river. Mention a specific day of the week.

_____

_____

2. Make up a sentence using *Doctor Chung* as a noun of address. Pretend the doctor is an important zoologist from a famous university in Canada.

_____

_____

3. Make up a sentence using *Dad* as a noun of address. Mention the name of a street in your sentence. Mention a special holiday.

_____

_____

4. Make up a sentence using the name of your dog (or cat) as a noun of address. Mention the name of a product you are going to give to your pet.

_____

_____

5. Make up a sentence using *Uncle Frank* as a noun of address. Mention a mountain range in Canada. Mention a famous Canadian park near the mountain range.

_____

_____

CHECKOUT

1. In titles of books, short stories, films, plays, and poems, do not capitalize unimportant words like *a*, *a*, *the*, *to*, *for*, and *at* unless one begins the title.

2. A noun of address is a proper noun that a writer or speaker is directly addressing in a sentence.

3. Nouns of address often indicate kinship relationships.

4. Acronyms are labels formed from the first letters of words of titles or names.

5. A header is the title of a section in a report, article, or paper.

Punctuation

Chapter Objectives

What will you have learned when you have completed this chapter? You will be able to

1. recognize that punctuation in English has rules, conventions, and purposes.

2. identify the standard rules for comma, colon, and semicolon use.

3. apply the standard rules for comma, colon, and semicolon use.

4. identify the standard rules for apostrophe use.

5. apply the standard rules for apostrophe use.

6. recognize the conventional uses of quotation marks.

7. apply the conventional standard rules for quotation mark use.

Chapter 14: Self-Test

Add commas, semicolons, colons, apostrophes, capital letters, and quotation marks wherever they are needed in the following paragraph. Check your answers with the Answer Key.

when alex wants to imagine spectacular scenery he thinks about the queen charlotte islands along the coast of british columbia. naden harbour for example is located at the top of graham island an important fishing area. as tourists travel by plane to naden they see serene meadows and rolling hills. If they are fortunate enough they can spot a small herd of sitka deer or the great majestic roosevelt elk these animals roam freely through the hills. sometimes tourists ask are there any bald eagles out today? instead of the magnificent eagle however visitors might see flocks of pacific crows that pester them for food. in this secluded wilderness the history of the haida a proud coastal first nations people is evident in the artefacts. walking along the shorelines, visitors can find the remains of old longhouses totem poles and old burial poles reminders of the haida past. fishing lodges like north island lodge employ some of the local haidas who work as fishing guides. in the summer months the fishing is remarkable the giant pacific chinook salmon and the enormous halibut called the vacuum cleaners of the sea make spectacular catches. during the winter, the northwesterly winds begin to blow and the once calm waters turn into a grey, raging sea.

The Comma

The most common punctuation mark in the English language is the *comma*. Also the most overused and abused, the comma's function is to separate, not join. Using too many commas makes reading just as difficult as including too few.

Here is an extremely long sentence. Its style isn't particularly good; however, it demonstrates how difficult it can be to read a sentence without commas.

During the parade one of the clowns who was riding a tiny decorated bicycle and pulling a wagon with a small dog in it and who was throwing candy coins and colourful balloons to the children suddenly stopped in the middle of an intersection preventing the parade from moving forward.

With commas added:

During the parade, one of the clowns, who was riding a tiny decorated bicycle and pulling a wagon with a small dog in it, and who was throwing candy coins and colourful balloons to the children, suddenly stopped in the middle of an intersection, preventing the parade from moving forward.

Rules can guide you to proper comma use in your writing. Read and think over the rules given in the next sections. As well as applying these rules in the sentence exercises, use them when you edit your own writing.

The Comma in a Series

A comma is used to separate three or more items in a series. The items may be words, phrases, or clauses.

Some books suggest that the comma before the *and* is optional; however, *Spotlight on Sentence and Paragraph Skills* suggests you use a comma before the *and*. In most cases, this comma helps clarify meaning. The comma in this situation is called the *serial comma*, or sometimes the *Oxford comma*. Journalists do not often use it. However, the serial comma is often recommended in academic writing.

Cheese, fruit, and biscuits make a traditional English dessert.

Restful sleep, adequate exercise, and good food are important to health.

Garden fork and shovel, hammer and mallet, and long-handled pruners and hand-held secateurs are useful tool combinations to have around the yard.

(Notice that pairs of tools are kept together as units by the use of the comma.)

The passenger, who arrived late for boarding, who delayed the ticket agent, and who required assistance with her small child, was a famous soap opera star.

Exercise 1   *Using the Comma in a Series*

Insert commas where they are needed in the statements below. Check your answers with the Answer Key.

1. His children enjoy playing hockey volleyball and soccer.

2. Mel's aunt knits Cowichan sweaters socks and gloves to sell at the Aboriginal Arts store.

3. Rice pasta and potatoes are high in carbohydrates vitamin C and riboflavin.

4. The aquarium has beluga whales killer whales and grey sharks on public view.

5. Mark Georgio and Austin play golf together on the weekends.

6. Allie discovered that some money an expensive pen and a calculator were missing from her desk.

7. Ajay and his cousin bought dishes a lamp three chairs and a bed for their apartment.

8. Mrs. Perez bought bananas cream bread and onions at the local grocery.

9. Bernice the grandmother and their neighbour go swimming on Tuesdays Wednesdays and Saturdays.

10. Breaking your promises forgetting special occasions and making excuses for yourself will not make you popular with your friends.

Exercise 2   Using the Comma

Work in pairs. Insert commas where they are needed in the statements below. Be prepared to share your answers.

1. Talking laughing and eating together, the group gossiped about their new teacher ski instructor and fitness coach.

2. Reading the article checking the label on the jar and analyzing the information, Marigold learned that zinc magnesium and calcium are minerals essential to the human body.

3. The company ordered green blue and red binders for the conference it was hosting.

4. Chrysler Jeep and Rover dealerships are found on Markam Avenue on First Street and on Bay Boulevard.

5. Turn left at the next light continue for four blocks and then turn right to get to the new arena.

7. The documentary animated film short movie and software demonstration were funny interesting and informative parts of the media conference.

8. Lunch for the campers tourists and dignitaries consisted of salads rolls fruit and fresh lemonade.

9. Daphne collects antique dolls doll furniture and doll clothing.

10. The chief of police the mayor and the head of security were meeting about the recent disaster.

Three More Comma Rules

The comma not only separates items in a series; it has other important functions as well.

1. Use a comma to separate a specific day and month from the year. Do not use a comma between a month and year if no day is given.
   May 12, 2007
   January 1, 2005
   May 2010

2. Use a comma to separate the names of towns, cities, and villages from the name of the province.
   Saskatoon, Saskatchewan
   Barrie, Ontario

3. Use a comma after an introductory expression at the beginning of a sentence to separate it from the rest of the sentence.
   On the contrary, Ramone was delighted with the plan.
   Having lost all his courage to ask Shula out, Devin left the party.

Exercise 3 Using the Comma

Insert commas wherever they are necessary in the following sentences. Check your answers with the Answer Key.

1. Paint stencils and round brushes were needed to make the decorative border.

2. Without a doubt Thomas is a wonderful carver father and friend.

3. After talking with my uncle I decided to take a trip to Brampton Ontario this year.

4. Appointed to the Land Use Committee on October 5 2005 Josef felt honoured as he waved to the press in Portage La Prairie Manitoba.

5. The family had a new baby on August 7 2004 moved their home to Sault Ste. Marie Ontario invested in a small business and bought a new car.

6. His branch office in Winnipeg Manitoba contacted the head office located in Calgary Alberta.

7. The peaches plums and lemons had all spoiled in the fridge.

8. The restaurant uses juicy bacon fresh lettuce garden tomatoes and homemade mayonnaise on its burgers.

9. After months and months of planning the new park was ready in Carrot River Saskatchewan on April 5 2006.

10. Wolves dogs and coyotes are members of the canine family.

11. With a huge sigh of relief the packer put the roses petunias cedars and shrubs on the truck.

12. Will anyone help me look for the address book the stamps and the computer labels?

13. After the ashes had cooled down in the ruins of the old building the fire investigator found an old metal chest full of silver coins.

14. Hurrying along after the bus Kristina skidded tripped and broke her ankle.

15. Read this article compare its ideas with Professor Lutz's theory and then write an essay.

Exercise 4   *Using the Comma*

Insert commas whenever you think they are necessary in the following sentences. Be prepared to share your answers.

1. The orchestra played rock and roll jazz and classical music at the concert.

2. Having said all he had to say Albert walked out of the meeting room.

3. Of course the agency in Hollywood California is looking for you.

4. Indeed our hotel in Banff Alberta was very expensive.

5. Please purchase salt sugar vinegar and spices for the pickling jobs.

6. Our best friend in Cranbrook B.C. has moved to Prince George B.C.

7. Tula married on September 22 1998 and was divorced in October 2001.

8. After all no one but you seems to care about it.

9. Plan to pick up the children drop off the videos and make supper tonight.

10. He drove trucks for Websters Sani-Moving Moves-R-Us and Big Guys.

11. Marking the exam papers Candace ordered a pizza a salad and a diet Coke.

12. After receiving a promotion on May 15 2004 Harry was fired on May 18 2004.

13. Depending on the weather the game may go on.

14. Kingston Ontario Hamilton Ontario and Regina Saskatchewan all have universities.

15. During a terrible winter storm many people in Montreal Quebec lost their power had no water and could not leave their homes because of the freezing rain.

Five More Rules of Comma Use

1. Use a comma before a coordinating conjunction (*and, but, or, so, nor, yet, for*) in a compound sentence.
   Elroy wanted to win the prize, but he had forgotten to buy a ticket.
   The drovers brought the cattle through town, and the dust from the herd settled everywhere.
   The orders were sent to Montgomery's office, or they went directly to central receiving.

2. Use a comma after a subordinate clause that begins a sentence.
   Because the sheriff forgot to lock the cell, the prisoner escaped.
   Since most of the family had left the dinner table, the baby felt lonely.
   Although the drawer jammed, I managed to open it.

3. Use commas between coordinate adjectives but not cumulative adjectives. (As explained in Chapter 11, *coordinate adjectives* are adjectives in a series. Because the adjectives are separate in meaning—you can put *and* between them—they can be switched in position. Cumulative adjectives, on the other hand, must be placed in a specific order.)

   (coordinate adjectives)
   Flex, my fitness instructor, was muscular, demanding, and rigorous.

   (cumulative adjectives: you cannot say *the alcoholic first woman*)
   The first alcoholic woman addressed the waiting audience.

4. Use commas to set off nouns of address or appositives. Remember that a *noun of address* directly addresses someone by name. An *appositive* defines who or what a noun or subject is.

   (noun of address)
   You will have to wait, *Uncle Johnny*, until we get to your apartment.

   (noun of address)
   When the champagne arrives, *Martha*, please propose a toast.

   (appositive)
   My coach, *Brian Flax*, used to be on the Olympic rowing team.

5. Use commas to set off interrupters or parenthetical expressions.
   Interrupters or *parenthetical expressions* are expressions that interrupt the flow of sentences. These expressions are put in the middle of a sentence to add emphasis or interest, but they are non-essential to its meaning.
   Conjunctive adverbs such as *however, moreover, nevertheless, then,* and so forth can be used as parenthetical expressions. They may add contrast or emphasis to the meaning and may be considered essential.

   (conjunctive adverb adding emphasis)
   The small company, *of course*, could not meet the supply.

   (conjunctive adverb adding emphasis)
   She is, *without a doubt*, the loveliest woman I know.

   (conjunctive adverb adding contrast)
   Karin, *however*, would not budge.

Exercise 5 Applying More Comma Rules

Insert commas where they are needed in the following sentences. Be prepared to share your answers.

1. One of the smallest kittens was very playful and it was always pestering its brothers and sisters.

2. After the chairperson adjourned the meeting the members of the committee went for a beer together.

3. So much of the treasure had been lost in my opinion to people's greed.

4. The opponent's arguments on the other hand were weak unsubstantiated and racist.

5. Although the golfers enjoyed the match they had hoped for better weather.

6. Leslie does not know your cousin but she wants to meet him.

7. I wish to say Mr. Nicks that the hot dishes at the buffet table are greasy tough and unappetizing.

8. We can of course call in an expert witness for the trial.

9. One of the most amazing animals at the show I understand was a pet raven.

10. As the house lights dimmed the audience thrilled to the first opening strains of the orchestra.

11. The Speaker of the House Lloyd Pamar nevertheless would not permit the jokes from the Honourable Member from Kicking Horse Pass.

12. If you happen to see a green mountain bike out back Dennis please let me know.

13. His latest novel is I believe his best.

14. The supervisor in fact must have been feeling unwell or he would be here this afternoon.

15. Our card game was cancelled we understand because the management finds the activity to be too boisterous impolite and inappropriate.

Commas and Restrictive and Non-restrictive Clauses

Since the information in a non-restrictive clause is not needed to define a noun, commas are not required around the clause. However, it is sometimes difficult to recognize whether a clause is restrictive or not. In such cases, you won't be sure whether to include commas.

Here are tips for deciding whether a clause is restrictive or non-restrictive:

1. Try reading the sentence without the clause in question. Is the subject defined without the clause?

   The dentist who spoke to our dental assistants' class is a very good speaker.

   If you remove the clause *who spoke to our dental assistants' class*, the sentence becomes this:

   The dentist is a very good speaker.

   Do you know which dentist the writer of the sentence is referring to? Without the clause, you cannot tell, so the clause is needed to define the subject. Therefore, the clause is restrictive.

   Now suppose you put commas around the clause; the sentence would look like this:

   The dentist, who spoke to our dental assistants' class, is a very good speaker.

   The commas indicate that the words contained between them are not necessary. Moreover, the commas may indicate that the words are a *parenthetical expression*. Remember that a parenthetical expression is not needed for meaning: the words add emphasis but no ideas. Such an expression may be included to add interest to the writing style.

   Here are other examples of parenthetical expressions:

   The webmaster, of course, had been trained at Preston Technical University.

   Her father, on the other hand, was talking to her French professor.

   The couple, naturally, were completely unprepared for the surprise party.

   Safa, along with his sister, will stay overnight in the dorm.

2. If you decide the clause is necessary, can you tell what distinguishing features the clause is providing for the noun?

   My neighbour who keeps Peking ducks has few slugs in his garden.

   My neighbour is distinguished by the clause *who keeps Peking ducks*. After all, not too many neighbours would have such pets. Therefore this clause is needed to distinguish which neighbour the writer is indicating.

3. Look for the relative pronouns *that* and *which*. *Which* is generally used for non-restrictive clauses, while *that* is most often used with restrictive expressions.

   The coffee that I left on my desk is gone.

   Mrs. Jones's Coffee, which is on sale everywhere, tastes bitter.

Exercise 6   *Writing Sentences with Commas and Clauses*

Work in pairs. Write sentences according to the directions, paying attention to where commas are needed. Be prepared to share your work.

1. Use *Justin* in a sentence containing a non-restrictive clause.

   _____

   _____

2. Use *cellphone* in a sentence that begins with a subordinate clause.

_____

_____

3. Use *briefcase* in a sentence containing a restrictive clause.

_____

_____

4. Use *noodles* in a sentence containing a non-restrictive clause.

_____

_____

5. Use *DVD* in a sentence that begins with a subordinate clause.

_____

_____

Exercise 7 Comma Review

Insert commas wherever they are needed in the following sentences. Be prepared to share your answers.

1. The detective the clerk and the constable from Yorkton Saskatchewan discussed the case.

2. Have you brought the salsa chips sandwiches and pop for the picnic Brad?

3. In the antique chest we found old-fashioned faded photos some old clothes and a silver ring belonging to a juggler who came from Lachine Quebec.

4. Thinking it over Reese rejected Nestor's offer but he nevertheless remained interested in keeping in contact.

5. In due course the old man who had lived all his life on Mulberry Street died.

6. The painting *Snow in Summer* had hung in the gallery for several years and it was finally sold in January 2004.

7. Breeding animals in captivity educating the public and setting up sanctuaries are by the way just part of the mandate of a modern zoo like the one in Calgary Alberta.

8. Although Queasley was a famous scientist he couldn't get a date.

9. The famous author Carol Shields who died of breast cancer in 2003 wrote about family love and finding one's place in the world.

10. Besides being rich in vitamin E whole unprocessed almonds contain magnesium phosphorus fibre iron and calcium.

11. Her son Monty plays the accordion the harmonica and the bongo drums and he has moreover been trained as a French chef.

12. Although Maddox has played football for two years with the Toronto Argonauts he played earlier in his career with the Edmonton Eskimos the Calgary Stampeders and the Ottawa Roughriders.

13. Slowly the fog rolled into shore and then it seemed to cover the small fishing boats the houses and the streets with a moist thick salty presence.

14. Walking home from work each day Collin noticed that his legs had become stronger indeed and lost energy had been regained.

15. I wish to speak to the manager Mr. Gimley over the loss of my account or I will be forced to bring the matter to the attention of my lawyer Verna Schwartz.

16. The cleaner who had mistaken the bin in the art installation as garbage was embarrassed by his error but the gallery owners were in fact somewhat amused by the incident.

The Semicolon

A *semicolon* (;) can work to join elements together. Use semicolons to vary your sentence style, but do not use them too often. They can become tiresome.

The semicolon has two main uses:

1. Use a semicolon to join two independent or main clauses in a compound sentence. The semicolon goes in front of a conjunctive adverb in a compound sentence. Remember to put a comma after the conjunctive adverb.
   My dog slept soundly by the woodstove; the cat was curled up beside him.
   We do not want any more junk mail delivered to our home; moreover, we will email the post office about our complaint.
   Wash those dark cotton jeans in cool water; otherwise, the dye will run.
   In Chapter 4 you will find a list of conjunctive adverbs.

2. Use a semicolon to separate phrases in a list when the phrases contain commas. Otherwise, your reader will not be able to distinguish the units.
   On the way home from work, he bought the chicken, potatoes, and oil; drove to the bank, dry cleaners, and drugstore; and called Taylor, Mary, and Zoe on his cellphone.
   Agatha Christie's *The Mouse Trap* will play on Tuesday, June 10 at 8:00 p.m.; on Monday, June 16 at 7:00 p.m.; and on Sunday, June 22 at 3:00 p.m.

Exercise 8 *Semicolon Use*

Supply semicolons and commas wherever you think they are needed in the following sentences. Check your answer with the Answer Key.

1. The experiment was a success therefore we should be able to publish our results in the spring.

2. Whenever they were afraid, the children would tell each other stories the activity seemed to calm them.

3. Sometimes Eleanor goes out with Amos however she does not plan to marry him.

4. The roses in the roadside park smelled like honey moreover they attracted hundreds of bees.

5. Forgetting to set his alarm, the graduate student was late for his thesis defence consequently the thesis committee was annoyed by his tardiness.

6. Clarice is arranging the chairs for the meeting Percy is organizing copies of the report.

7. Please put the extra strawberries into a bowl after you have washed and cleaned them otherwise they will spoil overnight.

8. Ryan performed a violin concerto for his fellow music students as a result he was seen to be a potential concert artist.

9. Nurse Sophie will assist the doctor in emergency she has the most experience of the whole nursing staff.

10. The two chemicals should never be mixed consequently they are stored in two different parts of the lab in two different types of containers.

11. The canoe trip was really relaxing for Theo and Stephen therefore they've decided to go on another one with three other friends from college.

12. Use this soft brush and air to clean the lens of the camera afterward replace the cap on the lens.

13. The University of Toronto is holding a symposium on family literacy delegates will attend from across North America, Europe, and Asia.

Exercise 9 *Correcting Semicolon Use*

Work together in a small group to correct the errors in the following sentences. Try using semicolons in your revisions. Be prepared to share your work.

1. The assembly stood when the president of the company entered the room; but everyone felt the tension in the air.

2. She would rather not go for a boat ride this evening; since she gets seasick easily.

3. An injunction against the protestors was delivered by the RCMP, however; the group did not leave the site.

4. I learned how to do some Spanish dances by taking an extension course at Green Leaf College, the instructor was competent; and he made the class a lot of fun.

5. Will introduced me to Ginny, his secretary, Mr. Tong, his boss, and Lucky, the doorman.

6. Salt the pasta after you have added it to the boiling water, otherwise, you may find you have oversalted it.

7. I plan to read all of Tolkien's novels, moreover, I plan to rent all three of Peter Jackson's movie trilogy.

8. Stand back from the elevator doors when the elevator is operating, they are unstable.

9. When Tess is photographing in bright light, she adjusts the shutter otherwise the picture may be overexposed.

10. The colourful brochures cost nearly $1000 to print, however they are really attractive and should bring in new business.

The Colon

The *colon* is an interesting mark in punctuation because readers pause briefly when they see it in their reading. You can use a colon from time to time when you want your reader to pause to consider an idea. However, do not overuse colons. Using semicolons and colons too often in your writing will make them lose impact.

Use a colon to introduce an idea that directly relates to a complete sentence in front of it. The colon signals anticipation for the reader: he or she expects to learn more.

Bring these items with you the first day of class: dictionary, paper, pens, and chewing gum. (complete idea comes before the colon)

His reputation was ruined: he had been spotted in the library reading a comic book. (complete idea comes before the colon)

Exercise 10 The Colon

Add a colon in each of the following sentences wherever you think one is necessary. If you think the sentence is correct as given, write **OK** after it. Be prepared to share your answers.

1. The sightseers brought important items sunscreen, bottled water, fruit, and trail mix.

2. Several features of a successful relationship include trust, humour, communication, and concern.

3. The instructions on the work order were clear do all repairs before four that afternoon.

4. I worried so much about my exams I developed anxiety attacks.

5. The guests arrived early for the party and organized the food hummus, pita bread triangles, vegetable dips, potato chips, crackers, salads, cold cuts, fruit, and wine.

6. Have you ever listened to the following radio stations online Classical FM, Underground 5, or Alternative Flow?

7. The Coast Salish Nations have deep ecological and traditional knowledge of their environment fish, beach foods, trees, and forest materials.

8. If you play your Walkman in class, the instructor gets very annoyed.

9. I suggest we try to find the following items at garage sales this Saturday a hammer, a small table for Granny, a tripod for my camera, and a snow blower in good condition.

10. The attendant at the concert directed Beth to row 14, but we were waiting for her in row 41.

Quotation Marks

Quotation marks show direct speech. In other words, these marks used at the beginning (") (opening quotation marks) and at the end of the speech (") (closing quotation marks) indicate to the reader the actual words of the speaker.

Hints for Using Quotation Marks

- *Use a comma to separate the speaker from the speaker's words.*
- *Place the period inside the closed quotation marks.*
  Aunt Lila said, "Please help me pick the flowers for her bouquet."
- *If the direct quotation is interrupted by identification of the speaker, use a comma and then closing quotation marks after the first part of the quotation. Do not use a capital letter to begin the second part of the quotation.*
  "As far as I can recollect," the witness replied, "no one was standing at the bus stop."

Other Uses for Quotation Marks

Use quotation marks around titles of songs, short poems, short stories, titles of chapters, and other short works.

They enjoyed reading Ruth Rendell's story titled "Surrender."

Bob Dylan's "All Along the Watch Tower" is one of my favourite songs.

Exercise 11   Quotation Marks

Supply commas and quotation marks where they are needed in the following sentences. Be prepared to share your answers.

1. Rolf said No one should leave the premises until the all-clear signal sounds.

2. The rain was coming down so hard Maureen explained I didn't see the other car.

3. Winston Churchill said Democracy is a terrible system but it is the best there is.

4. Worried that she would miss her plane Rita turned to me and said I have to go.

5. The littlest of the children spoke in a tiny voice Please sir may we have more?

6. Wishing to earn the respect of his friends and family Fen studied very hard and later told me I was very pleased to have done so well at school.

7. Wesley speaking to his dog in an excited voice said We should go for a walk now.

8. The aircraft controller said to the pilot You will have to adjust your landing approach.

9. Everyone wants someone to love them sobbed Gertrude and I am no exception.

10. The drama teacher said We must try to visualize who we are.

11. Have you ever heard the song Imagine by John Lennon one of the Beatles?

12. Dennis Lee's poem Alligator Pie is a favourite with the children at the daycare.

13. One of my best friends has just written a wonderful short story about his boyhood in India called The Summer of the Monsoon.

The Apostrophe

In general terms, the *apostrophe* is a mark of punctuation used in possessives and in contractions. You did some work with the use of apostrophes and possessives in Chapter 5.

Apostrophe and Possession

You may recall from Chapter 5 that an apostrophe is used when you want to show that a noun owns something.

the cat's claws
the worker's pay
the ship's sail

Here are some rules of possession:

1. If a noun is singular, use -'s.
   Michel's sweater   the dog's ear   the book's cover

2. If a noun is plural, use *s'*.
   cats' paws
   doors' hinges
   businesses' profits

3. If a noun has an unusual plural and does not end in -*s*, add -*'s*.
   children's game
   women's washroom

4. Most nouns can have a singular possessive or a plural possessive form.
   a person's rights
   people's rights

5. In relationship expressions such as *mother-in-law* and *brother-in-law*, add -*'s* to the end of the expression to show the possessive. Be careful of shared possession.
   my brother-in-law's car
   his mother-in-law's house
   my brother and sister-in-law's child

Exercise 12   *Possessives and Apostrophes*

Add apostrophes to the following. Check your answers with the Answer Key.

1. One of the teachers notebooks is missing.

2. They have located the childrens parents in the mall.

3. Were there any boys uniforms left on sale at the store?

4. Mrs. Sloan won't need to borrow Pamelas car after all.

5. The cars four tires were so bald that the driver had a difficult time controlling the vehicle.

6. Several pieces of glass were lodged in the windows frame.

7. Everyone who wishes can get the football players autograph for free.

8. "The Moonlight Sonata" is one of Beethovens most gentle compositions.

9. To prevent theft, please put the girls bicycles in the locker overnight.

10. One of my grandfathers eyes was a deep brown.

11. Sheilas purse was left on the cross-town bus yesterday.

12. He intended to stay out of harms way, but several incidents caused him trouble.

13. Her sister-in-laws lawyer used to work for the federal government.

14. One of the carts wheels has fallen off by the side of the road.

15. We will be listening to one of Philip Glasss compositions.

Apostrophes in Contractions

Use an apostrophe when you write a contraction. A *contraction* is a shortened way of expressing forms of some verbs and their auxiliaries, or some verbs plus *not*. Some instructors and professors may consider contractions to be too informal for academic writing. They are certainly part of everyday speech and written dialogue.

I am/I'm	he is/he's	she is/she's
we are/we're	they are/they're	you are/you're
I will/I'll	she will/she'll	we will/we'll
they will/they'll	you will/you'll	it will/it'll
I have/I've	he has/he's	she has/she's
you have/you've	we have/we've	they have/they've
it has/it's	who has/who's	who is/who's
cannot/can't	do not/don't	should not/shouldn't
would not/wouldn't	will not/won't	has not/hasn't

Exercise 13 *Apostrophes and Contractions*

Write contractions for the underlined expressions in each of the following sentences.

1. Mrs. Ferrier <u>will not</u> be attending the retirement lunch on Thursday.

2. At the entrance to the park visitors <u>cannot</u> buy permits for open fires since the ban on fires went into effect in April.

3. Freddy <u>has not</u> got the money to go to the soccer game in France this summer.

4. By using a survey, <u>they will</u> decide what to do with the government surplus of money.

5. <u>It has</u> been raining all week, and <u>I am</u> beginning to feel a bit depressed by it.

6. Maggie said she <u>would not</u> be able to help the grade six science class with their field trip.

7. <u>He had</u> lived in the Toronto region for most of his adult life.

8. For over a year, she <u>has been</u> planning a trip to Montreal.

9. <u>I have</u> been thinking about the first time I went climbing in the mountains.

10. <u>Let us</u> decide how many meetings <u>we will</u> need this semester.

Exercise 14 *The Apostrophe*

Some of the following sentences contain errors in apostrophe use. Repair the errors, or write **OK** if you think the sentence is correct. Be prepared to share your answers.

1. The lawyer was defending the right of the robot to it's vote.

2. All students are asked for their IDs when they use Northern Colleges library.

3. She exclaimed she didn't know who's fault it was, but she suggested it might be Joes.

4. We enjoyed looking over Chris's wedding pictures with her.

5. Whose got the time to read, anyway?

6. George's wife, Rita, called her brother's-in-law and invited them to dinner.

7. Maria's and Rodney's child, Reginald, always scored perfect As in his exams.

8. The sheriff's office called to ask us if we were interested in helping them with they're campaign.

9. No sooner had Terry's roof been repaired than his sink's began to leak.

12. Josh's learning habits need some work, but he is doing well considering the pressures hes under at home.

13. My mother-in-law's sweet potato pie won a blue ribbon at the pioneers fair.

14. The Workers Compensation Board is designed to help worker's injured on the job.

15. What she said would have hurt anyones feelings.

16. Elaine's and Wendy's opinions were strong and loudly voiced.

17. His son-in-law and daughter's business was doing extremely well in Richmond.

18. The teacher marked the errors with bright red Xs.

19. The little girls' bike was missing from the rack, and she cried when she told her mother the news.

20. Everyones idea of a good snack is different.

21. One of his dogs' paws was cut.

22. Its a shame that Louise doesn't know who's cat that is.

23. McDonalds food is fast and cheap.

24. Mrs. Kleins words' were lost in the wind as we walked near the ocean.

25. That condominium's price is far too high for it's location.

Exercise 15 Editing Practice

The following paragraph contains errors of the following types:

- comma use (including comma splices)
- semicolon use
- colon use
- apostrophe use with possessive case
- capitalization
- quotation marks

Read the paragraph. Correct each error you see.

How often does the average Canadian family go out to eat? According to the Canadian food guide to eating the average Canadian may not be so "average" after all. Some of Canadas statistics show that many Canadians eat out at least three times per month. Single Canadians tend to eat out more for various reasons they do not like to cook for themselves they do not want to eat alone and they claim it is cheaper. Not everyone agrees with the singles analysis of why eating out is preferred, Janice Hippman of the canadian restaurateurs association says Yes it is nicer to eat with other people. It makes the simplest meal taste better, however, many singles eat out because they are too lazy to cook or they simply don't know how to cook. On the other hand many families budgets do not permit too many trips to restaurants these days. It is no secret where most families will go out for their meals. McDonald's wendy's a&w burger king and taco time top the list. Hippman also reminds us that the traditional family meal may be a thing of the past most families have busy working parents and active children whose schedules do not always mesh.

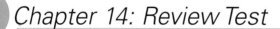

Chapter 14: Review Test

Read the following passage. Add capital letters, periods, commas, quotation marks, and apostrophes wherever necessary.

the royal jewels: an alberta designer and her charlies angel

farah fawcett liked queen bee design's silver and crystal shoulder-duster earrings so much she took them home from the set of alberta-shot *hollywood wives,* part II and wore them on *leno* shes the first celebrity to wear my designs says designer leanne gallagher whose weighty rings charm bracelets necklaces and earrings are hand-cut in sterling silver or gold luscious bunches of gem-

stone beads are paired with simple cuts and clean lines to create pieces that are unusual colourful

and unlike fawcett perhaps perfectly balanced theyre available at rubaiyat and kismet in calgary,

chachkas in vancouver and artworks in edmonton.

Western Living, December 2003, p. 10

ESL POINTER

Direct and Reported Speech

For direct speech, use quotation marks. However, sometimes a speaker or writer will report what someone else said rather than quote him or her directly. This speech is called *reported speech*.

Direct: "After one o'clock, the bar closes," said the bartender.
Reported: The bartender said that after one o'clock the bar closes.
Direct: "I feel woozy," cried Meena.
Reported: Meena said that she felt woozy.

Exercise 1   Group Activity: Changing Speech

Work in a small group to change each sentence according to the directions. Write your sentences in the spaces provided. Be prepared to share your answers.

1. Lon said that he was sorry he could not come with us to the art gallery. (Change reported speech to direct speech.)

   _____

   _____

2. The student responded, "I don't know how to answer the question." (Change direct speech to reported speech.)

   _____

   _____

3. Nazeer said he would help me study for my algebra test. (Change reported speech to direct speech.)

   _____

   _____

4. One of the women stated, "I have applied for a training course in computer information technology." (Change direct speech to reported speech.)

_____

_____

5. The teacher said, "I want you to prepare a title page for your reports." (Change direct speech to reported speech.)

_____

_____

6. The opera star, Rico Coos, said he enjoyed giving performances in our fine city of Toronto, Ontario. (Change reported speech to direct speech.)

_____

_____

7. The manager of the hotel said he would allow us to have our cat in the room, provided we paid a pet fee of $20. (Change reported speech to direct speech.)

_____

_____

CHECKOUT

1. A comma is used to separate items in a series. Some books suggest that the comma before the *and* is optional; however, *Spotlight on Sentence and Paragraph Skills* suggests you use a comma before the *and*.

2. Since the information in a non-restrictive clause is not needed to define a noun, commas are not required around the non-restrictive clause.

3. *Which* is generally used for non-restrictive clauses while *that* is most often used with restrictive expressions.

4. Quotation marks show direct speech.

5. In general terms, the apostrophe is a punctuation mark used in possessives and contractions.

part 4

Paragraph Writing

A *paragraph* is the basic building block of academic writing. It has a particular structure, including a topic sentence, major supporting ideas, and minor supporting details. It may end in a sentence that draws a conclusion from the paragraph's ideas or in a sentence that wraps up the main ideas.

Writing an effective paragraph involves composing a clear topic sentence and then developing this idea using specific, convincing points so that your reader is engaged and interested in what you have to say. This section will give you practice in reading and writing summary, descriptive, narrative, and explanatory paragraphs.

chapter 15

Summary Paragraphs

Chapter Objectives

What will you have learned when you have completed this chapter?
You will be able to

1. recognize what a summary is.

2. identify the purposes of a summary.

3. write a one-sentence summary.

4. write a paragraph summary.

A *summary* is a brief account of something using your own words. Lectures, books, articles, conversations, and ideas may all be summarized to some extent. You provide summaries in your life when someone asks you to report on an event you went to or a movie you saw. In a condensed way, you tell the person what went on, leaving in what you believe to be the most important parts and leaving out small, unneeded details. Summaries can also be useful to readers, because they offer a concise version of the original. For example, to help you decide if you want to watch a movie or not, you probably use the summaries or story lines given in magazines like *TV Week* or *TV Guide* or in the television schedules found in daily newspapers. Summaries are useful in the workplace, too. Busy people like corporate executives or government officials require summaries since they simply do not have time to read in full detail all the material needed on the job. In everyday life, shoppers can read information on products' packages in order to decide whether to purchase them or not. Book jackets, DVD wrappers, and magazine covers all provide different kinds of summaries for consumers.

Consider this advertising copy on a box of cereal:

You know you want to live a healthy lifestyle, but with all the demands of your busy schedule, you find that you're not always eating as you should. Nummy Flakes helps you get a good start to your day without fuss or muss. One cup of Nummy Flakes along with low-fat milk provides the nutrition you need along with the beneficial fibre you require.

Try writing a one-sentence summary of this. Include only the details you think are important. Use your own words.

Now, go back and reread the advertising copy. Then reread your one-sentence summary. Is there anything you would like to add or delete from your summary? Adjust it accordingly.

Compare your answer with the one below. What differences do you notice? Do you think your one-sentence summary is effective?

Possible answer:

Eating Nummy Flakes is a fast and easy way to get nutrition and fibre into your diet.

A vital skill in summarizing is knowing which ideas are significant and which are unnecessary. The significant points are called the *main ideas*; the smaller, less important ones are called *minor details*. Sometimes it is really quite difficult to tell which is which because not all structures or contexts are the same.

College and university instructors often ask students to summarize articles from professional journals. Summary writing, then, is one of the key skills you will need to be successful in an academic setting.

How Can Writing a Summary Help You?

Your preparation for writing a summary is what lays the foundation for critical thinking and persuasive writing. In order to achieve a deeper level of thinking, you must first understand the points or arguments being made. For example, if your assignment is to read an article written by an expert and then comment or compare the writer's position with another writer's (part of critical thinking), then you must first understand the two writers' points. This first step is necessary in order to interpret, analyze, and evaluate someone else's ideas. Furthermore, as you begin to think about a writer's points and then list them, you are helping to develop a deeper comprehension by carefully revealing to yourself what you are grasping. As you unravel the writer's arguments or ideas, you understand more and more. As you think your way through them, you also develop new insights on the topic.

Summary writing helps you become more accurate in your interpretations of someone else's ideas and better at selecting an author's significant points. At the same time, you will discover that writing summaries develops your recall of information. When you write an effective summary of an article, you demonstrate to yourself and to your instructor or professor that you understand the material. In this manner, you will begin to value your abilities to summarize as an important study tool.

Guidelines for Preparing a Summary

Different kinds of summaries are suited to different purposes. As an academic writer, you must use your summarizing skills in connection with articles, lectures, presentations, films, and chapters of textbooks. Understanding the vocabulary used in the material is really important.

Because preparation of summaries takes a surprising amount of work, you will find that guidelines help.

- A summary should contain the most important features of the original work.
- It should be balanced. It should treat all aspects of a writer's or speaker's points equally. It should not give special treatment to one point over another.
- It should be objective. You should leave your personal opinion out of it. Being objective means reporting on major ideas without letting your own bias interfere with your interpretation. Being objective takes practice.
- It should be as complete as you can make it. Leaving out significant ideas because you have run out of space or run over a given word count makes for an incomplete and therefore ineffective summary.

Exercise 1   *Group Activity: Writing One-Sentence Summaries*

Work together in a group of three. Write a single-sentence summary for each of the following short pieces. Use your own words. Be prepared to share your answers with the class.

Paragraph 1 Manreet had never been downhill skiing before. She had felt too embarrassed to tell her friends when she agreed to come on the ski trip. As they approached the ski equipment rental shop at the base of the mountain, Manreet wondered what story she could tell to convince them she was unable to go. She bit her lip anxiously.

Paragraph 2 Diego was certain he had locked his keys in his car. He shook his head in frustration, and with a short sigh walked back toward his office to retrieve his spare set. After a long, frustrating day, he was not surprised to feel his anger rising, but with each step he took in the calming evening breeze, his temper began to cool down. He looked up at the night sky and was astonished to see the myriad pinpoints of light glittering back at him. Almost like a cape that had been hugging his shoulders, he felt his bad mood lifting.

Paragraph 3 How often have you seen a butterfly fluttering by and wished you could make it linger? It's comforting to know you can. The solution is to plant nectar-producing plants and shrubs. A sunny part of the garden is best—both for flowers and butterflies. Make sure you have a diversity of plant material—both annuals and perennials, planted with succession of bloom in mind. Butterflies have a strong sense of smell, and when you see them "dancing" by they are seeking out the source of a particular fragrance. You will certainly be rewarded if your garden has what they are looking for.

—Joanne Outerbridge, "Butterflies"

Purposes of Writing a Summary

Keep your purpose in mind as you write your summary. Here are several different reasons a student might have for writing one:

- To use as a study tool
- To make research information more accessible
- To understand a writer's argument
- To show my professor or instructor that I understand the material
- To deepen my own comprehension
- To provide a tool for someone else to get the information quickly

Exercise 2   *Deciding the Purpose of a Summary*

Here are some summary assignments that students at university or college might receive. Using the list of purposes above, decide the purpose or purposes of each assignment. Check your answers with the Answer Key.

Assignment 1: In a sociology class, you are asked to visit a recreational site. You are asked to interview five people on the site. You are to provide a summary of your interview findings. What is the purpose of this summary?

Assignment 2: Your philosophy instructor asks you to summarize two philosophers' theories given in two different articles. What is the purpose of this summary?

Assignment 3: Professor Smiles, who teaches a first-year course in psychology, asks you to read and summarize the first four chapters of your psychology textbook for next week's class. What is the purpose of this summary?

Assignment 4: Your political science instructor asks you to critique the arguments for and against free trade given in a political debate. What is the purpose of this summary?

Assignment 5: In your business administration course you are given a group assignment called "Foundations of Business." You must work collaboratively with two other students. Each of you is responsible for reading three different articles as a basis for your project. What is the purpose of this summary?

Rules for Paragraph Summary Writing

When you write summaries as paragraphs, use the following six rules, adapted from Jeanne D. Day from the University of Notre Dame.

1. Leave out unnecessary information.

2. Delete information that repeats.

3. Whenever possible, cluster information under larger categories (this is called *super-ordination*), or use a more general term.

4. Select a topic sentence. (A *topic sentence* is a sentence in a paragraph that sums up the main ideas of the paragraph.)

5. If there is no topic sentence, invent one that fits.

6. After following steps 1 to 5, rewrite using your own words. Sometimes special terms must be used. Avoid quoting the author's own words, unless it is completely necessary to do so.

Applying Day's Rules of Summary Writing

Review the following example that illustrates how to apply the six rules.

Original Paragraph

World War I brought special horrors. Soldiers faced new weapons such as tanks, poison gas, airplanes and flame throwers. On the battlefields, soldiers on both sides often protected themselves by digging deep, muddy trenches and waiting there until instructed to attack. The area that lay between them and the enemy trenches was called "no man's land." When ordered to attack, the soldiers left their trenches and "went over the top" into no man's land. There they tried to dodge the artillery shells and machine gun bullets and swarm into enemy trenches. Many never made it across. (word count: 96)

—Susan E. Merritt, *Her Story II: Women from Canada's Past*

Summarized Version 1

This version applies Rule 1 (leave out unnecessary information) and Rule 2 (delete information that repeats).

World War I brought special horrors. Soldiers faced new weapons such as tanks, poison gas, airplanes and flame throwers. On the battlefields, soldiers on both sides often protected themselves by digging deep, muddy trenches and waiting there until instructed to attack. The area that lay between them and the enemy trenches was called "no man's land." When ordered to attack, the soldiers left their trenches and "went over the top" into no man's land. There they tried to dodge the artillery shells and machine gun bullets and swarm into enemy trenches. Many never made it across. (word count: 96)

Summarized Version 2

This version applies Rule 3 (cluster information under larger categories whenever possible or use a more general term).

World War I brought special horrors. Soldiers faced new weapons such as tanks, poison gas, airplanes and flame throwers. On the battlefields, soldiers on both sides often protected themselves by digging deep, muddy trenches and waiting there until instructed to attack. The area that lay between them and the enemy trenches was called "no man's land." When ordered to attack, the soldiers left their trenches and "went over the top" into no man's land. There they tried to dodge enemy fire and swarm into enemy trenches. Many died. (word count: 88)

Summarized Version 3

This version applies Rule 3 (more clustering, or combining, of information).

World War I brought special horrors. Soldiers faced new weapons on the battlefields, and for protection they dug trenches and waited to attack. They "went over the top" into no man's land toward enemy trenches while dodging opposing fire. Many died. (word count: 41)

Summarized Version 4

This version applies Rule 4 (select a topic sentence).

topic sentence

World War I brought special horrors. Soldiers faced new weapons on the battlefields and to protect themselves, they dug trenches and waited to attack. The soldiers "went over the top" into no man's land, and there tried to dodge enemy fire and swarm into enemy trenches. Many died. (word count: 48)

Summarized Version 5

This version applies Rule 6 (rewrite using your own words).

World War I brought special horrors. To offset innovative weapons in battle, soldiers used trenches from which they "went over the top" into no man's land and into enemy fire to overcome enemies in their trenches. Many died. (word count: 38)

Exercise 3 *Applying the Rules*

Use the six rules to construct several versions of a summary. Use the World War I summary versions as a model. Choose one of the following excerpts. Your summary should be 50 words or less. Be prepared to share your versions with students who have chosen the same excerpt as you.

Excerpt 1

The conception of this article and my answer to the search for a "National Hero" came to me one day while at my local skatepark. I heard a group of kids all excitedly whispering and flustered. Upon closer attention, I found out that they were just trying to figure out where they can get a pen. A pen, uh? I found my answer when I looked up again at the vert ramp and saw a huge group of kids surrounding a tall skater. As I skated over a bit closer, I realized what I should have known. The best skateboarder in the world, for who knows how long, Tony Hawk, was present, signing autographs and padding up to skate. No one was skating with Tony so I went up on the vert ramp to watch a few of his mesmerizing runs. To my surprise, Tony quickly acknowledged me with a smile and said, "Hey, how ya doin' today?" After the session I saw Tony taking off his pads and decided to formally introduce myself to him. He dealt with me, and the hordes of kids around him, in a real attentive and nonchalant brotherly type of way. He seems good with people casually interacting with him. He's just a big kid with god-like talent on his toy. (word count: 218)

Brad Edwards, "The Hawk Within," Smithgrind.com. (**www.smithgrind.com/index.cfm/ exclusives.hawk**) Courtesy of Brad Edwards and Gravity Skateboards.

Excerpt 2

Call me stubborn if you like. I was a quiet student at university, just wanting to become a teacher. And I did—and loved the job. In the 1970s I joined second-wave feminists in pushing the envelope of stereotypes and I rose on the professional ladder along with the men. I agreed that women can become judges or astronauts or play professional hockey and have value for whatever they do. The problem is that I did believe it, literally. So when in 1975 I had my first child, I threw myself into that role, too. I put in 18-hour days with no weekends or full lunch hours. I never had a real holiday or even an actual coffee break and I loved it. I prepared teaching material in reading, math, and history and I studied language development and infant massage. I learned about medical care, and a human life depended entirely on my care. Yet I was shocked to find that suddenly my social status had gone through the basement. Because I was now a homemaker my cheque was refused at a store. My credit card was turned down without a note from my husband. I was denied any salary and my husband could not even say our child was being cared for by a caregiver—because I was that caregiver. I was not allowed to contribute to the Canada Pension Plan, and most life insurance companies turned me down. I could not, on my own, even get bank credit. Now that really irked me, because I may have been doing a traditional role but I was not happy to be seen as a second-class citizen. I was particularly angered to see friends who, because of divorce, were forced to leave their children. The man who left them still could rule their lives by forcing them to choose certain careers and not others. I was irritated that one census form said "If you have been a homemaker all your life, indicate 'never worked.'" I could hardly believe it, but women's groups who had worked so hard to value women were actually now working to insult one role of women. Homemakers were the new pariah, and governments bought into this and would not consider us as "working" women. (word count: 377)

Beverly Smith, "Why a Mom Complained at the U.N.," *Canadian Parents* (**www.canadianparents.com**) Reprinted by permission of Canadian Parents Online Inc.

Excerpt 3

Just a short, 10-minute walk from Parliament Hill, Aboriginal Experiences feels like it's a world away. Situated on an island in the Ottawa River, this family-friendly attraction lets everyone experience Canadian Aboriginal culture first-hand. The two-hour Taste of Native Spirit tour begins with a guided walk through the small village of traditional dwellings. Each depicts a particular native lifestyle. The travelling life of plains hunters is seen in the highly portable teepees, while the longhouse suited the more settled life of the agricultural Iroquois. Local Algonquin people built bark-covered wigwams secured with spruce roots indigenous to the central Canadian forest. Dance performances by the seven-person Kehewin Native Performers from Alberta demonstrate traditional hoop, grass and jingle dances to the sound of the drum. Tots happily join in the final friendship dance. Children will enjoy opportunities to make souvenir crafts and participate in group discussion. Particularly useful for young ones is the talking feather used to help people take turns listening and speaking. Afterwards, Buffalo burgers, corn on the cob, and plank-grilled salmon are served up for lunch. (word count: 177)

Maclean's, May 24, 2004. Reprinted by permission of Betty Zyvatkauskas.

Writing Article Summaries

The following two articles, and the notes that follow each, will offer you useful practice in selecting relevant information and then combining it using your own words and the preceding guidelines.

Read the first article as if you had been asked to summarize its main points for the purpose of deepening your comprehension. Understanding the vocabulary is really important, too, so if there are any words that you cannot understand from their context, you may have to look them up in the dictionary.

As you read, keep in mind the six rules and the guidelines for summary writing. Then look over the set of notes following the article. Finally, you will combine these notes into an eight-sentence summary for extra practice.

Article 1

The following article appeared in a newspaper. Newspaper writers do not follow the same strict rules that academic writers do. For example, you will see that many paragraphs are a single sentence long. Some paragraphs do not have clear topic sentences. These differences stem from the fact that journalists, particularly those writing for newspapers, have a different style and form of writing. Their writing fits into single columns, so often single sentences work best. Whole paragraphs such as the ones academic writers construct would be so text-dense that they would look like black blobs on the paper. Besides, journalists are not writing for the same purpose or audience as academic writers. The job of journalists is to report the news in a concise way.

As a student, you may be expected to read articles from daily newspapers or popular magazines because the issues are current and the facts are relevant. Your professor or instructor will not expect you to write like a journalist, however, unless you are taking journalism or media studies. Most of the time, you must still adhere to the principles of good academic writing.

Cellphones Are Changing the Way We Interact

Andrew Flynn

Toronto—Cellphones are changing the way people interact around the globe—and not just the way they communicate, says the author of a new study on the devices.

From the instant global communicators to hip-slung totems of wealth and privilege, cellphones have influenced business, fashion and relationships.

"Little more than 100 years ago the fastest way of sending a message was effectively to send it with a messenger," says Sadie Plant, a British cultural scholar and author who undertook the study, commissioned by cellphone giant Motorola.

"We now find ourselves in a situation where it has become so ubiquitous, so common, it really is the kind of cyberpunk or science-fiction future where people do have a little communicating device in their pocket," she said in an interview.

Plant's study claims the cellphone has subtly changed the way men and women interact.

A group of professional women in Chicago told her they thought male colleagues showed off their phones "using them as symbols of status or even virility." A British survey suggested that many women used cellphones to deflect unwanted attention—60 per cent of lone women were found to be carrying a phone, compared with 47 per cent of men.

Even when not in use, cellphones were used as props to indicate worldly success. One anecdote from the study tells of a young man on his cellphone loudly discussing an important deal to impress a group of women on a crowded train—only to have the phone ring, exposing the call as fiction.

Some people have even kept a second cellphone to facilitate an extramarital affair, Plant noted.

"Of course every new technology is picked up for every conceivable purpose," she says, though more than one phone doesn't necessarily indicate foul play.

"It can be very useful to know if you should put your business hat on when the phone is ringing, or is it a very different kind of call?"

On the upside, Plant says, the cellphone may be starting to influence the age-old battle of the sexes over men's communication skills.

"When I was a teenager [boys] tended to be very uncommunicative and taciturn: Often they were not interested in using the ordinary telephone, whereas girls always had the reputation of chatting a lot on the phone," says Plant.

"But now it seems that the mobile phone has made it quite fashionable for the boys to be more communicative. I think that in turn spills out into their everyday behaviour."

In Japan, Plant noted that an entire generation of young people has come to be known as "the thumb generation" for their ability to type lightning-fast text messages on a small cellphone pad.

The behaviour has even spilled over into other areas of life, to the extent that teenagers have been observed pointing at things and ringing doorbells with their thumbs more often than index finger.

Mobile phones have become such a fixture in cities around the world that "many urban songbirds have become adept at impersonating mobile tones and melodies," Plant says in the study.

But they have also reached the developing world, where they are connecting regions that have never had land-line telephones.

"The most significant thing is to realize the extent to which the mobile phone is finding its way to parts of the world and to communities which in many cases have never had access to fixed-line phones," says Plant.

Free access to communication technology can improve social well-being and even act as a force for political change," says Plant.

"On the positive side, we have seen a shrinking of the world. Obviously, the mobile phone does allow news to travel very quickly, and clearly that can have a dramatic effect.

"There were some very interesting reports out of the Philippines earlier this year when they had a coup. A lot of people refer to that as the 'text-message solution' because (cellphone-based) messaging was primarily the way by which people informed each other about what was happening in the political situation and organized their demonstrations and meetings." (word count: 673)

Times-Colonist, October 29, 2001, B1. Reprinted by permission of the Canadian Press.

NOTES FOR SUMMARY

Notice that the writer of the following notes has tried to use his own words whenever he can. He has gone through the original reading and eliminated unnecessary information. He has also gotten rid of repetition. He has tried to combine and cluster whenever he could.

- Cellphones hugely influential in altering communication
- Sadie Plant, British researcher who did a study for Motorola, says cellphone communication is everywhere; even birds imitate their sounds
- Plant says cellphones have altered how the genders interrelate
- Some women say men use cellphones as status or sexual symbol
- More women (60%) than men (47%) carry one, survey found
- Cellphones used as props and for many other purposes
- Young men more communicative as a result of cellphones, Plant says
- In Japan, "thumb generation" uses text-messaging on cells
- Cellphones connecting distant regions of the world
- Plant says cellphone use can improve human relations
- Since news travels quickly via cellphones they can help political change

Exercise 4   *Group Activity: Combining Notes into a Paragraph Summary*

Work in a group of three to five people. Together, use the notes from "Cellphones Are Changing the Way We Interact" to compose an eight-sentence summary. Provide a clear topic sentence to begin your paragraph. Input your summary and make five copies.

Your instructor will ask you to exchange your copies with another group's. Review the other group's summary, and offer its members feedback by commenting on:

1. Clarity of the topic sentence
2. How the group has combined the sentences
3. How the piece flows from point to point

Article 2

The purpose of writing a summary for the next article is to demonstrate your understanding of the research findings it presents. Again, as you read the article, keep in mind the rules and guidelines of summary writing. Then look over the set of notes that follow. Finally, you will read a student's eight-sentence summary of the original article.

Single Parents' Children More Prone to Obesity

Canadian Press

Ottawa: Children raised by single parents are more likely to be fat than those in two-parent families, according to a national study released yesterday.

"While we suspected that family structure and physical activity were associated with the risk of becoming overweight or obese, this study confirms it," says Carmen Connolly, director of the Canadian Population Health Initiative.

The organization studied 7,216 children across Canada between the ages of seven and 11 and found that children raised by only one parent were 40 per cent more likely to be overweight.

That's likely due to the fact that many one-parent families have smaller household incomes and would be less able to offer healthy meal choices or encourage their child to take part in physical activity," said the study's lead author.

"Maybe you can't afford to put your kids in swimming lessons or dance class," speculated Mark Tremblay, professor of kinesiology at the University of Saskatchewan.

"You might be more inclined to use television or some multimedia technology in the home as a babysitter."

Children from high-income families were 24 per cent to 40 per cent less likely to be overweight or obese.

Any kind of physical activity—and not just sports but even dance, art and music—is a good preventive measure, the study found.

But kids who tended toward sedentary pastimes such as television and video games were more likely to put on the pounds.

Watching more than three hours of TV a day could increase the likelihood of obesity by more than 50 per cent, compared to watching less than two hours a day.

The findings, published yesterday in the *International Journal of Obesity*, provide valuable information for parents and schools who can help kids guard against developing unhealthy habits, Tremblay said.

For instance, parents may want to limit time in front of the TV and provide safe outdoor play spaces.

The study found unorganized sport more protective than organized sport because it tended to be frequent and goes further to developing a lifelong behaviour pattern of physical activity.

"If we've developed an appreciation and a habit for going to the park, going to shoot hoops or playing in the yard, then that might perpetuate through the later years," said Tremblay.

An earlier study by the same group found that having more siblings tended to reduce a child's chances of becoming fat—a finding explained by researchers as likely having to do with the amount of stresses on household resources.

The number of obese children in Canada has more than tripled in the past 15 years, the group says. (word count: 427)

The Province, August 13, 2003, A6. Reprinted by permission of the Canadian Press.

NOTES FOR SUMMARY

- Canadian Population Health Initiative studied 7261 7- to 11-year-olds, found that children of single parents are 40% more likely to be overweight
- Likely because single parents make less money, and so provide less-healthy meals and fewer physical activities
- They can't afford things like dance lessons—use TV etc. as a babysitter for their kids
- Kids with single parents 24 to 40% less likely to be overweight than kids in two-parent families
- Any physical activity—dance, art, music—can prevent obesity
- Kids who watch more than three hours of TV a day 50% more likely to be obese
- Preventative measures—limiting TV watching, safe play spaces outside, casual sports
- Children with more siblings less likely to be overweight
- Obesity rate tripled in past 15 years

SUMMARY PARAGRAPH

This is the summary that one student provided based on the notes above. Notice that Allen begins his paragraph with a clear topic sentence.

A recent national study showed that children reared by single parents are more likely to be overweight than those in two-parent families. The Canadian Health Initiative, sampling 7,216 children aged 7 to 11, found that there are three times as many obese children today as there were 15 years ago. And whereas kids raised by only one parent are 40 percent more likely to be overweight, children of high-income parents are 24 to 40 percent *less* likely to be overweight. The authors reason that, since single parents tend to have less money, they are not as able to provide their kids with healthy meals and to get them involved in physical activities. These children are thus more likely to engage in sedentary pastimes like watching TV—and watching for more than three hours a day ups their chances of being obese by 50 percent. Activities like sports, dancing, art, and music, in contrast, help prevent obesity. Interestingly, the study found that unorganized sports in particular—playing in the park, shooting hoops—helps develop a habit of physical activity that may sustain itself into the future. (word count: 105)

Allen Vivian

Here is how the assignment was evaluated:

- The summary paragraph should contain most of the points listed in the notes.
- Students should use their own words whenever possible.
- The paragraph should be 120 words or less.
- Students should use good paragraph form.
- Students should not write in fragments or note form.
- Students should use correct punctuation and grammar.

The assignment was marked out of 10 as follows:

4 marks for including most of the major points
2 marks for using their own words
2 marks for staying within the word count limit
2 marks for correct paragraph form, punctuation, and grammar

WRITING ASSIGNMENT 1

Summary Paragraph
Using the rules and guidelines in this chapter, write an effective summary paragraph for the following article. Your purpose is to demonstrate to your instructor that you have understood the material.

Your summary paragraph must be no longer than 115 words. Use correct paragraph form, including a topic sentence. Edit your work for correct punctuation and grammar. Be prepared to hand in your work.

The Ripe Stuff

Liz Pearson

When the scientists who study berries start making them a regular part of their own diets, you know they've got to be great! Here's the scoop.

Berries contain potent plant compounds called flavonoids and phenols. These antioxidants may help prevent conditions such as heart disease and cancer by battling free radicals before they can damage your cells.

Recent studies from the USDA Human Nutrition Research Centre on Aging at Tufts University in Boston claim that age-related declines in memory, balance and coordination were reversed in rats fed a diet rich in blueberries. Researches have also found that blueberries prevent mice from developing Alzheimer's disease, even when they were genetically predisposed to it. Berries appear to enhance brain health by protecting nerve cells from damage.

Animal studies suggest that different types of berries guard against various forms of cancer, including cancer of the colon, breast, esophagus and prostate. In a study from Ohio State University, rats exposed to a carcinogen and fed a berry-rich diet had 80 per cent fewer cancerous tumours of the colon. The plant compounds in berries appear to prevent cancer cells from forming. They may also stop cells from multiplying and even destroy them.

Berries may also help your heart by keeping your arteries relaxed and reducing damage to the inner lining of blood vessel walls. In addition, numerous studies on cranberries and, more recently, blueberries, have found they help fight off urinary tract infections by preventing bacteria from adhering to the bladder wall. Plant compounds in berries may also promote good vision by helping to protect or repair damaged eye tissue.

The No. 1 berry question I'm continually asked is: which berries are best? While blueberries get top billing for their antioxidant properties, lots of emerging research shows most other berries, especially cranberries, are good for your health. Black raspberries have even more antioxidant power than blueberries, but they're not easy to find in grocery stores. Your best bet may be to wait for summer, and go to a farm to pick them yourself.

Try to eat 1/2 to 1 cup (125 to 250 mL) of a wide variety of berries most days of the week. Fresh or frozen? That's up to you and may depend on where you live or the time of year. Frozen berries have the same nutritional value and disease-fighting potential as fresh ones. Strawberries and raspberries are more likely to have pesticide residues so always wash them thoroughly before eating or consider buying organically grown fruit. (word count: 415)

Chatelaine, June 2004, p. 33. Courtesy of Liz Pearson, Registered Dietitian.

ESL POINTER

Appositives

Writing summaries can help you develop your ability to combine ideas in interesting ways. ESL student writers tend to stay with simple sentences, because they know how to construct these sentences and they find they can control their errors more easily. These are two good reasons, but as a writer, you also need to develop sentence style.

One language element you can use to vary your sentence style is the appositive. An *appositive* is a phrase that provides more detail about the noun that precedes it.

Simple sentences: Calgary is the capital city of Alberta. It is world famous for its large rodeo. The rodeo is called the Calgary Stampede.

Combined sentence with appositives: Calgary, the capital city of Alberta, is world famous for its large rodeo, the Calgary Stampede.

Notice that the appositive *the capital city of Alberta* is contained by two commas. The second appositive, *the Calgary Stampede*, has a comma in front of it to set it off from the rest of the sentence.

Exercise 1   Group Activity: Forming Appositives

Work in a group of three students. Combine the following groups of sentences into one sentence by using appositives wherever possible. Be prepared to share your answers with other groups.

1. Nashwa is our coach. She was born in Egypt. She was a top athlete in soccer in her home city of Giza.

2. Kensington Market is found in Toronto, Ontario. It is located west of Chinatown. It contains produce stands, shops, cafés, and restaurants. It is multicultural.

3. Hazel Bishop was an American chemist. She was also a businesswoman. She invented a lipstick in 1949. The lipstick stayed on the lips a long time. She formed her own cosmetic company.

4. The Canada Food Guide was revised in 2002. It recommends that our diets include no more than 30 percent of calorie intake as fat. No more than 10 percent of fat calories should come from saturated fats.

5. The National Film Board of Canada was formed in 1939. It has produced more than 10 000 films. It has won more than 4000 awards. The NFB's head office is in Ottawa. Its operational headquarters is located in Montreal.

CHECKOUT

1. Preparation for writing a summary lays the foundation for critical thinking and persuasive writing.

2. There are several different reasons for writing a summary:
   - To use as a study tool
   - To make research information more accessible
   - To understand a writer's argument
   - To show the professor or instructor you understand the material
   - To deepen your comprehension
   - To provide a tool for someone else to get the information quickly

3. The six rules for summary writing are:
   - Leave out unnecessary information.
   - Delete information that repeats.
   - Cluster information under larger categories.
   - Select a topic sentence.
   - If there is no topic sentence, invent one that fits.
   - After following steps 1 to 5, rewrite using your own words.

chapter 16

Narrative Paragraphs

Chapter Objectives
What will you have learned when you have completed this chapter?
You will be able to

1. describe the four basic types of writing discussed in *Spotlight on Sentence and Paragraph Skills.*
2. tell if a piece of writing is an example of narrative writing.
3. write a narrative paragraph assignment.

Four Types of Writing

You will come across many different types of writing in your academic and leisure reading.

If you wish to tell a story, you will use a type of writing called *narrative writing*. In narrative, or story, writing, you move through what happens in a step-by-step fashion. You do not have to provide proof or evidence for your points. You are simply relating a series of events.

If you wish to describe something, you will use *descriptive writing*. In it, you describe how something looks, feels, tastes, smells, sounds, acts, or seems. You must use choice adjectives to make your description vivid and interesting for the reader.

If you wish to explain a process or how to do something, you will use *process* or *process analysis*. You explain how to do something, or how something is done. Your steps must be clear and must be presented in a logical way.

If you wish to convince or persuade your reader, you will use *persuasive writing*. You must state your position on a topic or issue and then develop clear reasons for this position. You must also use examples or more explanation to develop each of your points.

Exercise 1 Reading Four Types of Writing

Read each of the following paragraphs. Decide whether each paragraph is narrative, descriptive, process analysis, or persuasive. After each paragraph, write down its type. Be prepared to share your answers with the rest of the class.

Paragraph 1

My cousin Levi knows how to ripen green tomatoes easily. *First,* he strips all the tomatoes from his plants and brings them indoors. *Next,* he washes and dries each green tomato to be sure to get rid of mildew or disease on the surface. *Then* he lays five or six folded sheets of newspaper along a part of the kitchen counter that he does not use often. *After that,* he carefully lines up each tomato. *Then* he forgets about them for a few weeks. *Finally,* the tomatoes begin to turn a light pink followed by a slight orange until they begin to redden. The tomatoes provide a tasty addition to the family's diet without adding too much work for Levi.

Type of paragraph: _____

Notice how the words in italics help convey the idea of time. These words are called *transitions*, and they help the reader know where each steps begins and ends. (See Chapter 17 for more on transitions.)

Paragraph 2

I was *casually* walking by an *old-fashioned* jewellery store the other day when I spotted the *most beautiful animal* brooch I had ever seen. This *amazing* brooch was in the shape of a tiger. Its eyes sparkled with yellow gems that could have been chips of topaz. Its black stripes shone with black diamonds. At the end of its tail a *startling* red zircon twinkled in the light of the shop window. Although the little beauty caught my interest, I gasped and walked away after I noticed the $15 000 price tag!

Type of paragraph: _____

Notice that the words in italics add details to the description. Some of these words are adjectives that add colour and interest.

Paragraph 3

I do not agree with increasing rates for using public transit. First, I think the transit systems in our cities should be free to every citizen. To pay for operating and maintaining the system, we could use lottery money. We could have special lotteries for public transit, and all profits would be fed back. Furthermore, I believe that public transit could be operated more efficiently. If we cut costs, we would not have to keep raising rates. Cost cutting could come through using electric or battery power, using smaller and more economical buses, and redeveloping routes so that more users are on board. Therefore, I believe that by rethinking the idea of public transit our cities and bus riders would all benefit.

Type of paragraph: _____

Paragraph 4

My grandfather told me a story about how he was lost in the forest for two days when he was a little boy. He had been out berry-picking with the rest of the family. The day was hot and bright. My grandfather said he began to feel irritated by the heat, so he tried to move into the shade of the trees. He didn't notice he was moving farther and farther from his family. When he suddenly realized, he looked around but could not see anyone. He called and called, and even though his family answered, he was not able to move in the direction of their voices. He said he was so scared that all he could do was sit down and cry. Soon he could no longer hear their voices. After a few hours the sun started to set, so Grandfather knew he had better do something fast. His own father had taught him some important things about surviving in the bush. Grandfather tried to remember the teachings. He did recall that his father told him not to panic and to make a rough shelter out of tree boughs in case the weather got bad. Grandfather also remembered that his father had said to mark his own trail if he was going to find food or water. Grandfather knew which plants he could eat and which were poisonous. So he did the best he could, and after two days and two nights they found him, safe but a little shaken.

Type of paragraph: _____

Notice that the writer uses transitions to help his story move along. Keep in mind how important transitions are in your own written work.

Exercise 2 *Finding Four Types of Writing*

From magazine, newspapers, or Internet sources, find an example of each type of writing. Bring these samples to class. Your instructor might ask you to meet in groups to share the pieces and to discuss the following:

What did you like about the piece of writing?

Why is it (or is it not) a good example of the type of writing?

What do you notice about the writing style?

Keep a record of your discussion notes to use when you report your findings to the rest of the class.

Reading Narratives

Here are some examples of narratives. Notice that the writers begin with a topic sentence so that the reader will know what the paragraph is about. Work in pairs to answer the questions that follow each narrative. Be prepared to share your answers with the rest of the class.

Narrative 1: A Surprising Spider Story

Heather Maciorowski

The University of Manitoba Entomology Department had received a call from someone who had discovered a small tarantula resting on a bunch of bananas in the produce section of a local grocery store. Initially, the shopper thought the tarantula was simply a brown spot, but then, as the bananas were moved, the spot stretched its legs and tried to escape! The produce manager captured the spider in a jar and the Entomology Department was called: were we interested in this specimen?

I have always had a keen interest in insects as well as arachnids and so was dispatched to obtain "the prize"—a tarantula about the size of a toonie.

Back at the entomology lab, we housed our new guest in a terrarium. Now, the problem arose of what and how we would feed it. We placed grasshoppers and baby mice into the spider's new lair but neither proved to be of interest. It occurred to us that the tarantula might be dehydrated after its long journey hidden among the banana bunches, so I placed a Petri dish of water in the terrarium and watched as the tarantula approached the dish, lifted a foreleg and "tested" the contents. The tarantula then climbed into the water-filled dish and lowered its body into the water. I could almost hear an "aahhhhhh" as it soaked itself.

Thus rehydrated, we hoped the tarantula was ready to eat. One of the entomology professors kept a culture of large German cockroaches, which we thought might serve as a possible food source. Into the terrarium I placed a nice specimen bearing long thread-like antennae. The cockroach explored its new domain, antennae waving.

I watched as the cockroach approached the tarantula from the rear. One of the cockroach's antennae brushed the hairs on one of the spider's back legs. In a flash, the spider turned and grabbed the cockroach. Lunch had been served.

The tarantula lived in its terrarium for approximately a year and grew from the size of a toonie to the size of a saucer.

Dear Sad Goat: A Roundup of Truly Canadian Tales and Letters, Bill Richardson, ed. Reprinted by permission of Heather Maciorowski.

1. What did you find appealing in the story?

2. What surprised you?

3. What comments can you make about the writer's style?
   - Does she use effective adjectives?
   - Does she use effective comparisons?
   - Does she avoid clichés and vagueness?
   - Does she use a variety of sentence patterns?

4. Have you ever had something surprising like this happen to you? When? What was the experience like?

Narrative 2: Oh No, Ogopogo!

During the summer of 1990, our Hooge family gathering was at a campground between Summerland and Penticton. I had been looking forward to showing my father a business in Penticton for several years and this was my chance, so early Monday morning he and I headed into town. As we were rounding a small bay, my father said, "Look, there's the ogopogo." Intent on not being distracted from my mission, I glanced and said, "It's a log." He said, "No it's not," so I glanced again. It was moving, so I said, "It must be a wave from a boat." To this my father replied, "Do you see any boats?" So I looked again... the lake was smooth as glass and there wasn't a boat in sight. So I took a better look. Now, my eyesight at that distance (between 200 and 300 feet) is better than virtually anyone I've met, and what I saw was the side view of what appeared to be a long serpent swimming in the water. Its head was above the surface and was shaped like a sheep's head. The next 3 to 5 feet of its body was submerged, but the back 12–15 feet was breaking the surface of the water and it was leaving a wake. As I continued to watch, still not wanting to be distracted from showing my dad this business (and hopefully investing in getting me started in one), we rounded the little bay enough to see the creature from the back and it was definitely swimming like a big snake, smooth motion, forward and slipping toward the side. Walt Disney could not have created something more realistic looking. I am fully convinced that what I saw was the ogopogo... I am a believer. That evening my wife and brother and I returned to that bay and ended up talking to a couple pulling their boat out of the water. When I told them what I had seen, they said they had talked to an army sergeant from Vancouver who had witnessed the same thing in that location that day... and I heard from another local that this army sergeant had gone public with his sighting when he returned home.

Jack Hooge, **http://sunnyokanagan.com.** Courtesy of 20/10 Vision.

1. What did you like or dislike about the story?

2. What do you know about the legend of Ogopogo?

3. Do you know any other creature legends of Canada?

4. Have you ever had an experience with such creatures? When was your experience and what was it like?

Narrative 3: Volunteer Work Projects

Sylvia Rebelo and Cidalia Cota

The Destination Cuba Program from George Brown College has been participating in the Che Guevara Brigade for six years. Each year, the experience is unique. This year, the first two weeks of our stay were spent in Santa Clara in the dormitories of the Instituto de Sciencas—a medical school. Our focus in Santa Clara was working alongside Cubans, touring historical and cultural sites, and immersing ourselves in the Cuban culture.

Part of our work included painting the Casa Dos Abuelos—a seniors' home. Our painting time was limited, but some members of the brigade were able to use their artistic talents to create a spectacular, tropically themed mural that the seniors will be able to enjoy for years to come. Though our task was to provide a freshly painted residence for the seniors, our greatest pleasure came from the time we spent in conversation with them.

We also had the pleasure of working at *organopanicos* (organic farms). Here we spent our time picking weeds from row upon row of organic produce: guava, beets, carrots, lettuce, green beans and corn. The warm welcome and hospitality we received from the workers there made our experience that much richer. Not only did they take the time to share their knowledge of organic farming with us, they also provided us with an abundance of produce to take back to our residence. Our meals were much enhanced!

We also volunteered with the organic farm of the Instituto de Artes—an instructional art high school. We worked alongside Cuban students who were also doing volunteer work. We picked cucumbers and made the earth ready for planting by clearing away rocks. Working with the students was inspiring. It was great to see a young group of students giving back to the school they attend during the year.

Academic and Community Partnerships, George Brown College—Cuba (2002), Canada World Youth (**http://www.canadaworldyouth.org**).

1. Did the story appeal to you? Why or why not?

2. What transitions do the writers use?

3. Do you think these kinds of exchange projects are a good idea? Why or why not?

4. Have you ever volunteered for a project? What did you do? What was the experience like?

Narrative 4: Saskatoon Lad Olympic Winner

George Genereaux, 17-year-old Saskatoon school boy, today won the clay pigeon trapshooting championship at the Olympic games. Genereux's brilliant performance gave Canada its first Olympic gold medal since 1936.

Genereux won as Sweden's Kuut Holmquist missed the 24th of his final 25 shots to lose by one bird. Genereux had a point total of 192 out of a possible 200.

Holmquist needed a perfect round of 25 "kills" to tie the Canadian. Genereux's teammate, Roy Cole of Hamilton, placed 13th in the competition.

Genereux's eight-round total of 192 points was the figure he predicted earlier would win the championship. His scores for the eight rounds were 24–24–24–23–24–24–25–24, a remarkably consistent record.

Genereux is holder of the North American junior and Saskatchewan open trapshooting championships. The six-foot, dark-haired youth with the crew cut won the mid-western invitation trapshooting handicap in Winnipeg 1949 when he was only 14. In that same year and in 1950 he won the Manitoba-Saskatchewan junior championship.

He won the North American title last year.

Today's final shoot between the lad from the Canadian West and the 34-year-old Swedish furniture merchant was the second dramatic struggle between the two.

Today it looked as though another shoot-off were in prospect. On his last round, Genereux, the gallery's favourite, fired a 24 out of a possible 25, missing on his 24th shot to spoil what would have been his second straight perfect round.

The only competitor who could catch Genereux was Holmquist, shooting his first year in international competition. With Holmquist needing a 25 for a tie, and a shoot-off, it looked for a long time as though he would make it as 23 straight birds fell.

Then the Swede missed the 24th, just as Genereux had done before him, and the title went to Canada. It was Canada's first clay pigeon crown since W.H. Ewing of Montreal won it in 1908.

Genereux fired as his mother, Mrs. Catherine Genereux, watched from the gallery. He will receive his Olympic gold medal—Canada's first of the 1952 games—in a ceremony Sunday.

Genereux acquired his love for trapshooting by tagging along with his father hunting prairie chickens.

Saskatoon Star Phoenix [Souvenir Edition] July 26, 1952. Helsinki [CP], **http://library.usask.ca**
Reprinted by permission of The Canadian Press.

1. What do you notice about the style of writing in this article?

2. When was it written? Do you believe writing styles change?

3. Why is this story important, do you think?

4. Do you agree that there are "small heroes"? Why or why not?

Narrative 5: Aboriginal Culture and Spirit

Dave Yanko

La Ronge—In the early 1990s, Cree Elder Sally Milne decided she was going to become the best in the world at something. Precisely what that something was going to be, she didn't know. In fact at the time, she didn't know why she felt so compelled to excel.

Milne first considered cross-country skiing. She had very little experience with the winter sport. But the date of a popular, all-abilities competition was approaching and she thought the event might be a good opportunity to measure her potential. Before it arrived, however, event organizers asked her to provide some prizes in the form of birch bark bitings she'd just recently begun to create...

"I'm now one of the four most renowned bark biters in the world," Milne proclaims, her small smile growing into a hearty laugh as she adds: "There's a total of four of us in the world!"

Of course the last part is not true—Milne's humour is often self-deprecating and seldom far from the surface during a chat at the La Ronge Band RCMP office where she works as an Aboriginal resource person. The truth is that in less than 10 years, her exquisite designs have found their way into homes in Germany, Austria, England, Scotland, China, Australia and New Zealand. Here in North America, Canadian Governor-General Adrienne Clarkson and Hollywood movie star Bruce Willis are among those who own and admire her birch bark bitings.

Sally Milne has become the best at something. She's an Aboriginal artist with a global reputation. And she now believes she understands why she felt moved to attain her high standing.

"Society has to have a wider picture of who you are. It's like: Sally Milne is a well-known artist so, okay, we can take her seriously. That's what it's for. It's to gain credibility in the mainstream society."

Milne needs this credibility to maximize her reach and effectiveness as a teacher of traditional Native culture. And while she searched for it "out there," she now sees clearly that the means to achieve it were inside of her all the time. She believes her path was set out for her by the "Seven Grandfathers," spiritual keepers of the traditional Native principles of love, respect, honesty, peace, patience, courage and wisdom. She likens these laws to Christianity's Ten Commandments, except Native culture focuses on the "shalts" rather than the "shalt nots." And each tenet must be accepted as second nature before the next one can be learned.

"When the Grandfathers look at you they can see where your heart is at," says Milne. "You have to love yourself before you can love others. You have to respect yourself before you can respect others."

Aside from the public recognition it's given her, Milne's art plays an important role in her personal life. She says it gives her strength by connecting her to the beauty and tranquillity she knew as a young girl growing up on the trapline in the boreal forest of northern Saskatchewan. Yet she's disarmingly matter-of-fact about bark biting and the amount of effort involved in its creation.

It takes three or four weekends each summer to collect most of the bark required for a year's worth of bitings, she says. The most difficult and time-consuming aspect of the entire process is not the actual biting, but rather the peeling of thin layers of bark used for the designs.

"Once I've got the bark [prepared], then every once in a while I'll sit down to watch a movie and I'll make these bitings," says Milne. "Then I just stick them in books and forget about them."

Each biting is produced in a matter of minutes. She once created 83 or 84—she wasn't sure of the precise number—in one sitting. She has hundreds of the bitings, which she sells for as little as $15, filed in books throughout her home.

The intricate, symmetrical types are created by folding a segment of bark and "bruising" it with her teeth. Milne's designs typically depict butterflies, bees or dragonflies in a forest setting.

"I used to do a lot of spiders, too, but it seems nobody except me liked them."

Traditional Woodland Cree used bark bitings as templates for decorating baskets with quills. There was no "art for art's sake" in the nomadic lives of the Cree, according to Milne. Arts and crafts were used as decoration for necessities such as clothing, tools and utensils. The bitings were discarded after serving their purpose.

Milne credits her traditional upbringing on the trapline and her late entry into the infamous residential school system—she was 12 before she went to school in Prince Albert—with helping her to value the goals of balance and harmony in her adult life.

She says much Cree culture and spirituality was lost over the past century as traditional knowledge normally passed down by Elders was replaced by an alien culture imposed by Euro-Canadian schools and churches.

So well removed was the Lac La Ronge band from its roots, says Milne, that she and others interested in spiritual renewal were forced to go to Manitoba and Alberta to relearn much of the traditional knowledge and understanding behind Woodland Cree ceremonies and traditional spiritual practices.

Milne, who in 1984 began teaching Cree culture at the band school in La Ronge, reflects on the trials facing many Aboriginal peoples in a teacher's guide she wrote called *Living in a Good Way*. In it, she asks readers to imagine someone stripping them naked and permanently removing them from their homes and from everything they own.

"And then after a time, when your dignity, self-respect and pride are gone, this same someone comes and says: 'Come, from now on I'll look after you, your every need will depend on how I feel at the moment.'" The guide goes on to show how an understanding of traditional culture can help give Aboriginal youth the tools they need to lead balanced and fulfilling lives in modern times.

Today, in addition to her nine-to-five job, Milne is a medicine woman who specializes in the treatment of people suffering emotional problems, especially children.

She teaches a university extension class in Cree culture—she's the first person in Saskatchewan to teach a university class without having a university degree. And she's helped five young people earn their master's degrees by being their source of information on traditional aspects of Aboriginal knowledge.

"I tell the kids, 'Find out who you are and you can take it with you anywhere you go. It doesn't matter where you live or what you do—you can be a rocket scientist. But you still have to have this knowledge about yourself.'"

There was a point in Milne's young adult life when she began to doubt her traditional beliefs. She recalls thinking that maybe she'd been wrong all along. Maybe the people whose values she held dear really were as backward as some suggested.

"I thought the best thing to do was to go back [to the trapline] and see for myself," she said. "So I went back home and, by gawd, they were great!"

And with that, Sally Milne laughed heartily.

Virtual Saskatchewan, **www.virtualsk.com/current_issue/culture_and_spirit.html.** Courtesy of Dave Yanko, virtualsk.com.

1. What do you notice about the style of writing in the piece?

2. What do people admire about Sally Milne's work?

3. What teachings are spoken about in the article?

4. Do you create art of any sort? How did you get started? Why is your work important to you?

WRITING ASSIGNMENT 2 Narrative

Write a story paragraph (a narrative paragraph) of at least 300 words about an important event in your life. You should begin your paragraph with a topic sentence. Use separate paper. Double space your work.

CHECKOUT

1. *Spotlight on Sentence and Paragraph Skills* concentrates on three basic types of paragraph writing.
   - narrative
   - descriptive
   - explanatory

2. Some things to keep in mind when reading paragraphs:
   - Decide what you like about the piece of writing.
   - Examine whether it is a good example of a basic type of writing or not.
   - Notice the writing style.
   - Keep a record of your observations.

3. Reading can help improve your writing.

4. To be good at writing, you must practise.

chapter 17

Descriptive Paragraphs

Chapter Objectives

What will you have learned when you have completed this chapter?
You will be able to

1. use classification as a tool for arranging ideas in your writing.

2. apply different arrangements to your writing.

3. use comparisons such as similes in your writing.

4. analyze what makes up good descriptive writing by reading selected passages.

5. recognize a cliché in your own and others' writing.

6. recognize stereotypes in your own and others' writing.

7. write a descriptive paragraph about a place.

8. write a descriptive paragraph about a person.

9. write a descriptive paragraph about an event or situation.

Using Classification as a Tool

You may find that descriptions are easier to write than other forms of writing such as *persuasive* (written to convince the reader) or *expository* (written to inform the reader). Perhaps you prefer descriptive writing because you can base it on your experience, senses, and imagination. Perhaps you find descriptive writing simply more pleasurable.

As a writer, you can remember in your mind's eye what something looked like. You can recall how it smelled, tasted, felt, or sounded. In describing, you attempt to translate your sensations into words. Your imagination will often assist you because we are never able to remember sensations exactly: we can remember only the memories of an experience. To be able to describe something or an event so that it can be understood and appreciated by someone else is a remarkable and much-valued skill.

You often use descriptions in your life. You have probably found yourself describing a movie or television show to someone else. Or you might have explained to friends what some experience was like. If you tell them about travelling to another country, for example, part of your story will be descriptive. You may give details of what a place looked like, what buildings you saw, or what the food tasted like. Obviously, your description will contain many adjectives and other modifiers to add detail and interest.

As a writer, before you describe something, you must really concentrate on the thing you are going to describe. You must decide how you want to go about arranging your ideas.

One method of organizing involves classifying. *Classifying* helps you organize what you see, hear, taste, touch, smell, or feel. In doing so, you group your ideas or sensations into categories. For example, if you want to describe a particular flavour of a food to someone else who hasn't tasted it, you may classify the taste by making some comparisons with your own experiences. You might classify the taste like this:

sweet or not sweet
sour or not sour
bitter or not bitter
salty or not salty

After this first rough classification, you can settle on a more particular detail. You might decide to select the idea of sourness. Perhaps the flavour you remember had a hint of salt in it, too. So, you then decide that the taste was sour, yet salty.

Next you try to get your meaning across by applying your classification to a shared experience. In other words, you compare. You think of something that is sour—a lemon, perhaps. Then you think of something from your experience (and from the other person's, you hope) that tastes salty—a peanut. Your description might then be: "It tastes tangy like a lemon, but salty like a peanut." In describing the taste, then, you have done two things: you have classified and compared. First you classified the taste into categories, and then you compared it to something similar.

Two Methods of Classification

In general, there are two methods of classification:

1. from a general thing to a specific thing (large to small). This method of classification is sometimes referred to as *deductive thinking*. You use this general to specific classification in deductive thinking.

general	more specific	more specific	most specific
printed material	→ books	→ novels	→ *Space Vampires*

2. from a specific thing to a general thing (small to large). This method of classification is sometimes referred to as *inductive thinking*. You use this specific to general classification in inductive thinking.

specific	more general	more general	most general
toy poodle	→ dogs	→ mammals	→ animals

Of course, there are many other ways to classify, depending on your point of view and your purpose. When you write from a personal point of view, for example, your classification will relate to your own experiences and beliefs. If you are writing an English literature essay and intending to give broad information, your classification can be widened, made more global. Conversely, if you are writing a paper on marine biology, for example, you must use a highly specialized form of scientific classification.

Exercise 1 Classifying: Specific to General

Classify the items below from the specific (smallest) to the most general (largest) group. Think of all the items as nouns. Use a three-step classification in your thinking:

1. the item
2. a more general category to which the item belongs
3. the most general category to which the item belongs

You may check your answers with the Answer Key at the back of the book.

Example: Maxx jeans   →   pants   →   clothing

Item	More General Category	Most General Category
1. Bayer's aspirin	_____	_____
2. Toshiba microwave	_____	_____
3. Toyota Rava	_____	_____
4. drone	_____	_____
5. prickly pear	_____	_____
6. poutine	_____	_____
7. romaine	_____	_____
8. oyster	_____	_____
9. Big Mac	_____	_____
10. shoe	_____	_____
11. prime minister	_____	_____
12. parsley	_____	_____
13. spear	_____	_____
14. owl	_____	_____
15. swallowtail butterfly	_____	_____
16. lollipop	_____	_____
17. dictionary	_____	_____
18. teenager	_____	_____
19. whisk	_____	_____
20. engineer	_____	_____

You probably had to think quite hard about your answers—surprising when you consider that the items listed are common things. The difference is that you may not have thought about them in this way before.

Writing is also thinking—very actively. To consider things in a certain way in order to solve a problem or to get the answer to something else is called a *strategy*. Classification is one of the strategies you can use in thinking and writing. Your path to an answer becomes clearer.

Exercise 2 *Classifying: General to Specific*

Classify the items below from the largest category (general) to the most particular (specific) one. Think of all the items as nouns. Use a three-step classification in your thinking:

1. the most general category to which the item belongs
2. a more specific category to which the item belongs
3. the specific item

You may check your answers with the examples given in the Answer Key.

Example: education → post-secondary → Wallis College

General	More Specific	Most Specific Category
1. celebrity	_____	_____
2. appliance	_____	_____
3. hobby	_____	_____
4. wood	_____	_____
5. alcohol	_____	_____
6. food	_____	_____
7. emotion	_____	_____
8. invention	_____	_____
9. country	_____	_____
10. music	_____	_____
11. sport	_____	_____
12. travel	_____	_____
13. tool	_____	_____
14. herb	_____	_____
15. furniture	_____	_____
16. book	_____	_____
17. fear	_____	_____
18. recreation	_____	_____
19. family	_____	_____
20. poetry	_____	_____

Classification at Work in the World

The concept of classification is not just something found in a book like this one. You will notice the two methods of classification used all the time at work and home.

First consider how the specific-to-general classification can be used in different ways every day. Scientific knowledge is based on this strategy. For example, a scientist may be working on an experiment in his or her laboratory. He or she notices something specific happening in the experiment that has never happened before. The experiment is set up again and again, and the same surprising thing happens. From this series of experiments, the scientist discovers a new general idea and principle. Biology, the study of living things, also uses classification. Animals have been grouped into larger classes because of the specific traits they share. In addition, social science uses classification as a means of investigation. Police work, especially in forensic science, makes use of this strategy. A particular clue or set of clues leads to more general information. In this case, the general information might be the identity of the criminal.

In your everyday life, you use classification, too. You might be doing some house repairs. As you go along, you learn little specific bits of information that you can use in a general way. You might learn, for example, something about laying carpets when you make your first attempt. You can then apply this information to another room that needs carpet, and from there you can apply what you have learned to any situation that requires carpet-laying. Each time you do something, you become more expert at doing it because you learn something specific that can be applied in a general way.

Classifying from the general to the specific is another "real world" strategy you use in thinking and learning. In the work world, for instance, it is used all the time. Perhaps you are hoping to set up a business because you like being your own boss. You must decide what type of business to launch. Perhaps you want to begin in retail, with your own store. Now you have to decide on its location: where is the best place and why is it favourable? Then you have to ask yourself what merchandise will be sold. In short, you will soon recognize that each step in the planning process moves from the general to the specific.

Even when you are shopping, you are classifying. When you want to buy shoes, you must decide what style, what colour, and what price to pay. You also have to consider what is available in the stores. Even a trip to the grocery store will involve some classifying for you. You must decide what meals to plan, what fits your budget, and so forth.

Exercise 3 Classification at Work and at Home

Think of some of your own examples of how classification is used in the workplace and at home. Complete the chart below. Give two examples for each. Use the same three-step classification.

Example:

Item: Community

specific	more general	most general
paying taxes	civic duty	citizenship

general	more specific	most specific
civil society	voting	citizen's rights

Item: work world

Specific to General   General to Specific

_____   _____

_____   _____

_____   _____

Item: home

Specific to General   General to Specific

_____   _____

_____   _____

_____   _____

Comparisons and Descriptive Language

Using comparisons can also help you in your descriptive writing. *Comparison* means looking for similarities—in what ways two things are the same. You use comparisons a good deal of the time. Each time you say that something is like something else, you are comparing the two items.

You now have two tools to assist you in your writing. First, you may use classification to help your thinking, understanding, and organizing of ideas. Next, you make use of comparison, comparing an experience, appearance, or idea to something else. When you are looking for similarities, you will often use *like* or *as*.

Like and *As* Comparisons

You often compare two things by telling what something is like in relation to something else. You would almost certainly use the prepositions *like* or *as* to link the two ideas. These words help you show your reader that you are establishing a close connection or relationship between two concepts, ideas, features, or conditions.

Shane is angry <u>as</u> a troll today.
The buttons were <u>as</u> colourful <u>as</u> fruit salad.
Amil's guitar playing was <u>as</u> soothing <u>as</u> gentle waves.
My cousin Janice is <u>as</u> nosey <u>as</u> a terrier.
Her paintings look <u>like</u> my nightmares.
The dancer moved <u>like</u> a snowflake in the breeze.
The helicopter sounded <u>like</u> a gigantic washing machine.
When she sang, Belinda's voice was <u>like</u> a song sparrow's.

Like and *as* expressions are known as *similes*. You have probably noticed similes when you read poetry, short stories, and novels. Mystery writers and poets are particularly fond of using similes in their writing.

Writers have to use them carefully. Similes can be complete successes or failures. Ernest Hemingway, a famous American novelist who lived in the twentieth century, wrote a letter to the art critic Bernard Berenson. In it, he said "Similes could be like defective ammunition." In other words, although similes can have great power, they can also fall flat and not have much effect at all.

Exercise 4   Group Activity: Reading and Interpreting Similes

Work with two or three other students as a group, and read the following excerpts. Discuss the answers to the following three questions:

What two things are being compared?

How are these two items similar?

Why might the writer have chosen these two items for comparison?

Be prepared to share your answers with the rest of the class.

1. Diddy Shovel's skin was like asphalt, fissured and cracked. (Annie Proulx, *The Shipping News*)

2. The word *hand* floats above your hand / like a small cloud over a lake (Margaret Atwood, "You Begin")

3. We have taken the night / like a Persian black cat / into bed with us. (Irving Layton, "Nightfall")

4. bright glimpse of beauty / striking like a bell (P.K. Page, "After Rain")

5. The legs she stuck out into the sun were shiny and discoloured and faintly cracked, like old plates. (Alice Munro, "Hired Girl")

6. The day rose up around them like a sheet of fire and everything and everyone fell into a torpor. (Timothy Findley, *Not Wanted on the Voyage*)

Comparisons and Clichés

You may recall that *clichés* are overused expressions. When you are using comparisons, choose them carefully so as to avoid clichés. Some similes may be more common than you think. Consider these:

hungry as a bear	sunk like a stone	fit as a fiddle
sick as a dog	sweet as sugar	proud as a peacock
tough as leather	light as a feather	sober as a judge
clear as crystal	cute as a button	busy as a bee
blind as a bat	cool as a cucumber	old as the hills
neat as a pin	eats like a pig	dry as a bone
flat as a pancake	heavy as lead	pretty as a picture

strong as an ox	still as a graveyard	slept like a baby
worked like a slave	acted like a baby	as good as gold
roared like a lion	free as a bird	skinny as a rail
nutty as a fruitcake	drinks like a fish	wise as an owl
moved like a cat	slippery as an eel	smart as a whip
like walking on eggshells	straight as an arrow	yellow as gold
slow as a snail	brown as a berry	green as grass
stubborn as a mule	hard as steel	quick as a wink
hollow as a drum	pale as a ghost	black as pitch
dead as a doornail	mad as a wet hen	sly like a fox
free as the wind	warm as toast	right as rain

No doubt you have heard many of these comparisons. You may notice that common similes often involve animals. Whether their connotations are positive or negative, these images evoke strong feeling in cultures. But since most of these similes are used so frequently, they have become too familiar to have any impression on us at all.

Exercise 5 Using Like and As Comparisons

Add some similes of your own in the spaces below. Avoid using any clichés; instead, try to create original, thought-provoking comparisons. Use one or more words, and try to be descriptive. Add subjects to each of the sentences. Your instructor may wish to see this exercise, or you may be asked to share and discuss your answers with others in class.

Example: Riva was as elegant as a swan.

1. The _____ was as cold as _____.

2. _____ is as tiny as a _____.

3. _____ are as soft as _____.

4. _____ is as tall as a _____.

5. _____ has a voice like (a) _____.

6. _____ was as angry as a _____.

7. _____ is as nervous as a _____.

8. _____ has a face like a _____.

9. The traffic today was like _____.

10. The story was as boring as _____.

11. Use a simile in a complete sentence describing how your friend looked at a ceremony.

12. Use a simile in a complete sentence describing how proud your friend was when he became a father.

13. Use a simile in a complete sentence describing how friendly you are.

14. Use a simile in a complete sentence describing what someone's dress is like.

15. Use a simile in a complete sentence describing how happy a couple is.

Describing Places

Classification helps you think about things by putting them in an order you can understand. You learned that inductive and deductive thinking help arrange your classification in orderly ways and that *similes* can brighten your written expression. How would you use classification as a tool if you wanted to describe a place?

Suppose you wished to describe a house that you had lived in as a child. You would have to think of some way of arranging ideas so that your reader could easily follow your written description. In this case, classification would not mean conceptualizing by category. Instead, it would make better sense for you to think about using a spatial organization.

You need a plan for descriptive writing. First, you could provide a general context for the house by briefly describing its surroundings and the neighbourhood (*most general*). Next, you could classify your ideas by working from the outside of the house to the inside. You might describe the outside of the house using either a top-to-bottom or a bottom-to-top approach. After that, you could describe the inside—the overall floor plan or layout of the rooms (*more specific*). You would then have to think about how you would arrange your description of each room. Would you describe from left to right or from right to left? Would you use a top-to-bottom approach or the alternative (*more specific*)? You may conclude your piece by describing your favourite part of the house (*most specific*).

Conversely, you could describe the house from specific to general. For instance, you could start with your favourite room (bottom to top, top to bottom, left to right, or right to left) and then describe the rest of the rooms, followed by the outside of the house, the yard, your neighbours' places, and the immediate neighbourhood.

Or you also could organize your description from a different perspective altogether. You could use another person's point of view, one of your children's, for example, or the builder's. You could even imagine it from your pet's point of view. How would your cat or dog go about describing your place if it could?

You can see that there are a variety of ways to organize your ideas. You will think more clearly by using classification and choosing one point of view. If you use your classification wisely, it will help your reader to visualize the object, place, person, or experience you are writing about.

Exercise 6 Ordering Place Descriptions

Choose three of the places from the list below, and follow the instructions given. Write in complete sentences. Your instructor may wish to check this exercise or may have you share your answers with the class.

a fairground	a lunchroom	your office	a bakery
a restaurant	a daycare centre	a service station	a video arcade
an airport	a marina	a meeting room	a music store
a hotel	a florist's shop	a craft shop	the mayor's office
a nursery	a dock	a fish and chip shop	an equipment yard
a movie theatre	a ferry terminal	a church or temple	a hockey arena
a shopping mall	a schoolyard in summer		

1. Tell how you would begin your description. In other words, what sort of classification would you use: general to specific or specific to general?
2. Tell how you would arrange your description. Would you use a top-to-bottom or bottom-to-top approach? Would you describe from left to right or from right to left?
3. Next, provide some specific modifiers that you would use to describe the place. You may wish to consult your thesaurus.
4. Finally, use two *like* or *as* comparisons (similes) you want to include in your description.

Example: library

1. I would use a general-to-specific classification. I would begin by describing the outside of the building (from the roof to the main floor). I would then move from the outside steps to the inside. Once inside, I would describe the main floor only.
2. I would describe the main floor from the left to the right. I would begin with the information desk on the left and go right around the room to end with the copying machines.
3. Some modifiers I would choose are *sombre, eerie, strained, cluttered, enthralling, intense, overwhelming, silently, with a slouch, in a jumble,* and *stuffy.*
4. I might use *stuffy as a crypt,* the room was shaped *like a coffin,* and *the student was studying a book as intensely as a cat does a bird* for my comparisons.

Reading Other Writers' Place Descriptions

Did you know that reading can help improve your writing? Writers can learn many things about writing by reading others writers' work. You must learn to pay attention to how authors go about saying something in their writing. When you are learning about writing, you should be doing a lot of your own reading.

You can train yourself to read with the eyes of a writer. Start by noticing the word choices the author makes. What kinds of sentences has the writer constructed? What are some of the images you develop from what the writer has created? What sorts of details did the writer include? How effective was the writer's language in your opinion?

The following readings have been taken from well-known writers' works. Study each reading carefully with a writer's eye. Be prepared to answer some questions afterwards.

Selection 1

Beyond the gardens the ground sloped steeply down to the river, like a cliff with huge boulders sticking out of the clay. Paths threaded their way down the slope between the boulders and pits dug out by the potters, and bits of brown and red clay piled up in great heaps. Down below a bright green, broad and level meadow opened out—it had already been mown and the village cattle were grazing on it. The meandering river with its magnificent leafy banks were almost a mile from the village and beyond were more broad pastures, cattle, long strings of white geese, and then the familiar steep slope on its far side. At the top stood a village, a church with five "onion" domes, with the manor-house a little further on.

—Anton Chekhov, "Peasants"

Selection 2

He was lying on an old bedstead, which turned up during the day. The tattered remains of a checked curtain were drawn round the bed's head, to exclude the wind, which however made its way into the comfortless room through the numerous chinks in the door, and blew it to and fro every instant. There was a low cinder fire in a rusty unfixed grate; and an old three-cornered stained table, with some medicine bottles, a broken glass, and a few other domestic articles, was drawn out before it. A little child was sleeping on a temporary bed which had been made for it on the floor, and the woman sat on a chair by its side. There were a couple of shelves, with a few plates and cups and saucers: and a pair of stage shoes and a couple of foils hung beneath them. With the exception of little heaps of rags and bundles which had been carelessly thrown into the corners of the room, these were the only things in the apartment.

—Charles Dickens, *The Pickwick Papers*

Selection 3

I had about another five miles to drive, and the road, hardly more now than two black furrows cut into the prairie, was uneven and bumpy. The land was fenced on both sides of the road, and at last I came to a rough wooden gate hanging loosely on one hinge, and beyond it there was a cluster of small wooden buildings. The largest of these, the house itself, seemed at one time to have been ochre-coloured, but the paint had worn off and now it looked curiously mottled. A few chickens were wandering about, pecking at the ground, and from the back I could hear the grunting and squeaking of pigs.

—Henry Kreisel, "The Broken Globe"

Selection 4

Orry led him down a great, empty, glowing corridor and through a valve-door into a small room. "The Garden," he said aloud, and the valve-door shut; there was no sense of motion but when it opened, they stepped out into a garden. It was scarcely out of doors: the translucent walls glimmered with the lights of the City, far below; the moon, near full, shone hazy and distorted through the glassy roof. The place was full of soft moving lights and shadows, crowded with tropical shrubs and vines that twined about trellises and hung from arbours, their masses of cream and crimson flowers sweetening the steamy air, their leafage closing off vision within a few feet of every side. Falk turned suddenly to make sure that the path to the exit still lay clear behind him. The hot, heavy, perfumed silence was uncanny; it seemed to him for a moment that the ambiguous depths of the garden held a hint of something alien and enormously remote, the hues, the mood, the complexity of a lost world, a planet of perfumes and illusions, of swamps and transfor-mations.

—Ursula K. Le Guin, *City of Illusions*

Selection 5

The streets of most ancient Greek cities were muddy, filthy alleys, although a few were paved with slabs of fieldstone, with a dressing of mortar. There was no attempt at drainage. The stroller hardened to the cry: "Exit!" ("Coming out!") which meant that a load of refuse was about to be thrown into the street.

—L. Sprague de Camp, *The Ancient Engineers*

Exercise 7   *Responding to the Readings*

Refer to reading selections 1 to 5 to answer the following questions. Do your work on separate paper. Answer in complete sentences. Check your answers with the Answer Key.

Selection 1

1. What in general does the paragraph describe?

2. How does Chekhov describe the meadow? Find specific adjectives.

3. How does he describe the pastures?

4. What word does he use to describe the way the paths were laid out?

5. How does he describe the geese?

6. What two adjectives does he use to describe the river's banks?

Selection 2

1. What in general does the paragraph describe?

2. What adjectives does Dickens use to describe the table?

3. What other objects are found in the room?

4. What feeling do you get from reading the paragraph?

Selection 3

1. What in general does the paragraph describe?

2. How does Kreisel describe the house?

3. What adjectives does he use to describe the road?

4. How does he describe the gate?

Selection 4

1. What in general does the paragraph describe?

2. What adjectives does Le Guin use to describe the garden?

3. What smells can you "smell" as you read?

4. How does the paragraph make you feel?

Selection 5

1. What is de Camp describing here?

2. What language—emotional or non-emotional—does the writer use?

3. Are there many descriptive words in the passage?

You will have noticed that these reading selections describe very different places, some imagined, others perhaps experienced. Did you "read like a writer," as noted psycholinguist and reading expert Frank Smith suggests? Did you notice the arrangement of ideas in each of the selections?

If you look back at the first reading selection, you will see that Chekhov uses a general-to-specific arrangement of detail. As you read, you begin outside the village and move in to take a closer look. You get a general sense of the farmlands and their orderliness, and then you move to a specific feature of the village—a church.

In selection 2, did you notice that Dickens places you in a small, cramped space? He does not let you "leave" the confines of the miserable apartment. Instead, as a reader, you are forced to "look" around the place and take in all the specific details that add up to a description of poverty.

In selection 3 Kreisel uses a general-to-specific arrangement. He begins at a distance, and then moves the reader into the barnyard where he describes what animals he sees and hears.

If you turn back to selection 4 and reread it, you can see how specific Le Guin's details are. She has chosen a general-to-specific order, beginning on the outside and then moving into the special garden. As a reader, you get a sense of what is outside the glass roof of the garden and then feel as if your eyes are moving up and down, following the light and shadows and the twisted greenery on the trellis walls. You can smell the fragrance of the garden. As Le Guin takes you on a tour of the room, you can feel the space with your senses.

In selection 5, you will notice that de Camp's description is general, in that he refers to "most ancient Greek cities." You get a broad sense of the place rather than of a specific building or street.

These selections may help you think about arrangement of ideas and details in descriptive pieces of writing. You can learn a great deal by putting your writer's eye to work whenever you read description.

Preparing a Descriptive Paragraph

Useful Transitions

A valuable device for writers is the *transition*, a word or phrase that signals a change in thought. You might wish to use a transition for one or more of the following purposes:

- to add an idea
- to indicate a change in time or a step in a process
- to contrast a point
- to show a spatial relationship
- to provide an example
- to conclude a point

Useful Transitions for Writing Descriptions	
For Spatial Relationships	**For Adding Ideas**
across	also
next to	first
to the left	and
below	second
to the right	in addition
above	third
near	furthermore
between	last
nearby	next
close to	moreover
	besides
	finally

Transitions in Descriptive Writing

- I could tell by the way Juanita had decorated her room that she loved flowers. *First,* a large vase of yellow roses was on the side of her desk. *Next,* I noticed that the wallpaper was a pattern of white peonies and mauve clematis. *Finally,* the quilt on her bed was made up of floral fabric.
- My doctor's office is rather austere looking. A plain bookshelf sits *on the left of* the entrance to the office. *Next to* that is a brown couch upholstered in a faded corduroy. *In front of* the couch is a small table that holds magazines about fishing, curling, and golf. *On the other side of* the small table is the receptionist's desk where the office computer is proudly displayed. A large, lateral filing cabinet is fixed in the space *to the right of* the desk. *Nearby* a small green fern in a stand adds colour to the dingy tones of the office.
- *As* customers enter the new mall, they will be assailed by the smell of fresh bread coming from the baker's shop *to the immediate right of* the main entrance *and* the aroma of pizza wafting over from the pizzeria *on the opposite side.*

Writing Steps

Good writing takes hard work. By now you have probably recognized this rather troublesome truth. Writing is much more than learning lots and lots of rules. Writing is about doing writing—actively and frequently. To be good at anything, you must practise what you know and be prepared to learn from your mistakes and successes. Writing is not a single process.

It involves several stages:

1. prewriting (planning and thinking)

2. initial drafting (first attempt)

3. revising (rewriting)

4. editing (improving the effectiveness of phrasing, grammar, and sentence sense)

5. proofreading (finding typing errors, spacing problems, and careless mistakes such as missing a word, having words or lines repeating, missing page numbers, bad print quality, paragraph indentation, and so forth)

6. presentation (checking for correct pagination, title page, correct size of font, clear copy, and no spills or messes on the pages)

Ten Suggested Writing Steps to Follow

1. **Select an interesting topic.** Choose a topic that you know something about and that you find interesting. When you are assigned course work, you will usually be given a generous number of topics from which to choose. Select something engaging, challenging, or fun.

2. **Check the "fit" of the topic.** Take the topic and work with it for a few minutes. Write down what you think you know about it. Write down a rough plan for what

you would do with the topic. Then sit back and read what you have written. Does it look as if the topic has the fit you are looking for?

3. **Develop a rough writing plan.** Draw a line down the centre of a blank sheet of paper. On the left half of the page, jot down the main points you wish to discuss. On the right half, add details. Include some transition words in your notes to help remind you to use these words when you write.

4. **Be organized.** How you organize your material is just as important as what you have to say. Having lots of ideas is wonderful, but you must arrange them so that they can be understood. Just jotting down ideas as they "flow" to you is a fine technique for getting your writing started, but you will be the only person who can understand what your notes mean. Since your writing must be understood by your readers, it must be organized and clear.

5. **Write your first draft.** A *draft* is an attempt, an unpolished version of a piece of writing. Just start to write, consulting your rough writing plan from time to time. Be prepared to work through several drafts. Do not expect your first draft to be error-free.

6. **Let your ideas rest.** Leave your first draft overnight or for a day or two. Then reread it. You will notice what needs changing—what you will need to revise. Try writing a second draft with a mind to making it better. Think about improving word choice, clarity, sentence sense, and organization.

7. **Get an audience.** Have someone else read your next draft. Listen to what the person tells you. What parts did the person like? What parts did the person find difficult to follow? What changes will you make based on the person's comments?

8. **Revise.** Rewrite according to your reader's comments and your own sense of the phrasing, organization, and clarity of expression. You are almost at the final drafting stage.

9. **Proofread your final draft.** Read line by line. Look for careless errors in spelling, typing, spacing, pagination, omission, repetition, and punctuation. Use a coloured highlighter and highlight the proofing errors as you see them.

10. **Check the presentation of your final draft.** Prepare a clear title page. Centre the title. In the bottom right corner, type in your name, the course name and section, the date of handing in, and your instructor's name. Look through all the pages to be sure they are paginated correctly. Look for spills or smudges on the page, and prepare a fresh page if needed. Be certain you know what presentation your instructor prefers. You may think that a fancy 14-point font will delight him or her, but you may be surprised. Most instructors accept only 11- or 12-point font in certain fonts.

   Perhaps it may seem trivial to talk about presentation of an assignment, but you should know that it makes a difference. Instructors are busy people. They do not have time to translate your good intentions. Your professional-looking, carefully prepared paper will send a message to your instructor. A messy, haphazardly prepared assignment sends another.

Be patient with yourself as you work through your writing assignments. Writing will become easier with more experience. Expect that it will take effort. You will make some mistakes. Your writing will not be perfect, so be kind to yourself and allow the mistakes to benefit you.

Tips for Revising and Proofreading

1. **Separate the composer and the editor in you.** The composer side of you wants to write down ideas as fast as they come. The editor side of you wants to stop and correct every little error. Separate the composer from the editor. Don't worry about mechanical mistakes when you are first getting your ideas out on paper. When you compose or let your ideas get out on the page, you should think only of the ideas, and if they are meaning what you want them to mean and making sense at the same time.

2. **Edit selectively.** When you edit, you are looking for grammar errors, sentence-level errors, ineffective phrasing, errors in logic, and possible revisions. A good rule of thumb to follow is to select only one or two features to look for at a time. For example, if commas give you trouble, look for comma errors only. If you know that you have a bad habit of running ideas together, during the next reading look only for run-on sentences. Go line by line. Use a highlighter in a bright colour to help draw your attention to the error; this practice will make retyping and repairing easier for you. When you are proofreading, use a different-coloured highlighter. Proofreading errors are easy to overlook, so do the reading carefully, slowly examining one sentence at a time.

3. **Edit out loud.** You may find it difficult to "see" your paper after a while. Try reading out loud to yourself. This may seem a rather strange thing to do at first; however, you will find that it forces you to pay attention and hear what you have written. It also helps you to develop your own voice. This writer's voice will be your guide.

WRITING ASSIGNMENT 1   Description of a Place

Your first writing assignment is to describe a place. You may choose a topic from the ones below. The place you choose can be real or imagined.

Your description should be approximately 200 words long. Your lines should be double spaced. Remember to describe something; do not tell a story.

Your descriptive paragraph should contain a *topic sentence* (the sentence that lets your reader know what you will be discussing). A topic sentence is usually found at the beginning of the paragraph, but it can be placed in the middle or at the end. Sometimes the topic sentence is missing, and the reader must infer it. Ask your instructor where he or she prefers to see the topic sentence in your descriptive paragraph.

a bus depot	a hardware store	a graveyard	a bar
a navy base	a dog kennel	a marsh or swamp	a beach
your hometown	a movie theatre	a park	a car dealership
an ice cream stand	a fast-food outlet	a lake	a mountain resort
a camp site	an ancient ruin	a temple or mosque	a restaurant lobby

Describing People

Have you ever read about someone's life? Do you remember how engrossed you became by the details of that life? You may also recall how the description of the person's features helped you visualize him or her. The information about how people dressed, what they liked to do, how they behaved, and even what they liked to eat may all have seemed unusually interesting to you.

Descriptive language is one of your best tools when you describe people. If you use effective adjectives, adverbs, prepositional phrases, comparisons, and specific details, your descriptions of people will be interesting to read. Remember: Your reader wants to be engaged by the details you provide.

When you write about people, it is important for you to keep in mind that clichés and stereotypes can destroy your good intentions as a writer. Clichés, you will recall, are expressions that are tired; they have been worn out by overuse. If you use clichés in your writing too often, you may lose the interest of your reader. Consider the following.

Her hair was as black as coal.

This expression is a cliché and does not add effective detail. Your reader has seen and heard this phrase too many times.

Improved: Her hair was as black as the wing of a raven.

This expression is a little more effective because now your reader is visualizing how the person's hair is similar to the rich colour of a bird's wing.

More improvement: Her hair was as black as an autumn midnight sky.

This expression is becoming even more effective. Your reader can think of the deepness of the night sky and compare it to the colour of the woman's hair.

His legs were as skinny as toothpicks.

Your reader has seen this cliché once too often. If you chose to leave it in your description, you would deaden the impact.

Improved: His legs were as skinny as a chicken's.

Although this expression is a little more effective, it is still somewhat clichéd.

More improvement: His legs were as skinny as pencils.

Your description is becoming more effective. Your reader can now visualize the thinness of a pencil and compare it to the person's legs.

You must also be aware of using stereotypes when you are writing descriptions of people. If you use stereotypes, you run the risk of offending your reader, particularly if the stereotype you choose to use is one that is racially based. As you recall, stereotypes are unfair generalizations of people based on their race, colour, gender, religion, or occupation. In addition, you will find that most stereotypes are clichéd. Here are some stereotypes that have become clichéd and insulting:

"the feminist": a plain-looking, bespectacled, man-hating, intellectual young woman who cannot get dates

"the nurse": a voluptuous, blonde, sex-hungry young woman

"the blonde": a dim-witted, curvaceous sex kitten

"the athlete": an obtuse, muscle-bound, self-obsessed young man

"the scientist": a maniacal male genius who thinks only of his work

"the star": a spoiled, self-indulgent, egocentric, bad-tempered person

"the librarian": a prim, fastidious, humourless female

"the news reader": a trustworthy, dedicated, perceptive, knowledgeable person

"the politician": an ambitious, self-serving, unprincipled person

"the lawyer": an unscrupulous, greedy, manipulating male

"the gangster": a flamboyant, murdering, dim male American thug

After reading these stereotypes, you will probably be able to come up with more. Some stereotypes are more damaging than others, and some can even be flattering. However, they all frame people in particular ways, and thus diminish their individual complexity. So be cautious in creating your descriptions of people: do not let clichés and stereotypes compromise your portrayals and offend your readers.

Ordering Descriptions of People

Consider what you know about classification. How would you use it when you wish to organize ideas in a description of someone?

You have various arrangements to choose from:

1. general to specific

2. specific to general

3. outside to inside

4. inside to outside

5. most important feature to least important

6. least important feature to most important

If you choose general to specific, you may begin with a general description of the person and then discuss a specific aspect of him or her. For example, if you are going to describe a favourite coach, you may start with who the person is and what he or she is like in general. If you believe the person's patience is the most valuable trait he or she possesses, you might end your piece with a discussion of that. On the other hand, if you select a specific-to-general classification, you may begin with what you believe the person's most special characteristic is; then you may discuss what the person is like in a general sense.

Another effective means of organizing is outside to inside. Simply put, you may describe the person's appearance (outside) and then proceed to describe what the person is like (inside). Or, you may wish to reverse this arrangement (inside to outside).

Finally, you may find it useful to arrange details about the person in order of importance, from most to least important. Or you may work the other way around—from least to most important. In such an arrangement, you will want to think of your purpose. Are you trying to emphasize what is most important by placing it first? Are you trying to build your description so that the most important feature of the person is emphasized last?

All of these arrangements are equally effective. You must decide which one suits your purpose.

Reading Other Writers' Descriptions of People

Read the following descriptions of people written by well-known writers. Then answer the questions that follow.

Selection 1

Mrs. Thompson. a good deal older than Jeannie, had become her best friend. She was a nice, plain, fat, consoling sort of person, with varicosed legs, shoes unlaced and slit for comfort, blue flannel dressing-gown worn at all hours, pudding-bowl haircut, and coarse grey hair. She might have been Jeannie's own mother, or her Auntie Pearl. She rocked her fat self in the rocking-chair and went on with what she had to say.

—Mavis Gallant, "My Heart Is Broken"

Selection 2

He crossed his arms across his chest, fingers on each hand hanging over his elbows, thumbs hooked inside—crooked, stiff fingers, with huge, arthritic knuckles; a farmer's fingers: knuckles barked and scratched, one finger cut off just below the fingernail from an argument with a baler. She remembered when his hair, snow white, had been as brown as shoe polish. He said nothing, biting his lips together and not meeting her eyes, staring a little cross-eyed at the yellow wall beside her.

—John Gardner, *October Light*

Selection 3

Captain Crabbe was small. He had come as an undersized boy to the west coast of Vancouver Island and there he had stayed. He had been fairish and was not bald. His eyes were sad like a little bloodhound's eyes and pink under, but he was not sad. He was a contented man and rejoiced always to be joined again with his wife and his gangling son and daughter.

—Ethel Wilson, "From Flores"

Answer the following questions about the three descriptive paragraphs you have just read. Do your work on separate paper. Answer in complete sentences. Check your answers with those below.

SELECTION 1

1. Is Gallant's description of Mrs. Thompson vivid? What adjectives does she use that are effective in your opinion?

2. What sort of person does Mrs. Thompson seem? What helps you form your opinion of her?

3. What is a "pudding bowl haircut"? Describe what that haircut might look like.

SELECTION 2

1. Who is the person Gardner is describing? What adjectives help you imagine what this person looked like?

2. What sort of person is this character? How can you tell?

3. What does "one finger cut off just below the fingernail from an argument with a baler" convey about the character?

SELECTION 3

1. Based on Wilson's description, what sort of man do you think Captain Crabbe is?

2. Find an example of a simile in her description. Is the simile an effective one, do you think?

3. What adjectives does she use that you find especially successful?

The three paragraphs describe the outward appearance of several memorable characters. Notice what adjectives were chosen to give the characters life. If you closed your eyes and tried to visualize them, you would probably succeed in seeing these people just from the writers' descriptions.

In selection 1, you will notice that Mavis Gallant has included carefully selected adjectives. Mrs. Thompson does not just have legs—she has "varicosed legs." Her shoes are not just shoes—they are unlaced and cut open to be more comfortable. Her dress is no ordinary dress: it is a "blue flannel dressing gown" that she wears most of the time. Her hair, "coarse and grey," has been cut in a "pudding-bowl look." All these adjectives help you form the image of this character.

In selection 2, John Gardner describes an old farmer. Notice how he describes the old man's hands. The fingers are "crooked," "stiff," and "arthritic." The old farmer does not look at the speaker; he bites his lips and looks past her. From the description you can tell that the farmer has had a difficult, physically demanding life.

In selection 3, notice that Ethel Wilson portrays Captain Crabbe as someone who seems satisfied with his life and his work. He is aging but is not jaded. He still looks forward to being with his family. Wilson tells you that he has the sad look of a bloodhound, but is not actually like that. This is a good example of how someone's appearance can belie who he or she really is.

Exercise 8   Group Activity: Adding Modifiers to Descriptions of People

Work in a small group to complete this exercise. Choose five people to describe from the suggestions below. Think of possible modifiers to describe each one. Have one group member write down the group's ideas. Then select four expressions that you think would be appropriate to describe each person you have chosen.

Try to keep your images fresh. Avoid clichés, jargon, slang, and stereotypes if you can. Another group member can write in the selected expressions. Then write a sentence that includes your ideas. Be prepared to share your answers with other groups.

Example: a birdwatcher:

    1) alert

    2) in the brown, crumpled jacket

    3) camouflaged

    4) silently

The camouflaged birdwatcher in the brown, crumpled jacket sat silently alert.

Choice 1: a hockey referee

1) _____

2) _____

3) _____

4) _____

Sentence:

_____

_____

Choice 2: a lifeguard

1) _____

2) _____

3) _____

4) _____

Sentence:

_____

_____

Choice 3: a singer

1) _____

2) _____

3) _____

4) _____

Sentence:

_____

_____

Choice 4: a new employee

1) _____

2) _____

3) _____

4) _____

Sentence:

_____

_____

Choice 5: a security guard

1) _____

2) _____

3) _____

4) _____

Sentence:

_____

_____

Choice 6: a skateboarder

1) _____

2) _____

3) _____

4) _____

Sentence:

_____

_____

Choice 7: a young mother

1) _____

2) _____

3) _____

4) _____

Sentence:

_____

_____

Choice 8: a cashier

1) _____

2) _____

3) _____

4) _____

Sentence:

_____

_____

Choice 9: a chef

1) _____

2) _____

3) _____

4) _____

Sentence:

_____

_____

Exercise 9 *Improving a Descriptive Paragraph*

Below is a rather spare description of a child. Add some modifiers, using your thesaurus, to make this description more detailed and interesting. Rewrite your description on a separate piece of paper. Remember to avoid the problematic expressions: clichés, jargon, slang, and euphemisms. Have someone else in the class read your new description. Discuss your answer.

The small boy stood at the corner of two busy streets. He seemed to be waiting. His hands were by his sides. He looked down at the sidewalk.

Follow the same directions for this simple description:

A young soldier stood at attention outside the gates of the base. He was about 20. His gun was ready by his side. He remained fixed and his eyes stared straight ahead.

WRITING ASSIGNMENT 2 Description of a Person

The characters in Gallant's, Gardner's, and Wilson's descriptions come alive because of the vocabulary the writers have chosen. You can benefit from paying attention to how professional writers do their work. You can study how they craft their sentences, which words they select, how they make use of modifiers, and what they choose to describe in detail.

Your second writing assignment is to describe a person. Choose a topic from the ones that follow. The person you write about can be real or imagined. Your descriptive paragraph should contain a topic sentence. Your description should be approximately 200 words long and double spaced. Remember to describe something; do not tell a story.

a baseball or football fan	a carpenter	a woman waiting for the bus
a construction worker	a guitarist or pianist	a bingo player
a house painter	a lacrosse player	a rancher
a writer at work	a school principal	a child in a park
a television watcher	a jogger	a supermarket clerk
a deckhand on a ship	a television talk show host	a baker
a bank teller	a baby	a boxer

Describing Situations

Read the following description of what it felt like to someone when his father died:

After he was gone, we couldn't seem to talk, but instead, as if like dogs, we each took our sorrow to a different part of the house, not willing to share it.

—Barry Milliken, "Run"

This single sentence captures the author's feelings in a simple but poignant way. Notice how Milliken uses a comparison—a simile—between the grieving family and a dog's manner of dealing with pain: to take it to a private place and deal with it alone.

Description of a situation includes not only the scene itself but also someone's feelings about it. The best descriptions, in other words, encapsulate the essence of the experience. In order to make the situation believable, writers pay particular attention to the effect of their words on you as the reader. As a writer, you must also think about the influence your words can have.

Imagine you want to describe a family gathering. You could paint this picture in words with or without *emotive language*—expression that appeals to human emotions. If you chose to be objective about the situation, you might merely describe it as if you were recording it as a camera would. However, if you wanted your reader to get an emotional sense of the situation, you would use emotionally charged words to convey a particular feeling. Consider the following examples:

Objective writing:
The father was seated at the head of the table. He watched his family for several moments without saying anything. Then he began to carve the roast beef, and as the plates were passed to him, he loaded each with a slice of meat. Suddenly he began to laugh.

Emotive writing:
The harsh, haggard father was seated as sternly as a grey statue at the head of the long, quiet table. He watched his hushed family with silent disapproval for several painful moments. At long last, he began to carve the precious roast beef, and as the plates were dutifully passed to him, he carefully set a slice of succulent meat on each. Without warning and to the family's surprise, he unleashed deep roars of laughter.

The first example contains few descriptive words; the situation is described in a matter-of-fact manner. The second example contains modifiers that convey a sense of the situation: *haggard*, *harsh*, and *hushed* communicate a feeling of oppression as the father, like *a grey statue*, presides over the family dinner. You may also feel some tension when you read the words *silent*, *painful*, *dutifully*, and *unleashed*.

Denotation and Connotation of Words

Words can have an impact because they can manipulate your feelings and attitudes. As a writer, you should be aware of the denotation and connotation of words.

The *denotation* of a word is its exact, literal meaning. For example, if you looked up the word *home* in any dictionary, you would find its literal meaning: a place where your family lives, where you live, or the place you call your residence. The *connotation* of a word, in contrast, goes beyond its literal meaning; it's what a word suggests to a reader or listener. As well as its literal meaning, then, the word *home* is associated with feelings of love, comfort, and satisfaction.

On the other hand, you may associate the word *home* with feelings of anxiety, mistrust, and tension. In other words, connotations may be pleasant or unpleasant, positive or negative, depending on the individual and his or her experiences. Not all connotations are the same for everyone, but within cultures, certain words tend to connote meanings in predictable ways.

Exercise 10 Group Activity: Identifying Connotations

You may do this exercise as a class or in small groups. Together, think of 10 words that have strong connotations. Have one person write down the connotations, or associations, that each word has for each member of the group. The group should also consider whether some associations are clichéd or stereotyped. Each group should be prepared to share their answers with the entire class.

Situations Worthy of Description: Creating Impact

Many skilled journalists have developed an eye for choosing a particular detail of a situation as a way of interpreting the event for the reader or listener. In short, these writers have learned what is worth paying attention to. Similarly, photojournalists are capable of discovering something visually noteworthy in a scene.

When you are watching, listening to, or reading a news report, pay close attention to the journalist's language. You will likely find concise, descriptive passages. You may actually feel yourself transported to the place or event because the writer has skillfully "taken" you there.

Fiction writers can also transport you. Read the passages that follow and notice, if you can, your reactions to their descriptions. You will answer some questions at the end of the readings.

Reading Other Writers' Descriptions of Situation

Selection 1

The next day, right after supper, we were all seated in our armchairs, some in the shadows, others within the pale circle of light near the table where a glass lamp burned palely. We were talking about spectres, phantoms, and ghosts, while awaiting the old neighbour who was going to tell us about the inhabitants of the haunted house. He was late. Perhaps he had decided not to talk any more. His secret would die with him. The stove roared with a fire of red spruce.

—Pamphile LeMay, "Blood and Gold"

Selection 2

In the school yard clusters of people constantly formed and dispersed. Here and there reds and yellows and oranges made bright spots among the blue and grey suits and dresses. A baseball game was being played in one corner of the field. In the opposite corner the children's races were being run. The monotone of the announcer called: "Twelve and under. Twelve and under. Collect at the starting line. Will all those twelve and under collect at the starting line." A record of "The Maple Leaf Forever" was playing at the grandstand. Through the other noises the constant harangue of the basemen rose and fell to unnerve a procession of batters.

—W.D. Valgardson, "Dominion Day"

Selection 3

It was close to midnight when the hunchbacked tyrant Richard III, played by English star Alec Guinness, was finally slain, and Shakespeare's historical melodrama thundered to its conclusion. When Guinness and the rest of Richard III's cast took their bows, they were met by a five-minute standing ovation that's still talked about nearly half a century later. Not satisfied with applauding, many in the huge tent that housed the just-launched Stratford Festival began to cheer, weep and even embrace with un-Canadian abandon. Nathan Cohen, usually the country's most curmudgeonly critic, later rhapsodized that that July, 1953 debut was the single most memorable theatre experience he's ever had. "The people in business suits and the men in evening dress," he wrote, "the women in summer skirts and dresses and in gorgeous evening gowns, were screaming from the bottom of their throats, in praise, in gratitude, in a delirium of joy. I don't know how many times I heard it said, 'This is going to put Canada on the theatre map. We have finally come of age!'"

—John Bemrose, "Fifty Years of Stratford Magic," *Maclean's,* May 27, 2002

Responding to the Readings

Refer to reading selections 1 to 3 to answer the following questions. Do your work on separate paper, and answer in complete sentences. Your instructor may ask to see your work. Be prepared to share your answers.

SELECTION 1

1. What is the situation described here?

2. What feeling do you get from reading this?

3. What language—emotional or non-emotional—does the author use?

4. Give some examples of the words the author used to help you decide.

SELECTION 2

1. What does the paragraph describe?

2. What separate activities does Valgardson describe?

3. What adjectives does he use to describe the crowd?

4. What noises does he describe that you can "hear" as you read?

SELECTION 3

1. What situation is Bemrose describing?

2. Does he use many words with positive connotations? Find some examples.

3. Bemrose also quotes Nathan Cohen's words about the experience. What sorts of words does Cohen use to describe the situation? Select a few and explain whether you believe they have a positive or negative connotation.

4. What sense of the experience do you get from reading Bemrose's description?

Tips and Tools for Describing Situations

Imagine that you were invited to write about a special event, a graduation ceremony, a wedding, or a visit from a famous person. What words you selected, depending on their connotation, could sway your reader to experiencing the situation in a particular way.

TOOLS FOR DESCRIBING SITUATIONS

- Take advantage of common connotations of words.
- Work with positive or negative connotations.
- Use comparisons.
- Use choice modifiers.
- Use interesting similes.
- Plan the arrangement of ideas.

TIPS FOR DESCRIBING SITUATIONS

Here are two important factors for you to consider when you are planning to write about a situation or experience:

1. Know your purpose.

2. Know your audience.

YOUR PURPOSE

You must think about what it is you are trying to do. In other words, examine your intentions when you write about a situation or experience. Remember: Be careful with your choice of modifiers, since they will convey a particular feeling to the reader. Consider the answers to these questions as you plan your writing:

- Why do you wish to write about the situation?
- Are you trying to convey a particular feeling to your audience?
- Do you hope to leave the reader with a particular sense of the experience?
- Do you want the reader to have positive or negative feelings about it?

YOUR AUDIENCE

Your *audience* is the reader or readers you are intending to reach. It's important to consider who these readers are and how they will respond to your writing.

Think about various audiences:

the general reading public
members of a select group
other writers
university professors
college instructors
other students

Thinking about your audience will help you to shape your piece of writing. For example, if your description is for your university or college newspaper, you can expect that mostly other students will read it. Therefore, you will select language that you think would be appealing to and appropriate for them. However, if you are writing a description as part of your course work, a lab in chemistry, a journal entry of a patient's condition, a creative writing course, or a case study for a business administration course, your professor or instructor will expect you to follow a specified format or style. You would choose language that suits not only a reader of your work, but also an evaluator of it.

Ordering Descriptions of Situations

Organizing your written description of a situation will take some thought and planning. After you have considered the purpose and audience, you must decide what factors will help you organize your ideas.

- a specific "physical" arrangement of ideas
- an overall picture
- a particular part of an experience or situation
- an emotive sense you want to give the scene or experience

Thinking about Your Arrangement

The overall picture gives your reader a general sense of the scene. Perhaps you wish simply to give a broad overview because your purpose is to focus on the bigger picture. For example, to describe a rock concert, you may wish to talk about the general set-up of the concert setting, the crowd, the stage, and the performers. You may not want to concentrate on a specific person because you want the writing to describe the event itself. On the other hand, you may want to express the feeling of being at the concert—what it is like to be a part of the experience. You may centre your reader's attention on a specific moment at the concert when something remarkable happens. In this instance, you may also choose to select emotive language with connotations that convey a sense of excitement and wonder. Alternatively, you may choose to describe the most important part of the concert along with some lesser incidents. Any of these arrangements is workable and can be effective.

Exercise 11 Ordering Descriptions of Situations

Read each of the following situations. Then refer to the section on the arrangement of ideas. Decide which of the four possibilities seems most appropriate for the situation. Be prepared to explain why.

1. a rodeo

2. a movie debut

3. a religious ceremony

4. a hockey playoff

5. a drought

6. a family picnic

Exercise 12 *Group Activity: Describing a Photographed Event*

1. Choose two other members of the class.
2. Each member of the group should bring in a photo of some sort of event.
3. Put all the photos from the class in a pile.
4. Each group chooses one photo at random.
5. The group writes a description of the situation they think the photo represents.
6. Each group shares what they have written. Then they call on the owner of the photograph to tell the class what the event in the photo was.
7. Groups may compare impressions.
8. A member of the class may volunteer to input the descriptions and email copies to others.

WRITING ASSIGNMENT 3 **Description of a Situation**

Your next paragraph writing assignment is to describe a situation chosen from the list of following topics. The situation can be real or imagined. Your description should be approximately 200 words long and double spaced. Remember to describe something; do not tell a story. Your descriptive paragraph should contain a topic sentence.

a baseball or football game
a flood
a cricket match
a fashion show
a campaign speech
a pie-eating contest
a recital
a fire
a barn dance
the opening of an art gallery
a rescue operation
an air show
a wrestling match
a political debate
a snowboarding event
a tornado
a talent contest
a charity auction

CHECKOUT

1. Suggested writing steps to follow:
   - Select a topic.
   - Check the "fit" of the topic.
   - Develop a rough writing plan.
   - Be organized.
   - Write your first draft.
   - Let your ideas rest.
   - Get an audience.
   - Revise.
   - Proofread the final draft.
   - Check the presentation of the final draft.

2. When you are writing descriptive paragraphs:
   - Classify your ideas to organize what you see, hear, taste, touch, smell, or feel.
   - Include similes to brighten your written expression.
   - Avoid cliché comparisons.
   - Be aware of the denotation and connotation of words.
   - Choose adjectives and other modifiers that add detail and interest.

chapter 18

Explanatory Paragraphs

Chapter Objectives

What will you have learned when you have completed this chapter?
You will be able to

1. list important characteristics of the academic paragraph composition.

2. describe two types of useful outlines.

3. develop a clear topic sentence.

4. develop good supporting details.

5. write a wrap-up sentence to summarize the ideas of your paragraph.

6. use transitions correctly.

The Academic Paragraph Composition

Most academic paragraph compositions have a set form: they have an introductory sentence, called the *topic sentence*, that introduces the reader to the topic. They have major points that support the topic sentence. There are usually at least three major points, but you might see some paragraphs with four or five major points. Each major point requires more discussion so that the paragraph is a full development of its topic. The supporting details provide this extension by adding information to the major points. The information can be in the form of examples, steps, reasons, or more specific explanation. Paragraph compositions should end in a single wrap-up or concluding sentence. The wrap-up sentence draws the discussion to a logical end. Explanatory paragraphs explain something about a topic.

Outlines

A basic outline is a plan for writing. An outline helps you organize your writing. It helps you know what you want to say. Different kinds of outlines can be used for different kinds of paragraph compositions.

Two types of useful outlines are the *sentence outline* and the *point-form outline*.

In the first type, you use full sentences for all points, and in the second type, you write your points in short notes. In both paragraph outline types, write the topic sentence out in full.

Full-Sentence Outline

Topic Sentence: Gardeners can get beautiful begonias by using this helpful advice.
Point 1: They should be aware of what soil type works best.
Supporting Detail: Equal parts of compost, moist peat moss, sand, and perlite is the perfect growing medium.
Point 2: Gardeners should pay particular attention to the planting of begonia tubers.
Supporting Detail: The hollow side of the tuber is placed about 1.5 centimetres below the soil's surface; tubers should be watered well and protected from extreme cold.
Point 3: Finally, growers should recognize that early care given to begonias ensures healthy plants.
Supporting Detail: After shoots appear through the soil, gardeners should water the little plants regularly and make certain they receive plenty of light, but not the direct heat of the sun. They can give the baby begonias half-strength fertilizer when the plants reach 7 centimeters in height and can continue fertilizing the plants every two weeks until they reach maturity.
Conclusion or Wrap-up: The right soil mixture, planting conditions, and care will provide gardeners with a bounty of beautiful begonias.

Point-form Outline

Topic Sentence: Gardeners can get beautiful begonias by using this helpful advice.
Point 1: awareness of soil type
Supporting Detail: Equal parts compost, moist peat moss, sand, and perlite
Point 2: attention to planting of tubers
Supporting Detail: hollow-side placed about 1.5 cm below soil; tubers watered well and protected from cold
Point 3: recognize early care ensures healthy plants.
Supporting Detail: water shoots regularly; ensure plenty of light but no direct sun. Give half-strength fertilizer when plants reach 7 cm in height; continue fertilizing every two weeks to maturity
Conclusion or Wrap-up: use right soil mixture, planting conditions, and care

Developing Topic Sentences

The first sentence of your paragraph composition is called the *topic sentence*. The topic sentence tells the reader what the paragraph will be about. Your topic sentence should be clear and directing.

Topic Sentence 1: Being a young grandparent has its advantages.
Topic Sentence 2: Proper preparation for exam-writing is essential for any student.
Topic Sentence 3: Watching DVDs at home on an excellent system is more fun than going to a theatre.
Topic Sentence 4: To reinstall the program, a user should follow these steps.
Topic Sentence 5: A search and rescue team has four main responsibilities.

Do you notice differences in these topic sentences? What would you do to develop each one into a paragraph composition?

Topic Sentence 1: You will probably list and discuss the advantages. You may think of examples for your own life experiences to add as details.
Topic Sentence 2: You will list reasons and explain them.
Topic Sentence 3: You will talk about the differences between viewing at home and going to the theatre.
Topic Sentence 4: You will provide steps for the reader to follow.
Topic Sentence 5: You will discuss the four main responsibilities.

Exercise 1 *Planning Topic Sentences*

How will the writer develop each of the following topic sentences? Write a sentence or two about how you would go about developing each one into a paragraph composition. Be prepared to share your answers.

1. Métis beadwork is different from other Aboriginal beadwork in three important ways.

2. The sound system has four outstanding features.

3. Training for a racquetball tournament takes discipline.

4. Rising tuition rates are having an impact on students.

5. Emily Carr House has an intriguing history.

6. Organizing a fundraiser can be educational.

7. Amending the soil is the key to growing hydrangeas.

8. Shellacking is not the same as varnishing.

9. Vegetarianism has its advantages.

10. School vandalism can be prevented.

Exercise 2 *Developing Topic Sentences*

Develop each of the following topics into a clear, effective topic sentence. Your instructor may ask to see your work or may ask you to share your work with others.

1. going on a long trip

2. working part-time

3. arranging a blind date for a friend

4. operating a hair dryer

5. making popcorn in a microwave

6. choosing the perfect dance partner

7. developing a relationship with a person in your family

8. choosing an instructor at college or university

9. deciding on a career

10. managing your money

Exercise 3   Group Activity: Peer-editing Topic Sentences

Work in a group of three to five people. Make copies of the topic sentences you developed in the preceding exercise and exchange them with members of your group. You and your peers will edit these sentences together. Examine each topic sentence according to the following questions:

1. Does the topic sentence direct the reader clearly?
2. How would the writer develop the topic sentence into a paragraph composition?
3. What point of view would the writer use?

On the back of each group member's paper, write your responses. Be prepared to explain them to each writer.

Developing Supporting Information

Clear and specific supporting information is crucial to the effectiveness of your paragraph composition. Vague or generalized information will not be convincing.

Point: Many users do not use the Internet effectively.
Unconvincing Supporting Detail: People waste too much time.
Convincing Supporting Detail: People do not investigate how their browsers and search engines can help them; they do not study the helpful advice available on various sites.

Exercise 4   Group Activity: Composing Supporting Details

Work in a group of three to five people. The following is an outline for a paragraph containing three main points about public transportation. You and your group should think of two specific details for each of the major points. Make sure the points are specific and convincing.

Topic Sentence: Public transportation in most cities does not meet most users' needs.

Point 1: The city bus is usually not convenient for many passengers.

1. _____

_____

2. _____

_____

Point 2: Bicycle routes are underdeveloped.

1. _____

_____

2. _____

_____

Point 3: The disabled and elderly are not considered important passengers in public transportation services.

1. _____

_____

2. _____

_____

Exercise 5 Providing Reasons

Provide three reasons for each of the following. Your instructor may ask to see your work. Be prepared to share your answers.

Three reasons why eating green vegetables is good for you:

1. _____

_____

2. _____

_____

3. _____

_____

Three reasons why [insert title of a favourite movie] is such a good film:

1. _____

_____

2. _____

_____

3. _____

_____

Three reasons why golf has become so popular:

1. _____

_____

2. _____

_____

3. _____

_____

Three reasons why I hate getting up early in the morning:

1. _____

_____

2. _____

_____

3. _____

_____

Three reasons why I should get an A in my English assignment:

1. _____

_____

2. _____

_____

3. _____

_____

Point of View

A writer's *point of view* is the position from which he or she writes. The *first-person*, or *personal* point of view means a writer will use the pronoun *I*. This perspective may be used in narratives (stories) or when relating personal experience. Some instructors discourage this point of view in their students' writing. However, it is important to realize that different points of view serve different purposes, so at times it may be perfectly appropriate to use the first person.

While some instructors will accept the second-person (*you*) point of view, most prefer students to use the third person; that is, *he*, *she*, or *they*.

Check with your instructor about which points of view are acceptable in your assignments and which are not. Often your instructor will specify this in your course outline.

Developing Conclusion or Wrap-up Sentences

Each paragraph composition you write should end with a sentence that either wraps up the ideas of your paragraph or makes a concluding statement about them. A conclusion is something that follows logically from an argument. A wrap-up sentence serves to summarize or to tie off the ideas of a paragraph. Examples:

Because hiking is relatively inexpensive, good exercise, and soothing to the spirit, the municipal government should develop a trail on the outskirts of the city.

After Orlando had recovered from his experience, his friends helped him write a story about it for the university paper.

Exercise 5 *Writing an Outline*

Choose one of the topics below, and write a full-sentence outline for it.

Provide three major points and then provide supporting details for each of these points. Include a topic sentence and a concluding sentence in your outline. Your instructor may ask to see your work or may ask you to share your work with others.

1. self-employment

2. collecting posters

3. grooming your dog

4. a simple celebration

5. learning to swim

6. telephone manners

7. fresh water kayaking

8. salt water kayaking

9. listening to music online

10. bird flu

11. sunscreens

12. choosing a good book

13. mending a broken heart

Using Transitions

Transitions are single words or phrases used to indicate to a reader that one idea is ending and another idea is beginning. Transitions can also be used to show other relationships between ideas. (More information about transitions is found in the preceding chapter.)

USE 1

If you want to keep building on an idea, you may choose to use *emphasis* or *addition* transitions.

Mary loves everything about her new apartment. She enjoys the colourful, exciting neighbourhood. Having people over to her new place is her latest hobby.

This sentence reads as if the writer just strung some ideas together, but look what happens when we add transitions:

Mary loves everything about her new apartment. She *also* enjoys the colourful, exciting neighbourhood. *In addition,* having people over to her new place is her latest hobby.

Emphasis or Addition Transitions

moreover

also

furthermore

finally

in the same fashion

as well as

another

too

again

in addition

USE 2

If you want to tell a story or explain to the reader how something is to be done in a step-by-step fashion, you may choose transitions that help to show *time order* or process analysis. The italicized words in the following paragraph all show time order.

When I was little, my grandmother *used to* tell me stories. *First,* she would get me settled in her big feather bed. *Then* she would turn out the lights so that the moon shone over the bed, and she would become a soft shadow beside it. *After that* she would clear her throat and begin her story in a soft, clear voice. *Soon* I would be back in the Old Country and she would be a little girl again in a strange place far away. *In due time,* my eyes would get heavy and her voice would become more and more distant.

Time Order Transitions

first	during
soon	last
to begin with	early
in the first place	when
now	until
afterward	whenever
second	finally
eventually	as soon as
third	in due time
later	after
at last	while
next	before
then	prior to
after that	meanwhile

USE 3

If you want to show how ideas are different from one another, you would use *contrast* transitions.

Po is *different* from his brother.
Unlike bees, wasps can nest in the ground.
She enjoyed her trip to Washington; *however,* she detested going to California.
His opinions are *opposite* to mine.
They hadn't expected him to like the gift, *but, on the contrary,* he raved about it.

Contrast Transitions	
but	otherwise
on the contrary	despite the fact
in contrast	still
on the other hand	although
however	even though
nevertheless	opposite
yet	different

USE 4

If you want to talk about how things are the same, then you would use *comparison* transitions.

Her friend enjoyed fishing and *likewise* so did she.

The two workers decided to have lunch together, and *both* of them realized that they had similar interests.

She was *also* upset by the comment, *along with* the others.

Comparison Transitions
both
respectively
each
similarly
like
also
likewise
and
along with

USE 5

You may wish to show how something has caused something else, often referred to as a *cause–effect relationship*.

Because Roberta slept in, she missed her bus.
The small dog loved to dig; *as a result,* he was punished for the potholes in the garden.
It is getting toward the end of the month; *therefore,* I am running out of money.
She told the police a lie; *consequently,* she was put under suspicion.
The meeting broke up, and *accordingly* everyone went on her way.

Exercise 6 Using Transitions

Work in pairs. Insert a transition word that would make sense for each of the following sentences. Pay attention to how the ideas in each sentence relate to one another. Be prepared to share your answers.

1. She wanted the job very much; _____, she could not get her courage up to apply.

2. Many flowers grow well in Oshawa; _____, many people make a hobby of collecting new ones for their gardens.

3. The teenager saved his money. _____, he bought himself a quality stereo system.

4. Wrap the fish in layers of brown paper; _____ freeze it immediately.

5. Mrs. Cembrowski worked for the company for 25 years. _____, she got the recognition she deserved.

6. The baseball game was in extra innings. _____, it was still not very exciting.

7. Some puppies chew everything they're not supposed to; _____, some don't seem to want to bother.

8. Their candidate was born and raised in the community. _____, she was first employed at the local canning factory.

9. _____ areas of the town looked clean and appealing. The volunteer project had paid off.

10. The bonfire got out of control; _____, many hectares of the forest were soon engulfed in flames.

WRITING ASSIGNMENT 1 Explanatory Paragraph

Choose one of the topics you developed into an outline in Exercise 5, or any other topic mentioned in this chapter. Write an explanatory paragraph of about 200 words in length. Construct a clear topic sentence. You may choose to provide three reasons as your three major points. Use transitions, and make sure to include a concluding or wrap-up sentence.

Edit your paragraph before handing it in to your instructor. You may be asked to take part in a peer-editing exercise by bringing in your completed paragraph.

CHECKOUT

1. Different sorts of outlines can be used for planning and organizing different kinds of paragraph compositions.

2. When you make an outline, start with the topic sentence.

3. Develop supporting details and provide a conclusion or wrap-up sentence.

4. Use transitions in your writing to show relationships between ideas and to signal a change in your thought.

chapter 19

Readings

Questions for the Readings

1. Is the piece of writing an example of academic writing?

2. What is the writer's purpose in each piece of writing?

3. What is the piece of writing about? Summarize the topic in one or two sentences.

4. Is there a clear topic sentence? Underline it. If there is no clear topic sentence, develop one.

5. Into what general category can the topic be classified?

6. Who would find the topic significant? Is the piece written for lots of different types of readers? If it is written for a clearly defined group of readers, who are they?

7. Look closely at the punctuation of the piece. Does the writer use colons or semi-colons? Is punctuation used in any special way?

8. Can you find examples of punctuation being used to help the writer write more interesting informative sentences?

9. Does the writer use any cumulative adjectives?

10. Of what is the author trying to convince the reader?

11. Does the writer provide arguments? What are they?

12. How does the writer support these arguments?

13. Does the tone of the writing help convince the reader?

14. Is the vocabulary specialized? Under what circumstances is it necessary and appropriate to use a specialized vocabulary?

15. Does the writer use any euphemisms or clichés? Why were they used? Do they affect the tone of the writing?

16. Are similes used? Did you find any comparisons?

17. Does the writing selection contain different sentence patterns? Did you find simple, compound, complex, and compound-complex sentences?

Reading 1: Charity Cool

Pamela Klaffke

Pamela Klaffke is a writer, editor, and media consultant. "Charity Cool" is from her entertaining and informative book *Spree: A Cultural History of Shopping.* Klaffke taps into Canadians' love of shopping.

Fashion was not a consideration when the Salvation Army organized its Household Salvage Brigade in 1890s London. Rather, the venerable Christian charity put unemployed men to work collecting discarded household items, books, and clothing in an effort to provide jobs and pass the salvaged goods on to the needy.

The practice of recycling used items for charity blossomed in the first half of the 1900s, spreading across the U.K. and into North America. But charity shop shopping as we know it today didn't appear until mid-century. The English organization Oxfam International claims its first charity shop—opened in 1948 on Broad Street in Oxford—was the first such store in the U.K.

Oxfam filled its stores with donations from the community, reselling the goods at low prices and using the profits to fight global poverty and suffering. The patrons of charity—or thrift—shops were primarily the poor; people who could not afford the luxury of buying new merchandise.

The first hint of the merger of thrift and fashion was in the late 1960s when the free-spirited "hippie" movement emerged along with communal living and messages of peace. Like many organic youth movements (whether it be '60s hippies, '70s punks, or the grunge kids of the early 1990s), a look evolved and was ultimately co-opted by the mainstream who habitually rejected the politics and focused on the fashion.

In 1977 the first poster girl for thrift shop chic arrived, with no ties to youth movements or to poverty. In fact, she wasn't a real person at all, but a character on the big screen. Playing the title role in Woody Allen's *Annie Hall,* Diane Keaton became a fashion icon, pairing oversize men's suit jackets with long skirts, boots, and hats. Keaton and her onscreen alter ego made the eclectic, thrift shop look fashionable, although thrift shopping amongst the middle and even upper classes had yet to shed its undesirable stigma.

Thrift stores were equated with poverty, neediness, smelliness, filth, and beyond a select group of fashion-forward hipsters, thrifting was not an acceptable shopping activity. Scouring the racks for vintage or antique finds had become customary in certain circles, but thrifting in general didn't hit mainstream North America until the 1980s.

If you could pinpoint one individual who made the most significant impact on the rise of thrift-as-fashion, it would have to be Madonna. When the provocative pop singer burst onto the world music scene in 1983 with her self-titled debut album, then released *Like A Virgin* one year later, she quickly cultivated a loyal following of young female fans eager to imitate her signature ragamuffin, thrift shop style.

Another musical thrift style muse surfaced in 1991 when Hole front-woman Courtney Love took to the stage in baby doll dresses and smeared lipstick, bringing what was dubbed the "kinderwhore" look to the fore. Love, along with her late husband, Kurt

Cobain of the grunge posterband, Nirvana, influenced a shift in the thrift shop fashion look. From Love's thrift shop slips to Cobain's laid-back, disheveled style, the twosome had suburban kids around the world rifling through thrift store racks.

While Love and Cobain were tearing up the stage in their thrift shop finds, Los Angeles-based artist Jim Shaw was trolling charity shops for finds of his own. Since the 1970s, Shaw had collected kitsch and often very bad paintings found in thrift stores, never paying more than $35 for a piece. Ultimately, he amassed quite a collection (called Thrift Store Paintings) which has continually toured worldwide since the early '90s and is in part responsible for sparking interest in "bad art."

By the mid–1990s, thrift store culture was firmly entrenched as an acceptable modern shopping practice, and by the end of the decade two popular independent publications had been launched.

Pittsburgh, Pennsylvania resident Al Hoff was the first with the debut of her Thrift Score 'zine in 1994. A long-time thrifter who was at it years before it was fashionable, Hoff shared her finds, thoughts, and advice with fellow thrifters, eventually authoring a *Thrift Score* book for publisher HarperCollins in 1997.

1997 also saw the launch of *Cheap Date*. Founded by British editor Bay Garnett and her fashion stylist friend Kira Joliffe in London, *Cheap Date* soon attracted high-profile supporters and contributors, particularly in the fashion industry. Models like Karen Elson and Sophie Dahl were among those who appreciated *Cheap Date*'s anti-"lifestyle magazine" stance and aesthetic. *Cheap Date,* the book, was released in 1999.

The integration of thrift to fashion was complete when, in the late 1990s, the very charity stores which had been branded with such a negative stigma started isolating the items the staff felt could fetch top-dollar from the fashion conscious thrifter. Oxfam took things a big step further when it launched its Oxfam Origins (later renamed Oxfam Originals) stores to cater specifically to trendy thrift store shoppers, making true thrift shop bargains all the more rare and coveted.

Reprinted with permission from *Spree, A Cultural History of Shopping* by Pamela Klaffke (Arsenal Press, 2003).

GLOSSARY

co-opted—v. taking something over
eclectic—adj. mixed styles of clothing are worn as an outfit
icon—n. someone who always wears new styles
Oxfam—n. organization that works to end poverty, injustice, and inequality in the world
stigma—n. bad reputation
venerable—adj. respected because it is old and good

Reading 2: Consumers Seeking Citizen Brands

Sarah Dobson

This reading is from *Marketing Magazine*. It is a May 2003 study by the Montreal-based research agency Arnold Worldwide Canada which suggests marketing companies have to put in major efforts to restore trust with consumers.

After unsettling activities among organizations such as Enron, Worldcom, Global Crossing, Martha Stewart Omnimedia and Hydro One, "there's a clear and present crisis in human trust," says Lynn Fletcher, chief strategic officer at Arnold Worldwide Canada, speaking at the Canadian Marketing Association national convention and trade show in Montreal April 28. However, "there is a lot of hope for marketers even in times of distrust," she adds.

The Toronto agency recently conducted an online poll of 1,000 Canadians to produce *Canadian Mood and Mindset.* The survey found 82% of respondents felt executives put their own interests ahead of employees, 81% felt profits are considered more important than providing safe and reliable products, 74% believe the standards and values of corporate leaders have declined over the past 20 years, 83% said they would rather do business with a company whose values are similar to their own, and 88% said companies need to take their responsibilities to society and the community more seriously. The study also found 84% of respondents have walked out of a store or hung up the phone on a company, 58% complained to a company, 58% stopped doing business with a company they felt didn't treat them with respect, 36% avoided a company because their advertising was disrespectful, and 26% refused to do business with a company because of its social practices or policies.

Companies considered untrustworthy included Enron, Worldcom, Hydro One, Merrill Lynch, Nike, Shaw and Rogers, with untrustworthiness described as greedy, reckless, dishonest, secretive and selfish. Trustworthy companies included Tim Hortons, Zellers, the Bay, Roots, cbc.ca, President's Choice and Canada Post. The basics of trustworthy companies involve making good quality products and services, sold at a fair price, standing behind their offerings if something goes wrong, treating customers and employees well, doing no harm and giving back to the community.

Fletcher says consumers are moving towards a "citizen brand" which shares its values, delivers on its consumer promise and is conscious of a broader role in the community. Citizen brands include Tim Hortons, Canadian Tire, Body Shop, Starbucks, Ben & Jerry's, Saturn, President's Choice and Canada Savings Bonds, says Fletcher.

To win back consumers' trust, marketers should look into "respect marketing," says Fletcher. While companies might feel the exchange with consumers is about goods and services for money, for consumers it's also about time, energy and information.

Sarah Dobson, *Marketing Magazine,* 2003. Reprinted by permission of the publisher.

GLOSSARY

citizen brand—brand the buyer can always trust
respect marketing—honest advertising
respondent—person who provides information
standing behind—sellers promise their products are good
trade show—event where manufacturers show their products to buyers

Reading 3: Destructor

Arthur Black

Arthur Black is a well-known author who has won awards for his books of humour. This reading is from his book *Black by Popular Demand*. Black loves to play with the English language.

The lesson today concerns euphemisms. Linguistic Muzak. The pretty words and punchless phrases we use to cushion and deodorize our thoughts.

"Passing on" is a popular euphemism. So much softer and unfinal than "dying," "croaking," or "biting the dust."

"Expecting"—there's another dandy euphemism. It's vague and sexless, unlike such straightforward vulgarisms as "pregnant," "in calf," or "carrying a bun in the oven."

The military world is a veritable compost heap of euphemisms. They're the folks who gave us the "anti-personnel device" (read lethal explosive designed to shred flesh and pulverize bone). And who can forget "nuclear deterrent" (read annihilation of life coupled with long-term planet poisoning)?

There's another euphemism currently making the rounds. It's a real late-twentieth-century cutie.

"Sanitary landfill."

Roll it around on your tongue once or twice. Sanitary landfill. Might almost be the name of a new complexion cream. "Sanitary"—nice, clean, inoffensive adjective. "Landfill"—something to enrich the soil and eradicate all those unseemly pocks and craters.

It sounds almost as if we're doing the world a favour.

In fact, we're unloading our crap.

Shrink wrap, old supermarket bags, bald tires, rusty bedsprings, breakfast crusts, cat litter—not to mention greases, solvents, acids, alkalies, and a mad chemist's brew of toxic, cancerous gunk too various to catalogue.

And if we can believe the headlines, we're running out of places to bury the stuff. The city of Toronto, that megalomaniacatropolis on the barely flowing Humber, is currently dispatching outriders to most of the townships and counties within garbage-hauling distance of its borders. They hope to strike a deal with somebody—*any*body—who will agree to take Hogtown's garbage.

Toronto's not alone. There's not a Canadian city or town of any consequence that has to look too deeply into its municipal crystal ball to see the garbage piling up.

And this is in Canada, an underpopulated country with nearly four million square miles of back yard!

Makes you wonder what they do in less capacious countries. Is Portugal sinking under the weight of its trash? Is Belgium up to its eavestroughs in Glad Bags? What about England?

Actually, we don't have to wonder about one city in England. An ex-citizen of Nottingham recently wrote an explanatory letter to the editor of a Toronto newspaper.

The letter writer, one Ben Banham, recalled walking to school past a building known as the Destructor. Inside the building, "the waste was dumped on conveyor belts and sorted by hand. All metal was first removed, except cans, and sent to scrap metal yards. Butcher bones were sorted out and finished as bonemeal for gardens; bottles and glass jars were removed and recycled. The remainder went through the furnace and finished as ashes and cans. The cans were boiled and went to steel mills. That left tons of ashes, which had two uses. They were mixed with cement and made into cinder blocks... [which] were used to line the inside of the brick-built houses, also as partition walls inside, and plastered...

"It would be fair to say," writes Mr. Banham, "that scores of the numerous soccer stadiums in the country used tons of the ashes for several inches of drainage under the turf. Result: Nothing wasted."

Indeed. Mr. Banham says the Destructor handled and disposed of all the garbage of Nottingham, an industrialized city of 300,000.

But Mr. Banham is wrong on one count. Something was wasted: the lesson we ought to have learned from Nottingham.

Ben Banham is a senior citizen and the Destructor is a hazy memory. All the facts and figures cited above were true only when Ben Banham was a Nottingham lad.

And that was eighty years ago.

Arthur Black, author. Reprinted by permission of the author.

GLOSSARY

alkalies—n. chemicals that can burn your skin
butcher bones—scrap bones
complexion—n. skin of the face
dandy—adj. very good
deterrent—n. something that prevents
eradicate—v. completely remove
less capacious—smaller in size
megalomaniacatropolis—n. a huge city full of people with crazy ideas
outrider—n. a person who leads the way
too various to catalogue—too many to keep track of
unfinal—adj. not final
veritable—adj. real

Reading 4: You Are Here

Martin Silverstone and Kendra Toby

Sometimes rides in an amusement park can become famous. Here, Silverstone and Toby write about Le Monstre—a thrill ride in La Ronde park on an artificial island in the St. Lawrence River. Notice the point of view in this piece of writing.

You are Le Monstre, the tallest wooden twin-track roller coaster on the planet and the star attraction at Montreal's La Ronde Amusement Park. With 56 humans at your mercy, you plunge down to near-vertical drops, career through countless hairpin turns, and reach speeds of 97 kilometres per hour. Only seconds into the ride, you've earned your nickname—the scream machine.

Affectionately known to coaster buffs as a "woodie," you were built in 1985 to fill a nostalgic demand for old, wood-style rides. You've come a long way from your simple beginnings in St. Petersburg, Russia, where, in 1610, coaster pioneers covered wooden slides with ice. Two hundred years later, your ancestors debuted on tracks in Paris under the moniker Montagnes Russes.

Soon your kind became the centre of attention at Coney Island, New York. Passengers paid a nickel to climb to the top of a 15-metre tower to board and ride the Gravity Pleasure Switchback Railway—the first modern-day roller coaster. Your predecessors roared into the 1920s with more than 1,500 rides operating across North America. Plagued by safety concerns and maintenance problems, fewer than 200 coasters remained in operation in the 1960s, when engineers embraced steel as the material of choice.

Steel, however, cannot reproduce your clackety-clack sound, carried by the breeze of a Montreal summer night, or your "picket fence" effect, caused by the blur of 450,000 board feet of British Columbia fir rushing by. To many, you are considered the crowning achievement of William Cobb, the dean of coaster-builders. He knew better than anyone how to take advantage of the Newton postulate to which you and all your kin owe their success—what goes up must come down.

Your "up" begins with the steady click, click, click of the lift chain slowly hauling you at a 30-degree angle to a height equivalent to a 13-storey building. At the crest, you offer a torturous moment of chilling anticipation—and a great view of the Montreal sky line for those brave enough to open their eyes—before momentum and gravity take over. Riders feel their weight triple as you compress them in the valleys with a stomach-churning G force of 3.5, greater than the force felt by space-shuttle astronauts at liftoff. As you whiz over a hump, your passengers feel the weightlessness of minus 2 Gs.

In the trade, you are known as a twister. Your immense bulk has been condensed, and your tracks intertwine like a giant pretzel, bisecting 18 times. Every steeply banked turn convinces passengers that you will fly off the tracks, hurtle them into the chilly St. Lawrence River, or collide with an overhead beam. These delicious fears are your most crucial attributes, but annual stress tests and x-rays ensure that you are statistically safer than a game of pool.

When you thunder into your last set of heart-stopping twists and rolls, passengers breathe a sigh of relief. But you have one last surprise in store—Cobb's trademark "whoop-de-dos." These little rises and dips transform you into a bucking bronco over the home stretch. As you screech to a halt, your white-knuckled passengers disembark and stumble away, wobbly-kneed. Chalk up another victory for Le Monstre.

Martin Silverstone, Editor; Kendra Toby, Editor. Reprinted by permission of the authors.

GLOSSARY

bisecting—v. dividing into two equal parts
career—v. to swerve about wildly
condensed—v. made thicker
crowning—adj. ultimate
debuted—v. appeared in public for the first time
hairpin turn—a turn greater than 90 degrees
momentum—n. Physics: mass multiplied by velocity
moniker—n. name
Newton—n. 1642–1727, English mathematician
postulate—n. a claim
predecessors—n. those who came before
statistically—adv. probably, most likely
switchback—n. a railway track with steep ups and downs
torturous—adj. painful, out of shape

Reading 5: The Health Effects of Pesticides
David R. Boyd

David R. Boyd is an environmental lawyer and senior associate with the University of Victoria, British Columbia. He is the author of *Unnatural Law: Rethinking Canadian Environmental Law and Policy* (UBC Press, 2003).

The health impacts of pesticides can be divided into two main categories—acute effects and chronic effects. Acute effects occur after heavy exposure and are well documented. Chronic effects develop in response to lower levels of exposure over longer periods of time. Because so many potential factors are involved, it is more challenging to conclusively prove a cause-and-effect relationship between pesticides and chronic health impacts.

According to the World Health Organization, there are about three million cases of acute pesticide poisoning in the world each year. The vast majority of these cases occur in developing countries. Statistics are not available in Canada, but in the United States, there are between 10,000 and 20,000 physician-diagnosed injuries and illnesses ascribed to pesticides annually. Many of the people harmed by pesticides are farmers, farm workers, and children. According to the Canadian Association of Physicians for the Environment, presently acceptable levels of aldicarb on watermelons are such that a small child could easily consume enough of the pesticide to experience acute toxicity, including vomiting, seizures, and respiratory failure.

In the past, the chronic impacts of exposure were overlooked. There is still considerable uncertainty about: the effects of recurrent exposure to low levels; cumulative, interactive, and long-term effects; effects on reproduction; and differential sensitivity according to factors such as people's age, gender, and size. However, peer-reviewed medical and scientific studies have established links between pesticide exposure and various forms of cancer, birth defects, developmental abnormalities, neurological effects, reproductive effects, lung damage, and decreased immune function. It is vital to understand that although pesticide residues in food and water occur at very low levels, measured in parts per million or parts per billion, these low levels may still be dangerous to human health and the environment.

Scientific evidence is accumulating that some pesticides are among the chemicals that disrupt endocrine systems. By mimicking hormones, endocrine-disrupting chemicals may harm the reproductive system, suppress the immune system, and impair normal development of intelligence. These impacts may not be evident until years or even decades after exposure, posing a huge challenge to scientists and medical researchers. According to the Standing Committee on the Environment, about 60% of the agricultural pesticides applied in Canada are known or suspected endocrine disruptors.

Certain groups of Canadians are particularly vulnerable to health impacts from pesticides, including farmers, the Inuit, infants, and children. Studies conducted by Health Canada indicate that farmers using pesticides may suffer from increased rates of fetal loss, and an inability to conceive. Inuit women in Canada's north suffer from high concentrations of pesticides in their breast milk. Persistent pesticides that travel long distances and accumulate in the food chain contaminate the Inuit's traditional food supply. Infants and children are at greater risk from pesticides than adults, particularly their neurological, behavioural, immune, hormonal, and reproductive systems. Infants and children ingest more pesticides relative to their body weight as they are exposed to pesticides at home, in public places, and through air, water, food, and behaviours such as eating dirt and putting hands in their mouths.

David R. Boyd, Senior Associate, POLIS Project on Ecological Governance, Faculty of Law, University of Victoria. *Unnatural Law: Rethinking Canadian Environmental Law and Policy* (UVC Press, 2003); **www.unnaturallaw.com**; **www.polisproject.org**; **www.environmentalindicators.com.**

GLOSSARY

acute—adj. sudden and very bad

aldicarb—n. a chemical substance used to kill pest insects

chronic—adj. lasting a long time

decreased immune function—less able to avoid illness

differential sensitivity—some people are more sensitive than others

disruptor—n. something that interferes with

endocrine—adj. endocrine glands secrete substances into the blood

fetal loss—death of a fetus

ingest—v. eat or swallow

neurological—adj. refers to the study of the human nervous system

peer-reviewed—examination by persons who have credentials in the field of study

physician-diagnosed—identified by a doctor

statistics—n. evidence, verification

well documented—proven and well-known

Reading 6: Attracting the Good Bugs

Sheena Adams

Sheena Adams is an author and gardening expert. Her article provides practical information to those wanting to improve the health of their garden with the use of biological pest controls.

The use of beneficial insects to suppress pest insects is one of the oldest forms of biological control practised in our gardens. The idea is simple: attract and host these helpful garden residents and allow them to take on the role of a natural pesticide. As a bonus, they will also aid in pollination and aeration for a healthier garden. In effect, by encouraging a natural ecosystem that is good-bug friendly, you can enjoy both a reduced pest population and less damage to your plants.

What we consider "bad" bugs are primarily vegetarians, eating only plants, while "good" bugs consume other insects. To attract these good bugs into your garden, and keep them happy enough to stick around and start a life cycle, you will need to consider three basics: water, shelter and food.

Providing water to beneficial insects during the summer is simple. A birdbath or shallow pan with clean water will do, but be sure to add a few large rocks for the insects to perch on. Low puddles, ponds, creeks and other natural water sources will also work.

Shelter is the next step. The key is to ensure that good bugs have a stable habitat with protection from mowing, rototilling and other disturbances. Permanent pathways, plots of cover crops, perennial borders, large rocks and shrubs will provide beneficial insects with adequate permanent housing. And in the vegetable garden, a small crop cover plot such as buckwheat or rye will give bugs a place to shelter on hot summer afternoons.

When looking for their meals, beneficial insects will source out sweet nectar (for carbohydrates), pollen (for protein) and pest insects and/or their larvae and eggs. Beneficial insects can easily eat several times their weight in pest bugs, but that doesn't mean they will eat all the pests; they know better than to cut off their food source. They will, however, reduce the population to a minimal level that healthy plants can easily resist.

The annuals and perennials we plant provide insects with nectar for food, as well as foliage for nesting. In order to feed beneficials throughout the season, plant early, mid and late-bloomers with ferny or fragrant foliage in which the insects can nest. Favourite annuals of good bugs include scented geraniums, marigolds, alyssum, cosmos, zinnias and sunflowers. Popular herbs are lavender, parsley, chives, coriander, dill, fennel, tansy and thyme, while favoured perennials include echinacea, asters and daisies, as well as columbines and golden rod. The columbines provide early-season food, whereas the golden rod feeds later in the season when other perennials have finished. Beneficial insects are also attracted by such plants as blanket flowers, bachelor's buttons, butterfly bush, carrots that have gone to seed, feverfew, coreopsis, lady's mantle, yarrow, milkweed and Queen Anne's lace.

Of the common pests that regularly invade our gardens—aphids, caterpillars, slugs, snails, whitefly and weevils—all luckily have a natural predator that we can easily attract. Ground beetles will attack slug eggs; hover flies and ladybugs will go after aphids; and parasitic wasps will control caterpillars. In the soil, an application of beneficial nematodes will help to reduce weevil and leather jacket larvae. Whitefly may also be controlled by beneficial nematodes and hover flies. If you want a head start on increasing your natural predator population, or you find your initial resident population rather small, you can add to it by purchasing beneficials at local garden centres or from mail-order insect companies on the Internet.

Once you have established a balanced insect population, be extremely careful when it comes to the use of chemical insecticides. Good bugs are particularly sensitive. Alternatively, some bad bugs have been able to build up a resistance to certain products. Therefore, if a spray is applied or drifts in, it can quickly ruin the ecosystem that you have worked so hard to create.

So, when hunting through your garden for beneficial critters and insects, be sure to give a thank-you to the earthworms, hummingbirds, butterflies and spiders for their help in aerating, pollinating and controlling pests. And be sure to encourage them to stick around.

Reprinted with permission, Sheena Adams; Garden Wise, Canada Wide Magazines & Communications.

GLOSSARY

adequate—adj. enough to support life
aerating—v. adding air to soil
beneficial—adj. improving health
biological—adj. pertaining to life and living beings
ecosystem—n. interacting system of living organisms and physical environment (rain forests, deserts, coral reefs, grasslands, or a rotting log)
foliage—n. the leaves or needles of a plant
host—v. provide shelter and food for
nectar—n. sugary liquid produced by many flowers
nematodes—n. microscopic worms that live in soil
perch—n. something like a tree branch to rest on
perennial—adj. a plant that lives for three years or more
pollen—n. powdery fertilizing element of flowering plants
pollinating—moving pollen within a plant or between plants
predator—n. an animal that hunts other animals for food
stable habitat—a safe place to live

Reading 7: Eating Humble Pie

David Suzuki and Holly Dressel

David Suzuki, professor emeritus with UBC's Sustainable Development Research Institute, and environmental activist Holly Dressel are well-known environmental authors. In this reading they present a short analysis of the potential for negative environmental impacts attached to some products of biotechnology.

We have been told that genetically engineered (GE) material just disperses in nature, but in fact, it is remarkably permanent. Biologically engineered genes and DNA have been found to persist in soil organisms, in insects, pollen and especially in water, and have been found in agricultural ditches as much as a kilometre from an original site. The antibiotic-resistant marker genes used in the process have survived digestion by cattle and even bees, and therefore pose a threat of increased antibiotic resistance up and down the food chain. This is one reason why the technology is under a *de facto* ban all across Europe. The genes themselves are not confined to the original, patented plant, but can be spread by wind and pollen to other varieties of the same crop, and even to wild relatives. Canada is already having tremendous problems with genetically engineered canola, which has not only spread its herbicide-resistant trait to other canola, but is now affecting its many wild relatives, creating what are being termed "super weeds." The situation is so serious that one reason the Canadian Wheat Board is actively fighting the introduction of herbicide-resistant GE wheat, apart from market considerations, is that the species has many wild relatives that could become forever contaminated with herbicide resistance.

Bacillus thuringiensis, or Bt, is a natural insecticide. A gene encoding the lethal characteristic of this bacillus has been injected into many varieties of crops, including corn, potatoes and cotton, even though it affects not just pests, but a broad spectrum of benign organisms such as Monarch butterflies and lacewings, and beneficial micro-organisms in the soil. There are concerns that it could hold dangers for human consumption over the long term. Biotech firms also admit that crops engineered to contain the Bt gene will accelerate the natural process of insect resistance that has made so many other pesticides obsolete. For that reason, they suggest a complicated system of planting "refugia," or non-Bt crop species at specified distances from the main crop, to make sure there are still insects in the area who haven't been able to create a genetic tolerance to the Bt gene. The refugia are not only complex and difficult to maintain; studies have shown that few farmers, even in the First World, abide by such regulations for Bt crop use, which only marginally slow down the resistance process in any case. Once insects are all resistant to Bt, critics say, the biotech companies will then produce increasingly dangerous and poisonous pesticides for use on our food crops.

And of course, like all the products of the Green Revolution, genetically engineered seeds tend to replace local crop diversity with one, patented variety; in fact, from the developing company's point of view, that's their main purpose. So, like IR–8 rice or Holstein cows, Bt corn and Round-up Ready Soy are already displacing scores of existing, non-GE, non-hybrid varieties, which could, with all their genetic potential and local suitability, become extinct like so many others before them. Finally, like all Green Revolution varieties, GE crops demand large amounts of water and very strict regimes of chemical inputs, fertilizers, herbicides and, in the case of all but the Bt varieties, pesticides. Not only are these regimes difficult for the small farmers most capable of producing large amounts of food to maintain; they place a still greater burden of industrial chemicals and water pollution on the earth.

It's obvious even from this thumbnail analysis that biotechnology conforms to four out of the six criteria that Bill McDonough listed as characterizing the First Industrial Revolution: "pollutes soil, air and water, requires thousands of complex regulations, destroys biodiversity and cultural diversity, and produces things that are so highly toxic they require thousands of generations of people to maintain a constant vigil." Indeed, while biotechnology's potential benefits are very high, its potential for negative impacts borders on the cataclysmic. Certain products of biotech, like the recently revived "terminator" gene, could, if spread by pollen to other plants, destroy the ability of large numbers of plant species to ever reproduce themselves again. What that would do to agricultural productivity doesn't bear thinking about.

Good News for a Change, copyright © 2002 by David Suzuki and Holly Dressel. Published by Greystone Books, a division of Douglas & McIntyre Ltd., and the David Suzuki Foundation. First published in 2002 by Stoddart Publishing, Ltd. Reprinted by permission of Greystone Books.

GLOSSARY

antibiotic-resistant genes—these may protect bacteria from antibiotics
benign—adj. not harmful to health
biodiversity—n. the many different species of animals, plants, fungi, and micro-organisms
biotech firms—businesses that market products of biotechnology
biotechnology—n. the use of genetic engineering for practical purposes
broad spectrum—lots of different types
canola—n. the oilseed rape plant from which canola oil is derived
cataclysmic—adj. very destructive
de facto ban—a ban that is in effect but is not legally authorized
disperses—v. scatter in different directions
DNA—n. deoxyribonucleic acid used to store genetic information
encoding—v. converting into a different form
genes—n. sets of instructions that control biological development and function
genetic engineering—a laboratory science that studies how genes behave
Green Revolution—international effort to eliminate hunger by improving crop yield
herbicide-resistant—not harmed by herbicides
marginally—adj. very small
marker genes—genes put into plants making them resistant to herbicides or antibiotics
patented plant—growers of this plant must pay royalties to the patent holder
regimes—n. strict rules controlling how and when things must be done
resistance process—gradually more and more insects become resistant to an insecticide
thumbnail analysis—a brief preliminary study or investigation
trait—n. inherited characteristic such as tolerance of insecticides or herbicides
vigil—n. the watching out or standing guard to make sure nothing bad happens

Reading 8: Reflexology

Epilepsy Ontario

Reflexology can enhance well-being and is harmless in nature. This reading relates a little of the history of this relaxing treatment and gives details of its typical characteristics and techniques.

Reflexology involves applying pressure to specific points on the foot which are believed to correspond to different parts of the body. The technique can involve the feet, head, ears or hands, although foot reflexology is the most common. Both feet are worked on during the course of a full session, as the body is seen to be a whole unit.

Ancient pictographs show Egyptians massaging their feet, while old texts and illustrations show that the Chinese, Japanese, and Indian people all worked on their feet to combat illness. The current theory of linking various parts of the foot with specific parts of the body was developed in the early 1900s by Dr. William H. Fitzgerald, who called the system "zone therapy." In the 1930s, Eunice Ingham, a nurse and physiotherapist who used zone therapy, refined the system, identifying especially sensitive areas she called "reflex points" and creating a map of the body as represented on the feet.

In a typical session, the reflexologist will begin by gently massaging your feet. Then, the reflexologist will begin applying pressure to the reflex points thought to correspond to your health problems. S/he will treat one foot first, then the other. No instruments are required, but some practitioners use devices such as rubber balls to apply some of the pressure. If you have foot problems, such as severe calluses or corns, the therapist may refer you to a podiatrist for treatment since reflexologists do not treat food disorders. Sessions typically last from 30 to 60 minutes.

Some reflexologists claim that manipulation of the feet reduces the amount of lactic acid in the tissues and releases tiny calcium crystals which accumulate in the nerve endings of the feet. This restores the free flow of energy from the feet to the corresponding organs. Others speculate that pressure on the reflex points may trigger the release of endorphins, chemicals in the brain that naturally block pain. Some practitioners claim that the reflexology leads to a state of relaxation that opens the blood vessels and improves circulation. Still others credit a detoxifying effect, suggesting that the manipulation dissolves crystals of uric acid that settle in the feet.

Although some people claim that reflexology can help control seizures, there have been no major clinical trials to verify the effectiveness of reflexology. It is recommended, even by its advocates, that reflexology be used as an adjunct to conventional therapy.

Alternative and Complementary Therapies, Information Library, Epilepsy Ontario, Thornhill, Ontario, Canada L4J 4P8, **www.epilepsy.org**, July 3, 2004. Reprinted by permission of Epilepsy Ontario.

GLOSSARY

adjunct—n. something that helps the primary treatment
advocate—n. someone who recommends
ancient pictographs—old paintings on rock walls
calluses—n. thickened, hardened areas of skin
correspond—v. to match or be the same as
detoxifying—v. changing something harmful into something safe
lactic acid—chemical compound that can cause muscle pain
manipulation—n. touching with skillful use of the hands
reflex points—points on the body that relate to organs
specific—adj. particular
uric acid—organic compound, small amounts are in human blood and urine
whole unit—everything works together, like a system

Reading 9: Northern Threads

Dane Lanken

This reading, from *Canadian Geographic*, explores the cultural significance of clothing specially designed by a culture to meet fierce Arctic conditions.

One sees less skin clothing today in the Far North than in former times. The availability and convenience of factory-made clothes from away have cut into traditional Inuit apparel as thoroughly as anywhere else. But that is not to say fur parkas and pants have disappeared. As [the] photos from the book *Uvattinnit: The People of the Far North,* by Montreal photographer Karim Rholem, make clear, Inuit of all ages still cherish their time-honoured outfits.

"We can't talk about saving our language and culture and not include our clothes," says AaJu Peter, an Iqaluit law student and teacher with a particular interest in traditional Inuit skills. "They're very much a part of our identity. But there's another reason to hang onto them too: there are no better clothes. The woman's *amautik* (with its child-carrying pouch) is still the most practical jacket, and nothing else has come along that is as warm or more appropriate on the land."

Educational strategy in Nunavut today is to introduce children to modern and traditional economies. Thus at school, they learn computer skills as well as how to prepare skins and sew the sophisticated clothes that kept their forebears warm for centuries. "It is thanks to that technology we are here today," says Peter.

Caribou (*tuktu*) and two seal species, the ringed (*nattiq*) and bearded (*ugjuk*), provide the basic materials of Inuit costumes. All are found throughout the Arctic world—the seals in shallow waters off land or pack ice, the caribou on even the most northerly islands.

Traditionally, women prepared the hides by repeated scraping, using the *ulu,* a curve-bladed knife. Depending on use, skins were sometimes dehaired, and sealskins, in particular, were softened by stamping and chewing. Seals were hunted year-round and caribou in the fall, so late fall, while it was still light, was the clothes-making time of year.

Two layers of caribou were the usual winter wear, an inner layer with the fur facing in and an outer layer with the fur out. A two-layer caribou outfit weighed only about four kilograms, perhaps half of what a matching non-Inuit winter ensemble would weigh, and was not affected by the buildup of humidity that can plague woven materials, such as wool, in cold climates. The ringed seal provided parkas and pants for spring and fall and boots year-round, while the tough skin of the big bearded seal went for soles, belts and laces. Other creatures—polar bears, musk ox, wolves, dogs and waterfowl—provided trim and sometimes whole garments. Rainwear and babies' waterproof pants were made of gut.

Before the arrival of Europeans, skin clothes were sewn with ivory needles and, sinew thread cut from the long, strong tendons in the caribou's spinal column and hind legs. There were a variety of stitches used, including the "waterproof stitch," by which soles were sewn to sealskin boots in a way that left no holes for moisture to penetrate.

In her wonderful book about Inuit clothing, *Sinews of Survival,* Betty Kobayashi Issenman lauds this stitching as "unequalled in the annals of needlework." Indeed, a skill worth preserving.

Courtesy of *Canadian Geographic* Magazine.

GLOSSARY

annals—n. year by year narrative accounts of historical events
availability—n. easy to obtain
caribou—n. Arctic deer with large antlers in both sexes
cherish—v. to like and care for something a lot
ensemble—n. a coordinated clothing outfit
Far North—area of the earth's surface above latitude 50 degrees N
ivory—n. hard smooth white material from the tusks of animals
laud—v. express approval of
parka—n. heavy winter jacket usually with a hood
plagued—v. having too much of
pouch—n. bag-like container for carrying things
sinew—n. tendon that connects muscle to bone
skin clothing—clothing made for humans from the hides of animals

Reading 10: Secrets of a Streetwise Cyclist

Karen Campbell Sheviak

The author of the following selection emphasizes that knowledge and skills are important to cycling safety and enjoyment. Even experienced cyclists can benefit from taking a defensive cycling course.

I'm riding my bike on the streets of downtown Toronto—and when I say on the streets, that's exactly what I mean: not on the sidewalk, not hugging the curb but in the middle of a lane on one of the busiest streets in one of the busiest cities in Canada. I never thought I would feel comfortable doing that. My biking experience had, for the most part, been limited to suburban settings: roads with wide lanes and little traffic, and bicycle paths through serene parks.

I'm on the first day of a Can-Bike course that teaches defensive cycling to experienced adult cyclists who want to improve their skills and feel more comfortable riding in traffic. Before I took the course, I was one of those people who assumed that, because I knew how to ride a bike and was familiar with basic safety issues and the rules of the road, I could just put on a helmet and go. But Can-Bike was a real eye-opener. The course revealed misconceptions and gave me some invaluable tips for safe city cycling.

- Ride on the road instead of the sidewalk. Cycling on the sidewalk increases the danger at intersections, because drivers aren't watching the sidewalk for cyclists to ride into the road and they expect traffic coming off the sidewalk to be at walking speed, not cycling speed. Plus, pedestrians have been injured and even killed in collisions with cyclists riding on the sidewalk.

- Don't hug the curb; ride in the lane. I used to hug the curb all the time because I didn't want to be too close to the traffic. It's actually safer to ride farther out, where you're in the drivers' field of vision and you have room to manoeuvre if something goes wrong. And you should stay away from the curb when you're stopped, as well. Many cyclists move to the curb at red lights so they can remain seated on their bike with one foot resting on the curb. This moves them out of the flow of traffic—and out of drivers' field of vision—at the most dangerous place for cyclists: intersections.

- Keep your eyes up and look ahead while you're cycling. If you do this, you can spot obstacles, such as an open car door or a large pothole in the road, well ahead of time so you can plan to avoid them, rather than react at the last minute. The more traffic there is, the farther ahead you should look, because there will be more things happening that you have to react to.

- Look, signal, then look again. The second time you look is called the "lifesaver shoulder check." It gives you one last chance to make sure that the coast is clear before you turn or change lanes.

"A lot of people who cycle haven't thought about the rules of the road since they were kids," says Barb Wentworth, a bicycle-safety planner for the City of Toronto and a Can-Bike instructor. "Can-Bike teaches cyclists how to be more aware of the risks on the road and gives them the skills to avoid those hazards."

Can-Bike does this by emphasizing four basic principles: manoeuvrability, visibility, predictability and communication (MVPC). You can remember it with the phrase "most valuable person cycles."

"Even if people never take a Can-Bike course, if they make decisions with those terms in mind when they're cycling, they'll make the right decisions," says Darrell Noakes, a Can-Bike instructor and national examiner in Saskatoon.

Reprinted by permission of the author.

GLOSSARY

defensive cycling—techniques that improve cycling safety
field of vision—visible area (usually 160 degrees) when looking straight ahead
hugging—v. keeping close to
invaluable—adj. of more value than can be measured
know-how—n. the skill and knowledge to do something
manoeuvre—n. control movement and direction
misconception—n. an incorrect idea
shoulder check—look over cyclist's shoulder to see what's behind

Reading 11: A Hummer of a Good Time

Mark Feenstra

Freelance writer Mark Feenstra's love of the outdoors takes him to many exotic places and experiences. This travel article recounts impressions of a Hummer in the natural surroundings of Whistler, British Columbia.

In case you're not up on your latest hip-hop artist vehicles of choice, allow me to briefly explain what a Hummer is. Picture an overgrown jeep, so wide that the passenger and driver could hardly touch hands if they fully extended their arms. They're so tough they include drainage plugs in the floor in case the vehicle is submerged.

I'm sure you're thinking this may possibly be the most useless of all car innovations, but there are recorded cases of Hummers being towed out of lakes, drained and started up again with no repairs. Previously only utilized by military personnel, the Hummer has lately seen widespread use as an extravagant highway advertising gimmick or as toys for those with more money than they know what to do with, and no inclination to ever get their vehicle dirty.

Now that we have that out of the way, let me explain how my girlfriend, Abbie, and I came to find ourselves cruising through Whistler Village in one. As it turns out, an old friend of mine had found work for the summer doing all-terrain Hummer tours up Blackcomb Mountain. When I called him to see if he was available for coffee, he explained that he just happened to have room for Abbie and I to jump in on the evening's sunset tour, free of charge.

Abbie and I are what you'd call environmentalists and have been known to hug a tree or two while consuming granola. Riding around in a gas guzzling tank was not normally something we would consider doing, but it was free and it would be the first time in a while I had seen my friend, so off we went to meet him. Sure enough, the big red beast of a mutated jeep pulled in, blaring music from the local pirate radio station. We watched it park diagonally across two spaces and out popped my grinning friend in a faux beaver fur cap, flaps sticking out at right angles to his head. After a brief reunion and introductions to my girlfriend, we were off to pick up his other three clients for the evening ride.

Since the Hummer was being used for sightseeing tours, it had been converted to add a two-seater bench in between the back seats and two bucket seats in the rear. It was in these back seats we sat, and somehow the fur hat had made it back there as well to end up on Abbie's head. The interesting thing about being in a bright red Hummer is that when you drive through a busy town like Whistler, people turn and stare, not that we minded one bit; after all, we could drive over any of their vehicles without even spilling our coffee.

Once we pulled off the main roads there was a brief stop so that our guide could deflate the tire pressure with the flick of a switch in order to gain better traction on the steep terrain ahead. After cruising up a grade that would make most cars smoke and sputter, we reached a level plateau with a steep embankment on one side.

Just as I noticed that there were tire tracks heading up a nearby vertical section, my friend pointed the vehicle straight at the tracks and began to drive up them. Driving about fifteen feet up the side of the hill, he put the Hummer in park and made some wise crack about coming up here to watch the stars. If I had reached my arm straight behind me, I would have been able to touch the ground due to the angle we were sitting at.

Before we even had a chance to be fully amazed at our verticality, he backed down out of the spot, pulled around and proceeded to reverse up into the same position. We were now staring pretty much straight down at the ground and expecting the whole thing to tip over at any second. I'm sure there were some sort of safety regulations which had to be met, but it was at this point that I noticed the roll bar was at eye level and if we went over, then the back two seats, which aren't normally supposed to be there, might suddenly disappear. Among other feats of vehicular prowess, he further demonstrated the ability to drive over ditches and varied terrain where there were often only three wheels making contact at any time.

Soon the automotive acrobatics were over and we continued our journey up through the trees and to the top of the mountain. As we rode up we attained better and better viewpoints of the scenic village below just before melting into evening fog patches. Shrouded in mist, the tall skinny trees took on an ethereal feel and I was glad that we had been able to experience this, despite our excessive gas usage.

Around this time my friend was also well into his guide speech about the possibility of seeing bears, telling us that there used to be a man employed by the tour companies with the name of Crazy Willy, or something equally ridiculous, who would put on a bear costume and jump out to scare the tourists (when I pressed him on it later, my friend told me that this story was entirely true).

Although he mentioned that bear sightings were quite common up here, we were all surprised to come across a mother and two cubs playing on a patch of leftover winter snow. The only noise to be heard was the occasional snap of a camera shutter as we sat and watched the bears frolic beneath a misty sunset backdrop. Neither Abbie nor myself had seen a wild bear before and I couldn't imagine a better setting for a first viewing. My friend later told me that out of his numerous bear encounters, this was surely the most impressive.

We finished the tour by heading to one of the upper lodges and watching the sun sink below the distant peaks. Then we returned back down to paved roads where we paused briefly to ooh and aah as the Hummer re-inflated its tires.

I don't know that I'd be able to cough up the money to pay for one of these tours, but it was definitely an enjoyable and beautiful experience. Since I'm great at rationalizing things, I figured that since Abbie and I are environmentally responsible 99% of the time, we could afford to break habit once in a while and do something like rampage up a mountain in a gas-eating Hummer. Hey, at the very least, it's a new experience under our belts.

Mark Feenstra, freelance writer. Reprinted by permission of the author.

GLOSSARY

all-terrain—adj. can be driven off-road over steep, rocky, rolling, hilly land
embankment—barrier made of earth
ethereal—adj. unusually light and delicate
faux—adj. something made to resemble something else
gimmick—n. clever, attention-seeking device
mutated—v. changed accidentally
plateau—n. flat area of land higher than the land around it
prowess—n. a superior ability that you can learn

rampage—v. act recklessly
utilized—v. put to use
verticality—n. spatial property; uprightness
wise crack—a sardonic joke

Reading 12: Tommy Prince, Canadian Hero

Laura Neilson Bonikowsky

Laura Neilson Bonikowsky is a writer living in Edmonton, Alberta. She is the associate editor of the *Canadian Encyclopedia*. In this article she writes about Tommy Prince, Canada's most decorated Aboriginal war veteran.

German soldiers on the front line near Anzio, Italy, thought little of the peasant farmer weeding his field near their emplacement. The field had been torn up by shelling, the crops all but gone. The soldiers watched disinterestedly as the farmer slowly worked his way along the field, stopping once to tie his shoelaces. Finally, the farmer stopped his work, shook his fist at the Germans and then the Allies, and returned slowly to the farmhouse.

The seemingly innocuous farmer was actually a highly trained Canadian soldier, a marksman and an expert at tracking and making his way unseen around the enemy. His name was Thomas George (Tommy) Prince and he'd gained many of his skills growing up on the Brokenhead Ojibway Nation reserve, north of Winnipeg.

For Tommy, like most young men on Canadian reserves, World War II meant the chance for a job and three square meals a day. However, Aboriginals were routinely rejected, for health reasons but also because of their race. Tommy was turned down several times, despite more than meeting the requirements for recruitment. He persisted and was finally accepted on June 3, 1940. He was assigned to the first Field Park Company of the Royal Canadian Engineers. He accepted every challenge that came his way and excelled as a soldier.

By 1942 Tommy was a Sergeant with the Canadian Parachute Battalion. He was posted to the first Canadian Special Service Battalion and was among a select group of Canadian soldiers sent to train with an American unit to form a specialized 1600-man assault team. They became the first Special Service Force (first SSF), known to the enemy as the "Devil's Brigade." The name was adopted by Hollywood as the title of a 1968 portrayal of the elite unit. Tommy was portrayed as "Chief."

The first SSF soon saw action. In Italy, Tommy volunteered to run a communications line 1400 m to an abandoned farmhouse less than 200 m from a German artillery emplacement. Tommy set up his observation post in the farmhouse and for three days reported on the activity in the German camp.

On February 8, 1944, shelling severed the wire. Tommy, disguised as a farmer, found and repaired the break in full view of the enemy, while pretending to tie his shoes. His courage resulted in the destruction of four German tanks that had been firing on Allied troops. He was awarded the Military Medal for "exceptional bravery in the field."

Tommy continued to distinguish himself. In the summer of 1944, the first SSF entered Southern France. Tommy walked 70 km across rugged, mountainous terrain deep behind German lines near L'Escarene, going 72 hours without food or water, to locate an enemy bivouac area. He reported back to his unit and led the brigade to the encampment, resulting in the capture of over 1000 German soldiers. He earned the Silver Star, an American decoration for gallantry in action, as well as six service medals. Tommy was honourably discharged on June 15, 1945 and went home to Canada.

Tommy returned from fighting Nazi racism to a country that denied him the right to vote in federal elections and refused him the same benefits as other Canadian veterans. The business he'd entrusted to a friend failed in his absence. Facing unemployment and discrimination, Tommy re-enlisted and served with the Princess Patricia's Canadian Light Infantry. During two tours of duty in the Korean War he won the Korean, Canadian Volunteer Service and United Nations Service medals. He was wounded in the knee, and was honourably discharged on October 28, 1953.

Tommy Prince is known as Canada's most-decorated Aboriginal war veteran. He was also a brave and remarkable man with an impish sense of humour, a man who beat his own demons, including alcoholism. Tommy had a strong sense of civic duty and a fierce pride in his people. He said "All my life I had wanted to do something to help my people recover their good name. I wanted to show they were as good as any white man." He dedicated himself to attaining increased educational and economic opportunities for Aboriginal peoples.

Laura Neilson Bonikowsky. Copyright © 2004 Historica Foundation of Canada, **www.histori.ca**.

GLOSSARY

bivouac—n. temporary camp for soldiers
brigade—n. military regiments and supporting units grouped for a specific purpose
emplacement—n. place where a military weapon is positioned
encampment—n. temporary living quarters for soldiers
excelled—v. was superior
impish—adj. playful
innocuous—adj. not likely to harm or disturb
marksman—n. soldier skilled in shooting
recruitment—process of getting recruits for the military
sergeant—noncommissioned military officer
shelling—heavy fire of artillery

Reading 13: Our Cat Goes to Heaven

Margaret Atwood

Margaret Atwood is one of Canada's most famous, popular, and prolific writers. She often writes humorously about serious issues. The following selection displays Atwood's wit.

Our cat was raptured up to heaven. He'd never liked heights, so he tried to sink his claws into whatever invisible snake, giant hand, or eagle was causing him to rise in this manner, but he had no luck.

When he got to heaven, it was a large field. There were a lot of little pink things running around that he thought at first were mice. Then he saw God sitting in a tree. Angels were flying around with fluttering white wings; they were making sounds like doves. Every once in a while, God would reach out with its large furry paw and snatch one of them out of the air and crunch it up. The ground under the tree was littered with bitten-off angel wings.

Our cat went politely over to the tree. Meow, said our cat.

Meow, said God. Actually it was more like a roar.

I always thought you were a cat, said our cat, but I wasn't sure.

In heaven all things are revealed, said God. This is the form in which I choose to appear to you.

I'm glad you aren't a dog, said our cat. Do you think I could have my testicles back?

Of course, said God. They're over behind that bush.

Our cat had always known his testicles must be somewhere. One day he'd woken up from a fairly bad dream and found them gone. He'd looked everywhere for them—under sofas, under beds, inside closets—and all the time, they were here, in heaven! He went over to the bush, and sure enough, there they were. They reattached themselves immediately.

Our cat was very pleased. Thank you, he said to God.

God was washing its elegant long whiskers. *De rien,* said God.

Would it be possible for me to help you catch some of those angels? said our cat.

You never liked heights, said God, stretching itself out along the branch, in the sunlight. I forgot to say there was sunlight.

True, said our cat. I never did. (He preferred to forget an episode with a fireman and a ladder.) Well, how about some of those mice?

They aren't mice, said God. But catch as many as you like. Don't kill them right away. Make them suffer.

You mean, play with them? said our cat. I used to get in trouble for that.

It's a question of semantics, said God. You won't get in trouble for that here.

Our cat chose to ignore this remark, as he did not know what "semantics" was. He did not intend to make a fool of himself. If they aren't mice, what are they? he said. Already, he'd pounced on one. He held it down under his paw. It was kicking and uttering tiny shrieks.

They're the souls of human beings who have been bad on earth, said God, half-closing its yellowy-green eyes. Now, if you don't mind, it's time for my nap.

What are they doing in heaven then? said our cat.

Our heaven is their hell, said God. I like a balanced universe.

GLOSSARY

elegant—adj. pleasing; excellent

episode—n. distinct incident that contributes to a whole

littered—adj. scattered about untidily

raptured—v. transported

semantics—n. study of the meaning of language

testicles—n. male organs that produce spermatozoa

Reading 14: Governments as Gambling Addicts

Sol Boxenbaum

Sol Boxenbaum is CEO of Viva Consulting Family Life Inc., a Montreal non-profit organization that treats gambling addicts. He is a well-known advocate and educator. In the following selection, Boxenbaum discusses the potential danger of gambling addiction brought on by video lottery terminals.

The most addictive form of gambling, the video lottery terminal (VLT), can be found in just about every neighbourhood bar, bowling alley, family restaurant and pool hall in Quebec. Neon signs invite one and all to play a game that provides the provincial government with $1.5-million of net revenue every day of the year.

Before governments discovered how much money could be made from it, gambling was illegal in Canada, and many considered it to be immoral. Now we face the first generation of Canadian children growing up in a society where gambling is not only legal, but sanctioned by governments that profit from its proceeds. These children are future gambling addicts: They need to be told that there's a reason VLTs have been called "electronic crack cocaine."

In Quebec, Loto-Québec, which owns, operates and regulates more than 14,000 VLTs, isn't warning anyone that these machines are potentially addictive. The absence of clear warnings about the dangers of VLTs is the basis for a class-action suit against Loto-Québec launched by lawyer Jean Brochu on behalf of an estimated 119,000 VLT gamblers throughout Quebec. While Loto-Québec has sought to quash some aspects of the suit, the Quebec Court of Appeal ruled last week that the suit can go ahead as filed. A trial date will soon be set.

This unprecedented lawsuit—believed to be the first against a government gambling agency—is being watched worldwide and could lead to similar suits. The suit, which seeks almost $700-million in damages to compensate VLT addicts for counselling and legal fees, is built on the premise called "duty of care," which places an obligation of including a safety warning on any potentially harmful product or activity.

To this day, Loto-Québec has not placed clear warnings on VLT screens. Its slogan "Let The Game Remain A Game" is not a genuine warning about the potential dangers of VLT gambling (imagine the tobacco industry labelling their product with a mere "Smoke Responsibly"). Yet an estimated 10 per cent of Quebec's population play VLTs on a regular basis; an estimated 125,000 of them are compulsive gamblers.

My firm counsels many who seek help for gambling addiction in English-speaking Quebec. Nine out of 10 problem gamblers we treat are VLT gamblers. Their gambling has major implications in terms of quality of family life, resulting often in conjugal violence, child poverty, and even homicide.

What VLT gamblers aren't being told is that they are competing against an electronic random-number generator that makes their chances of winning highly disproportionate to the potential maximum "jackpot" offered in Quebec. Nor are they told that their chance of winning does not increase with length of time played or amount of money fed into the machine. People who develop problems with VLTs crave an escape from reality—and increasingly, from the damages their gambling has already caused. Despite knowing that $500 is the most they can win, many VLT players have gambled away their life savings. Pathological gambling has the highest attempted suicide rate of all addictions.

Studies conducted at McGill University indicate an alarming increase in the number of people under 25 now experiencing gambling problems. By not warning young people about the dangers of VLT gambling, Loto-Québec is gambling with their futures.

Sol Boxenbaum, CEO of Viva Consulting Family Life Inc., a Montreal non-profit organization that treats gambling addicts.

GLOSSARY

addictive—adj. causing dependence
compulsive—adj. difficult to resist
conjugal—adj. between a wife and husband
crack cocaine—purified and potent form of cocaine that is smoked
highly disproportionate—much too large or small by comparison
homicide—when one person kills another
immoral—violating principles of right and wrong
mere—the minimum facts
pathological—diseased
quash—declare invalid
random-number generator—software application used to choose numbers haphazardly
unprecedented—there has never been one like it

Answer Key

Chapter 1: Parts of Speech

Self-Test

1. Words are classified according to how they function; these word classifications are called the *parts of speech*.
2. a) names a person, place, thing
   b) takes the place of a noun
   c) shows action by showing what the subject does or links the subject to the rest of the sentence
   d) describer or modifier of a noun
   e) describes or modifies verbs, adjectives, or other adverbs
   f) describes or modifies nouns, adjectives, or adverbs in the sentence
   g) word that joins
   h) word of expression

Exercise 1 *Word Position and Part of Speech*

1. a) adjective
   b) verb
   c) noun
2. a) verb
   b) adjective
   c) noun
3. a) noun
   b) adjective
   c) verb
4. a) verb
   b) adjective
   c) noun
5. a) verb
   b) noun
   c) adjective
6. a) verb
   b) adjective
   c) noun
7. a) adjective
   b) verb
   c) noun

ESL Pointer Exercise 1 *Word Order*

1. The three Japanese students arrived in Canada last spring.
2. Samir usually dislikes noise in the apartment after midnight.
3. The committee celebrated the athlete's superior accomplishments.
4. Will we meet you at the coffee shop at seven o'clock?
5. Chan often mixes paint for the hardware store.
6. Amal noticed the new student in the cafeteria yesterday.
7. Her party usually includes several guests from Africa.
8. The swimmer always wears goggles in the pool.
9. Anton and Blaz arrived in Canada from Germany during the winter.
10. Our family usually enjoys hot porridge on a cold morning.

Chapter 2: The Basic Sentence

Self-Test

1. No	5. No	9. Yes	13. Yes
2. No	6. Yes	10. No	14. Yes
3. Yes	7. Yes	11. No	15. No
4. Yes	8. Yes	12. No	

Exercise 1 Identifying Sentences

1. Yes	5. No	9. Yes	13. Yes
2. No	6. Yes	10. Yes	14. Yes
3. Yes	7. Yes	11. No	15. Yes
4. No	8. No	12. No	

Exercise 2 Finding Subjects of Sentences

1. Compound subject—Shing, neighbour
2. Simple subject—lawyer
3. Compound subject—he, band
4. Compound subject—student, technician
5. Simple subject—deer
6. Simple subject—spokesperson
7. Compound subject—uncle, grandfather, brother
8. Simple subject—captain
9. Compound subject—glassmaker, apprentices
10. Simple subject—dolls
11. Compound subject—miser, money
12. Compound subject—guests, pets
13. Compound subject—cucumber, cream cheese
14. Compound subject—Mr. Alnoor, sons
15. Compound subject—harpist, cellist, pianist

Chapter 3: Four Sentence Types

Self-Test: Part 1 Identifying Types of Sentences and Adding End Punctuation

1. Q, ?	5. E, !	9. Q, ?	13. C, .
2. C, . *or* !	6. E, !	10. S, .	14. Q, ?
3. C, .	7. Q, ?	11. Q, ?	15. S, .
4. S, .	8. C, .	12. C, .	

Self-Test: Part 2 *Changing Statements to Questions*

1. Do they enjoy learning English?
2. Does this new book belong to her?
3. Does he drive to Hamilton once a week?
4. Did the class meet on the third floor?
5. Did the store open at nine?
6. Does she often go out of town?
7. Did he wear an old coat to do the chores?

Exercise 1 *Finding Fact or Opinion*

1. O	4. O	7. O	10. O
2. F	5. O	8. F	
3. F	6. F	9. O	

Exercise 4 *Identifying Types of Sentences*

1. S, .	5. Q, ?	12. E, !	19. S, .
2. S, .	6. S, .	13. S, .	20. C, .
3. E *or* S (depending on the emotional impact the writer wants to make), . or !	7. C, .	14. Q, ?	21. S, .
	8. S, .	15. C, .	22. E *or* S, ! or .
	9. Q, ?	16. S, .	23. Q, ?
4. E *or* C, . or !	10. C, .	17. S, .	
	11. C, .	18. Q, ?	

Chapter 4: Sentence Patterns

Self-Test: Part 1 *Identifying Patterns*

1. 2	5. 4	9. 1	13. 1
2. 3	6. 3	10. 2	14. 1
3. 1	7. 2	11. 3	15. 4
4. 1	8. 3	12. 3	

Self-Test: Part 2 *Identifying Clauses*

1. The organist is an undercover agent for the police.
2. he pretends to be working.
3. The worst job was being a line cook
4. Quebec City is a special place to visit
5. Four men got out of the car

Self-Test: Part 3 *Constructing Patterns of Sentences*

Have your instructor or a classmate check your answers to this section.

Self-Test: Pattern One Sentences Part 1: Identifying Sentences

1. not a sentence
2. sentence
3. not a sentence
4. sentence
5. not a sentence

6. sentence
7. sentence
8. sentence
9. sentence
10. not a sentence

Self-Test: Part 2 Identifying Subjects and Predicates

1. *subject*: many cooks; *predicate*: like to grow fresh herbs
2. *subject*: a fiddler and a drummer; *predicate*: played every day outside my shop during the festival
3. *subject*: his career in politics; *predicate*: was finished in 2004
4. *subject*: the small, sleek brown otter; *predicate*: caught two small crabs for breakfast
5. *subject*: our relatives; *predicate*: will be at the terminal to meet us next week
6. *subject*: Ramone and Cecile; *predicate*: were engaged over the weekend
7. *subject*: Jasper National Park in Alberta; *predicate*: contains the largest icefield in the Canadian Rocky Mountains
8. *subject*: Duncan; *predicate*: spotted a small sailboat on the horizon
9. *subject*: Toby's children; *predicate*: take ballet lessons at the community centre
10. *subject*: Brandon, Manitoba; *predicate*: has a major university

Self-Test: Part 3 Identifying Pattern 1 Sentences

1. S	4. No	7. S	10. No
2. No	5. S	8. No	
3. S	6. No	9. S	

Exercise 1 Identifying Pattern One Sentences

1. 1	5. 1	9. 1	13. No
2. No	6. No	10. 1	14. No
3. 1	7. No	11. 1	15. No
4. 1	8. 1	12. 1	

Exercise 3 Identifying Pattern One Sentences

1. 1	5. 1	9. 1	13. 1
2. 1	6. 1	10. 1	14. No
3. No	7. No	11. 1	15. No
4. 1	8. 1	12. No	

Exercise 4 *Identifying Pattern One inside Pattern Two Sentences*

1. <u>Several of the technicians were away for special training</u>, but <u>no one had been hired to replace them on the job</u>.
2. <u>Sometimes Rob stops for supper at fast-food outlets</u>, and <u>he loves to order the largest burger with extra cheese</u>.
3. <u>Some dogs have waterproof coats</u>, and <u>they can stay relatively dry even in heavy rain</u>.
4. <u>I was at a dance last Friday night</u>, and <u>I met a great new guy from New Zealand</u>.
5. <u>Please freeze this extra fish</u>, and <u>package up the salad for lunch tomorrow</u>.
6. <u>Health care workers walked off the job in Edmonton</u>, and <u>their union leader made an announcement about their complaints</u>.
7. <u>He was not sponsored in the race</u>, but <u>he ran anyway</u>.
8. <u>A backbencher from the provincial government apologized for his error</u>, and <u>he offered to resign his position on the committee</u>.
9. <u>The newest hybrid cars are becoming popular</u>, but <u>they remain too pricey for the average consumer</u>.
10. <u>Calgary firefighters were called to a house fire in the early morning</u>, but <u>they were unable to save the dwelling</u>.

Exercise 5 *Identifying Conjunctions*

1. nor (not either)	6. but (contrast)	11. or (choice)
2. for (reason)	7. or (choice)	12. but (contrast)
3. and (add)	8. yet (contrast)	13. nor (not either)
4. for (reason)	9. and (add)	14. or (choice)
5. so (consequence)	10. but (contrast)	15. for (reason)

Self-Test: *Pattern Three Sentences* Part 1: *Identifying Pattern Three Sentences*

1. No	4. 3	7. 3	10. 3
2. 3	5. 3	8. No	
3. No	6. No	9. No	

Self-Test: Part 2 *Clauses in Pattern Three*

1. <u>Maxie wishes to apologize</u> (because she took your car).
2. (When the dinner begins), <u>tell us some of your favourite jokes.</u>
3. <u>Oda married Carla at the University of Regina</u> (when they were both physics students).
4. The paint (that I bought for the dining room) <u>is a bright yellow rather than a creamy one.</u>
5. <u>Please disregard</u> (what the pilot says to you during the flight).
6. <u>Most of the time the singer entertains on the cruise ship</u> (although he would prefer to be in Las Vegas).
7. <u>No one suspected</u> (that the mild, wrinkled, old woman was the bank robber).
8. (If the announcer forgets how to pronounce your name), <u>please assist him.</u>
9. <u>She has been the curator of a major museum in Toronto</u> (since she graduated with a master's degree in fine arts.)
10. (Before we light the birthday candles on our cake), <u>let's all make a wish!</u>

Exercise 7 *Identifying Types of Clauses*

1. [When the paint factory allowed effluent into the stream], <u>thousands of salmon fingerlings died.</u>
2. <u>The diamonds glittered</u> [as they lay in the snow].
3. <u>Do not hesitate to call me</u> [if you have concerns].
4. [After you add the eggs], <u>stir the dumpling dough rapidly.</u>
5. <u>The heat from the July sun is not good for lettuce</u> [because the leaves wilt easily].
6. <u>The school district is promoting a new reading program for kindergarten classes</u> [as it relates its complete literacy offerings in its current brochure].
7. <u>His website features pink poodles, dancing popcorn, and a blinking robot</u> [when you click the "enter" button].
8. <u>The light</u> [that comes in from the street] *disturbs my sleep.*
9. <u>The bartender</u> [who runs this place] *is an old friend of the duke's.*
10. <u>She studied the map</u> [which confused her even more].

Exercise 13 *Identifying Pattern Four Sentences*

1. No	4. No	7. No
2. 4	5. No	
3. 4	6. No	

ESL Pointer Exercise 1 *Identifying Pattern One Structures*

1. S-V-ADV	5. S-LV-N	9. S-LV-N	13. S-V-O
2. S-V-O	6. S-LV-ADJ	10. S-LV-N	14. S-V-O
3. S-V-O	7. S-V-ADV	11. S-V-O	15. S-V-ADJ
4. S-LV-ADJ	8. S-LV-ADJ	12. S-V-ADV	

Chapter 5: Noun and Pronoun Usage

Self-Test: Part 1 *Noun and Pronouns*

1. *herd* is a common, concrete, collective noun.
   elk is a common, concrete noun.
   grass is a common, concrete noun.
   course is a common, concrete noun.
2. *Sumi* is a proper noun.
   faith is a common, abstract noun.
   ability is a common, abstract noun.
   choices is a common, abstract noun.
3. *Mount Rose Bakery* is a proper noun.
   biscotti is a common, concrete noun.

Self-Test: Part 2 *Attributive Nouns*

1. They are building an innovative <u>town</u> hall next to the <u>community</u> centre.
2. What <u>furniture</u> store sells <u>leather</u> chairs?
3. At the meeting, we discussed <u>employee</u> benefits for the new salespeople.

4. <u>Nanaimo</u> bars, one of my favourite desserts, are so fattening.

5. From the terrace, Ivan and Mary Rose are watching the <u>Spanish</u> dancers.

Self-Test: Part 3 *Functions of Nouns*

1. Bernice; her husband—subjects
   camp—object of the verb *operate*
   Saskatchewan—object of the preposition *in*
2. lieutenant—subject
   supervisor—subject complement
   mission—object of the preposition *during*
   (*rescue* is an attributive noun here)
3. gang—subject
   thieves—object of the preposition *of*
   mountains—object of the preposition *in*
4. candidates—subject
   parts—object of the preposition *for*
   actors—subject complement
5. candles—object of the verb *set out*
   beach—object of the preposition *on*
   memorial—object of the preposition *during*
   friend—object of the preposition *for*

Self-Test: Part 4 *Possessives*

1. the bride's bouquet
2. Ross's sweater
3. the monkey's cage
4. the company's policy
5. the children's toys

Self-Test: Part 5 *Noun Plurals*

1. foxes
2. teeth
3. wrenches
4. trays
5. kisses
6. volcanoes
7. people
8. lunches
9. samples
10. candies

Self-Test: Part 6 *Pronoun Cases*

1. Who was first over the finish line?
2. His barking all night disturbs my sleep.
3. Zachary and I play in a band on the weekends.
4. The chief investigator whom the agency had hired was a drunkard.
5. It was actually she who rode the motorcycle.

Self-Test: Part 7 *Pronoun Agreement*

1. Everybody should remember to bring <u>his or her</u> backpack on the hike.
2. Few of those boards <u>are</u> useful for the tree house.
3. One of the students <u>wants</u> to arrange the ski trip.
4. The government must be accountable, and <u>it</u> should do <u>its</u> duty to the people.
5. When the last person leaves the building, <u>he or she</u> should lock the steel doors.

Exercise 3 *Finding Proper Nouns and Abstract Nouns*

1. delight (abstract), <u>Uncle MacIntosh</u>
2. Ramjit, <u>Commercial Avenue</u>, <u>Main Street</u>
3. hope (abstract), <u>Academy of Fine Art</u>, music (abstract), <u>Montreal</u>
4. frustration (abstract), <u>Nazim</u>, <u>Coke</u>, <u>Mazda</u>
5. solution (abstract), <u>I.M. Moved</u>, *<u>Introductory Physics</u>*, problem (abstract)
6. <u>Harbour Towers</u>
7. Happiness (abstract), <u>Fang Yin</u>, dream (abstract)
8. <u>Hull</u>
9. community (abstract), <u>7–Eleven</u>
10. fame (abstract), melody (abstract)
11. <u>Suzette</u>, <u>Kleenex</u>, sadness (abstract)
12. doubt (abstract), sleep (abstract), <u>Mrs. Guptah</u>
13. health (abstract), <u>Health Canada</u>
14. <u>Samson</u>, <u>Delilah</u>
15. <u>Miss Soto</u>, fright (abstract), life (abstract), <u>MediaSport Technology Building</u>

Exercise 5 *Identifying Types of Nouns*

1. recreation (common/attributive)
   director (common/concrete)
   English (proper/attributive)
   passengers (common/concrete)
   Jamaican (proper/attributive)
   cruise (common/abstract)
2. idea (common/abstract)
   Premier Wrangler (proper/concrete)
   office (common/concrete)
3. Pamela (proper/concrete)
   outline (common/concrete)
   report (common/concrete)
   Pacific (proper/attributive)
   dolphin (common/concrete)
4. California (proper/attributive)
   sea (common/attributive)
   lions (common/concrete)
   tricks (common/abstract)
5. Ling (proper/concrete)
   Chinese (proper/attributive)
   tea (common/concrete)
   breakfast (common/concrete)

Exercise 6 *Functions of Nouns*

1. *Dictator* is the subject of the sentence; *guests* is the object of the verb; *stories* is the object of the preposition *with*.
2. *Character* is the subject of the sentence; *book* is the object of the preposition *in*; *chef* is the subject complement after the linking verb *is*; *hotel* is the object of the preposition *at*.
3. *Santoso* is the subject of the sentence; *notes* is the object of the verb *is taking*; *meeting* is object of the preposition *of*; *Society* is object of the preposition *of*.
4. *Allen* is the subject of the sentence; *steward* is the subject complement after the linking verb *is*; *union* is the object of the preposition *in*.
5. *Fielder* is the subject of the sentence; *ball* is the object of the verb *threw*; *baseman* is the object of the preposition *to*.
6. *UPS* is the subject of the sentence; *packages* is the object of the verb *delivered*; *floor* is object of the preposition *to*; *tower* is object of the preposition *of*.
7. *Danh* is the subject of the sentence; *trip* is the object of the verb *won*; *British Isles* is the object of the preposition *to*.
8. *Helen* and *Vi* are both subjects of the sentence (compound subjects); *reporters* is the subject complement after the linking verb *were*; *scene* is object of the preposition *on*.

Exercise 9 *Forming Possessives*

1. tomorrow's news
2. two birds' nest
3. the Toors' cat *or* the Toor family's cat *or* the Toor family cat
4. the woman's slippers
5. Shakespeare's plays
6. one man's wallet
7. the nation's affairs
8. joint ownership: Bob and Ami's car
9. the committees' ideas
10. the surgeon's skills
11. the geese's calls
12. Dickens' novels *or* Dickens's novels
13. the day's soup
14. Joan's feelings

Exercise 10 *Forming Plurals*

1. rodeos
2. trays
3. bubbles
4. flurries
5. wives
6. solos
7. turkeys
8. elves
9. churches
10. risks
11. boxes
12. waves
13. bunches
14. worries
15. keys
16. halves
17. children
18. species
19. fences
20. policies

Exercise 11 *Recognizing Pronouns*

1. The glistening sea (it)
2. Alf and Shorty (they)
3. The clock (it)
4. Benny and Klaudia (they)
5. Collin (he)
6. Hot chocolate (it)
7. The students and their coach (they)
8. Luke (he)
9. Boris (you)

Exercise 14 *Pronoun Agreement*

1. Squirrels and chipmunks are related and their habits are similar.
2. The police officer was stopping traffic along the highway, and he was asking drivers questions. (*or* she)
3. Has everyone given his or her consent to have his or her pictures taken on Friday? (The original sentence may stand, however, since it uses inclusive language and is smoother. Check with your instructor.)
4. Some of the printer cartridges have dried up.
5. Jana dislikes films that depict violence because they tend to oversimplify situations.
6. The young soccer coach gave me a book to read, and it will improve my winning psychology.
7. Few workers spend time developing their safety knowledge on the job.
8. Many of those books smell musty.
9. A person usually doesn't want to show how he or she feels.
10. The curriculum committee has filed its report.

ESL Pointer Exercise 2 *Demonstrative Pronoun Agreement*

1. Those
2. These
3. this
4. these
5. This
6. this
7. these
8. this
9. These
10. those

Chapter 6: Verbs

Self-Test: Part 1 *Identifying Types of Verbs*

1. buys (action)
2. is (linking)
3. do (auxiliary); want (action)
4. has (auxiliary); tried (action)
5. becomes (linking); eats (action)
6. invited (action)
7. are (auxiliary); throwing (action); is (auxiliary); leaving (action)

Self-Test: Part 2 *Recognizing Transitive and Intransitive Verbs*

1. bought (T)
2. speaks (INT)
3. ran (INT)
4. buttered (T)
5. remain (INT)

Self-Test: Part 3 *Auxiliary Verbs and Their Functions*

1. do (E)
2. can (M)
3. had been (T)

4. was (T)
5. Were (T)
6. Will (T)

7. must (M)

Self-Test: Part 4 *Identifying Verb Phrases*

1. is calling
2. should be expecting
3. must remember
4. Have seen

5. has been acting
6. Were staring
7. must have been saving

Self-Test: Part 5 *Identifying Verb Tenses*

1. will be able (future)
2. must have planned (present)
3. are trying (present)
4. will be staying (future)
5. were completing (past)

6. did give (past)
7. are becoming (present)
8. will work (future)
9. was interfering (past)
10. had made (past)

Self-Test: Part 6 *Adding Correct Forms of Verbs*

1. takes or took
2. takes
3. ride

4. fell, broke
5. bent
6. begun

7. thought

Self-Test: Part 7 *Forms of Tenses*

1. had been chasing (past perfect progressive)
2. is having (present progressive)
3. brightened (simple past)
4. must have been paying (present perfect progressive)
5. pretends (simple present)
6. has left (present perfect)
7. will be pleased (future perfect)

Exercise 1 *Recognizing Action Verbs*

1. frighten
2. opened
3. engulfed

4. brew/drink
5. ordered
6. grow

7. blessed/applauded
8. wants/thinks
9. writes/reports

10. enter

Exercise 2 *Identifying Intransitive and Transitive Verbs*

1. ordered (T)
2. refused (IN), to answer (T)
3. spoke, responded (IN)
4. voted (IN)

5. vacations, becoming (IN)
6. broke, will forgive (T)
7. pruned (T)
8. threw, got (T)

9. pretended (IN), to be (T)
10. prepared (T)
11. concentrated, did look (IN)
12. appealed, remained (IN)

Exercise 4 *Identifying Auxiliary Verbs*

1. may/would
2. will
3. has/has
4. might

5. might/will
6. has
7. became/will
8. has

9. Did/did
10. will
11. do
12. May

13. must
14. would
15. were

Exercise 7 *Identifying Time of Verbs*

1. will be marking (future)
2. were cracking (past)
3. is arresting (present)
4. will speak (future)
5. had received (past)
6. do grow (present)
7. has slipped (present)
8. will wait (future)

9. were smoking (past)
10. did protest (past)
11. had forgotten (past)
12. will forgive (future)
13. are ripening (present)
14. were moving (past)
15. is expecting (present)

Exercise 8 *Identifying Tenses*

1. was bargaining (past progressive)
2. slid (simple past)
3. will have been broadcasting (future perfect progressive)
4. is promising (present progressive)
5. has been slipping (present perfect progressive)
6. will brew (simple future)
7. have waited (present perfect)
8. will have exceeded (future perfect)
9. take (simple present)
10. have been studying (present perfect progressive)
11. will be planning (future progressive)
12. were fighting (past progressive)
13. had not understood (past perfect)
14. had been working (past perfect progressive)
15. has supplied (present perfect)

Exercise 9 *Transforming Tenses*

1. Maybe they found out about us.
2. George is entering to win the horseshoe throwing contest.
3. The choir was giving a lovely performance.
4. No one will have been cycling on the new bike path since the flooding of some sections.
5. Layer cakes were a favourite at birthday parties in the 1950s.
6. Are you mowing the lawn for your in-laws?
7. Several of the witnesses had been refusing to give testimony.
8. Children from several classes are planting a garden along the south wall of the school.

Exercise 11 *Using Correct Verb Form*

1. sold (sell)
2. sung (sing)
3. written (write)
5. freezes (freeze)
6. ridden (ride)
7. tore (tear)
8. sank (sink)

9. grown (grow)
10. leaves (leave) or left
11. promise *or* promised (promise)
12. spoken (speak)
13. eat (eat) or ate
14. broken (break)

15. knew (know)
16. taken (take)
17. ate (eat)
18. rose (rise)
19. slept (sleep), missed (miss)
20. drawn (draw)

ESL Pointer Exercise 2 *Changing Modals*

1. The landlady <u>can</u> raise the rent in my apartment building. (The modal auxiliary verb indicates ability.)
2. I <u>should</u> *or* <u>must</u> confess to the lie I told you. (The modal auxiliary verb indicates obligation.)
3. The paddlers <u>may</u> *or* <u>might</u> *or* <u>could</u> *or* <u>would</u> set off tomorrow if the weather is calmer. (The modal auxiliary verb indicates possibility. Notice the slight changes in meaning with each modal.)
4. Miss Ramos <u>may</u> *or* <u>might</u> *or* <u>could</u> be hired as the new vice-chair of academic operations. (The modal auxiliary indicates possibility. *Would* is not the best choice of modal since it usually is supported by a condition named in another part of the sentence.)
5. When my cheque arrives at the bank, I <u>can</u> take Yvette out to dinner. (The modal auxiliary indicates ability.)
6. The firefighters <u>should</u> *or* <u>must</u> protect themselves from serious injury by taking advanced training. (The modal auxiliary indicates obligation.)
7. Her children <u>may</u> *or* <u>might</u> *or* <u>could</u> perform at the concert at the university tonight. (Change the modal auxiliary to one that indicates possibility. *Would* is not the best choice of modal since it usually is supported by a condition named in another part of the sentence.)
8. If anything goes wrong with the plan, Alric <u>will</u> telephone us. (The modal auxiliary verb indicates determination.)
9. These cookies <u>should</u> *or* <u>must</u> be baked at 350 degrees for 18 minutes. (The modal auxiliary indicates obligation.)
10. Come-by-Chance, Newfoundland, <u>may</u> *or* <u>might</u> *or* <u>could</u> be one of the most interesting place names in Canada. (The modal indicates possibility.)
11. With a new excellent coach and money from a private donor to practise and compete, Violet <u>may</u> *or* <u>might</u> *or* <u>could</u> ski in the 2010 Olympics in Whistler, British Columbia. (The modal auxiliary indicates possibility.)
12. If you wake up early in the morning, you <u>should</u> *or* <u>must</u> assist with breakfast preparation for the guests. (The modal auxiliary indicates obligation.)

Chapter 7: Modifiers

Self-Test: Part 1 *Adjectives and Adverbs*

1. adverb, adjective
2. adjective, adjective
3. adjective, adjective, adverb, adverb, adjective
4. adverb, adverb, adjective
5. adverb
6. adverb, adjective
7. adverb, adjective
8. adverb, adjective, adjective
9. adjective, adjective, adjective
10. adverb, adjective, adjective

Self-Test: Part 2 *Prepositional Phrases*

1. We slowly paddled our canoe [in the still waters] [of Moose Lake].
2. Go practise your flute [in the back room].
3. [Without a care] [in the world], the puppies gambolled [in the grassy field].
4. Sometimes [in the evening] they go [for a relaxing stroll] [along the beach].
5. Where will you store your bicycle [during the harsh months] [of winter]?

Self-Test: Part 3 *Comparative Adjectives*

1. loveliest
2. better
3. prettier
4. best
5. taller
6. cooler
7. better
8. tighter
9. worst
10. brighter

Exercise 1 *Identifying Adjectives*

1. A <u>sudden</u> storm caused <u>extensive</u> damage to the <u>maple</u> tree in the park.
2. An <u>electrical</u> short in an <u>old</u> iron was the cause of the <u>house</u> fire down the street.
3. Yesterday I called the <u>new</u> plumber to come to fix the <u>leaky</u> faucet.
4. My neighbour is <u>cantankerous</u> at the best of times.
5. Bleach is a <u>caustic</u> substance found in <u>many</u> <u>kitchen</u> cupboards.
6. His argument was so <u>compelling</u> that we all agreed with him.
7. The <u>toasted</u> <u>tomato</u> sandwiches tasted <u>scrumptious</u>.
8. The <u>scraggy</u> brush was very <u>dense</u> near the <u>railway</u> tracks.
9. The pet was confined to the <u>dark</u> basement of the <u>family</u> house.
10. This <u>vanishing</u> cream eliminates <u>ugly</u> wrinkles.
11. Mr. Castillo's <u>carefree</u> attitude is <u>refreshing</u>.
12. In a <u>peaceful</u> part of the forest the <u>young</u> stag settled in for an <u>undisturbed</u> rest.
13. The <u>short</u>, <u>sharp</u> blade of this knife is <u>effective</u> for cutting mangoes.
14. The <u>serpentine</u> front of the <u>antique</u> <u>oak</u> chest of drawers made it very <u>valuable</u>.
15. The <u>civil</u> war was <u>devastating</u> to the <u>tiny</u> <u>African</u> country.

Exercise 3 *Recognizing Adverbs*

1. <u>Apparently</u>, the courier was <u>quite</u> lost on his new route.
2. On the weekends, Mel <u>regularly</u> visits his father at the nursing home.

3. <u>Finally</u>, Arlene spoke <u>calmly</u> to the angry tenant.
4. The sailboat appeared to float <u>effortlessly</u> on the peaceful ocean.
5. The leafy vegetables should be <u>coarsely</u> chopped and <u>quickly</u> stir-fried.
6. The archaeologists <u>unexpectedly</u> discovered an ancient text deep in the cave of the desert mountain.
7. During the campaign, Estella was <u>certainly</u> brilliant in the debate.
8. <u>Yesterday</u> the children were <u>happily</u> painting the back fence a bright green.
9. <u>Indeed</u>, many of the speakers were <u>strongly</u> opposed to the motion.
10. Krystal was concentrating <u>so</u> <u>deeply</u> that she did not hear me enter the study room.
11. <u>Today</u> we went about our unfinished business <u>efficiently</u>.
12. Wynn kissed the baby <u>tenderly</u> and <u>softly</u> closed the bedroom door.
13. The colt <u>awkwardly</u> frolicked on the grassy field.
14. <u>Suddenly</u>, Arnold swept his arm <u>backward</u> and <u>clumsily</u> knocked over Mrs. Piettla's favourite vase of flowers.
15. The artist <u>painstakingly</u> daubed vivid points of colour as he hummed <u>cheerfully</u> to himself.

Exercise 4 *Identifying Adverbs*

1. After a few drinks, we found ourselves <u>merrily</u> singing around the piano.
2. She is <u>equally</u> disturbed by the ugly rumour.
3. Lucy is <u>rather</u> short but is <u>apparently</u> good at basketball.
4. Mr. Lucas is <u>constantly</u> worrying about his huge property taxes.
5. The thief <u>quietly</u> entered the hotel room and <u>systematically</u> rummaged through the guests' luggage.
6. Randolph stood <u>approximately</u> 3 metres from the crowd before he began speaking <u>calmly</u>.
7. We were <u>just</u> leaving when the alarm rang <u>sharply</u>.
8. Are you <u>quite</u> sure you must leave <u>tomorrow</u>?
9. The boisterous children were playing together <u>contentedly</u>.
10. Our boss was <u>busily</u> directing us toward the meeting room.
11. <u>Apparently</u>, the husband was <u>considerably</u> older than his wife.
12. She strained <u>intently</u> as she listened at the outer door.
13. Because I was <u>quite</u> late, I had to eat my supper <u>unceremoniously</u> in my room.
14. Guadalupe stared <u>coldly</u> at her supervisor, and then with a sweeping motion she pushed her chair <u>backward</u> and smirked <u>crookedly</u> at him.
15. The guests were <u>visibly</u> upset by the minor earthquake that had rumbled through the resort town.
16. We were <u>definitely</u> opposed when the chairperson <u>wildly</u> preached her point of view.
17. <u>Quite</u> <u>often</u> the nanny will <u>cheerfully</u> take the children to the community centre.
18. I <u>almost</u> forgot my car keys when I got <u>extremely</u> busy <u>today</u>.

Exercise 8 *Prepositions*

1. above	4. on	7. down	10. beside
2. under	5. against	8. between	
3. across	6. up	9. before	

Exercise 10 *More Objects of Prepositions*

1. The road <u>to</u> the house (O) is long and winding.
2. The old cat became too hot <u>in</u> the sun (O).
3. The scholar <u>of</u> the month (O) was given a trip <u>to</u> Ottawa (O).
4. Her husband made repairs <u>to</u> the large family van (O).
5. I was talking <u>to</u> the woman (O) <u>in</u> the blue suit (O).
6. The editor <u>of</u> the paper (O) was sued <u>by</u> the city councillor (O).
7. An officer <u>from</u> the RCMP (O) visited the criminal justice class.
8. <u>In</u> the afternoon (O) the children built a fort <u>from</u> old boards (O).
9. The tips were divided <u>among</u> the staff (O).
10. The temperature rose <u>during</u> the day (O).

Exercise 11 *Prepositions Misused*

1. Yes, I am tired. *or* Yes, I am somewhat tired.
2. They worked hard. *or* They worked fairly hard.
3. I bought it from him.
4. Let's end it.
5. We will start wearing slacks today. *or* We will start wearing slacks effective today.
6. I bought it from someone.
7. Where is he?
8. I don't think she knows where she is going.
9. The paper blew out the window.
10. Look through the window at the snow. *or* Look out the window at the snow.

Exercise 12 *Identifying Types of Prepositional Phrases*

1. Marek and Hans hid the boat <u>under the bridge</u> (ADV).
2. <u>At night</u> (ADV) we can spot many sparkling stars <u>in the sky</u> (ADJ).
3. The baby <u>with the big brown eyes</u> (ADJ) was staring <u>at the bright lights</u> (ADV) <u>of the toy</u> (ADJ).
4. Go <u>through the doors</u> (ADV) and follow the stairs <u>to the right</u> (ADJ) <u>of the entrance</u> (ADJ).
5. The cowboy <u>with the 10-gallon hat</u> (ADJ) won the bucking contest.
6. <u>After surgery</u> (ADV), she did not understand the doctor's advice <u>about her diet</u> (ADJ).
7. <u>For two weeks</u> (ADV), Amir was sick <u>at home</u> (ADV) <u>with the flu</u> (ADV).
8. <u>Inside the submarine</u> (ADV), the crew was preparing <u>for war</u> (ADV).
9. <u>Under the porch</u> (ADV), we found an old blue bottle full <u>of strange stones</u> (ADJ).
10. The early ferry arrived <u>on time</u> (ADV) <u>for a change</u> (ADV).
11. The politician gave a speech <u>about world poverty</u> (ADJ) <u>to the conference delegates</u> (ADV).
12. <u>Outside the theatre</u> (ADV) the rain fell <u>on the waiting patrons</u> (ADV).
13. The technician and the controller will stop work <u>at seven o'clock</u> (ADV) and go <u>for supper</u> (ADV).
14. The load <u>of wash</u> (ADJ) was ruined <u>by the dye</u> (ADV) <u>from her orange pyjamas</u> (ADJ).
15. <u>About midnight</u> (ADV), the campers heard an eerie howling <u>from the dark woods</u> (ADJ).

Chapter 8: Verbals

Self-Test: Part 1 *Identifying Gerunds and their Functions*

1. touring around the countryside (subject)
2. practising the piano (object)
3. singing (subject complement)
4. playing baseball (subject)
5. telling stories of the old country (object)

Self-Test: Part 2 *Identifying Infinitives and their Functions*

1. to wait (subject)
2. to hum (object)
3. to worry (subject complement)
4. to draw (subject complement)
5. to please her employer (subject)

Self-Test: Part 3 *Identifying Participles and their Functions*

1. stretching, modifies *kitten*
2. rushing off, modifies *Dottie*
3. feared, modifies *one*
4. Crashing, modifies *waves*
5. soothing, modifies *Music*
6. adopted, modifies *daughter*

Self-Test: Part 4 *Correcting Errors with Verbals*

1. Yoni's pushing you to complete the project may provide you with motivation. (possessive case in front of a gerund)
2. After teaching the dog tricks all afternoon, I found the cat became jealous. (dangling participle: add a subject noun or pronoun for the participle to modify)
3. Sheena's running too hard and too long may injure her ankles over time. (possessive case in front of a gerund)
4. Regaining her strength, Louisa shifted the suitcase into another position. (dangling participle: move the subject noun for the participle to modify)
5. In the college play, his younger sister wanted to act eagerly and with passion. (Split infinitive: remove the adverbs from the middle of the infinitive. Reorganize the sentence for smoother reading if needed.)
6. The car's stalling made Mr. Brooks angry. (*Stalling* is a dangling participle. Reorganize the sentence.)

Exercise 1 *Finding Gerunds*

1. no gerund
2. gerund
3. gerund
4. gerund
5. gerund
6. gerund
7. no gerund
8. gerund
9. gerund
10. no gerund

Exercise 3 *Possessive Cases and Gerunds*

1. Velma believes your running for office is entirely silly.
2. Without his glasses, the counsellor was not seeing the student's frowning.
3. She was not aware of the municipality's warning posted outside the gate.
4. Their blocking your promotion at the firm was unwarranted.
5. Our kneading the dough made the bread soft and luscious.
6. The diplomat's describing the attack in the airport was fascinating.
7. The school board requires the parents' signing the release forms.
8. I don't like Frederico's cheating on his wife.
9. His understanding the directions is critical.
10. The registrar has approved your transferring to another program.

Exercise 4 *Identifying Infinitives and Infinitive Phrases*

1. to cry
2. to help you, to get ahead
3. to be afraid
4. to let you in
5. to swim the lake this year
6. to sing
7. to plague him
8. to gain the agent's attention
9. to do, to act
10. to shake the hand

Exercise 8 *Identifying Participles and Participial Phrases*

1. Watching the stars through a telescope
2. Frowning
3. roasted
4. Presenting the young man with a medal, decorated
5. Jerked, flaming
6. Standing his ground
7. Preparing the nest, gathered, frenzied
8. Kicking the mound with his foot, approaching
9. Absorbed in his mathematics problem, advancing
10. Roaming the meadows

Exercise 10 *Identifying Differences between Participles and Gerunds*

1. volunteering (gerund)
2. having no place to park (participial phrase)
3. taught from age three by a famous composer (participial phrase); respected (participle)
4. no participles or gerunds
5. whimpering (participle); stepping (participle)
6. created during or just after local showers (participial phrase); polarize (participle)

7. planning ahead for a party (gerund phrase)
8. after surviving a near death experience (participial phrase)
9. laughing all the way to the bank (participial phrase); moulded (participle)
10. having been compromised by the drug (participial phrase); compelling (participle)
11. burned (participle); deepening (participle)
12. hunting (gerund)
13. speeding in a school zone (gerund phrase)
14. baking cookies for the children (gerund phrase)
15. harnessed (participle); using solar panels in our homes (gerund phrase)

Chapter 9: Subject–Verb Agreement

Self-Test: Part 1 *Identifying Subjects of Sentences*

1. bell, alarm
2. Basketball, hockey, football
3. Either
4. noise
5. Leaving a relationship after ten years
6. queen
7. Cellphones, laptops
8. Yan, she
9. women
10. Dancing, swimming
11. box
12. Sue

Self-Test: Part 2 *Subject–Verb Errors*

1. sounds
2. has
3. asks
4. is
5. travels
6. is
7. is
8. plays
9. stops
10. like
11. are
12. are
13. The sentence could be correct as it stands if the writer means *not one single photo* is worth saving. *None of those digital photos are worth saving to your hard drive* means more than one.
14. is
15. are

Exercise 1 *Identifying Subjects*

1. Romeo
2. cups, saucers, Chenoa
3. None
4. players, coach, referee
5. issues, union
6. flood, people
7. basket
8. statue
9. To make special ethnic dishes
10. Having diabetes
11. herd, I
12. No one, some
13. reasons, McLooney
14. bar
15. fruit, vegetables
16. Most, some
17. Nobody

Exercise 3 *Identifying the Subject of Sentences*

1. Gretta
2. Mr. Loo, Mrs. Singh, Ms. Wong
3. cellphone, licorice, calculator
4. number
5. Being correct all the time
6. sun, roads, family
7. tellers, manager
8. Buying clothes for your children at garage sales
9. Ulrich, cousin
10. ingredient
11. Angelina, chocolate, peanut butter
12. Having a small stature
13. chickens, rooster
14. subject
15. majority

Exercise 5 *Identifying Subject–Verb Agreement Type*

1. have
2. is
3. knows
4. is
5. feels
6. was
7. sits
8. is
9. contain
10. is
11. was
12. disagrees
13. is (There is no specific rule, except that *conducting stem-cell research studies* is a gerund phrase acting as the single subject of the sentence.)
14. is
15. was

Exercise 7 *Repairing Subject–Verb Agreement Errors*

1. flows
2. is
3. OK
4. OK
5. are
6. is
7. was placed
8. were
9. attempts
10. attests
11. OK
12. wants
13. were
14. has
15. OK
16. have
17. OK
18. OK
19. OK
20. was
21. is
22. is
23. were

Exercise 9 *Editing for Subject–Verb Agreement Errors*

Ken enjoys the outdoors, but he notices that in the fall there (seems) to be a swarm of wasps everywhere he goes. Although none of the wasps (have) stung him, Ken (remains) curious about them. Some of the female wasps (appear) a bit more aggressive than others, especially as the season (comes) to a close. Ken knows that wasps (are) a social insect, so he often searches for the nest. A group of guards (remains) at the entrance of the nest to protect the queen inside. Neither the guards nor the queen (appears) to notice Ken. Disturbing the nest or killing the wasps (is) unthinkable. Ken, along with his children, (enjoys) cautiously watching the activities of wasps. Over the years, the family (has) learned many curious facts about them, and nobody in the family (has) been stung yet.

Chapter 10: Sentence Faults

Self-Test: Part 1 Recognizing Sentence Faults

1. F	4. CS	7. RO
2. CS	5. P	8. RO
3. P	6. F	

Self-Test: Part 2 Repairing Parallelism Faults

You may think of other solutions than those given here, so check with your instructor.

1. Downloading the new software from the Internet and configuring it with his other programs took Charlie four hours yesterday. *or* To download... to configure
2. The new building on campus is bright and spacious with lounge spaces for students. *or* The new building on campus is bright, spacious, and comfortable for students with lounge spaces. *or* The new, bright, spacious building on campus has lounge spaces for students.
3. Spending time with your children is interesting and challenging.
4. Meredith is appreciated as not only generous but also as humorous.
5. The company dislikes the complaints more than the customers do.
6. Bryce walked to the mall but not to his work.
7. The clerk talked to the customer for 20 minutes and demonstrated the power of the paper shredder. *or* ... has been talking ... and demonstrating ...
8. My cousin likes to read widely, deeply, and intensely.

Self-Test: Part 3 Repairing Different Types of Sentence Faults

You may think of other solutions than those given here, so check with your instructor.

1. My mother was wrapping the small gift, smiling to herself, and humming to a tune on the radio. (The fragment needs a subject.)
2. Wind and solar power are two natural sources of energy; they do not deplete or pollute the earth or its atmosphere. *or* Wind and solar power are two natural sources of energy that do not deplete or pollute the earth or its atmosphere. *or* Wind and solar power are two natural sources of energy. They do not deplete or pollute the earth or its atmosphere.
3. Gerald was *or* is *or* has been fighting off a cold and the flu before his exams.
4. The drainage of wetlands around developing cities has had a destructive influence on bird populations; water fowl have fewer and fewer places to feed and to nest. *or* make two separate sentences *or* Because the drainage of wetlands around developing cities has had a destructive influence on bird populations, water fowl have fewer and fewer places to feed and to nest.
5. Because the concert was not a success, it will be cancelled next season. (Add another clause to repair the fragment.)
6. How many single Canadians actually visit bars and really meet new people there? *or* How many single Canadians actually visit bars? How many really meet new people there?
7. Stacie's planning of the student elections was the most successful ever. (Add a verb to repair the fragment.)

Self-Test: Part 4 *Parallelism Faults*

1. In order to meet the nursing qualifications in the province, you must possess the following: a Bachelor of Science degree from a reputable university, the ability to speak and write English fluently, and some demonstrated clinical experience.
2. Neither the German shepherd dog nor the alarm worked to stop the burglar.
3. Luke was better in physics than he was in graphic art. *or* Luke was better in physics than in graphic art.
4. "Tiger oak" is the term used to describe maple wood that has striped grains and mottling.
5. Svettla paid more for the two rattan chairs than her husband did.

Exercise 1 *Finding Run-on Faults*

1. RO	4. OK	7. OK	10. RO
2. OK	5. OK	8. RO	11. RO
3. RO	6. RO	9. OK	12. OK

Exercise 4 *Finding Run-ons and Comma Splices*

Answers can vary. Check with your instructor.

1. He gave his old car to Helena, unfortunately she cannot afford to pay for insurance. **CS** Add a semicolon after *Helena* or make two separate sentences.
2. OK
3. Because of the dangerous wildfire, the Ministry of Forests ordered an evacuation of the area after three days of rain, the alerts were lifted people were allowed to return home. **CS** Add a semicolon after *area* and *lifted* or make three separate sentences.
4. No one realized the mistake everyone was too busy looking after business. **RO** Add a conjunction like *because* or *since* between the two sentences, or put a semicolon between *mistake* and *everyone*. You may also choose to write two sentences.
5. Some webpages are really difficult to navigate, often the side bars are distracting, and the colours are too busy. **CS** Put a semicolon after *navigate* or write two sentences.
6. Gay cruises have become lucrative for cruise lines last year major companies reported a 26 percent increase in ticket sales. **RO** Put a semicolon between *lines* and *last* or make them separate.
7. OK
8. Where was Izo when I needed him, was he with the inspector on the roof? **CS** Make two separate questions.
9. OK
10. I am not certain how the thief entered the building the police suspect that he or she gained entry through the unlocked window. **RO** Put a semicolon between *building* and *the* or make two separate sentences.
11. OK
12. An HIV-positive man is facing criminal charges because apparently he did not inform his sex partners he had a moral and legal obligation to do so. **RO** Make two separate sentences starting with *His sex partners* or put a semicolon in front of *his*. The second choice creates a rather long sentence.

Exercise 9 Parallelism Faults

1. Working with children is stimulating, challenging, and rewarding.
2. Not being able to speak the language causes confusion, frustration, and embarrassment.
3. To prevent crime, to attend to victims of accidents and crimes, and to apprehend safely those suspected of crime are a police officer's responsibilities.
4. Being sound of mind and strong in body, the elderly man was able to live quite happily by himself. *or* Being mentally sound and physically strong, the elderly man was able to live quite happily by himself.
5. Three of the issues the committee will have to deal with right away are as follows: camp maintenance, staff recruitment, and camp promotion.
6. His doctor advised him to eat less, exercise more and not smoke at all. *or* His doctor advised him to eat less, to exercise more, and not to smoke at all.
7. For many people, attending AA meetings is first embarrassing, possibly even humiliating, then helpful, and finally successful.
8. A high level of motivation, experience in problem-solving, and unconcern about your every decision are necessary if you hope to run a successful business.
9. Influential factors in any nation's economic regression are these: bad management of natural resources, unwise policies regarding national debt, and the inflationary demands of unions.
10. Although the first applicant seemed scared and shy, the second was composed and outgoing.
11. Not only did we see smoke, but we also noticed flames.
12. She looked for work in the want ads of *The Ottawa Citizen* and in the employment pages of the university's student paper.

Exercise 11 Finding and Repairing Different Sentence Faults

Answers for repairs will vary; check with your instructor.

1. **FRAG** Suggested repair: The shooting suspect was believed to be the victim of a lover's quarrel.
2. **P** Suggested repair: A faulty gas meter and a leaking hose short-changed the customer at the service station. *or* The customer at the service station was short-changed because the gas meter was faulty and the hose was leaking.
3. **FRAG** Suggested repair: Fay Wray, made famous in her role in the 1933 classic, *King Kong*, was born in Cardston, Alberta, and died at 96 in New York City.
4. **RO** Suggested repair: Some experts warn many schools could collapse during an earthquake [insert colon or semicolon] these buildings are more likely to fall down than any other kind.
5. **P** Suggested repair: The Iron Man competition included the following events: swimming, cycling, running, and shooting in the fastest time.
6. **P** Suggested repair: The Abbotsford International Air Show takes place every August, has average attendance of 200 000, and hosts representatives from 25 countries.
7. **P** Suggested repair: City taxpayers should vote not only on wage increases but also on new services.
8. **P** Suggested repair: Regina's show will include local experts in health, in fashion, and in beauty.
9. **P** Suggested repair: When summer arrives, Hector has yard work such as mowing the lawn, weeding the flower beds, and trimming the dead branches of shrubs and small trees.
10. **CS** Suggested repair: Paul wanted to start a car repair business in his hometown; however, he could not raise the capital he needed.
11. **P** Suggested repair: Air Canada has been restructured to give it protection against its creditors and to keep the company operating.

12. **FRAG** Suggested repair: The wrestling team was told their new coach who came from China had been in Olympic competitions.
13. **P** Suggested repair: In a recent study, researchers found that grandmothers are more important than money in improving the quality of children's lives.
14. **CS** Suggested repair: Nadia is a vegetarian (insert semicolon) consequently, she won't be ordering the main course of *filet de boeuf en croute*.
15. **P** Suggested repair: Wilton found affordable, good-looking, and quality accessories at the small shop.

Chapter 11: Improving Sentence Style

Exercise 1 *Misplaced Modifiers*

1. During the last holiday our family ate almost 3 kilograms of chocolates.
2. The student irritated nearly every student in our economics class.
3. While he was having coffee, Mr. Mazur spotted a deer in his vegetable patch.
4. A man who had lost his glasses and had a small brown dog asked us for help.
5. Tonia is writing a research report in her philosophy class about Jean-Paul Sartre.
6. When it is almost autumn, remove the plant from the garden and store it in the greenhouse.
7. A tall yellow vase that Claude had purchased sat in the hallway.
8. You will need to cook only one casserole for the dinner.
9. At the store I bought fresh flowers which I gave to a dear friend.
10. Jen saw a destitute old lady in raggedy clothes walking down the street.
11. Although fewer than expected, the parents who did turn out for the rally were very angry.
12. Kora-Lee wrote nearly all of her term paper yesterday.
13. I saw a church with a white steeple as I walked up the hill.
14. Peggy, who was talking excitedly with her friend, adored the puppy in the pet store window.
15. The player simply ignored the referee who blew his whistle.

Exercise 2 *Identifying Active or Passive Voice*

1. passive	4. active	7. active	10. passive
2. active	5. passive	8. passive	
3. active	6. passive	9. passive	

Exercise 3 *Changing Passive to Active Voice*

Your answers may vary. Check with your instructor if you need help.

1. The women's club (or other subject) gave Maude a gift of a pearl brooch.
2. Farmers raise sugar beets in southern Manitoba.
3. Collin (or other subject) discovered a rare salamander among the rocks on the eastern coast of the island.
4. The volunteers (or other subject) sorted the children's school supplies by grade and district.
5. At noon on the Internet, Ethan completed the registration for advanced physics.
6. The movers packed the boxes and labelled them carefully.
7. Soon after sunrise three of the hunters spotted a male moose.
8. The officer fined only one of the campers $250 for not having a permit.

9. Hasim raised the point that student parking permits were entirely too pricey.
10. The mallard duck (or another subject) made a hollow and lined it with thick reeds; then she laid five light green eggs.

ESL Pointer Exercise 1 *Adjectives and Commas*

1. former heavyweight (cumulative)
2. firm, final (coordinate)
3. sensible, satisfying (coordinate)
4. disgraced, disqualified (coordinate)
5. rotting wooden (cumulative)
6. expensive fire truck (cumulative)
7. recent political (cumulative)
8. approved flight (cumulative)
9. costly waterfront (cumulative)
10. fabulous, sunny (coordinate)

Chapter 13: Mechanics

Self-Test: Part 1 *Applying Seven General Rules of Capitalization*

1. Certainly we serve Valley Farms vanilla, strawberry, and chocolate frozen yogurt made from fresh fruit grown in the Annapolis Valley and from milk from Ontario.
2. The English class took a tour of the Perksy Library on the grounds of the University of Passmore.
3. Before October 9, 2005, Ellie must have work done on her Ford Mustang.
4. I really enjoy chopped Spanish peanuts on the sundaes I purchase from Dairy Queen.
5. Andy, do you know if Bingo's Pizza Place puts Greek olives on their special pizza?
6. The trip to Hamilton, Ontario, on January 15, 2004, made Thomas so tired that he missed two days of teaching at George Johnson Elementary School.
7. The Royal Bank of Canada accepted my cheque from the Bank of Hong Kong.
8. Our instructor of Japanese told us to purchase the book *Haiku from the Heart*.
9. Has Wallace ever worked with an Apple computer before he took his course at the Alberta Institute of Technology?
10. On August 15, 2004, the twins, Barney and Bernie, received a huge carton from the Big Brick furniture store on Fourth Street.
11. Mr. Gervais read an excellent book for gardeners called *Special Plants for the Canadian Garden* published in Toronto, Ontario, in 2002.
12. Dave, please prepare the hall by sweeping the floor, washing the dishes, and stacking the chairs.
13. He owned three businesses: a restaurant, a hotel, and a dry cleaning store in Sidney, N.S.
14. Buy some Kleenex, Pepsi, Old Dutch popcorn, and Island Farms butter.
15. The journalist who is studying German interviewed Mrs. Ludlum at the Canadian embassy in Zurich Switzerland.

Self-Test: Part 2 *Applying Seven Special Case Rules for Capitalization*

1. Gary's specialist, Dr. Chung, wants Gary to come to Westside Hospital for some tests.
2. Their family wants to travel to Sri Lanka in April for the Buddhist New Year.
3. Through PATS (Pacific Animal Therapy Society) Sharlene takes her Scottish terrier to visit the elderly.
4. Armand's email read: "The meeting was TOO long for my tastes!"
5. The header for the chapter was "Seven Rules for Spanish Punctuation."
6. The Stone Age describes an early time in the development of human cultures, before the use of metals.

7. Uncle Arthur plays the Hawaiian guitar with great style and enthusiasm.
8. Before the rally at Miracle Stadium, several Olympic contestants spoke with President Bush.
9. The title of the section should be as follows: 'Medicinal Flowers of Ontario.'
10. The song "Like a Virgin" was playing on the radio when my husband Arlo proposed to me.
11. The cruise ship, *Caribbean Cool*, was docked in the inner harbour last week, so many residents of Victoria were able to tour the facilities on board.
12. The Dragon Boat Festival held every summer in Vancouver, B.C., attracts thousands of visitors.
13. Professor Hector Elmez will give a lecture tonight entitled "Costs of the Spanish Civil War."
14. Ms. Buckley, my neighbour, purchased a 2005 red Toyota Solara.
15. On Mother's Day, they purchased the perfume called Sensi by Giorgio Armani, a box of Godiva chocolates, and a large bouquet of roses called Fragrant Cloud to give to their beloved mother.

Exercise 1 *Applying the First Seven Rules of Capitalization*

1. Montreal, Quebec
2. Kraft marshmallows
3. Irish coffee
4. my friend Peter
5. Kelley's Bar on Broad Street
6. the Park Building on First Avenue
7. the author Ann Rice
8. the film *Pirates of the Caribbean*
9. Councillor Monica Shempsky
10. the poet Phyllis Webb
11. the province of Prince Edward Island
12. the new territory of Nunavat
13. Moose Jaw, Saskatchewan
14. the television show *Space Cops*
15. Blue Sky Valley
16. short story writer Alice Munro
17. the cookbook *Vegetarian Snacks*
18. the village of Pemberton, B.C.
19. the Canadian Tire store
20. Teachers Credit Union

Exercise 2 *Capital Letters*

1. Enid read the book *The Understanding of Hope* by Philip Renner. (Italics are the same as underlining here.)
2. Does the Red River flow through Manitoba?
4. Clark Kent bought a small condo in Ottawa, Ontario.
5. Moira's children enjoyed watching the movie called *The Princess and the Pea*.
6. Louise works in Squamish, B.C., but her husband works in Toronto, ON.
7. *Such a Long Journey* is a lovely book that Kaitlin will enjoy.
8. The Rocky Mountains are found in Alberta and British Columbia.
9. Baldev will call Ontario Hydro to have the temporary power connected.
10. On Saturday we bought a large Pepsi and a McCain's pizza and watched the movie *The Hitchhiker's Guide to the Galaxy*.

11. The College of the West offers a course in breaking quarter horses and in learning the trade of the farrier.
13. The cafeteria offers Dasani and Perrier water but does not sell carbonated soft drinks such as Sprite, Dr. Pepper, or Mountain Dew.
14. Herbert's favourite mystery novel is *The Spy Who Came in from the Cold.*
15. Disney's movie *The Lion King* was popular with children.

Exercise 4 *Using Seven More Rules of Capitalization*

1. Would you please tell Officer Bailey I will see her at five after I speak with Superintendent Burbles?
2. Chief Engineer Patterson spoke to Mayor Simpson about the city strike.
3. Would you buy a new Chevrolet from Tim Brown Chevrolet, Aunt Arthie?
4. The reporter from the *Globe and Mail* spoke to Alderman Dawson about the fire in Bixby's Department Store.
5. The Golden Age of Greece refers to a time of great stability and culture when democracy was born.
6. Sister Monique, a Carmelite nun from Saskatchewan, wrote a powerful article on various child-rearing practices among First Nations peoples.
7. The parent spoke to Principal Brown about her son's progress in school.
8. Many children are fascinated by how Stone Age people lived.
9. Every March Japan holds the Doll Festival called Hinamatsuri.
10. King Arthur and the Knights of the Round Table were said to live in the Age of Chivalry.
11. In June El Salvador celebrates a special holiday called School Teachers' Day.
12. Mothers Against Drunk Driving, or MADD, began as a grassroots movement.
13. The header was titled "The Klondike Gold Rush of 1897."
14. Mannfred named his rowboat *Lily of the Valley* after his favourite flower.
15. Why don't you consider using David Austin roses, Mother, in your English country garden?

Chapter 14: Punctuation

Self-Test

When Alex wants to imagine spectacular scenery, he thinks about the Queen Charlotte Islands along the coast of British Columbia. Naden Harbour, for example, is located at the top of Graham Island, an important fishing area. As tourists travel by plane to Naden, they see serene meadows and rolling hills. If they are fortunate enough, they can spot a small herd of Sitka deer or the great majestic Roosevelt elk: these animals roam freely through the hills. Sometimes tourists ask, "Are there any bald eagles out today?" Instead of the magnificent eagle, however, visitors might see flocks of Pacific crows that pester them for food. In this secluded wilderness, the history of the Haida, a proud coastal First Nations people, is evident in the artefacts. Walking along the shorelines, visitors can find the remains of old longhouses, totem poles, and old burial poles, reminders of the Haida past. Fishing lodges like North Island Lodge employ some of the local Haidas, who work as fishing guides. In the summer months, the fishing is remarkable; the giant Pacific Chinook salmon and the enormous halibut called "the vacuum cleaners of the sea" make spectacular catches. During the winter the northwesterly winds begin to blow, and the once calm waters turn into a grey, raging sea.

Exercise 1 Using the Comma in a Series

1. His children enjoy playing hockey, volleyball, and soccer.
2. Mel's aunt knits Cowichan sweaters, socks, and gloves to sell at the Aboriginal Arts store.
3. Rice, pasta, and potatoes are high in carbohydrates, vitamin C, and riboflavin.
4. The aquarium has beluga whales, killer whales, and grey sharks on public view.
5. Mark, Georgio, and Austin play golf together on the weekends.
6. Allie discovered that some money, an expensive pen, and a calculator were missing from her desk.
7. Ajay and his cousin bought dishes, a lamp, three chairs, and a bed for their apartment.
8. Mrs. Perez bought bananas, cream, bread, and onions at the local grocery.
9. Bernice, the grandmother, and their neighbour go swimming on Tuesdays, Wednesdays, and Saturdays. (You might interpret *the grandmother* as an appositive in this sentence.)
10. Breaking your promises, forgetting special occasions, and making excuses for yourself will not make you popular with your friends.

Exercise 3 Using the Comma

1. Paint, stencils, and round brushes were needed to make the decorative border.
2. Without a doubt, Thomas is a wonderful carver, father, and friend.
3. After talking with my uncle, I decided to take a trip to Brampton, Ontario, this year.
4. Appointed to the Land Use Committee on October 5, 2005, Josef felt honoured as he waved to the press in Portage La Prairie, Manitoba.
5. The family had a new baby on August 7, 2004, moved their home to Sault Ste. Marie, Ontario, invested in a small business, and bought a new car.
6. His branch office in Winnipeg, Manitoba, contacted the head office located in Calgary, Alberta.
7. The peaches, plums, and lemons had all spoiled in the fridge.
8. The restaurant uses juicy bacon, fresh lettuce, garden tomatoes, and homemade mayonnaise on its burgers.
9. After months and months of planning, the new park was ready in Carrot River, Saskatchewan, on April 5, 2006.
10. Wolves, dogs, and coyotes are members of the canine family.
11. With a huge sigh of relief, the packer put the roses, petunias, cedars, and shrubs on the truck.
12. Will anyone help me look for the address book, the stamps, and the computer labels?
13. After the ashes had cooled down in the ruins of the old building, the fire investigator found an old metal chest full of silver coins.
14. Hurrying along after the bus, Kristina skidded, tripped, and broke her ankle.
15. Read this article, compare its ideas with Professor Lutz's theory, and then write an essay.

Exercise 8 Semicolon Use

1. The experiment was a success; therefore, we should be able to publish our results in the spring.
2. Whenever they were afraid, the children would tell each other stories; the activity seemed to calm them.
3. Sometimes Eleanor goes out with Amos; however, she does not plan to marry him.
4. The roses in the roadside park smelled like honey; moreover, they attracted hundreds of bees.
5. Forgetting to set his alarm, the graduate student was late for his thesis defence; consequently, the thesis committee was annoyed by his tardiness.
6. Clarice is arranging the chairs for the meeting; Percy is organizing copies of the report.

7. Please put the extra strawberries into a bowl after you have washed and cleaned them; otherwise, they will spoil overnight.
8. Ryan performed a violin concerto for his fellow music students; as a result, he was seen to be a potential concert artist.
9. Nurse Sophie will assist the doctor in emergency; she has the most experience of the whole nursing staff.
10. The two chemicals should never be mixed; consequently, they are stored in two different parts of the lab in two different types of containers.
11. The canoe trip was really relaxing for Theo and Stephen; therefore, they've decided to go on another one with three other friends from college.
12. Use this soft brush and air to clean the lens of the camera; afterward, replace the cap on the lens.
13. The University of Toronto is holding a symposium on family literacy; delegates will attend from across North America, Europe, and Asia.

Exercise 12 *Possessives and Apostrophes*

1. One of the teacher's notebooks is missing.
2. They have located the children's parents in the mall.
3. Were there any boys' uniforms left on sale at the store?
4. Mrs. Sloan won't need to borrow Pamela's car after all.
5. The car's four tires were so bald that the driver had a difficult time controlling the vehicle.
6. Several pieces of glass were lodged in the window's frame.
7. Everyone who wishes can get the football players' autograph for free.
8. "The Moonlight Sonata" is one of Beethoven's most gentle compositions.
9. To prevent theft, please put the girls' bicycles in the locker overnight.
10. One of my grandfather's eyes was a deep brown.
11. Sheila's purse was left on the cross-town bus yesterday.
12. He intended to stay out of harm's way, but several incidents caused him trouble.
13. Her sister-in-law's lawyer used to work for the federal government.
14. One of the cart's wheels has fallen off by the side of the road.
15. We will be listening to one of Philip Glass's compositions.

Chapter 15: Paragraph Writing

Exercise 2 *Deciding the Purpose of a Summary*

Answers may vary. Some assignments may have more than one purpose.

Assignment 1: To make research information more accessible

Assignment 2: To understand a writer's argument; to show my professor or instructor I understand the information

Assignment 3: To use as a study tool; to deepen comprehension; to show my professor or instructor I understand the information

Assignment 4: To understand a writer's argument; to show my professor or instructor I understand the information

Assignment 5: To provide a tool for someone else to get the information quickly; to make research more accessible

Chapter 17: Descriptive Paragraphs

Exercise 1 Classifying: Specific to General

1. Bayer's aspirin, pill, drug
2. Toshiba microwave, oven, appliance
3. Toyota Rava, car, vehicle
4. drone, bee, insect
5. prickly pear, cactus, plant
6. poutine, snack, food
7. romaine, lettuce, vegetable
8. oyster, shellfish, animal
9. Big Mac, sandwich, fast food
10. shoe, footwear, clothing
11. prime minister, official, person
12. parsley, herb, vegetable/plant
13. spear, weapon, tool
14. owl, bird, animal
15. swallowtail butterfly, insect, animal
16. lollipop, treat/sweet/snack, food
17. dictionary, book, reference
18. teenager, youth, person
19. whisk, utensil, tool
20. engineer, professional, person

Exercise 2 Classifying: General to Specific

1. celebrity, singer, Luciano Pavarotti (or other)
2. appliance, refrigerator, Whirlpool (or other brand)
3. hobby, modelling, WW II airplanes
4. wood, soft, pine
5. alcohol, liqueur, Drambuie
6. food, picnic, sandwiches
7. emotion, sadness, grief
8. invention, telephone, cellphone
9. country, Canada, The North
10. music, jazz, fusion
11. sport, team, hockey
12. travel, space, rocket
13. tool, knife, cleaver
14. herb, kitchen, oregano
15. furniture, chair, lounger
16. book, mystery, *The Hound of the Baskervilles*
17. fear, loss, death
18. recreation, outdoor, skiing
19. family, canines, dog
20. poetry, children's, nursery rhymes

Exercise 7: Responding to the Readings

SELECTION 1

1. the countryside and a small village in Russia
2. bright green, broad, level, mown
3. broad, steep
4. threaded
5. long strings, white
6. magnificent, leafy

SELECTION 2

1. a poor, rundown room
2. old, three-cornered
3. old bedstead; tattered, checked curtain; medicine bottles' broken glass; child's bed on the floor; dishes; shelf; shoes; rags and bundles
4. gives the reader a depressed, rather sad feeling

SELECTION 3

1. an old farm
2. ochre-coloured, worn paint, curiously mottled
3. two black, uneven, bumpy furrows
4. rough wooden gate hanging loosely on one hinge

SELECTION 4

1. a garden in a futuristic city
2. soft, moving, tropical, steamy, hot, heavy, perfumed, cream, crimson
3. the perfume of the flowers, the steamy air, the greenery of the lush garden
4. a calm, soothing feeling; appeals to the senses through the perfumed air, the sight of the beautiful flowers, and the soft, shimmering lights

SELECTION 5

1. the streets of an ancient Greek city
2. non-emotional language
3. few descriptive words

Index

391